A SHORT HISTORY OF THE CIVIL WAR

A SHORT HISTORY
of the
CIVIL WAR

James L. Stokesbury

WILLIAM MORROW AND COMPANY, INC.

New York

It is the policy of William Morrow and Company, Inc., and its imprints and affiliates, recognizing the importance of preserving what has been written, to print the books we publish on acid-free paper, and we exert our best efforts to that end.

Library of Congress Cataloging-in-Publication Data

Stokesbury, James L.
 A short history of the Civil War / James L. Stokesbury.
  p. cm.
 Includes bibliographical references and index.
 ISBN 0-688-11523-3
  1. United States—History—Civil War, 1861–1865. I. Title.
 E468.S86 1995
 973.7—dc20   95-7093
                      CIP

Printed in the United States of America

First Edition

1 3 5 7 9 10 8 6 4 2

BOOK DESIGN BY SUSAN HOOD

For Kevin and Shauna, Mike and Lisa, and Brianna

Acknowledgments

This book, like some of my earlier ones, was written while I was on sabbatical leave from teaching duties at Acadia University, and I am pleased to acknowledge the university's generosity in granting me the leave. Acadia also supplied me with travel grants which, in the course of several summers, enabled me to visit many of the battlefields of the Civil War, an inestimable advantage for anyone attempting to sense the spirit of that terrible conflict. My colleagues in the History Department, and at the university generally, have always been most supportive of my work, and in the context of this particular study, I wish especially to thank two good friends: Dr. Graham Adams of the Department of English, who insists, undoubtedly wisely, that I shall never truly understand the South until I come to terms with William Faulkner; and Dr. Bruce Matthews of Religious Studies, who for years has either loaned me books or fed me with reviews to keep me up to date on what is appearing in print.

A number of readers have similarly taken time to send me material, and I must mention particularly Mr. John Gearing of Gaithersburg, Maryland, and Mr. Tom Kelly of New Canaan, Connecticut.

Any errors of fact or interpretation in this work are my own.

It would be impossible to say too much, or even nearly enough, about the constant support and encouragement of my wife, Elizabeth, who has borne patiently with my absentminded stare as she tries to tell me things I need to know, while I am off in my imagination on some distant battlefield, and who has fretted sympathetically over sore shoulders acquired from extended sessions at the word processor. To her, as always, goes my most profound gratitude, for everything.

Contents

CONTENTS

Maps

Part I

1861:

PLAYING AT WAR

Chapter 1

From Washington to Charleston

HE ELECTION of Abraham Lincoln as the sixteenth president
of the United States in November of 1860 set the stage for
division, secession, and civil war. Americans had gone through
angry and bitter election campaigns before, but until this point, they
had always managed to live with the result, even when it produced
such victors as William Henry Harrison, who died within a month of
taking office, or when the whole electoral scene had been confused, as
it was in 1824, when Andrew Jackson won a plurality in the popular
vote but John Quincy Adams was chosen by the electoral college. Why
then should the election of Lincoln have been any different? Why could
the country not survive this as it had other political upsets before?

Elections in the nineteenth century were a serious and complex business. In the 1860 contest, the country was split into sections, and there
were four major candidates. The election was held on the 6th of November, and it took a few days, in this age before instant electronic
information, to get all the votes organized and counted. Nonetheless,
it was soon certain that Lincoln had indeed won, with enough of a
margin that he would not be tricked out of his victory—the electoral
college did not even meet until February—and the announcement of
his election threw the country into an uproar.

But the winner remained strangely elusive on the great questions of
the moment. Candidates, indeed, once they had been nominated by
their parties, were not even supposed to campaign; they were expected
rather to sit at home, preferably on the front porch in a rocking chair,
and treat the whole matter as if it were of little interest to them—
displaying, in other words, the detachment of a true statesman. They

3

might receive friends, advisers, and potential office-seekers, but the undignified hurly-burly of the actual election was left to underlings. In this election, it was true, Stephen A. Douglas, the famous "little giant," the candidate of the northern Democrats, had vigorously stumped the nation. More prescient than most, Douglas saw tragedy on the horizon, and he spent his strength in an attempt to avert it by securing his own election. All to no avail. The country seemed on the edge of an irrevocable split, and Lincoln's triumph was the proof of it.

By rights, Douglas should have won. The Democratic Party had been the last of the great national institutions holding the country together. The other three parties that fielded candidates were all factions or splinters, cobbled together recently out of one crisis or another. Lincoln's party, the Republican, was a mere six years old, had run for its first presidential election only in 1856, and was identified exclusively with the northern part of the country. The Constitutional Union Party was a marriage not of convenience but of desperation, between the old, now moribund, Whigs and the anti-foreign Know-Nothings, and its only claim to support was that it fielded a southern presidential and a northern vice presidential candidate. Finally, there were the southern Democrats, who by insisting on their own man, former vice president John C. Breckinridge of Kentucky, split the party and deprived Douglas of his victory. Thus Abraham Lincoln, with a mere 1,700,000 votes out of four and a half million, became the sixteenth president of the United States.

Though he had repeatedly insisted that the southern, slave-holding states had nothing to fear from him, Lincoln's election became the signal for the dissolution of the union. Southern leaders had convinced themselves that a victory by the "black Republicans" would be absolutely intolerable to their section and their interests, and the more rabid among them immediately acted upon that conviction.

The leader in the move to secede was the state of South Carolina. It had provided many of the statesmen of the early republic, most notably John C. Calhoun, the great champion of states' rights, and Carolinians cherished their tradition of dissent. They cherished it so much and so vociferously that one annoyed southern newspaper editor of the fifties had characterized the state as "too small to be a country, too big to be a lunatic asylum." Now, in December, the state held a convention and voted to secede from the United States. South Carolinians began arming, and made moves to seize federal property within their borders.

In Washington, D. C., the outgoing president, James Buchanan, watched all this with a jaundiced eye. Buchanan was a reasonably astute but not terribly strong or active politician. He had done well, he thought, merely to survive his four years as president. He did so by generally favoring the southern position on the issues that divided the country, and that favoring in turn had done a great deal to create the present situation. By the turn of the year, however, most of the southern members of Buchanan's cabinet had resigned, and, now supported by stronger union men, he was showing more backbone than he had previously done. He refused to receive commissioners from South Carolina, and he announced that he would resist with force if the state overtly confiscated federal property. The issue centered around control especially of Fort Sumter, sitting in the mouth of Charleston Harbor, an offense to the touchy pride of South Carolinians.

Meanwhile, the fever of secession spread. Early in January state troops from Georgia took over federal forts there; southern senators met in Washington and agreed to recommend secession to their home states. Mississippi announced its secession on the 9th, Florida the next day, and Alabama the day after that. By the 1st of February, Georgia, Louisiana, and Texas had also gone. These all sent delegates to a convention that met at Montgomery, Alabama, on February 4. Within a week they had written a constitution and elected a president.

Jefferson Davis of Mississippi was one of the South's most experienced politicians, a position he had obtained somewhat by default. In his own mind he was always a soldier, and he had in fact been educated as one. Born in 1808, he had graduated from West Point in 1828 and spent seven years in the army before becoming a planter in Mississippi. He entered politics before the Mexican War and was elected to the U.S. House of Representatives, but resigned to serve as colonel of the 1st Mississippi Rifles; he came home from the war with a wound, a reputation for bravery, and a high opinion of his own military abilities. Returning to politics, he was a senator and a very successful secretary of war in President Franklin Pierce's cabinet. In the Senate, he was one of the most forceful advocates of southern rights, and regularly threatened secession if those rights were not respected. He would have infinitely preferred a military command to the presidency of the Confederacy, and he might well have been better suited to it. Nonetheless, he was the choice of the Montgomery convention, so of course he accepted. Whether or not the president of the new nation would need any military knowledge was a still unanswered question.

Abraham Lincoln, indeed, was doing his best not to answer it. The working of the government had not caught up with the potentiality of the new technology. In spite of the advent of both railroads and the telegraph, there was still a long hiatus between the election of a president and his taking office. Lincoln was not to be inaugurated until March 4, so the union of the states was largely broken before he assumed responsibility for it. During these months he remained as quiet as possible; he had repeatedly insisted the South had nothing to fear from his administration, that he had no designs against the institution of slavery where it then existed—an important concession and qualification both—but he would say little more than that.

In this, he did not disappoint expectation, because most of the people who counted politically in the United States did not have high expectations of Lincoln anyway. Few men so revered since their death have been so poorly regarded during their lives as Lincoln was.

Abraham Lincoln was far from being the backswoods buffoon that many Americans thought him. Born in Kentucky in 1809, the son of a poor family, Lincoln was largely self-educated; he had in his youth been a laborer, a storekeeper, and a postmaster. He taught himself the law by reading law books, and was admitted to the Illinois bar in 1836, gradually building a small practice and a sound reputation in his home state. He had served several terms in the state legislature, and in 1847 was elected to the House of Representatives in Washington. He was there for only one term, and was little known; his most important opinions were against slavery and against the Mexican War. He spent a good part of the next decade explaining that while he was opposed to the war, he was not opposed to support for the men who had fought it.

In 1856 he became a Republican, and ran for the Senate against Stephen A. Douglas. In the course of the campaign, the two opponents engaged in a series of debates that brought Lincoln to national prominence. The issue was basically the right of the national government to limit the spread of slavery into new territories, and the two men hammered out their own positions, and away at each other's. Widely reported and subsequently published in book form, the debates still make fascinating reading; to imagine the setting and the audience—a great crowd of men, some of whom had ridden for miles, standing in the sun for five or six hours listening to two men standing on a platform debating, their voices unaided by artificial amplification—is to gain a great deal of respect for the intelligence and political seriousness of Americans in the mid–nineteenth century.

Lincoln lost the election, but was regarded as the coming man among the Republicans. He was still a dark horse when the party met at Chicago in July of 1860 to nominate a presidential candidate, but he was most Republicans' second choice, and he won the nomination on the third ballot.

———

In February of 1861, the president-elect took a leisurely route to Washington. The nearer he got to the capital and to his inauguration, the worse the situation looked. By the time he reached Philadelphia, there was wild talk of an assassination plot, so he departed from his planned route and virtually sneaked into his own capital.

Meanwhile, various politicians in Washington were attempting to produce last-minute compromises that would save the union. None of these worked; the final positions of either side were simply irreconcilable: preservation of the union versus separation.

Many thought that if the country were to be saved, Lincoln's cabinet would have to do it, for few had much confidence in the new and untried president. The cabinet, by contrast, consisted of men long used to the arena. Yet more perceptive observers might have noted that a weak man would not have picked assistants of the caliber Lincoln did. As secretary of state he chose William H. Seward of New York, an ex-Whig, a senator since 1849, and Lincoln's leading opponent for the Republican nomination in 1860. Abrasive, abusive, ambitious, Seward was believed by many men, especially himself, to be the real power in the new administration; easterners could tell themselves that he at least was capable of running the government. Westerners could put their faith in Salmon P. Chase, who became secretary of the treasury, and who represented the more radical abolitionist wing of the Republican Party. Chase knew little about finances, but everything about politics, and Lincoln valued his opinions. The same was true of Montgomery Blair, an able lawyer and politician who became postmaster general, and Gideon Welles, a competent secretary of the navy whose chief claim to fame is an intimate insider's diary of Civil War Washington. Lincoln's only major mistake was in appointing Simon Cameron as his secretary of war. In 1860 Cameron had delivered Pennsylvania to Lincoln, and the secretaryship was his reward; Lincoln appointed him with strong misgivings, which were fully justified by corruption and mismanagement, and within a year Cameron was shipped off as minister to Russia, about as far away as Lincoln could get him.

It was possible, then, for political men to assure themselves that if the new president was not up to the mark, at least Seward, or Chase, or *someone*, would be able to make the government work. Still, here was a new party, and a new chief executive, neither of whom had ever held major office, trying to deal with the greatest crisis of the century. The omens were not good.

Lincoln had been in Washington for a week and a half before Inauguration Day, and had received a great many visitors and office seekers, but he still had not given much of himself away, a point that, again, might have impressed people had they not been too busy watching Seward play the viceroy. Lincoln appeared one of the few calm men in the capital, but was it because he knew everything, or because he knew nothing?

On March 4, President Buchanan called for Lincoln where he was staying at Willard's Hotel, and they rode together in an open carriage to the Capitol. Troops were much in evidence, several hundred regulars, and a couple of thousand volunteers in a variety of impractical uniforms. There was an air of unwonted martial bustle about the city. A temporary platform had been erected before the east face of the still unfinished Capitol building, and there the inauguration ceremony was held. Some thirty thousand spectators had gathered to see the event. Lincoln took the oath of office, sworn in by the chief justice of the Supreme Court, Roger B. Taney. Ironically Taney, a man of immense legal knowledge and personal rectitude, had delivered the majority decision for the Court in the Dred Scott case, and thus had done a great deal to cause the crisis now engulfing the nation.

Before taking the oath, Lincoln delivered his inaugural address. It characterized the man; it was brief, it was eloquent, and it went right to the heart of the matter. Lincoln stated that the union was perpetual and could not be broken; he offered, he said, no threat to the existing institution of slavery; therefore there was no need for secession, and the issue of secession, of war or peace, was squarely up to the South: "You can have no conflict without yourselves being the aggressors." He offered conciliation, and he offered goodwill, but there was the distinct possibility of war in his message, and he did not shrink from it. Indeed, when all the millions of words by and about Lincoln are sloughed off, the absolute core of the man appears: He faced facts; he saw the world as it was.

Such ability was increasingly rare as the month wore on. Two days after Lincoln's inauguration, President Davis of the Confederate States of America issued a call for 100,000 volunteers for twelve months' service, and by early April, the new nation had 35,000 men enlisted and armed. Meanwhile the Upper South, the West, and the border states twisted and turned. North Carolina narrowly voted against a secession convention; the margin was less than two hundred votes out of more than 90,000 cast. In Texas, old Sam Houston came out against secession, but Texas had been largely settled by southerners, and Houston was lost in the whirlwind of emotion. President Davis sent commissioners to Washington, but Lincoln refused to meet with them, on the grounds that to do so might imply recognition of the legitimacy of the new government. Arizona voted for secession; Arkansas voted against it; Virginia did the same, then sent unionist representatives to Washington who told Lincoln he should be firm for the union, but that any use of force would send Virginia into the arms of the Confederacy. Thus while Lincoln tried to make some sense of his new world, all around him were busily trying to deny the reality of it.

The issue finally narrowed down to Fort Sumter, in itself a totally unimportant piece of real estate, but symbolically a bone in the throat of Charleston Harbor and thus of the whole Confederacy. Away back in December, Major Robert A. Anderson, in command of the federal garrisons in Charleston, had moved his few troops from Fort Moultrie, indefensible on a sandbar north of the harbor, to the newer Fort Sumter out on its island. Charlestonians, who had been noisily demanding the turnover of all federal property, moved into Moultrie and denounced Anderson's move as a treacherous outrage. By April there had been many attempts to resolve the problem of the fort. Indeed, by April it and Fort Pickens, down in Florida, were the only federal holdings left in the Confederacy; everything else had been quietly taken over.

The Washington government, seeking to avoid an overt clash, agreed not to reinforce the garrison at Sumter, but Lincoln and his cabinet, after getting contradictory messages from Anderson, did decide to try to resupply the fort. To this end, they ordered a small squadron of ships south. By the second week in April, all was confusion. The Confederates, under the command of a Louisianan as flamboyant

9

as his name, Pierre Gustave Toutant Beauregard, had ringed the harbor of Charleston with batteries. Anderson did not know if or how long he could hold out, and in his several meetings with Confederate officials he managed to confuse himself as thoroughly as he confused them. Seward was whispering half-promises to Confederate representatives, and one of the ships detailed for Charleston had already been sent off privately by the president to Fort Pickens. In other words, under the stress of the situation, normal communications and reactions were breaking down. Each side would subsequently charge the other with bad faith, but that was not really the truth of the matter; the truth was that neither was fully in control, either of events or of itself. Human beings do get tired; they get angry, confused, and impatient, and they take actions which, in the cool light of later reflection or the calm of an academic study, seem foolish and self-destructive.

Thus the Washington government thought it could skate along the fine line between resupply and reinforcement, and it was wrong. The Confederates thought they had elicited a promise from Anderson to evacuate the fort; they thought they had a promise from Seward that an arrangement could be reached. But neither of these was unconditional, and neither Anderson nor Seward was in a position to make them so. Finally, it must be noted that there were those on either side, but especially among the Confederates in Charleston, who did not really want an accommodation; they wanted a little action.

That was what they got. Anderson finally told the Confederate commissioners that he would be forced to evacuate the fort, unless resupplied, by midnight on April 15. The Confederates, knowing the resupply ships were on the way, decided not to wait. At four-thirty on the morning of the 12th, the batteries in Charleston Harbor opened fire. A rolling deluge of shot and shell hit the fortress, driving the defenders into the bombproofs. Charlestonians rushed into the streets, happy and excited, to shake hands, hug, and congratulate each other. Men and women on foot and in their carriages flocked to the waterfront to watch the great event. The waiting and the tension were over at last. The soldiers were mostly local boys, and they gave civilian friends and neighbors the honor of touching off the cannon, and firing a shot at the hated Yankees cowering on their little island. It was truly a great occasion.

All through the 12th the roar continued, as the batteries kept firing on into the night. By mid-day of the 13th, the attackers had fired

4,000 shells. Sumter itself was a mess, with casemates broken and guns dismantled, and much of it on fire, though there had been almost no actual casualties. Finally, at two-thirty on the afternoon of the 13th, Anderson surrendered. Conceded the honors of war, he insisted on firing a 100-gun salute as part of his departure. Midway in the salute, one of the guns burst, ironically causing the only fatalities of the entire episode. Anderson and his men went aboard ship—the relief squadron—and sailed away to the North, to be received as heroes.

Two days later, President Lincoln issued a proclamation calling for 75,000 volunteers for three months' service to suppress the rebellion.

———

Thus the election of Abraham Lincoln led almost inexorably to division, secession, and war. Yet on the face of it, it is difficult to understand why that should have been so. Lincoln in his campaign and in his public utterances after the election repeatedly denied that he posed any threat to the southern part of the country, or to its institutions—meaning slavery—and, setting aside the normal confusions and contradictions of life, he did his best to live up to his intentions, in spite of secession and the overt seizure of federal property in the South. If one probes deeper into the nation's past, however, it becomes apparent that Lincoln's election was less the cause than the excuse for the crisis. The causes themselves went back almost to the very beginning of American history, or at least to the beginning of English settlement on the continent, and were rooted in the diverging paths different sections of the country had taken since then. A war in which more than 600,000 men died needs something beyond a mere excuse.

Chapter 2

From Settlement to Secession

AMERICANS HAVE disagreed about almost every aspect of the Civil War, including even what to call it. Though "the Civil War" is now generally accepted, in the years immediately after it ended it was often called "the War of the Rebellion," as in the publication of the official records. Southerners tended to like "the War of Southern Independence," which created parallels with the American Revolution, and some northerners, though not many, preferred "the War to Free the Slaves." This never really gained much popular support, because southerners denied that they were fighting to keep the slaves from being freed, and the majority of northerners denied that they were fighting to free them. The term "Civil War" is in fact a fairly neutral one, which carries little tangential baggage, while any of these other names carries too much implication as to causes and motivations, and is thus unacceptable to one segment or another of opinion.

What then were the root causes of the Civil War? Scholars and citizens alike have argued that question ever since the war ended, defending different points of view, and it would be bold to the point of foolhardiness to assert that any one problem, or any specific series of problems to the exclusion of others, caused the war. There were all sorts of difficulties, yet it may be said that the difficulty that most of the others centered around, that came to subsume all the other dissatisfactions, and that focused the national anger, was the issue of slavery and its preservation, limitation, or extension. Lincoln himself remarked that the war was about slavery pure and simple, and he should have known.

Slavery was not a problem when the original colonies were first settled in the seventeenth century. In that era slavery was a simple fact of life. The African slave trade was already well established in the Caribbean and in Latin America. One of the great humanitarians of the Catholic Church, Bartolomé de las Casas, nicknamed "the Apostle of the Indians," had written against American Indian enslavement, but his alternative solution to Spain's labor problems was the importation of African slaves to take the place of the Indians. The English and northern Europeans broke into the trade in the 1570s, and the first Africans brought to the new colony of Virginia were "twenty negars" sold by a Dutch ship in 1619. Slavery as an institution was not confined solely to Africans, however. At the time of the English Civil War, in the 1640s, there were still several thousand legal serfs, slaves in all but name, living in England, and during the mid-century, thousands of English were sent out to the plantations of the West Indies as slaves, transported convicts, indentured servants, or in various other unfree conditions.

The two important differences between these Europeans and Africans were that, first, the Europeans were slaves as a result of some act they had committed, or were supposed to have committed, and there were still some legal constraints on how they might be treated, while the Africans were regarded simply as property, bought and sold; and more importantly, Europeans tended to die rapidly in the living and working conditions of the tropics, while Africans managed to survive them. Very gradually, Africans supplanted whites as slaves, and eventually slave labor became almost entirely African. By the mid–eighteenth century, African slave labor was an integral part of the economic system of the southern American colonies, and considered absolutely essential in those climates where tobacco, rice, and, a little later, cotton were grown. There were slaves in all the colonies, of course; many northern merchants and shipowners brought home a slave or two for household use, but the northern climate and economy were such that slavery there was always marginal rather than vital. Even the slave trade itself, southern polemicists to the contrary, was never more than a small segment of the northern shipping business.

From very early days, slavery introduced an uneasy relationship in southern life. There was always the underlying threat of revolt. This was more imagined than real, because of the peculiar conditions of southern American life: slaves never made up more than about one third of the population, and they were relatively isolated in small groups and subsumed within the larger white community on farms and plantations, most of which were fairly small holdings with fewer than fifty slaves. Nonetheless there was a constant subterranean fear among white southerners, and in fact, one authority counts at least two hundred attempted slave plots or risings in the century and a half before the Civil War.

One result of this was a perpetual ambivalence in white southern life and attitudes, well illustrated in such writings as the famous Civil War diary of Mary Boykin Chesnut: the slaves are warm-hearted, loyal people—yet they might rise up and murder their owners; the slaves are far more trouble and need far more care than they are worth—yet the South cannot function without them; southerners are kind and caring masters—yet southern men constantly abuse slaves and have forced sexual relations with slave women, a fact which Mary Chesnut, though a good nineteenth-century lady, acknowledges surprisingly openly, with particular disdain. White southerners thus did not like living with slaves, but became convinced they could not live without them.

By the time of the American Revolution and the formative, constitution-making years of the new republic, slavery was a fixed institution. It is often pointed out ironically that the stirring words in the Declaration of Independence, "that all men are created equal, that they are endowed by their Creator with certain unalienable rights, that among these are life, liberty, and the pursuit of happiness" were written by the slave owner Thomas Jefferson. White Americans ignored the role played by blacks in their revolution, and in creating a free republican society they again tried to ignore that they possessed in the midst of it an indigestible lump of servitude.

When they came to write a constitution, they could neither avoid slavery nor get rid of it, so they achieved a compromise which defied logic and had as its only justification the fact that it was acceptable to the writers. For purposes of enumeration and apportionment of representatives, they treated a slave as three fifths of a person, even though, in almost every other context, they treated slaves as property rather than as persons. To make this compromise acceptable to northern members of the Constitutional Convention, from areas where there were few slaves, they agreed to forbid further importation of slaves after 1808. Beyond that, when most of the framers of the Constitution contemplated the problem of slavery, they seem simply to have hoped it would gradually go away.

This hope was disappointed by several different developments. Americans expanded south and west, and the Gulf Coast was opened up to settlement and to slave agriculture. The biggest cause of the continuation of slavery, however, was the population explosion in Europe and the concurrent advent of the Industrial Revolution. The immediate agent of change was a gifted Yankee tinkerer named Eli Whitney. Working in Georgia as a tutor, he developed a little machine that would pick the seeds out of cotton, a hitherto laborious process done by hand. He not only made a fortune for himself, he also made a fortune in cotton production for thousands of southerners: "You cannot make war on Cotton! Cotton is King!" And of course, a totally inadvertent by-product of King Cotton was the continuation, and the expansion, of slavery. So much for the vague hope that the problem would go away.

Since it refused to go away, Americans were then faced with the question of what to do about it. To that question alone they might conceivably have found an answer, but human questions seldom exist in isolation. For the United States, one of the fastest-growing and most dynamic societies of its day, there were a great many other questions to be answered as well, and the pace of change was almost staggering. Indeed, one thing that made the slavery issue assume ever-increasing importance was that change was distributed unevenly. For a variety of reasons, the northern part of the country was changing more rapidly than the southern. The American Industrial Revolution, a spin-off from the European one, began on the rivers of New England, when Yankee traders took their money and began putting it in cotton mills and other large "factories" on the Merrimack and the Connecticut and the Housatonic rivers. Then came the era of canal building, soon to be followed by the railroads. Though it did not look so on the map, the most efficient access to the interior of America ran through New York City, up the Hudson and across to the Great Lakes, and then out to the old Northwest Territory, what we would now call the Midwest and the Great Lakes states. As the rocky hillside farms of New England gave out, sons moved west to Ohio or Illinois, and the wave of westward migration lapped to and across the Alleghenies and into the great central basin of the continent. The same process of migration occurred in the South, too, and southerners moved to the Louisiana Purchase area, and pushed beyond that into Texas. So Indiana entered the union in 1816, Mississippi in 1817, Illinois in 1818, and Alabama in 1819.

Problems arose with the admission of new states. Southerners developed the first sense that they were being threatened, that there was a danger of them becoming a minority in the running of their own government, that their interests were to be disregarded by a more rapidly growing and larger whole. This sense, becoming a fear, led to a series of compromises in the construction of the nation. In 1820, the Missouri Compromise admitted Maine as a "free" state, and Missouri as a "slave" state, in an attempt to preserve the balance between the two types; in addition, an amendment barred slavery from any territory in the Louisiana Purchase north of latitude 36°30'. The compromise was a triumph at the time, but it set the pattern for subsequent deals; from now on, southerners would demand that the slave and free states match each other in numbers; this would necessitate that slavery be legal even in places where it was an impractical form of labor. The union would finally be wrecked on the rock of a hypothetical right.

From the 1820 compromise to the 1850s, affairs went manageably, perhaps even smoothly. The twenties were dominated by tariff questions, with northern manufacturers wanting high tariffs to shelter them from better and cheaper British goods, and southerners wanting low tariffs so they could trade their agricultural produce for imported finished goods. South Carolina was so incensed at what it considered northern bullying that it adopted a doctrine of "nullification," announcing it had the right to override federal legislation if it chose to do so. President Jackson threatened to use force against the recalcitrant state, but eventually another compromise was reached, and the issue slowly faded. What did not fade, however, was the problem of who had the power to do what. In other words, what was the true sovereign authority, the individual state or the federal union?

It was a peculiarity of the American system that that question had not been satisfactorily answered in the constitution. Originally the states had regarded themselves as being independent, sovereign entities; several, in joining the federal union, had explicitly said so, and had even reserved the right to get out again if they thought it in their best interest to do so. New England, for example, had discussed withdrawal from the union at the time of the War of 1812. But in the years since then the feeling had grown that it was really the federal union that was the repository of ultimate authority, that the United States was one nation rather than a mere conglomeration of several little nations.

At least that feeling had developed for some people, most notably those who had most to gain from such a sense. There were areas where men felt not heartened but threatened by the growth of such central power; in the Old Northwest states, there was a good deal of resentment at being held in thrall to the manufacturing power of the East. And in the South, of course, there was the fear that the section, which hitherto had more or less dominated the national life—five of the first fifteen presidents had been from Virginia alone—was now doomed to minority status. Southerners began to feel increasingly besieged in their own country. And feeling so, they went on the offensive.

It was a confusing time, for the country was on the whole doing well economically. Southern cotton producers fattened on the never-ending demand for their product, northern manufacturers found ever more profitable schemes to invest in. By 1840 there were more than twice as many miles of railroad in the United States as there were in Great Britain, the home of the railroad. Cotton was the leading industry in the country, and immigration was growing in a steady stream. Yet the problems, the imbalances, the feelings of dislocation, persisted. No sooner was one issue resolved than another one cropped up.

In 1833, for example, the Nullification Crisis finally ended in the spring with a new tariff bill drawn up by Henry Clay. In December the American Anti-Slavery Society was organized in New York, dedicated to the abolition of slavery. There had been abolitionists around for some time, of course, and the most outspoken of them, William Lloyd Garrison of Newburyport, Massachusetts, had already been publishing his newspaper, *The Liberator*, for two years. Most people, even in the North, regarded the abolitionists as dangerous radicals, the lunatic fringe on the whole question of slavery. Garrison himself was nearly lynched in Boston in 1835; he was doomed to twenty more years of thundering in the wilderness, but his day would come.

All the issues that faced the growing country came increasingly to be defined in terms of slavery, and how they affected the balance between slave and free. When Texas revolted against Mexico, and won its independence, the Texans sent a delegation to Washington to demand either admission to the union or recognition as a new nation. President Jackson, just as he left office, chose to recognize their independence, because Texas was a slave territory, and to admit it as a state

17

would upset the balance in Congress, and give a majority to the slave-holding side.

In the 1840s the central government, especially under President Polk, adopted an aggressively expansionist stance; it went to war with Mexico over the southwestern frontier, and threatened war with Britain over the northwest. Some Southerners began fantasizing about the "Golden Circle," a great and highly imaginary slave-holding empire that should encompass the entire Caribbean and Gulf of Mexico; it was indeed fantasy, though filibusters such as William Walker played at making it reality—it was more than play for Walker; he was shot in 1860—but it would return in another form to haunt the Union as a subversive organization during the Civil War.

Henry Clay of Kentucky, "the Great Compromiser," both one of the great statesmen and one of the great schemers of his era, bought the country a few more years of troubled peace with the Compromise of 1850. He introduced in the Senate a bill that he thought would resolve all of the existing questions about slavery, admission of new states, and the balance of sections. Opposition was prolonged and vigorous; Senator Seward of New York did much to ruin his subsequent chances of becoming president by denouncing slavery and proclaiming that "there is a higher law than the Constitution." On the other side, Senator John C. Calhoun of South Carolina told the North that it must both agree to the extension of slavery and stop agitation about the issue. Thus the lines were clearly drawn, and it was a measure of Clay's ability that he managed to push his compromise through in a series of five acts. Yet even that brought the country closer to division, for one of the five, a sop to the South, was a strong law for apprehending fugitive slaves.

The issue simply defied efforts to make it go away. To Southerners, a slave might be three fifths of a person when it came to counting him for representation in Congress, but a slave was all property, like a stray cow or a runaway horse, if he tried to flee to the North or to Canada. Southerners bitterly resented that northerners—actually, a minuscule number of them—helped slaves escape, and the whole issue was one of those matters clouded in mythology. Very few slaves did manage to escape; there was indeed an "underground railway," but it was far less organized than the term implies, and what there was, was mostly a matter of sympathetic and helpful free blacks rather than whites. Most of the abolitionists had little or nothing to do with it.

The new Fugitive Slave Act that came out of the Compromise of 1850, however, empowered federal commissioners to catch runaway slaves, denied the blacks any judicial recourse, and penalized citizens for refusing to support the authorities. Northerners felt shamed by the sight of blacks led off in chains, and many states passed personal freedom laws that virtually contradicted the federal law—playing, in other words, the same game of nullification as South Carolina had done twenty years earlier. By its insistence on its "rights," the South was giving increasing ammunition to the abolitionist cause.

Even more ammunition came from an unlikely source. In 1851, in response to the new laws, a woman named Harriet Beecher Stowe, the wife of a professor at Bowdoin College in Maine, began publishing *Uncle Tom's Cabin* as a newspaper serial. Issued as a book in 1852, it sold 300,000 copies in the first year, and seven million eventually. It was a literary phenomenon—by contrast, Herman Melville's entire output in his life was just over 50,000 copies—and for many people it turned slavery from an abstract legal question into a burning moral drama. On meeting Stowe in 1861, Abraham Lincoln remarked, "So this is the little woman who wrote the book that made this great war."

Bitterly resented in the South, the book inflamed the sectional rivalries becoming ever more important in American life. But so did everything else. Next on the list was the issue of a transcontinental railroad and the route it should take. Fortunes would be made and lost on the choice, and, at least indirectly, blood would be shed, for the railroad question led to the fateful problem of Kansas.

Senator Stephen A. Douglas wanted the western railroad to run from Illinois, his own state, and to get that, he moved to organize the territory of Nebraska and bring it in as a state. Southerners objected; Nebraska was north of 36°30', and would therefore be a free state, and upset the precarious congressional balance. All right, said Douglas; split it in two, call the southern part Kansas, and bring it in as a slave state; Douglas could be pretty flexible on such matters. Others could not; the proposed Kansas was still north of 36°30', so bringing it in as a slave state violated the time-honored Missouri Compromise. All right, said Douglas again, let the inhabitants decide for themselves whether they wanted to be a free or a slave state. To him it was a matter of deals and accommodations, but this new specter he rather casually conjured up—Popular Sovereignty—doomed Kansas to a bloody period of violence, split the country, helped split his party, focused sectional antagonisms, and in short, did much to cause the eventual breakup of the union.

Kansas itself became "Bleeding Kansas," a territory of mobs and gangs, of lynchings, shootings at night, rigged elections, and literally murderous rivalries. It finally had two legislatures, one "slave" and one "free," and two constitutions, and the issue was not resolved until the Civil War itself subsumed it.

Blood in Kansas, and blood on the floor of the Senate. In May of 1856, Senator Charles Sumner of Massachusetts, an outspoken antislavery radical, delivered a slashing speech on the Kansas issue. Three days later Preston Brooks, U.S. representative from South Carolina, marched into the Senate chamber and fiercely beat Sumner with his cane. The Yankee senator was permanently crippled, and did not return to the Senate until 1859. Northerners and sympathetic southerners alike were appalled, but Brooks also received hundreds of canes in the mail from enthusiastic supporters.

The next year the Supreme Court handed down its decision in the famous Dred Scott case, which had dragged on in one form or another for years. It was argued that Scott, a slave, had been effectively freed when his master took him north of the 36°30' line. Chief Justice Roger B. Taney wrote a convoluted decision denying that a black could be a citizen, and ruling that an American citizen—that is, Scott's master— could not be deprived of his property by the simple act of moving from one part of the country to another, a decision that made the whole Missouri Compromise, and the entire edifice of accommodation built since 1820, unconstitutional. In other words, according to Taney, slavery was legal—anywhere and everywhere in the United States.

Again there was a howl of southern triumph and a storm of northern protest. The pro-slavery interests seemed everywhere to be on the offensive, and in Congress, in the White House, in the Supreme Court, they appeared to be carrying the day.

The ironic, indeed tragic, element in all this was that the more successful they were, the more demanding the slavery interests became. They not only wanted to have their way, they wanted everyone else to agree willingly that they *should* have their way. And every time they met opposition, they responded by threatening secession. Very few slaves were going to be taken to Kansas, yet they wanted Kansas to be a slave state; even fewer were going to be taken to New Mexico, but they wanted that to be slave territory, too. No southerners at all were going to move to Wisconsin and set up a slave plantation, yet the logical implication of the Dred Scott decision was that they should be able to do so, in the impossible event that they should want to. In pursuit of such hypothetical rights, they sundered the national institutions that had held the country together, and eventually they sundered the country as well.

The Democratic Party was the last of these great national institutions to go. The other national party, the Whigs, was moribund, a pale ghost of the strong force it had been for a generation. After 1852 it split, and those of its members willing to accommodate slavery, the "cotton Whigs," moved into the Democratic ranks, while those opposed, the "conscience Whigs," became Republicans. The Democrats held together through the 1856 election, putting Buchanan in office in the face of a surprisingly strong showing by John C. Frémont, the Republican challenger, but that was about as far as they got. Historian Kenneth Stampp contends that the year 1857 was decisive; between Kansas, Dred Scott, and a host of lesser problems, the Democrats began to come apart. Douglas, the leading man of the party, and Buchanan, the president he helped elect, quarreled. By 1858 it was becoming increasingly obvious that there were really two Democratic parties, a northern one, in great disarray, and a southern one, ever more dominant and ever more demanding that its views be accepted by the whole.

Thus as the decade of the fifties neared its end, there appeared both less and less room for compromise, and fewer and fewer institutions capable of bringing it about. The extremists were more vocal than ever. Early in 1859 the Southern Commercial Convention called for the reopening of the African slave trade, an idea occasionally bruited in the South for about twenty-five years but seldom given serious consideration. And later in the year, on the other side, John Brown tried to raise a slave revolt.

Brown, from Connecticut, was a fanatical abolitionist; he had taken part in the fighting in Kansas, and under normal conditions, would have been tried and convicted of murder. Now, with the support of wealthy and frustrated abolitionists, some of whom knew what he was doing, others of whom were careful not to know, he decided that further violence was the only answer. To this end, he and some twenty followers seized the federal arsenal at Harpers Ferry, Virginia, on the night of October 16. Overrun within a day by troops commanded by

Colonel Robert E. Lee, Brown was tried for treason. Before he was executed, he turned the trial into a showcase for his opinions. No one has ever been able to show definitively whether Brown was crazy or sane, or how much he was of either. Like many similar people, he was able to conduct a clever defense, and to appear, to those predisposed to regard him as such, as a martyr. To pro-slavery people he looked like the Fiend incarnate, the personification all of that was evil in the North, and the realization of their worst fears.

Personification and fear were indeed a large part of the problem. When Lincoln, in the closing paragraph of his inaugural address, appealed to "the better angels of our nature," he was invoking an attitude that had been largely submerged by the stresses and strains of the last few years. One should not think that sectionalism, slavery, and states' rights were the only matters claiming Americans' attention; there was a bank panic in 1857; the North was torn by anti-immigrant feeling, producing the Know-Nothing Party and anti-foreign legislation in such states as Massachusetts; the Mormons were in near revolt in Utah; gangs fought in the streets in New York City. But again and again the country came back to the split between North and South, and under repeated assault, the national consensus was breaking apart.

Faced with this, northerners and southerners developed a largely fictitious picture, a stereotype, of each other. To northerners, the typical southern male was a hard-drinking, hard-riding wastrel, living off the sweat of the slave, boastful, bullying, threatening, fiscally and morally irresponsible, at best a romantic fool and at worst a sadistic beast. The northerner was just the opposite: he was mature, conscientious, careful, rational—a modern man. The southerner, by contrast, saw himself as religious, chivalrous, sensitive, a responsible steward of his people, white and black, and a proud guardian of his state's heritage. But he saw the northerner as a mean-spirited, hypocritical, money-grubbing capitalist, whining about the poor black slaves while keeping his own workers in conditions worse than slavery, determined to grind the South down through tariffs and to have his own way with the nation.

All of these pictures were of course ridiculous, and it would be equally absurd to assert that all Americans held these views of other Americans. But enough Americans held them to give some credence to the statement that the sections of the country were indeed breaking apart, and that people in any section were in the process of mythologizing and thus dehumanizing the people in another section. And dehumanizing your enemy is the first step in the process of killing him.

Most people, of course, simply wanted to live their lives and get on with their affairs. The abolitionist of the North remained a marginal rather than a dominant figure. Few northerners were willing to fight to free the slaves; indeed, relatively few northerners cared a hoot about the slaves, and to the extent that people did care, it was largely the feckless actions of the South that made them aware of the issue. Well into the war itself, Lincoln had to be very careful of how he handled abolition, for the fear of what support any firm advocacy of it might cost him.

The southern situation was even more complex. Most southerners were in fact not slaveholders, so the section was actually in thrall to a dominant minority, those who owned slaves or had a vested interest in supporting the slave system. That system had trapped the South in a time warp; immigrants came to the North because only there could they make headway; free labor of the type most immigrants could do was unable to compete with southern slave labor. Southerners said they preferred not to have the immigrants anyway, but in so doing, they denied their section the dynamic forces of free labor and investment capital that were transforming the North and leaving the South behind.

There, finally, lay the root of the problem. The United States as a whole was expanding and evolving very rapidly into a modern mixed-economy mid-nineteenth-century society, and the South was not keeping up. Because it was not, its traditional domination of the national scene, especially in politics, was slipping. Faced with that, southern leaders developed a siege mentality; threatened by external forces they could neither fully understand nor readily adapt to, they responded with repeated threats: Give us our way or we shall leave. For many years, they successfully staved off the future, and they did get their way. But in the process, they eroded the national will to compromise and ultimately destroyed the institutions capable of achieving further accommodation. When the last of those institutions, the Democratic Party, split into northern and southern factions in 1860, the election of Abraham Lincoln as the first Republican president was all but assured. And southerners already knew what they would do if that happened.

But they did not know what the result of their action would be.

Chapter 3

Choosing Sides

WRITERS HAVE often asserted that the outcome of the Civil War was simply inevitable, the North so outweighing the South that there was really no contest. If such were truly the case, then one would have to ask why the men of 1861, who could count as well as authors a century later, were as stupid as they would seem to be. For if the outcome was a foregone conclusion, the Confederates were remarkably stubborn in resisting it, and the Union equally incompetent in attaining it.

Stating the matter thus baldly reveals how silly the assertion actually is. After Lincoln called for 75,000 men for three months' service, he consulted with his army commander, Winfield Scott; the latter offered the opinion that *maybe* 750,000 men could put down the rebellion in three years. Lincoln was appalled; but even then Scott had underestimated what it would take to do the job.

Far from being a clear-cut matter of arithmetic, the war was an extraordinarily close thing, and at any one of several points, or for any one of many factors, it could have had a different ending. If, in the end, God did prove to be on the side of the big battalions, that was a result of the process of the war itself, and of the decisions, wrong or right, made by the participants in it. Historians, as a rule, prefer to argue against the concept of inevitability—to accept it would put them out of business. But so do most human beings: who among us would rather trust to the wisdom of statisticians than take arms against our fate?

It is necessary first of all to assess the resources available to either side, to see how they balance out. That is a balance that must not,

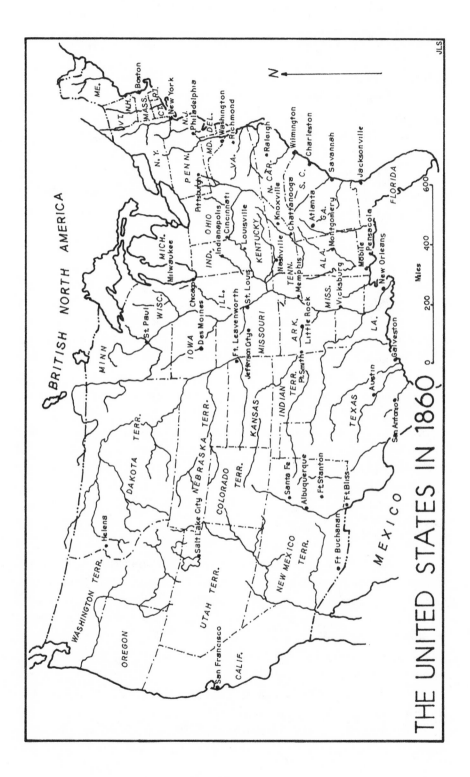

THE UNITED STATES IN 1860

however, be taken in isolation; it is also necessary to consider the aims of either side, for if they each had different assets, they each also had different aims. Finally, it is particularly germane to consider the choices made and roles played by the border and middle states. Had any or any number of them chosen a different side from the one they joined, then not only would the balance of forces have been changed, but the geostrategic picture would have been so significantly altered that the entire conflict would have proceeded differently. The choices those states made, however, were a part of the war itself, so it is useful to assess the relative strength of the combatants first, and then to discuss which way the middle states moved and why they did so.

―――

At the time of the attack on Fort Sumter the United States consisted of all the territory of the present contiguous mainland. Neither Alaska nor Hawaii had yet been acquired. Much of the West was as yet unsettled by Americans; California, acquired in the Mexican War and admitted as a state in 1850, and Oregon, admitted in 1859, remained isolated. There were thirty-four states, the latest of them being Kansas, admitted only in January of 1861. The census of 1860 gave the country a population of 31,443,321. That figure suggests a degree of precision, a precision that soon fades into estimates upon breaking the country in two.

Of the thirty-four states, eleven seceded to form the Confederate States of America. They counted a population of about nine million, which left something more than twenty-two million for the Union. Four slave states, Delaware, Maryland, Kentucky, and Missouri, remained in the Union. In all of the middle states, however, not just these four, men made individual choices. Though Kentucky was a Union state, there were Kentucky regiments in the Confederate army, and though Tennessee was a Confederate state, there were Tennessee regiments in the Union army. East Tennessee was a hotbed of Union loyalism throughout the war, and Lincoln nearly drove his generals to distraction wanting to send forces into that area. On the other side, Jefferson Davis was similarly plagued by refugee Kentucky politicians assuring him the population would support a Confederate invasion of its territory. The population of western Virginia was so overwhelmingly loyal to the Union—and resentful of eastern domination—that it seceded in turn from Virginia, and was admitted as a state of the Union in 1863. So it went, and the Confederacy may be said to have had a population of roughly nine million, and the Union of twenty-two million.

But of the nine million Confederates, perhaps three million were slaves, and the figure may have been as high as three and a half million. How these people should be counted depends almost entirely upon the sympathies and predilections of the counter. Almost unanimously they wanted a Union victory, and would not willingly assist the Confederacy; on the other hand, as slaves, there was little they could do about it, unless and until they were liberated by Union military action. Even if they preferred not to support the Confederate war effort, they necessarily supported the Southern economy, and at times, they made an actual military contribution, often being used, for example, to dig fortifications in one place or another.

Setting aside this vexing issue, we have perhaps six million white people in the Confederacy, some less but most more committed to their cause. Twenty-three states remained in the Union, or twenty-four if West Virginia be counted, with a population of twenty-two million. But of that, California and Oregon contributed very little in manpower to the war, and again, the population of the four middle slave states must be split. It is probably roughly correct to say that a Confederacy of six million faced a Union of twenty-one million, giving the Union a manpower superiority of three and a half to one.

Much has been made of the superior manufacturing capacity of the North as opposed to the essentially agricultural economy of the Confederacy. This has been overstated, in part because it has been romanticized. The mythology of the "Lost Cause" pitted the natural and agricultural South against the artificial manufacturing North. The northern states, and especially the northeastern states, were indeed relatively highly industrialized, and there is no doubt that the much stronger and more balanced economy of the Union was better suited to modern warfare than was the more highly agricultural South. Confederates hoped to offset this by imports from Europe, paid for with their cotton, but the Union blockade cut off a good deal of that possibility. As it went on, however, the Confederacy proved surprisingly adept at developing its own manufacturing capacity. The fact was that both societies were agriculturally based—in the nineteenth century *all* societies were that—but the North was marginally more industrialized than was the South, the margin was a large one, and it was an extremely important one.

The best case in point for this issue would be railroads. The American Civil War was really the first railroad war, though the new means of transportation had been used, in a hesitant way, in both the Crimean War and in the short Franco-Austrian War of 1859. In this war, however, Americans would make railroads the sinews of their armies and the object of their operations. Here the Northern advantage is clearly shown.

In the Union's territories there were some 22,385 miles of track. Though this was split among competing companies, and here and there was impeded by different gauges, so that cars from one line could not operate on another, it nonetheless formed a coherent transportation system. That system proved less than needed, as well as a source of immense profit and possible corruption for its owners and operators; one of the notorious profiteers, for example, was Lincoln's first secretary of war, Simon Cameron, who was also a vice president of the Pennsylvania Railroad. Early in 1862 the federal government passed the Railways and Telegraph Act, giving Lincoln the power in effect to nationalize the railways if necessary, and under that threat the operators set uniform rates and got along with the government. The government also set up the United States Military Railroads, and operated its own lines in the active theaters of war.

The Confederacy had only 8,783 miles of track at the start of the war, owned by more than a hundred companies. Some of the roads were but a few miles long, and were used, for example, to bring cotton to steamboat landings. Only about a quarter of the lines were major systems, and again they had different gauges and modes of operation. The Confederate government, whose whole reason for existence was resentment of centralized authority, was far more reluctant than its federal enemy to control and organize the railroad system, and the early weaknesses of the Confederate transport net are some measure of the relative positions of the two combatants. Eventually, indeed, the whole Confederate transportation apparatus collapsed, but that having been said, it should also be pointed out that by the middle years of the war, the Confederates were very effectively utilizing what they had, and were transferring troops from one threat to another almost more efficiently than was the North.

Much was made at the time of the importance of cotton; Southerners believed that, as cotton and its manufacture was then the leading industry of the United States, and as Britain and France were both dependent upon Southern suppliers for their cotton industries, this would give them the necessary leverage to gain recognition of their independence. Even if the North did fight, they told themselves, British and French recognition would mean foreign loans, possibly foreign alliances, and thus Confederate victory. Unfortunately for them, the years immediately before the war had produced bumper crops, so when the war began, Europe was able to get along for some time without fresh imports. By the time that surplus was used up, other factors were taking effect, and European recognition was withheld. Cotton was indeed important, and it was manipulated as a factor in the economy of war, but it did not prove to be nearly the all-important lever that Confederates had hoped it would be.

National finance, the ability of either side to sustain the war effort fiscally, was another area where comparisons may be drawn. The total wealth of the Union was infinitely greater than the total wealth of the Confederacy, as was the ability of the Union to mobilize that wealth for war purposes. The best evidence of this is the matter of what happened to either side's money. In this situation, mere legitimacy counted for a lot, and the Union, like the English Parliament in the seventeenth century, could claim such legitimacy. So in the North, the national institutions simply continued to function, and the North had far less difficulty than the South raising the money with which to wage war.

In fact there are really two issues here: one was the matter of the total national wealth; the other was how to translate that wealth into disposable form for war purposes, that is, how to produce money as distinct from wealth. There had for many years been disagreements in the United States over the simple matter of money; generally speaking, agriculturalists and working people favored paper money, while business interests favored "hard" money, gold and silver, less liable to depreciation. However, as in every major war, the supply of hard money quickly proved far too small for the nation's needs. In the North, banks were faced with a near panic as early as late 1861, indeed, as soon as it became apparent the war was not going to be over in a hurry. Investors and creditors began hoarding their gold and silver, and the war economy threatened to come to a halt because there was no money available to lubricate it. Faced with this, early in 1862 the federal

29

government began issuing paper money, "greenbacks," so called because they were green on one side. Eventually about $450,000,000 was in circulation in paper money. The important thing about the greenbacks, however, was not how many there were, but how valuable they were; at their lowest, in mid-1862, the greenback dollars were worth ninety-one cents of "hard" money, a 9 percent depreciation, virtually negligible in time of war.

The Confederacy, by contrast, had to start from nothing. Its Congress began by passing the Bankers Loan and issuing bonds to the value of $150,000,000. Later they raised a Produce Loan, against the cotton crop of Southern planters. Eventually they went to an income tax and even an agricultural tax in kind, that is, one paid in items rather than in money. But they never really had enough specie to back their finances, and of course they too issued paper money. Unlike its Northern counterpart, however, Confederate money rapidly depreciated. By early 1864 the Confederate secretary of the treasury, Christopher G. Memminger, was reduced to such desperate measures that the Confederacy refused to accept its own money as payment for bills. Before their collapse, the Confederates had run up a national debt of more than $700,000,000, and had experienced inflation of 6,000 percent; their money, the visible expression of their national credit, was worthless. The wonder is, as authorities have noted, not that their finances were so chaotic, but that they managed to last as long as they did in the face of it.

From the foregoing it might indeed appear that the outcome of the war was inevitable, but two factors in particular militate against this view. The first is that the war had to last long enough for the weight to matter. If, for example, the Confederates had somehow managed to win it by 1862, then the long-term inability of the Confederate government to finance the war effort would not have been a matter of concern. History is replete with instances of a weaker state defeating a greater in some lightning attack. So the relative ability of either side to sustain a long war became a factor as a result of the war itself; in other words, it was a matter of the battlefield.

The other factor, which has received a little less notice, is that the aims of the two combatants were quite different, were indeed as disproportionate as the means they possessed to wage the war. The Confederacy had no real designs on the Union; it simply wanted to be quit of it. Except for a few feeble attempts to round out its western borders by forays into New Mexico, the South wanted only to be left alone. It was thus fighting a war whose ultimate aim was simply the defense of its own territorial integrity. It did, of course, carry the war occasionally into the North, but that was a matter only of operational strategy, not of long-term national policy. So all the Confederacy had to do was sustain itself, demonstrate its viability by showing that it could not be conquered, and eventually it would win the war.

The Union set itself a far more difficult task: Lincoln proposed to restore the national authority. That was a polite way of saying the Union intended to destroy the Confederacy, absolutely, totally, lock, stock, and barrel. When the war was ended, the Confederacy should utterly cease to exist. This went beyond even Clausewitz's renowned aim of war: to force the enemy to accept one's will. Here was war carried to a totality of aim seldom seen by the modern world of the nation-state. Napoleon might have wanted to conquer Europe, and he repeatedly lopped off chunks of Prussia, and he put his own brothers on the thrones of Spain and Naples, but he did not expect Prussia, or Spain, or Naples, to disappear as entities. To destroy a nation of six, or nine, million people is a major undertaking, and a far greater task than simply sustaining one against external attack for a period of time. If the Union intended to do what Lincoln said he intended it to do, however judicious the language by which he disguised his war aims, it was going to need all the power it could mobilize, and that, ultimately, was pretty nearly what it did need.

––––––

Through all of this, as was suggested above, the position chosen by the middle states was crucial to the course of the conflict. In the immediate aftermath of Fort Sumter, both Confederate and Union volunteers flocked to the colors. Bands played north and south, and all the pretty girls told all the brave young boys they could love only a soldier. William T. Sherman had already taken a sorrowful leave of friends and supporters, resigned his position as superintendent of the Louisiana State Seminary of Learning and Military Academy, and headed back north, his duty clear to him. John C. Pemberton was a Pennsylvanian, but he had married a Virginian. As Sherman came north, he went south. For others the path was less clear. George H. Thomas of Virginia

31

decided to stay with the old flag, in spite of offers from his state and the disapproval of his sisters, who never spoke to him again. Throughout the border and middle states, tragic scenes took place as families were split, in many cases never to be reunited. For what we consider as entities—this state or that state—were in reality thousands of agonizing individual choices, as men and women argued and prayed to discover their rightful path and place.

Two Eastern Seaboard slave states remained in the Union, Delaware and Maryland. In the former, there were less than two thousand slaves, and most people disapproved, mildly, both of slavery and of secession. Nonetheless, the state had gone for John C. Breckinridge, the Southern Democrat candidate, in the 1860 election, and the people of Delaware were almost as united against coercion of the South as they were against secession. Given its sentiments and its location, Delaware presented little threat to the Union.

Maryland was both more complex and more important, surrounding as it did the district of the national capital. The western upcountry part of the state was largely Unionist, but the eastern part was pro-Southern, and in fact saw some of the earliest blood of the war. On April 19, the 6th Massachusetts Regiment, marching through Baltimore on its way to Washington, was attacked by a pro-secession mob. Hustled and pelted with stones, the soldiers opened fire, and got through the city only at a cost of four soldiers and twelve civilians. The state's governor, Thomas Hicks, refused to call the legislature into session, knowing it would demand at least a secession convention. Only when Federal troops clearly dominated Baltimore did the state government finally meet, and even then Maryland was held for the Union largely by political chicanery, including a number of illegal arrests of politicians.

Virginia was the first state to secede after Fort Sumter. Two days after Lincoln's call for volunteers, the state adopted a secession bill; even more important, ex-governor Henry Wise moved to seize the federal arsenal at Harpers Ferry and the navy yard at Gosport near Norfolk. The weak federal garrisons tried unsuccessfully to burn both, which were soon in Confederate hands. Officially Virginia did not secede until May; in fact, although originally voting against it, most of the state was by now "wild for secession," blaming Lincoln for starting the war, and joining enthusiastically in the new Confederacy, which reciprocated by moving its capital from Montgomery in Alabama to Richmond.

North Carolina was far less enthusiastic than its neighbors either

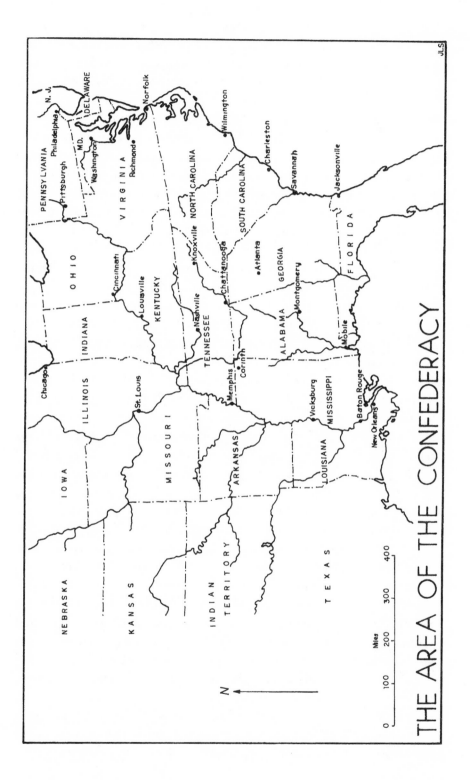

THE AREA OF THE CONFEDERACY

NEBRASKA

IOWA

KANSAS

INDIAN
TERRITORY

TEXAS

MISSOURI

ARKANSAS

LOUISIANA

ILLINOIS

INDIANA

OHIO

PENNSYLVANIA

KENTUCKY

TENNESSEE

MISSISSIPPI

ALABAMA

GEORGIA

FLORIDA

SOUTH CAROLINA

NORTH CAROLINA

VIRGINIA

MD.

DELAWARE

N. J.

Chicago

St. Louis

Memphis

Vicksburg

Baton Rouge

New Orleans

Mobile

Montgomery

Corinth

Nashville

Knoxville

Chattanooga

Atlanta

Louisville

Cincinnati

Pittsburgh

Philadelphia

Washington

Richmond

Norfolk

Wilmington

Charleston

Savannah

Jacksonville

N

Miles

0   100   200   300   400

JLS

north or south. Union sentiment was strong, especially in the western counties, and the inhabitants of the Old North State tended to regard Virginians as too full of themselves and South Carolinians as hotheaded fools. Yet the logic of geography and ultimately of sentiment pulled them toward the Confederacy. When Lincoln called for volunteers, Governor John Ellis replied that such a call was unconstitutional and a usurpation of power by the federal government. He refused to call the state militia into service, and on May 20 North Carolina seceded and joined the Confederacy, the last but one of its members to do so.

The last of them was Tennessee, and the state was torn apart by the decision. It was a peculiar split, for the eastern part of the state, mountainous, peopled by small freeholders, poor, proud, and fiercely independent, was solidly for the Union; while the western part, more prosperous and cultivated, was for secession. In January the state's voters turned down secession by a four-to-one margin, and refused even to call a convention to consider the issue.

The voters reckoned without their governor, Isham G. Harris, so strong for the South that he earned the sobriquet "the War Governor of Tennessee." After Fort Sumter, he pushed through legislation calling for military liaison with the Confederacy, and began recruiting troops, eventually producing about 100,000. The eastern counties refused support, and made some feeble moves to secede from Tennessee as Tennessee was seceding from the Union, but Harris sent his troops in and held the territory for the state, and ultimately for the Confederacy. These east Tennessee Unionists were the people Lincoln wanted so much to help, but he was unable to do so for most of the war.

The only other state that actually seceded was Arkansas, but its adherence to the Confederacy was less a foregone conclusion than might appear from its position on the map. Governor Henry M. Rector was himself an ardent secessionist, but his citizens were not as single-minded as he was. As early as February of 1861, he had state troops seize the federal arsenal at Little Rock, but next month when he called a secession convention, the delegates voted against him and adopted a wait-and-see attitude instead. After Sumter, Rector by himself refused the federal call for volunteers, and then called a second convention. This time Arkansans followed him, though many did so reluctantly, and the state seceded in early May. Like most of the other border states, it remained divided, and for a good part of the war, it had two rival governments.

Of all the states at issue, that left only Kentucky. What was it to do? Lincoln knew how important it was strategically: "I *hope* I have God on my side—but I *must* have Kentucky." Kentuckians themselves hardly knew what course to choose. Economically they were Southerners; by tradition and inclination they were pro-Union, very proud of Kentucky statesmen, notably Henry Clay, who had done so much to keep the Union together over the last couple of generations. The governor, Beriah Magoffin, was an idealist, accused of being a traitor by either side; he decided that the only hope for the entire country lay in Kentucky remaining neutral, a buffer between the two factions, until wiser counsels should prevail. He would have put the issue of the state's secession to a plebiscite, but his pro-Union legislature refused to authorize it, fearing the voters might go South. Magoffin called out the state militia, which promptly divided into two. Then he allowed Confederate recruiters into the southern part of the state, and the Union set up recruiting offices across the Ohio River to attract Kentucky volunteers.

Kentucky neutrality was a chimera; the state could go either way, and it was largely a question of which side played its cards more carefully. In the event, President Lincoln won the trick; he was much more at home in this game than Jefferson Davis with his logical, legalistic mind. To Davis, since Kentucky neutrality was a sham, he treated it as such, while Lincoln played along with it. Davis was soon undercut, anyway, by the unauthorized action of Leonidas K. Polk, his western commander, who simply sent troops into Columbus, Kentucky, a useful port on the Mississippi. Federal troops under Ulysses S. Grant occupied Paducah in retaliation. Magoffin called for an alliance with the United States, but Lincoln simply dragged his feet, whereupon Magoffin abandoned his high-minded neutrality and called for help. Kentucky for the Union.

There was one other slave state, Missouri, sticking up west of the Mississippi like a large bastion. Its solidity on the map was the only solid thing about it, though. The state was divided several ways, but until Fort Sumter the moderates held sway against a newly elected and strongly pro-secession governor, Claiborne F. Jackson. In early May Jackson set up a training camp outside St. Louis and garrisoned it with the state militia, like himself pro-Southern. However, he had not counted on Nathaniel Lyon.

Lyon was a redheaded, hot-tempered Connecticut Yankee in the U.S.

35

Army, strongly Republican and violently anti-Southern after serving in Bleeding Kansas. Though he was only a captain, he was a man of action. Suspecting that Claiborne planned to use his militia to take control of the federal arsenal in St. Louis, Lyon dressed up as a woman and toured the militia camp. He teamed up with Francis P. Blair, Jr., one of the Missouri's leading Unionists, son of one of Lincoln's big backers and brother of the postmaster general. Taking their own troops, they surrounded the militia's Camp Jackson and by a preemptive dawn strike disarmed the opposition. Unfortunately Lyon then paraded his prisoners through St. Louis, causing a riot in which twenty-eight people were killed. Claiborne denounced all this as foreign invasion, and declared for the Confederacy, moving the capital to Jefferson City and leaving Lyon and Blair in possession of the state. Lincoln immediately promoted Lyon from captain to brigadier general. The state was subsequently torn apart, with two rival governments, and large numbers of men serving on both sides, in a ratio of about two and a half to one in favor of the Union. Little columns fought back and forth across the state for much of the war, though it generally was treated as a Union state from now on. Lyon himself was killed at the battle of Wilson's Creek in August, characteristically taking the offensive against an enemy that outnumbered him two to one.

The path chosen by any of these border states was thus a mixture, of politics and often of political sleight of hand, tending off into violence and ultimately regular military action. As in all of America's wars, men were willing to go long distances to fight. Arkansas and Louisiana troops helped the Confederate Missourians at Wilson's Creek, and an Iowa regiment fought on the side of the Union Missourians. Farther west, Texans attempted to extend their control into New Mexico, and state troops under Lieutenant Colonel John R. Baylor fought a little engagement with Federal soldiers at Mesilla, northwest of El Paso, in July. It was well into the summer before the general battle lines were drawn: Virginia, Tennessee, and Missouri were to see the most battles of the entire war, as armies moved back and forth, asserting or losing control of vital territory and communication arteries.

So by September the sides were chosen; men had made their choices, stepped forward, held up their hands or put their names on the line. The time for speeches and patriotic poses was over. It was time now for fighting.

Chapter 4

Opening Operations

THE VOLUNTEERS flocked in. North or South, there was no lack of men willing to fight. President Davis had called for 100,000 men, and had already armed and equipped a third of them before the Union stirred itself. Lincoln's call for 75,000 was spurned by the secessionist states, but brought a fierce growl of response throughout the North. Almost every state could have doubled its quota of regiments, and there was a sudden run on military books, as men of ambition tried to transform themselves overnight into officer material. The first call, for three-month men, brought in 91,000. In May Lincoln issued another call, for three years' service this time, and by the first of July, there were 310,000 troops in federal service. On the 4th of July, giving a traditional holiday speech to Congress, Lincoln asked for 400,000; the legislators responded by voting 500,000.

Part of the response stemmed from the fact that there was already a very active militia movement in the country, so it was full of young men playing at soldier anyway. These were quickly embodied in state service, and showed up wearing a variety of bizarre uniforms, including anachronistic Revolution-period coats or exotic North African baggy trousers. Many units clung to their bright uniforms even after they discovered what good targets they made.

But there was more to the rush to war than mere playing. Americans on either side were firm in their convictions, Southerners that they had been wronged by the growth of government and were justified in withdrawing from the compact, and Unionists that the compact, and the experiment it represented, were a noble enterprise that must not be allowed to fail. Men on both sides appealed to the sacrifices of their

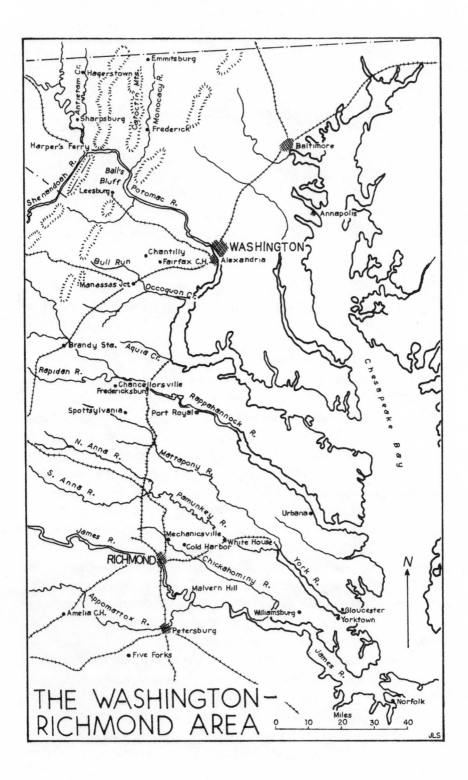

THE WASHINGTON–RICHMOND AREA

Emmitsburg

Hagerstown
Antietam Cr.
Catoctin Mts.
Monocacy R.

Sharpsburg

Frederick

Harper's Ferry

Baltimore

Shenandoah R.

Ball's Bluff

Leesburg

Potomac R.

Annapolis

Chantilly
Fairfax C.H.
WASHINGTON
Alexandria

Bull Run

Manassas Jct.

Occoquon Cr.

Brandy Sta. Aquia Cr.

Chesapeake Bay

Rapidan R.

Chancellorsville
Fredericksburg

Rappahannock R.

Spottsylvania

Port Royal

N. Anna R.

Mattapony R.

S. Anna R.

Pamunkey R.

James R.

Mechanicsville

White House

Urbana

RICHMOND

Cold Harbor

Chickahominy R.

York R.

Malvern Hill

Appomattox R.

Amelia C.H.

Williamsburg

Gloucester
Yorktown

Petersburg

James R.

Five Forks

N

Miles
0   10   20   30   40

Norfolk

JLS

grandfathers; both claimed to represent the legitimate heritage of the Revolution. The war could in this sense be seen as honoring a debt to the heroic past. The people of the Civil War generation often expressed their sentiments in exalted language which may sound a little artificial to a later generation, but the feelings so expressed were obviously sincere to them—they were willing to risk dying for them. Thoughtful men of course deplored the fact that a family disagreement had come to blows—but since it had, better to fight and have done with it. As they have done repeatedly since, men regarded the war as a necessary purging, a blood sacrifice that would make society, either one, whole and pure. The war would thus become a rite of passage to maturity, for both individuals and the nation as a group.

So the armies gathered. In Washington and Richmond harassed officials rushed frantically about, trying to buy equipment, trying to match men and matériel, trying to fend off office-seekers, trying to separate the charlatan from the patriot. In the space of three months the United States forces increased 2,700 percent; at the same time the Confederacy created an army even while creating a government to manage it. On both sides it was a mobilization unmatched in scope and rapidity before or since.

What that translated to in the field was exponential confusion. The state units sent to the front all had different drill, different words of command, different forms of doing things. Most of them elected their officers; some of the officers were competent, some were fools. Some units arrived well equipped and reasonably well disciplined; some arrived as little more than mobs. The regular-army officers and the volunteer officers, some of whom were retired or resigned West Point graduates, tried desperately to make sense out of the whole matter.

Gradually it transpired that there was a Federal army around Washington, largely encamped on the Alexandria side of the Potomac. And there was a Confederate army somewhere south of it down in northern Virginia. Faced with the fact that his first three-month volunteers would soon be ready to go home, President Lincoln decided that they ought to do something before they left, and that what they ought to do was go beat up that Confederate army. If that sounds somewhat amateurish, that indeed is just what it was, but Lincoln was not a free agent. On the one hand, he had his soldiers despairing that the volunteers could ever be taught to march in step and keep their ranks dressed; on the other, he had every newspaper editor in the country shrieking at him and lambasting the government for its spineless inaction. For if there were no lack of men willing to fight, there were even more men ready to inspire them to do it. For belligerence, bellicosity, and bombast, it would be hard to beat the popular press of the Civil War era; they knew all, they told all, they were never wrong, and they made fortunes pointing out other people's short-comings. So the Southern editors cried, "On to Washington!" and the Northern editors clamored, "On to Richmond!" and it was necessary to do *something* to still the noise.

Lincoln's troubles began at the top. The commander of the United States Army was Winfield Scott, a great soldier whose experience went all the way back to the war of 1812. It was Scott who suggested that Lincoln blockade the South, it was he who told the president how many men he would need to fight the war. But Scott was in his mid-seventies, unwell and unable to sit a horse. Lincoln needed a field commander. He first offered the position to Robert E. Lee, he who had commanded the troops against John Brown, but Lee decided to go with his home state of Virginia. Lincoln's second choice was Irvin McDowell. There were reasons for this, but none of them was particularly germane. McDowell had been in the Adjutant General's office; he was well-known in Republican circles in Washington, and he was the protégé of Salmon P. Chase. He had never in his entire career commanded troops in the field. His chief claim was that he was probably as good as anyone else; his chief drawback was that every other officer around knew he was no better than anyone else.

Still, McDowell knew the rudiments of what ought to be done, and he drew up an operation order that looked fairly sensible. The situation was this: A Confederate force of uncertain strength was centered around Manassas Junction in Virginia, about thirty miles southwest of Washington. It was commanded by the hero of Fort Sumter, General Beauregard. Then across the Blue Ridge in western Virginia, around Winchester, there was another Confederate force, commanded by Joseph E. Johnston. This latter was to be held by Union troops under the command of Robert Patterson, a Pennsylvania state general. McDowell could thus advance straight against Beauregard, and since he should substantially outnumber him, he ought to beat him.

On July 16 the great advance on Richmond began. McDowell's army struck its tents on the heights of Alexandria, and marched off to glorious war, the colors flapping in the breeze, the bands playing, and the troops in high spirits. Two days later and twenty miles down the road, hungry, tired, blisters breaking on their feet, the road behind them littered with all the junk they had thought they might need, the mob staggered into Centerville and collapsed. The officers spent the night of July 17–18 cursing, while the men wandered around, trying to find their regiments in the dark, lost, lonely, and thoroughly sick of soldiering.

That same day, Johnston got a telegram from Richmond, telling him McDowell had advanced, and directing him to march to aid Beauregard if he could do so. It happened that he could indeed do so, for Patterson, not understanding what he was supposed to do, had taken counsel of his own fears and retreated northward. He could hardly be blamed; in the War of 1812, after all, which was where he had learned his soldiering, they had not had all this nonsense with telegrams. Johnston put his men on the road, heading southeast toward Manassas. Meanwhile Beauregard, who in fact had about 20,000 troops, spread them along ten miles of a little creek called Bull Run and waited to see what might happen.

On the morning of the 18th, McDowell sent forward one of his five divisions, under Brigadier General Daniel Tyler, as a sort of reconnaissance in force, but told him not to get into trouble. A little too enthusiastic, Tyler got into a fight at two of the fords over Bull Run, and had his troops mauled by the well-positioned Confederates. This skirmish spread sufficient confusion among both the Union ranks and their commanders that for the next three days the army did nothing much at all, cooked rations, sorted out lost soldiers, and brought up a few units from the rear. In that interval the Confederates did much better. Most importantly, a large part of Johnston's command arrived; surprise!—he had not marched his men the full fifty miles from Winchester to Manassas; he had put them on trains of the Manassas Gap Railroad. With his troops plus a few others, the Confederates now had about 32,000 men in hand, and even more expected hourly.

With their troops on the field and as organized as they were going to get, both commanders developed their battle plans, and both decided to do the same thing. Each proposed to turn the other's right, roll up a flank, and destroy the enemy. McDowell was the more energetic of the two, and he got his people moving first, though his columns stumbled into each other and spent several hours of the early morning shoving and sorting themselves out. Nonetheless, they were still ahead of the Confederates, and Beauregard was rudely startled from his leisurely breakfast at the Wilbur McLean house when a cannonball crashed into the kitchen. The experience of this battle, incidentally, so unnerved Mr. McLean that he

41

decided to move his family, and he settled in Appomattox, southwest of Richmond, for the remainder of the war.

Beauregard still persevered in his intention to attack, and began issuing orders to put his right wing in motion. In fact, his staff got their written instructions so confused that one brigade crossed Bull Run and advanced out in the open, one prepared to attack, and one did nothing at all. By mid-morning, with the right-flank Confederates milling around, Beauregard finally realized that his left was under heavy pressure—the Federals having at last got themselves shaken out—and that he was in fact faced with a crisis.

Up at that end of the battlefield, Brigadier General Nathan G. "Shanks" Evans had refused his flank, and was now fighting desperately along Young's Branch, a little brook perpendicular to Bull Run, trying to hold back the Federal pressure. He was supported by Bee's and Bartow's brigades, but the opposition kept building up, and finally lapped around his open left flank. The Rebels went back up and over Henry House Hill, steadily at first and then at a run, and by late morning, the battle was beginning to fall apart for them.

Unfortunately for McDowell, all this was more the result of good luck than of good management, for the battle was hardly being managed at all. Once a commander had set things in motion, he was dependent on what his subordinates told him or what his staff could find out. McDowell marshaled his forces around the Henry House Hill, but the Confederates, even though badly outnumbered, did better. Troops under Thomas J. Jackson arrived, more were on the way, and the Confederates, pushed off the hill, came back again. Union artillery pounded them for a few moments, but were then decimated by an attack of the 33rd Virginia; the Virginians had blue uniforms, and the gunners had held their fire just too long.

By mid-afternoon the fight had stabilized around the Henry House Hill. McDowell had several brigades in line now, a bit mixed up but still full of fight. The Confederates too had steadied their line, mostly due to Jackson's efficient eye for a position: "Look at Jackson's brigade; it stands like a stone wall! Rally behind the Virginians!" As the Federals came forward a last time, newly arrived Confederates of Edmund Kirby Smith's brigade came crashing in on their right flank, and the attack fell apart. The Federals frayed out and went back, slowly at first, then, as they crossed Bull Run, as fast as they could.

The flight did not stop until it got all the way back to Alexandria.

McDowell tried in vain to halt the army at Centerville, but whenever a unit would try to rally, someone would sound an alarm, and off they would go again. Many units collapsed; many more, footsore and disgusted, marched hour after hour, grumbling and cursing. The way was a shambles, full of abandoned wagons, civilian carriages overturned and left by owners who had come out from Washington to see the fun, drunks, fools, whores, all the garbage a beaten and retreating army leaves behind it. The Confederates, almost as exhausted and at least as confused by their victory as the Yankees were by their defeat, could not develop an effective pursuit. Beauregard ordered it, but the two brigadiers he sent out fell to quarreling over who was in command, and after wandering around a while picking up trash, the Rebels gave it up.

The First Battle of Bull Run, or First Battle of Manassas, as the Confederates called it, was the first major battle of the war. Given that, both sides had done rather well; either one could have won it. The men had fought certainly as well as could have been expected. The North sustained just under three thousand casualties, and the South just under two. A few of the field commanders had done pretty well. On the Confederate side, Jackson, otherwise a bit of an eccentric, had handled his troops very nicely, and there had been some good cavalry work done by a dashing young fellow named J.E.B. "Jeb" Stuart. The Union too had a few good brigade leaders, including Fitz John Porter and William Sherman, and what would become a Federal hallmark, good artillery.

Higher command was a little shakier, naturally so. In their entire history, Americans had never fought on this scale before. Each of the armies alone was as big as both sides in any previous American battle, and it takes a great deal of practice to be able to move 30,000 men around the countryside in a coherent way. McDowell had divided his army into five divisions, but had not managed to control them very well. Several thousand Federal troops spent the day marching vaguely here and there, and listening to the sound of distant gunfire. On the Confederate side, the matter was even more confused; Johnston ranked Beauregard, but generously set himself to organizing the arriving troops, while letting Beauregard fight his own battle on his own ground. Beauregard was lucky to have the help, which allowed him to redeem faulty dispositions and an erroneous concept of the battle. He was even luckier in that he won. McDowell had no such saving grace. Obviously, both sides still had a great deal to learn, but the Confederates seemed to have a little less to learn than the Federals.

While Confederate newspapers exulted that the war was all but over, it actually began. Polk and Grant maneuvered out along the Mississippi, and played games with Kentucky neutrality, and Lyon held Missouri for the Union. Strange things happened in western Virginia, too. The area where Ohio, Kentucky, Pennsylvania, and Virginia all met— the area that would become the state of West Virginia—was one of the vortices of the war. Activity swirled all around it, but little could actually be accomplished there, except the losing of reputations, or perhaps the making of them.

George Brinton McClellan had resigned a promising but slow career in the Army to become chief engineer of the Illinois Central Railroad in 1857. In 1861 he was living in Cincinnati and was president of the Ohio and Mississippi Railroad. The governor of Ohio, William Dennison, commissioned him as a state major general and gave him command of Ohio's volunteers. McClellan threw himself into the job of organizing and training the raw troops with a fierce energy. Handsome, full of activity, dynamic, McClellan impressed everyone he talked to, so much so that Lincoln was induced to give him a major general's commission in the regular army, a far more desirable plum than a commission in state or even federal volunteer forces, and appointed him commander of the Department of the Ohio. This put McClellan right up there next to Winfield Scott, which was almost where McClellan thought he deserved to be.

In June McClellan, commanding 20,000 troops, invaded western Virginia. There was a little bit of confused fighting, but the Confederates, with a mere 5,000 men in the area, all parceled out a regiment here, and two or three regiments there, were not able to offer a great deal of resistance, and McClellan soon secured the area. Though the fighting was pretty small in scale, and McClellan himself did not actually do any of it, his reports made his campaign sound like a backwoods version of Napoleon's famous Italian campaign. The newspapers were soon calling "Little Mac" the "Little Napoleon," and he began striding around with his hand tucked inside his tunic front and dictating to several secretaries at once. Small though the victories were, they were still victories, and the North badly needed some of those. So when Lincoln looked around for a general to supersede the unfortunate McDowell, his eye lit upon McClellan. To a generation that still read

Sir Walter Scott, it was "young Lochinvar is come out of the west" all over again. McClellan arrived in Washington five days after Bull Run, ready to save the Union.

There were yet other areas where the war was gaining momentum as the summer of 1861 went on. When Lincoln had first discussed an overall strategy for the war with Winfield Scott, the old general had suggested a far different idea from the "On to Richmond!" fever. He thought that by blockading the South's ports, and sending a force down the Mississippi, one might isolate the area and allow time for people to come to their senses. Gradually he refined the concept; economic pressure might squeeze the Confederacy to death. He called it a boa constrictor idea; when the newspapers got wind of it, they thought for some reason that the anaconda was a more appealing snake, or at least that the term tripped better off the tongue, so the plan became "Scott's Anaconda."

Lincoln had to be very careful in this. There were two particular problems. Any activity at sea to impede trade meant possible collision with Great Britain, and the British approved of a blockade only if they themselves were imposing it. Britain was already envious of a dynamic young America, and the British political classes seemed far more favorably disposed to the Confederacy, and to the Southern point of view, than was at all desirable. Lincoln must therefore constantly look over his shoulder, for fear he might see on the horizon a British fleet coming to the rescue of the Secessionists.

The legal aspect of this was even more tortuous. Theoretically, the imposition of a blockade was an act of war, and Lincoln was doing his best to assert that this was not a war between two sovereign states, but rather the suppression of an illegitimate rebellion by a legitimate government. If he proclaimed a blockade, he would in effect be acknowledging the existence of the Confederacy.

He got around this by a bit of sophistry that would have delighted the British had they thought of it themselves. He did not proclaim a blockade; instead, he announced his intention to proclaim a blockade at some indeterminate point in the future. Meanwhile, the federal government would take all the necessary preliminary steps, including patrolling Southern ports and interdicting access to them, so that when the blockade should actually be proclaimed, it would be an effective one, and not just a paper one. Having solved the legal problem, the government then set about solving the reality of it.

At first the task appeared insurmountable. The Confederate coastline was more than 3,500 miles long, and there were about 180 possible sites for loading or offloading cargo, from major ports such as Charleston and New Orleans to little swamps and bayous. Not only was the job enormous, but there was almost nothing with which to accomplish it. The pre-war navy was a motley collection of steam frigates, sailing sloops of war, and slowly rotting smaller craft. Of its official count of ninety ships, a full eleven were lost at Norfolk, and a mere twenty-three remained for the Union to employ, and several of them were on foreign stations. However, Gideon Welles and his indefatigable assistant secretary Gustavus Fox set to work. Money was no problem now, and contracts were let and designs approved—for double-ended paddle steamers, for small gunboats, for big steam frigates, and for a curious "ironclad battery" designed by a cantankerous Swedish engineer named John Ericsson. Meanwhile, Navy agents along the East Coast and the Ohio and Mississippi bought everything that would float, and a few things that would not. Tugboats, lumber schooners, riverboats suddenly found themselves hoisting a commission pennant, mounting a few guns, and going off to war. Southerners might laugh, and the British might snort, but in August Admiral Silas Stringham and General Benjamin F. Butler occupied Hatteras Inlet and gained a base for blockading the Carolina coast, and later in the fall Commodore Samuel Du Pont occupied Port Royal Sound in South Carolina. By the end of the year the Atlantic and Gulf squadrons were getting organized, and in 1861, one out of nine ships that attempted to enter or clear a Southern port was intercepted. So the squeeze began.

———

The danger of foreign intervention, as perceived by Lincoln and his government, was indeed a real one. Britain and France almost immediately recognized the belligerency of the Confederacy, a move that was considered by both North and South to be halfway to full recognition. Full recognition would, or could, have meant credit, loans, and possibly even military alliances for the Confederacy, and any one or all of those might be the margin of victory. When the newly appointed United States minister to Great Britain, Charles Francis Adams, complained to his hosts of their move, they replied that there was little less than that that they could do; after all, the Confederacy was certainly and self-obviously in existence as a belligerent, and to deny that would be ridiculous. Fortunately, Adams was the very epitome of the Bostonian at its best, and he was quite at home with the British aristocracy, where form and character counted for a great deal; he could talk to Lord Russell and Lord Palmerston very much on their own terms. That was a very good thing, for Adams and the government he represented were soon faced with a major crisis, one that had the potential to change the course of the war.

The Confederacy of course sought to effect European intervention on its behalf, and in an attempt to do so, Jefferson Davis sent commissioners to Britain and France. If they succeeded in gaining recognition, they would become ambassadors. The two, James M. Mason and John Slidell, with their families and staffs, got to Havana on a blockade runner. There they transferred to a British vessel, the RMS— for "Royal Mail Steamer"—*Trent,* and headed for England in style.

As their mission had been well advertised, they were intercepted in the Bahama Channel by the USS *San Jacinto,* Captain Charles Wilkes commanding. Wilkes was a vigorous officer; he had no orders to act as he did, but he fired a shot across the *Trent*'s bow. The British captain pointed indignantly to his Royal Mail pennant and kept on. Wilkes fired another shot, whereupon the Englishman hove to. The American then sent a boat across, boarded the packet, and demanded the surrender of Mason and Slidell; over outraged sputtering, the two Confederates were escorted to the *San Jacinto.*

In the United States the story was greeted with delight, and Wilkes became an instant hero; this was exactly what Britain had done back at the turn of the century, and Americans had bitterly resented it; finally the biter was bitten. But in Britain the event was greeted by a national cry of anger: How dare anyone but a Briton violate the sanctity of the ocean! There was a shout for war: Ally with the Confederacy, and show these impudent Yankees once and for all whose ocean it is. The government decided to reinforce the British garrisons in their Canadian colonies.

Lincoln's government was seriously embarrassed by all this. To cave in to Britain risked political disaster at home; to stand firm risked war. Secretary Seward squared the circle; he sent the British government a stiff note, thanking them for recognizing the principle the Americans had defended in 1812 and acknowledging their wrongdoing at that time. That being said, he added that Wilkes had acted without orders, and he released Messrs. Mason and Slidell and sent them on their way. To further sweeten the pill, and perhaps to remind Britain that her empire was not entirely invulnerable, he offered the use of an American port, ice-free in winter, for the passage of their Canadian reinforcements. Both the American public and the British government were able to read what they wanted to see in Seward's response, and thus the Union staved off, for the moment at least, outside intervention.

Mason and Slidell, in the aftermath, turned out to be a poor catch. As a U.S. senator, Mason had authored the Fugitive Slave Act of 1850. He did not endear himself to London society, which found it much preferred Adams after all. Slidell, also a former senator, was a rather slippery character, which meant he fit in well in Napoleon III's Paris, but Napoleon III was as inconstant as the wind, and Slidell never accomplished a great deal, no matter how much at home he felt.

———

So fall slid into winter, and by now the battle lines were clearly drawn. Choices had been made, and men and women would have to live, or die, by them. Neither side had yet demonstrated the ability to wage effective large-scale war. Except for Bull Run and possibly Wilson's Creek out in Missouri, there had hardly been any real battles at all. That was all still to come.

But the preliminary work had been done. The Confederacy had made a remarkable start, stamping not only armies but indeed a government out of the very ground. Scholars are prone to dwell on the shortcomings of President Davis and his cabinet and officials; they should rather marvel that a national government as effective as this one was had been produced in so short a time, especially by a society whose whole reason for existence had been the denial of an overriding national principle. The Union might for the purposes of argument deny the legitimacy of the Confederacy, but it could hardly deny the fact of it. There it was, in arms and patently capable of asserting both its existence and its independence.

Yet the Union government had done remarkably well also. After a slow start, which still leaves doubt as to Lincoln's recognition of the task ahead of him, the federal government was gathering momentum for the struggle it could now see lay before it. A half million men were under arms, the Navy was growing by leaps and bounds, and if the central government could just manage to coordinate all its wealth and power, and apply it effectively, it should be irresistible. The great chief of the German general staff, Helmuth von Moltke, characterized the war as "a conflict of armed mobs chasing each other around the bush." So far he was pretty well correct. That, however, was about to change.

Part II

1862:

LEARNING

Chapter 5

Building Armies

THE CREATION of the armies that fought the Civil War was both a monumental and an absolutely unprecedented task. Even at the time of the French Revolution, when the Terror had decreed the levee en masse and attempted to mobilize the entire country, it had not achieved the degree of articulation of the Civil War era. The entire pre-war army, a mere 16,000 men, would have been about half of either force at Bull Run, and Bull Run represented but a fraction of the armies then at the disposal of the two opposing sides. If 1861 demonstrated that neither had as yet learned how to handle such masses, that is hardly a matter of surprise: no one had any experience of this magnitude before, and it was naturally going to take time to find or develop men who could do it. Indeed, much of the history of the Civil War can be explained in these terms—of a search for men who were intelligent enough, and experienced enough, and who had the right mental attitude, to wage the first modern war.

The officer ranks of each side therefore become a key to what happened. Who were the officers? Where did they come from? What kind of knowledge and experience did they possess? Answering these questions may help in some degree to explain the war.

Perhaps the first point that comes to mind in any review of the officer corps is the dominance of West Point over the war. The United States Military Academy, founded in 1802, essentially turned out engineers. There was what might appear to the uninformed an odd pecking order: graduates chose their branch of service in order of their class standing, and habitually the top of the class went to the engineers, then the artillery, and finally the cavalry and infantry at the bottom. After the

War of 1812, the curriculum was developed to the extent that a smattering of tactics, strategy, and military history was added to the basic engineering core, and professors such as Dennis Hart Mahan developed the military art and tried to adapt it to North American conditions.

For most of the pre-war generation, West Point graduated about fifty to sixty young officers a year, which meant there were about 1,200 graduates in the generation before the war. Given, however, that there were only 1,100 officers in the United States Army, that some small number of them were not West Pointers, and that a great many of them had been around two or more generations, this meant there was a surplus of graduates. Thus a great many had left the army between graduation and the Civil War. For a variety of reasons, civilian life offered more or different attractions, and many men, knowing their educations were valuable, resigned their commissions. On the Northern side, for example, McClellan had become a railroad executive, Sherman was the president of a southern college, and Grant had failed at a variety of commercial positions. For the South, Polk left immediately after finishing West Point and became an Episcopal bishop; Daniel Harvey Hill was superintendent of the North Carolina Military Institute and had been a professor of mathematics; and Thomas J. Jackson, class of 1846, was the Professor of Moral Philosophy and Artillery Tactics at Virginia Military Institute.

Since the Confederate States Army was all to do from nothing, men such as these, as well as those who resigned directly from the U.S. Army, such as Albert Sidney Johnston and Ambrose Powell Hill, moved with little friction into command positions. The most important influence on them was probably how close they were, or how well known, to Jefferson Davis. A West Pointer himself, and a former secretary of war, Davis knew the military scene intimately, probably too much so, and his predilection for certain officers was a major factor in the South's command structure.

The situation in the North was a little more complicated. Those serving officers who had stayed with the old flag continued to hold their rank and perform their functions, but Lincoln and his government, and his whole military establishment, were far less dependent upon the "regulars" than might have been expected. The regular army, though enlarged for the war, remained somewhat exclusive, and Winfield Scott in the closing days of his tenure of command was determined not to have the real soldiers diffused throughout some amorphous mass of part-time civilians. Most of the Union army therefore consisted of what were officially called "United States Volunteers," and commissions in these forces were heavily influenced by the separate states, which were responsible for raising the regiments to fill their quotas for the federal government. Thus General Patterson, who failed in western Virginia, was a Pennsylvania general. Grant was a colonel of Illinois infantry, and his commission as a brigadier general was of United States Volunteers. Only after Vicksburg was he transformed from a volunteer into a regular-army officer again. And such brilliant soldiers as Francis Barlow, a lawyer who enlisted as a private in the 12th New York and finished as a major general of United States Volunteers, never did get a regular commission. Neither did William Bartlett, a Harvard junior who enlisted the day Fort Sumter was fired upon, and rose to be a brevet major general, losing a leg and being four times wounded in the process. Giving rank as a volunteer officer was one way to avoid clogging the regular system, and perhaps the most famous example of that was George Armstrong Custer, a brigadier general of volunteers while still officially a first lieutenant in the regular army. At the end of the war he reverted from major general of volunteers to lieutenant colonel in the regulars.

Men such as Barlow and Bartlett were examples of what worked well with the system. There were other examples of what worked poorly. State governors, or even the harassed federal government, often granted commissions on the basis of political patronage or for other unmilitary reasons. The notorious Benjamin F. Butler, for example, was a Massachusetts militia general and was the first brigadier general of U.S. Volunteers appointed by President Lincoln. Another Massachusetts politician, Nathaniel P. Banks, offered his services as a general, and Lincoln could not refuse him—he was too important politically. Daniel Sickles got his commission because he was a leading War Democrat from New York.

Only the war itself would sort out these men, the good and the bad, the talented and the stupid. The two difficulties with that were, first, that the war killed good and bad indiscriminately, and second, once on the ladder of command, an officer was free to rise to his own level of incompetence, and while he did so was entitled to the consideration of his rank. Both sides were thus stuck throughout the war with the potentially disastrous results of unwise early appointments to high command, a Polk in the South, a Butler in the North. This, it may be concluded, is a common problem with armies undergoing a vast enlargement at the start of a war. France in 1792, and Britain in 1914, for example, experienced the same sort of difficulty.

———

In Brussels in 1815, the Duke of Wellington was asked if he could defeat Napoleon; Wellington pointed to a British soldier gawking at the sights, and replied, "It all depends upon that article there." Officers might be the brains of an army, but the blood and bone and muscle was provided by the ordinary soldiers. What were they like, these young men of 1861 who were stubborn enough, or brave enough, or perhaps foolish enough, to stand up and be shot at for an idea? In the entire course of the war there were nearly three million of them, North and South, very close to one person in every ten of the entire population of the United States before the war.

Mostly they were young; the average age of enlisted men in the war would be in the very early twenties; as a rough rule one might say the men were in their early twenties, the company-grade officers in their late twenties and early thirties, the field-grade officers in their late thirties and early forties, and the brigade and higher officers in their late forties and early fifties. There were of course exceptions in either direction. Edwin "Bull" Sumner commanded a corps in the Army of the Potomac, and was in his sixties; both of his sons also became generals; and Galusha Pennypacker of Pennsylvania was a captain at seventeen and a major general at twenty-one. John Sanders of Alabama was a brigadier general at twenty-four, and did not live to be twenty-five; David Twiggs, the oldest officer of the old army to go South, was seventy-one when the war began, but he was too old for active service.

But the enlisted men, especially before conscription was brought in, were usually young. In both armies they were recruited territorially; that is to say, they joined companies made up from their own towns and villages, and then were put into units by counties and states. A great many of them, in the beginning, came straight from local militia units already in existence. There were positive and negative aspects to this; on the one side, the young soldier felt better away from home if he was surrounded by friends going through the same experience as he was. There was an enormous comfort in that, and a great boost to the spirit. In times of peril, soldiers often encouraged each other by saying they must make the folks at home proud of them. But the cost could be terrible; a bad battle might well destroy the youth of an entire town all at once, and often did; companies or whole regiments could be virtually wiped out in a single charge, and with them the hopes and future of a little town in Vermont or Mississippi.

The initial calls for volunteers were quickly oversubscribed, and these men who enlisted in late 1861 or early 1862 were the backbone of both armies for most of the war. The expiry of the enlistments of these three-year men in the North brought a manpower crisis in late 1864; retrospectively, the government should have enlisted them for three years or the duration, whichever was longer, rather than three years or the duration, whichever was shorter. In the first enthusiasm of the war, men would still have gone; later they were more wary.

As it was, the federal government was besieged by state governors begging that their quotas of regiments be increased. The regimental system, in universal use among armies of the day, proved to be a drawback in the way it was administered, especially in the North. Officially a regiment should consist of from eight hundred to a thousand men, and most of them did, to start out. Southern regiments were a little smaller, and soon were a great deal smaller. On both sides, the commissioning of officers was a perquisite of the states, and every time a state raised a new regiment, it could commission a new batch of officers. Existing regiments, mustered into federal service, were less susceptible to this political interference. The tendency, therefore, was to let the older regiments wear down until they virtually disappeared, and to raise wholly new ones in their places. The system was not quite as bad as it sounds, for once an officer had proved himself, he could usually get reappointed to a new regiment in his state. But it still did admit of playing political favors, and it was very hard on the soldiers in the ranks. Month after month they would watch their unit—their home— waste away, until there were not enough of them left to do anything. It also meant that new soldiers had to learn everything from scratch, without the inestimable advantage of being filtered in, a few at a time, to a veteran unit where they could become seasoned. As it was, older, worn-down regiments scoffed at the big new ones who had yet to see action, and the new ones made all the mistakes that new soldiers have always made and that the veterans might have helped them avoid had the two groups been put together.

One peculiarity that is worth noting is the prevalence, more particularly on the Northern than on the Southern side, of foreign-born troops. In mid-century the United States was in the midst of a great tide of immigration, so much so that the situation had spawned the Know-Nothing Party, basically a nativist party; in the 1850s Massachusetts had even passed a law denying immigrants the vote as a reaction against the Irish immigrants coming in. But these immigrants, however badly they were sometimes treated in the land of opportunity, were willing to fight, and numbers of Northern regiments were almost completely made up of such men. Some two hundred thousand German immigrants fought in the Civil War; many of them were veterans of the 1848 revolutions, and the little wars they had spawned, and there were regiments and whole divisions in which the language of command was German. President Lincoln had commissioned Alexander Schimmelfennig less because of his knowledge than because of his name; the name, Lincoln wryly remarked, ought to be worth thousands of German recruits. Unfortunately the Germans tended not to do well, either in their commanders or in their battles, and they were regarded, probably unfairly, as inferior soldiers by the rest of the army.

Both sides had large Irish contingents, and the Army of the Potomac contained an Irish Brigade, commanded by General Thomas Meagher, a former revolutionary transported to Tasmania by the British government. It was made up mostly of New York regiments, with some additions from Massachusetts and Pennsylvania. The German regiments, by contrast, tended to come from the northwestern states out around the Great Lakes. Other nationalities were represented in smaller numbers on both sides. Some of the Louisiana Zouave regiments, for example, were almost exclusively French.

One significant group that was initially totally unrepresented was American blacks. In spite of the fact that this war would eventually prove to be very much about slavery—whatever the war's origin was thought or said to be—few people in 1861 or 1862 thought that black men ought to fight in it. Initial attempts on the part of free blacks to enlist were usually rebuffed, and protestations by the few black leaders that their people should participate were met either with indifference or embarrassment by the government. For a surprisingly long time, white Americans insisted that this was a white man's war—though the Confederacy was willing to ally with Indian tribes out in Arkansas and Missouri. Eventually, of course, any blood would do, even for the Confederacy, but that stage was a long time being reached.

The army tended, as armies do, to cook all these disparate ingredients down into a homogeneous whole. As units were mustered into state and then federal service, they went through a training process designed to transform them from civilians and individuals into soldiers. The recruits trained in camps in their home states, and when they had been uniformed and taught how to march and shoot, their unit was inspected and then formally mustered into United States service. Then, usually by train or boat, they went off to active service.

Though writers of books tend naturally to dwell on battles, surprisingly little of the soldier's life is spent in them. Most of it goes in filling in the time, drilling, doing fatigues, moving here or there, and waiting for something to happen. In both armies, through the winter of 1861–62, there was a great deal of waiting. The new commander of the Army of the Potomac, General McClellan, was a great believer in drill and reviews, and his army settled into its camps around Alexandria, doing its successful best to ignore the Rebels. Meanwhile, the army drilled. The tactical systems of the day were highly complex, and soldiers had to learn all the successive moves: forming up, guiding by the center, guiding by the right, facing to the front, or the rear, or the left or right flank, moving by companies, by columns of companies, by columns of division, firing by volley, firing independently, and on and on and on. One sympathizes with the officer, leading his regiment in an attack, who came up against a bog, and eventually shouted out in frustration, "Boys, git acrost that swamp and form up on t'other side now!"

Slowly, the army was whipped into shape. McClellan was a great one for grand reviews. The soldiers would form up, regiment after regiment, vastly impressed with themselves; the bands would play jaunty airs, and then up would sweep the little general, surrounded by gorgeous staff officers, and escorted by Rush's Pennsylvania Lancers, with their lance pennants flapping bravely in the breeze. It was a long way from the smoke and terror of Bull Run, but under these conditions, it was fun to be a soldier. To greater or lesser degree, other armies in other venues were doing the same thing, and all along the border between the United States and the Confederate States of America, boys practiced their close-order drill, did their camp duties, wrote letters home, and waited for something to happen.

The armies themselves were the several points of the spears, but an army does not just happen, and it certainly does not live independently. On both sides, governments made vast efforts to sustain and supply the forces they were creating. This was naturally easier for the North than for the South. The North not only had more manufacturing capacity of its own, but it had the established credit and the existing organization needed for the process. It had mills and factories that could readily be converted to war production, and the brick beehives of Lowell and Lawrence were soon turning out thousands of pairs of blue trousers and dark blue fatigue jackets, and the armory in Springfield geared up to increase tenfold its production of rifles. Not only that, the federal government was in a position to buy abroad and pay hard cash for what it got. The soldiers found themselves armed with weapons from every arsenal in Europe, from first-class Enfield weapons bought in England, to cranky old Suhl muskets bought from Austria, hastily converted from flintlock to cap-and-ball firing mechanisms. The South went through the same process, but it started from a smaller industrial base, and as a revolutionary government, had a harder time raising money and paying for what it bought abroad, though as always, plenty of European dealers were eager to speculate and make money from other people's troubles. War is such a lavish consumer that it always makes a great market. On balance, the Confederacy did very well for most of the war; with what it manufactured at home, captured from the Union, and bought abroad, it managed to sustain the war effort far longer than might originally have been anticipated.

Still, it was in the North that the sinews of modern war were first fully created, and much of that was due to Edwin M. Stanton, one of the least-liked and greatest men in this or any war. A successful lawyer, Stanton had been attorney general under President Buchanan; he returned to private life after Lincoln's election, but remained a power in Washington, and was associated with the anti-Lincoln faction—as who was not?—until January of 1862. He and McClellan were friends, and both thought Lincoln was not up to his job, a fact on which they often commiserated. The two were together when a message arrived from the White House appointing Stanton secretary of war in place of Simon Cameron, and the story is that when McClellan asked Stanton what he was going to do, Stanton replied, "Do? I am going to make Abraham Lincoln president of the United States!" Stanton always thought a little too much of himself, and it soon became apparent that it was Lincoln who was master, and Stanton was his man, and the best secretary of war in the United States, and possibly in all of history. He was a meddler, but he got things done, whether it was jailing crooked contractors or prosecuting newspaper editors who revealed military information to the Confederacy. Above all, he supplied armies; he presided over a War Department that produced endless quantities of guns, clothing, food, wagons, paper, ammunition, and the thousand things an army needs. A good administrator and a bad hater, next to Lincoln himself he was almost indispensable to the Union, and the two came to have a very close, if often stormy, relationship. The Union was lucky to have him.

The Confederacy did not have his equal. President Davis went through five secretaries of war, a couple of whom were very bright indeed. One, Judah P. Benjamin, may have been the most intelligent man on the whole continent, and he would have been a more than competent secretary had Davis let him alone. But Davis the onetime warrior and former federal secretary of war could not stay out of his own War Department, and Benjamin lasted only six months before becoming the Confederacy's new secretary of state; he was replaced by George W. Randolph, another highly competent administrator. Randolph brought in conscription and tried to get Davis to focus on the western theater, and he lasted only eight months, again driven off by Davis's interference. After that Davis settled on James A. Seddon, a Virginian of very poor health who let Davis make all the major decisions, and who thus held on to his post almost until the end of the war.

Both governments were constantly faced with internal opposition on the running of the war. In the South there were several sources of this, and some authorities have argued that the particularism of the separate states, and their resistance to control by the central government, was what ultimately cost the South the war. Since resistance to central authority was the whole *raison* of the Confederacy, this thesis has a certain plausibility to it. Other writers have argued equally convincingly, however, that this was a relatively unimportant factor, and that actually the Confederate central government functioned pretty well, and got along at least as well as could be expected with its component state counterparts. But there were other factors or factions at work. The Confederate politicians from the border states, in effect politicians in exile, always exerted a disproportionate influence, and like exiles everywhere, always promised a great deal more than they could ever actually deliver. There was also a "western bloc," trying unsuccessfully to distract Davis from Virginia and make him aware of both potential and danger across the mountains. And finally, there were those politicians in Richmond who were motivated simply by their intense dislike for Jefferson Davis, and opposed him just because he was the man he was. In his way Davis was a great man, and with a little more luck or better timing, he might have been the father of his country, but he was also an easy man to dislike, and there was no lack of men who fought him simply for that reason alone.

Lincoln too had his enemies, of course, and Washington had as many factions, or more of them, as did Richmond. Especially in these early days of the war, men were still learning how to handle themselves, and there were plenty of men who thought they knew far better than the president what ought to be done. In Congress there was the whole spectrum of opinion, from those who were still against the war, or any form of coercion at all, to those Radical Republicans, the far left of Lincoln's own party, who wanted war to the knife, and considered Lincoln far too squeamish to fight as they wanted to fight. They soon set up a Committee on the Conduct of the War, and any general who was considered soft on their main issue had to operate with one eye over his shoulder. What happened to General Charles P. Stone was a case in point. In October of 1861 Stone was commanding a division on the Maryland side of the Potomac. Ordered to help dislodge some Confederates on the other side, he pushed a brigade across the river to Ball's Bluff, where it got trapped with no supports and no line of retreat. In the shambles that followed, the brigade suffered nine hundred casualties out of 1,700 men. Stone was called before the congressional committee, meeting in secret, and ended up being arrested and thrown in a military prison, where he languished for more than six months, though no charges were ever preferred against him. The Radicals had their own charge: "unsound on the question of slavery." That was not an indictable offense, but if they had their way it would be, and any general who failed to realize that had better watch out.

Stone was merely a scapegoat, of course; from the Radical point of view, the real target was McClellan, and as the winter went on, as the army took shape, as the country watched and waited and the newspapers demanded action, the Young Napoleon became more and more the focus of attention. What was he going to do, and when was he going to do it? Everyone wanted to know, even Lincoln.

The president indeed was incredibly patient with his new general, a patience which McClellan returned with ill-disguised contempt. Lincoln tried to find out what McClellan proposed to do; McClellan would not tell him. Lincoln tried to suggest something he might do; McClellan dismissed this as mere amateurism. Lincoln proposed he might move; McClellan was not ready. Lincoln pointed out that it was expensive to keep a huge army doing nothing; McClellan pooh-poohed all this civilian nonsense. When McClellan snubbed the president, Lincoln mildly replied, "I will hold General McClellan's horse for him if only he will do something." Eventually of course even Lincoln lost his patience: "If General McClellan does not propose to use the army, perhaps President Lincoln might borrow it for a while."

Finally, of course, even McClellan knew he had to act. When Lincoln told him a straightforward advance south on Richmond seemed the most sensible move, McClellan loftily set aside such a silly idea. How simple, how childish, how *civilian* the president was! Advancing south overland would simply lead to another Bull Run. McClellan came up instead with a far more intriguing idea. He would do a flanking move by water, and be in Richmond before the Rebels knew what he was up to.

Meanwhile, while McClellan entertained politicians and made fun of his leader, while the Army of the Potomac stretched and stirred in its encampments, while spring rolled across the land, other armies in other theaters started to move. The grass greened, the trees blossomed, the blood ran high. Both sides now had armies at least half-prepared; it was time for real war now.

Chapter 6

Western Operations

THE ATTENTION of both Washington and Richmond was centered largely on northern Virginia, and what might happen around the two capitals. But in this war, ironically, what happened farther away turned out to be of more lasting importance to the war's direction. By late 1861 or early 1862, the general battle lines had been drawn. Missouri and Kentucky had both basically been held for the Union, and Tennessee had essentially been lost to it. The "frontier," then, between the two belligerents ran up the Potomac, across the mountains, and then dipped south through the western reaches of Virginia—this the disputed area that would in 1863 become the state of West Virginia—and from there along the southern border of Kentucky to the Mississippi River. Of course, since the Union expected to restore its authority over all the national territory, it did not acknowledge that this was a frontier, and since the Confederacy intended to claim Kentucky and possibly even Missouri as its own, it too treated the border as nonexistent. A peculiarity of war, and especially of civil war, is that men are forced to define their views in ways that often may not conform to reality.

By the end of 1861 both North and South had developed a command structure for the western theater. Unfortunately, neither of them had solved the problem very well; the South never would solve it, and the Union would only after a long period of trial, error, and the eventual success that changed the strategic geography of the area.

In November, when the Federal command was shuffled around, the War Department established a new series of departments, restructuring for war the administrative framework of the pre-war period. Such de-

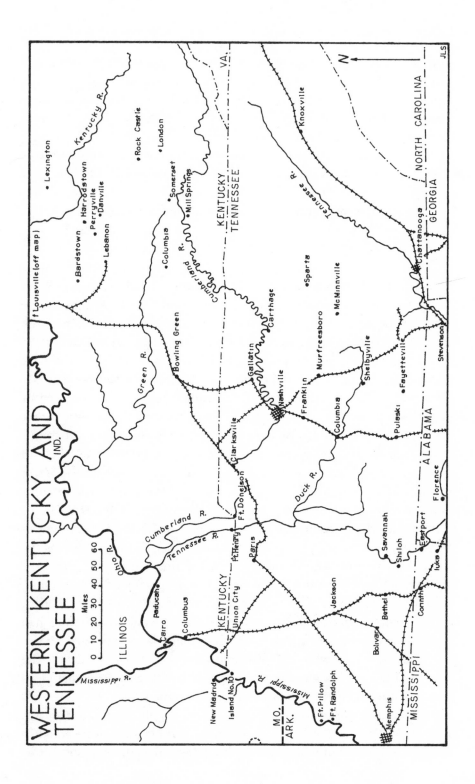

WESTERN KENTUCKY AND TENNESSEE

partments became the basic territorial organization of the war forces of both sides, and they were the support system that kept the operational armies in the field. In the Union there were actually sixty different departments, with their boundaries redrawn and overlapping at different times. Many of them, of course, such as the Department of Oregon, had little to do with the war in a direct way. Those along the "frontier" between the two countries were, however, the focus of events. In this western theater, General David Hunter commanded the Department of Kansas, in which relatively few regular operations were carried out. Far more important, indeed crucial, was the next one east, the Department of Missouri, commanded by Henry Wager Halleck.

Halleck was an odd fish, with a high-domed forehead and slightly poppy eyes. He had written several books on both law and military science, had married well and made a fortune. His classmates at West Point had nicknamed him "Old Brains," and he had taught at the Academy while he was still an undergraduate. He resigned from the Army in 1854, but at the start of the war Winfield Scott recommended to Lincoln that he be reappointed, which he was, and given the rank of major general in the regular army. At that time he was ranked only by Scott, McClellan, and John C. Frémont, the man he relieved of command in Missouri. A list of those four senior commanders might well suggest why the Union took so long to win the war. In Missouri, Halleck soon brought some order to the chaos Frémont left behind him, but he did have one glaring gap in his experience: he had never commanded troops in the field. He did, however, have a field commander of some promise, if at that point little more: Ulysses S. Grant.

Halleck's department was joined on the east by the Department of the Ohio; the division between the two of them was just east of the twin Tennessee and Cumberland rivers, and this fact would be of some significance as operations developed. The Department of the Ohio, which included most of Kentucky, had been commanded by William T. Sherman, he who had done well at First Bull Run; but Sherman had come close to a nervous breakdown while there, largely because he was one of the few men who had sufficient sense to realize how terrible the war was likely to be. He was relieved in November by Brigadier General Don Carlos Buell, a man whose flamboyant name belied a prosaic personality. Though this all sounded reasonably efficient, in fact it was not, for Halleck and Buell, as department commanders, were equal in status, though not in rank, and each took his orders direct from Washington. Any cooperation between them was going to be largely fortuitous.

———

The Confederacy was better off in command terms. Davis and his cabinet acknowledged the importance of the western theater, and even recognized the necessity for some unity of command there. The solution to the problem was, in Davis's eyes, Albert Sidney Johnston.

Johnston was in fact thought to be the best soldier in the Confederacy. He had the usual West Point background, with the added distinction of having once been secretary of war for the Republic of Texas. At the outbreak of the Civil War, he was in the regular army, in command of the Department of the Pacific. He resigned his commission when Texas seceded and made a hazardous journey back east. Immediately upon Johnston's arrival, Davis appointed him a full general of the regular army of the Confederacy, and gave him the whole of Confederate Department No. 2 to command. That in effect was all of the territory from Arkansas to the Appalachian Mountains, so the Confederates had at least a unified command with which to face their enemies.

Unfortunately, that was about all they did have. Under his subordinate commanders, Leonidas Polk in the west and William J. Hardee in the east, Johnston had only about 43,000 men. Halleck and Buell outnumbered him at least two to one, and perhaps three to one, depending upon what soldiers in their departments were counted.

The Union not only had lots of men, it had lots of plans, and the one worked against the other. Lincoln wanted Buell to advance into east Tennessee, to relieve the Unionist civilians there. Buell got only as far as Mill Springs, where one of his division commanders, George H. Thomas, the earlier-mentioned Virginian who stayed north, won a handy little battle. But Buell went no farther, because he did not want to advance into east Tennessee; he wanted to advance southwest toward Nashville. And that was what he eventually did, though he forgot to coordinate with Halleck about doing so. And since Buell was going off on his own, Halleck did the same, and he gave permission to Ulysses Grant to move south, up the Tennessee and Cumberland rivers. Grant moved out on February 2, about 20,000 strong, supported by the gunboat squadron of Commodore Andrew H. Foote.

Where they cross the Tennessee-Kentucky line, the two rivers are only about eleven miles apart. Each was defended by an earthwork, Fort Henry on the Tennessee and Fort Donelson on the Cumberland, but neither fort was really defensible, as both had been located and built in response to the politics of secession rather than with an eye to military operations. When Grant's gunboats arrived, in advance of his infantry slogging through the February mud, the Confederates abandoned Fort Henry and the garrison escaped overland to Fort Donelson.

Thus with hardly a shot fired, Grant had breached the center of the Confederate defense position. He soon sent some of his gunboats ranging upriver, burning railroad bridges and generally making a nuisance of themselves in north-central Tennessee. Meanwhile, he sent Foote's other boats back to the mouth of the Tennessee River, and then up the Cumberland, and after a week of soaking rain, he marched his army, now up to 25,000, east against Fort Donelson.

Here Confederate Commander General John B. Floyd proposed to make a stand with his 15,000 men. The fort stood on a commanding height and was a much better proposition than Fort Henry had been. The Rebels beat off a premature attack by Foote's gunboats, wounding the Union naval officer, and looked to be in decent condition when Grant got his troops up and invested the landward side of the fort on the night of February 14–15.

On the 15th Grant went off to confer with Foote. Meanwhile, Floyd launched a breakout attack, and actually succeeded in punching a hole in the Union line. Then he lost his nerve and recalled his troops to their own positions. Then, in a complete funk, he turned over command to Simon Bolivar Buckner while he himself, attended by Gideon Pillow, escaped from the post. Both Floyd and Pillow feared they might well be shot as traitors. The next morning, the trapped Buckner asked for terms, and Grant responded with the first of the concise phrases that would contribute to his fame: "No terms can be offered except immediate and unconditional surrender." Buckner grumbled at this lack of chivalry, and surrendered, along with 11,500 troops. It was the most signal Northern victory so far in the war. A week later, in his parallel but independent advance, Buell occupied Nashville. Between them, Grant and Buell had broken the Confederate defense of the west in two.

———

With Federal gunboats ranging as far up the Tennessee as Muscle Shoals in northern Alabama, and with thousands of Confederate prisoners on their way north, the Richmond government at last awoke to mortal peril. It ordered 15,000 reinforcements up from the Gulf Coast, from Mobile and from New Orleans, with Braxton Bragg to command them. It could not spare troops from the east, but it sent another hero, General Beauregard, to aid Albert Sidney Johnston. A little bit of self-serving here: Beauregard had quarreled with everyone in the east, and they were glad to be rid of him. But Johnston was equally glad to have him, so much so that he placed him in command of his western front, located at Jackson, Mississippi, while he himself retained a smaller number of men facing Buell south of Nashville.

The Southerners put together a plan. Over the next month they concentrated their forces. Johnston moved south as far as Huntsville, Alabama, and then west to Jackson, forced into this roundabout concentration by Federal control of the Tennessee River. Meanwhile the energetic Beauregard called in troops from everywhere, even from Polk, isolated up in western Kentucky. By the end of March, they had 40,000 men ready to march against Grant's advance.

Henry Halleck considered himself a great scholar, but apparently he had never read Napoleon's famous remark, "Ask me for anything but time." While the Confederates mustered their isolated and endangered forces, Halleck shuffled about. The victories at Henry and Donelson redounded greatly to his credit, in spite of the little he himself had to do with them. Now he was somewhat at a loss as to what he should do next, so he undertook a campaign against Washington, on the general line of "why I should be given supreme command in the west." He temporarily relieved Grant from field command, then eventually put him back there. Finally he ordered his army forward, and the Federals advanced south almost a hundred miles across the whole width of Tennessee, aiming toward Eastport, Mississippi, where the Tennessee River cuts the northeast corner of that state before bending into Alabama.

Early in March, Halleck won his fight to command Buell, and was given authority over the 50,000 troops at Nashville. Halleck immediately sent off long letters telling Buell what he wanted him to do, and Buell responded with equally long letters explaining why he could not possibly do it. Finally Buell lurched into motion, and got as far south as Columbia, Tennessee, a march of thirty-some miles that took him thirteen days to make. Here he was held up by a burned bridge over the Duck River, flooded but still not one of America's major waterways, for another ten days. Finally he got across and headed for a juncture with Grant, camped with six divisions, 35,000 men, on the west bank of the Tennessee at a little speck on the map called Pittsburg Landing.

This was a place of potentially great opportunity. From here the Federals could cut the rail line leading west to Memphis and east across the northern part of the Gulf states to Chattanooga; they could operate against Memphis itself, or they could strike south into Mississippi, for Corinth and Tupelo and points south. Grant and Buell together would have 85,000 men, and would constitute a formidable and very dangerous force.

Of that fact Sidney Johnston was as well aware as anyone, but it was Beauregard who convinced him to act before it was realized. His troops had moved and concentrated faster than the Federals, and he now planned to move north with his 40,000 and destroy Grant's army before Buell finally joined it. He disposed his men in four corps, under Generals Polk, Bragg, Hardee, and John C. Breckinridge, the Kentuckian who had been Buchanan's vice president but who had gone south when Kentucky remained in the Union. Johnston, with Beauregard acting as second-in-command, put his men on the road and started stealthily moving north.

The stealth soon gave way to cursing and shouting and shoving, as thousands of Confederates tried to move along the few clogged dirt trails and rutted tracks through the thinly populated territory northeast of Corinth. Brigades ran into each other at crossroads, or overtook each other, or were shoved aside as wagon trains and guns tried to get the right of way. Confederate staff work was in its infancy here, and it took three days to move the fifteen miles into contact. By then Beauregard had had second thoughts; surely, he reasoned, the Federals now knew all about this threat, and they must be preparing a trap. Maybe the Confederates should not attack after all. Johnston demurred; by late afternoon of April 5 he had his troops in line, where he had wanted them at dawn two days earlier. There was little sign of Federal activity. They would let the men get some food and a bit of sleep, and in the morning see what might happen.

On the other side, all was blissful ignorance. Grant had five of his six divisions nicely camped in a triangular position next to the Tennessee; his sixth division, under Lewis Wallace, was about five miles downstream, guarding his communications back north. Grant himself had gone off to Savannah, Tennessee, even further downstream, where he was meeting the first of Buell's advance, finally coming into at least supporting distance.

The five divisions at Pittsburg Landing were spread along the rolling countryside, W.H.L. Wallace, Stephen Hurlbut, and John A. McClernand in the northern part of the field, and the divisions of Benjamin Prentiss and William T. Sherman to the south. Sherman, over his nervous exhaustion as a departmental commander, was now back in a divisional command, and in early April he was indeed not quite as nervous as he should have been. In this he echoed his commander, for Grant expected that an attack, in the unlikely event it came at all, would be from the northwest. He had no patrols out, Heaven alone knew what his cavalry was doing, and on the eve of battle Grant was reporting to Halleck that he really anticipated nothing at all in the way of trouble. Of this notion he was about to be very cruelly disabused. The Confederates had finally sorted themselves out, and for the Union army the dawn was going to come like thunder.

———

Sunday morning, April 6: In the Union lines the troops were up early on a bright sunny day. Soldiering was not such a bad life, really, not for the boys who were used to splitting logs or hoeing turnips, and who got up before the sun anyway. There was the smell of coffee and of bacon frying and the boys teased and joshed each other with the kind of banter soldiers have used since Julius Caesar, and still do: "He's in for life, boy. . . . He found a home in the army. . . . Why, sure, the army gave him his first pair of shoes. . . . " Then there was some popping of musketry to the south, probably the pickets clearing their pieces after the night's dampness. Just because your company had no pickets out did not mean another company did not. Someone else caught the duty, for that was the way the army worked. Some fellow who rode around on a horse was responsible for putting all that together.

The popping became more insistent. General Prentiss had indeed sent out a patrol, and at about daybreak they bumped into skirmishers in front of Hardee's line. A nasty little fight developed, and four more companies of Federals came out, then a whole brigade. The fighting spread along the southern end of the Union position, as more and more troops stood to arms, hastily abandoning their morning routine. By eight o'clock the fighting was general, and Sherman and Prentiss were both in trouble.

The Confederate plan had been to hit hard on the Union left, its own right, and drive the Federals away from the Tennessee River, back up against several swamps and creeks that formed the inner boundaries of the battlefield. But their dispositions did not lead to this, and the assaulting forces instead spread out more or less evenly along the line, and got all intermingled as they deployed. The corps commanders rode here and there, grabbing brigades and regiments as they came to hand, and feeding them into the line wherever they could. By mid-morning the Confederates were roughly aligned—from west to east, Hardee, Polk, Bragg, and Breckinridge—and they were pushing hard.

But the Union side was not the utter shambles that has sometimes been suggested. Both Sherman and Prentiss had had just enough time to get their troops formed before the attack struck, and they fell back slowly and stubbornly. Both called for help from the divisions farther to the rear, and as Sherman's left gave way, it was replaced by troops from McClernand's division. Prentiss was forced back by the weight of the Rebels, but Hurlbut's men came up in support and took over part of the line on either side of what came to be called "the Hornet's Nest." Grant himself, downstream, heard the roll of gunfire and came hurrying back to the battlefield to find his subordinates handling themselves well. He set up a straggler line to catch the strays, sent word to Buell's troops to hurry their march, and looked to securing his flanks. He wanted to stabilize his line, but by late in the morning he had failed to do so.

The Confederates continued pushing, and one after another, the Federal units fell back. Prentiss in the center was ordered to hold at all costs, an order he interpreted literally. In the Hornet's Nest he drew up what was left of his division along a little slightly depressed lane, subsequently called "The Sunken Road," in imitation of Waterloo. Here his division stood until it withered away. A mere hundred yards in front of it, the Confederates massed their guns and opened a deadly fire on the Union lines.

By midday the battle had more or less stalled. Grant was still in serious trouble; everywhere along his line he had been driven back, and in his rear area, and under the bluff overlooking Pittsburg Landing, literally thousands of men had sought shelter, some wounded, some panicked, some crazy, some simply lost and bewildered. There, it looked as if the army were totally defeated, and men fed upon each other's fears. But the rear of a battlefield always looks that way. What counted more was those increasingly thin blue lines facing the Rebels, and their ability and willingness to hold on through the storm.

For though the Confederates had carried the ground all along the line, they had nowhere succeeded in making a clean break in it. They had driven the Union soldiers from their tents and their breakfasts, Rebels grabbing coffee and hardtack on the run, but now they were exhausted from three days of marching and short rations, and fear and noise and confusion worked on them as well as their enemies. The attacker may have whatever exhilaration the initiative grants him, but he needs it more than the defender does; the attacker has to get up and go forward, while the defender merely has to manage to stay where he is. By early afternoon the battle was up in the air, a question of who could last longer, or who could find some reserves.

Prentiss was still holding to his sunken road, with Hurlbut on his left and W.H.L. Wallace on his right. His determined stand had attracted increasing attention from the Confederates, but this had come at the expense of the rest of the field, and they had let themselves get sucked into concentrating here, against the toughest nut of the Union line. Eleven times the Confederates charged against his position, and still could not break it, though they slowly isolated it from the rest of the Federals.

The situation did not improve. Shortly after noon, Albert Sidney Johnston had been wounded in the leg, a little matter that he refused to bother with. He led one of the charges against Prentiss personally. By mid-afternoon he was dead; the little wound had been a severed artery, and Johnston's boot was full of blood and he himself falling out of the saddle, dying, before anyone paid any attention to it. Beauregard assumed command of the army, and kept on pushing, but there was a fatal flaw in this now: he had no more reserves to finish off his victory. He finally pushed Prentiss's supports away, left and right, and at the end of the afternoon the troops in the Hornet's Nest, what was left of them, out of ammunition and cut off, surrendered. But it was too late by then to exploit any more than this.

Night fell over the most terrible battlefield yet seen on the American continent. In many places the exhausted soldiers slept on their arms, and in the darkness it was difficult to tell the dead from the sleeping. Little parties wandered over the field, tracing the path they had fought, and looking for friends and comrades. East of the Hornet's Nest was a little peach orchard, and the dead and wounded lay thick with the broken blossoms around them. Just beyond that was a small shallow pond, and it reflected red in the torchlight, tinged with the blood of the wounded who had crawled there for a drink of muddy water, and died on the verge of the pond. A slow, soaking rain began in the night.

The Confederates were all but used up. They had been on the very knife-edge of victory, and unable to carry it off. Or unwilling: as darkness fell, Beauregard canceled a last effort because he believed Grant could not be reinforced during the night, and could be finished off at leisure come morning.

He was wrong. During the night Union gunboats kept up a slow but annoying fire from the river, randomly throwing shells at the Confederate lines. And even worse, back at Pittsburg Landing boat after boat crossed over from the eastern shore, bringing the first of Buell's troops. Grant's own sixth division, that under Lew Wallace, arrived at last. By morning, the Federals had four new divisions, 20,000 fresh men, with which to take up the contest.

Beauregard had none. He expected some reinforcements under General Earl Van Dorn, but they did not appear. Still, he believed he yet held the initiative. He slept the night in Sherman's captured tent, after sending off a grandiloquent message to Richmond announcing a great victory, and saying that he would complete it the next day.

The next morning, when Beauregard went to claim his victory, he found the fickle prize had flown. The Union gunboats were still there harassing his flank, the Union gun-line was still to his front, the Union divisions he had so roughly handled yesterday were still there—and 20,000 new troops of Buell's army were there as well.

Indeed, Buell's troops began their own advance on the Union left soon after daybreak, and drove slowly but steadily ahead, pausing as they went to allow new formations to filter into the line. Then Sherman's division, over on the other flank, took it up, and by mid-morning the battle was general, with the Federals pushing hard and the Rebels holding on for dear life. The fighting was every bit as bitter as it had been the day before, and regiments and whole brigades withered away. Patrick Cleburne's brigade of Hardee's corps started April 6 at a ration strength of 2,750; it mustered 900 on the morning of the 7th, and at night had 58 men present for duty. The fighting swelled up and whirled around Shiloh Church, a little crossroads about five miles from Pittsburg Landing, and the Confederate lines bent farther and farther back. By noon Beauregard knew he was done, and it was time to save his army. It took him a couple more hours to accept the decision fully, but about mid-afternoon he issued orders for a retreat. Slowly the army drew off southward, its retreat covered by Breckinridge's reserve corps.

Once they recovered their original position, the Union troops lost their drive. Both sides were utterly exhausted, and as the Rebels pulled off, the Federals more or less collapsed on their lines. Neither of these armies had been involved in a great, full-scale battle before, and the psychic shock was enormous. Men staggered around, or sat and stared vacantly, or shivered uncontrollably. They could hardly believe what they had been through. The evidence before them was visible enough: trees stripped of their leaves and limbs, ground torn up by shot and shell, bodies everywhere, and parts of bodies, and trails of blood, dead men and animals all over the place, an absolute charnel house spread over square miles. As an initiation to war, Shiloh was about as terrible as one could get, the casualties almost fourteen thousand on the Union side, and nearly eleven thousand on the Confederate. Grant claimed a victory, as indeed it was, though dearly bought, and Beauregard was forced to explain why what he had said was a victory turned out to be a defeat, which he found very hard to do.

With the Confederate field army in the west so badly depleted, Halleck now had a glorious opportunity to do extensive damage. Not only was he in the Confederate heartland, but there was good news from the Gulf Coast as well. A mere two and a half weeks after Shiloh, New Orleans fell to Federal forces.

————

The Crescent City of the South was a prize of immense strategic and commercial importance; even in 1861 it was a major city, with a population of 170,000, handling the commerce of the whole Mississippi Valley, busy, cosmopolitan, flamboyant, dangerous, and unhealthy. The Confederate government knew that this was a key city, but had relied on nature and existing works to protect it. The natural defenses consisted of the Mississippi River itself, a hundred miles below the city consisting of bayous, swamps, currents and twisting and constantly changing channels, all very unpleasant country for either men or ships. The fortifications consisted of a few works around the city, and more importantly, two permanent forts on the river down near its mouth, Jackson on the west side and St. Philip on the east, slightly above it. These had been improved with chains on barges, and hulks sunk in the fairway, and with their eighty guns, were thought to be impassable. The forts had about eight hundred men in them, and Confederate commander General Mansfield Lovell had several hundred more militia in position around New Orleans itself. He repeatedly asked Richmond for more support, but Richmond had other things to worry about.

Lovell of course was not the only one aware of New Orleans' importance. On the Union side, Commodore David Porter decided as early as the fall of 1861 that the city could be taken. It took him a while to convince anyone else of this. Porter was an active and energetic officer, but he suffered from being a little too political: Gideon Welles said he was "given to Cliquism." Nevertheless, Porter managed to sell his idea to Welles, and gradually the mission took shape. The Navy would do most of the work, which was fortunate, for the troops detailed for the expedition, largely from New England, were put under the command of Benjamin F. Butler. Late in 1861, there was some snooping around the passes at the mouths of the river, and a heavy Confederate ram, the *Manassas,* had beaten up some Union seagoing vessels that got caught in narrow waters. In December the Federals landed on Ship Island, and Butler used it as a staging point for his troops. This could be interpreted in several ways, and Lovell chose to think it portended expeditions against the Gulf Coast, but not against him.

Meanwhile the Federal navy gathered its strength for a major passage of arms. Porter himself took command of a fleet of about twenty mortar boats, clumsy things each armed with a huge thirteen-inch mortar, designed to lob shells into the forts and blow them up. The "real" naval vessels were commanded by Porter's adopted older brother, Rear Admiral David G. Farragut. A veteran of the War of 1812 and a Virginian who had gone north, Farragut was initially distrusted by the Lincoln Republicans, but rescued from obscurity by Welles and put in command of the Western Gulf Squadron. Now, with his flag flying in the new steam sloop *Hartford,* and twenty-some other oceangoing vessels under his command, Farragut was going to get his chance to demonstrate both his skill and his loyalty.

Farragut hoped to make a dash up the river, adding surprise to his other advantages, but nature worked against him. The sandbars across the mouths of the Mississippi gave it a depth of only fifteen feet, and Farragut's deepwater ships drew from sixteen up to twenty-three. It took him a month to work his ships over the bars and into deeper water at Head of Passes, which he finally did by April 8. By now Lovell knew he was in trouble, but he could not convince his superiors of that; after all, the day before the Federal ships cleared the bars, many of Lovell's troops, or potential reinforcements, were fighting for their lives up at Shiloh.

The next obstacle to the Union advance was the two forts some miles up the river. Farragut and Porter opened up a bombardment of them by the mortar boats, but after a week this had had little effect. During that time, however, some of the smaller, more maneuverable Federal ships had broken the chain that the Rebels had stretched across the river, and had marked or even removed some of the sunken hulks blocking the passage. Farragut decided to force his way past. He was also faced with the possibility of attack by Confederate rams, which were still being completed, and he knew that the longer he waited, the greater the eventual danger.

On the evening of April 23 Farragut went round his fleet, seeing that all his orders were understood and preparations made: topgallant masts stepped down, sandbags piled as extra armor, splinter nets hung, all those things in fact which turned a ship from a thing of grace and beauty into an ugly but useful fighting instrument. At two in the morning he hoisted the signal to advance, two red lanterns in the *Hartford*'s mizzen rigging, and off they went.

It looked far more perilous than it turned out to be. The ships blasted away at the two forts in succession; the forts fired back into the flame-filled night. In line ahead the ships steadily plowed up the channel, brushing aside the remains of barges, chains, and other devices the Confederates had hoped would halt their progress. The work was close enough that the gunboat *Pensacola* drew up abreast of Fort St. Philip, and Yankee sailors and Rebel gunners could yell curses at each other while they sponged and loaded their guns. A Rebel tug pushed a fire raft against *Hartford*'s side, but the sailors sank it by dropping cannonballs on it, and then sank the tug as well. A Rebel ram hit the steam sloop *Mississippi,* and the two, tangled together, went careening off across the river, then the ship got clear, fired more broadsides at Fort Jackson, and proceeded on upstream. It took a couple of hours for the entire action to be concluded, but for each individual ship, there was no more than a few minutes' hard work. All were hit, a couple were stopped by obstructions or rudder damage, but none was lost.

With that, New Orleans was doomed. Farragut spent a day patching up his fleet and getting the hundred-odd miles up the river, and he anchored off the city on the afternoon of the 25th. The city itself was chaos. The Confederates had set fire to anything they thought might be useful to the enemy, including thousands of bales of cotton stored and waiting for blockade runners, and the mob, always volatile in New Orleans, had run amok, rampaging through the streets and, as mobs usually do, taking out its frustrations by looting stores and getting drunk. While harridans stood on the river levees shouting insults at the Federal ships, the unfinished Confederate ironclad *Mississippi* came drifting downstream, a mass of flames, the city's last hope gone up in smoke. Farragut sent a party of Marines ashore, and after some confusion and a great deal of abuse and bluster, they succeeded in hoisting the United States flag on the city hall.

Downstream the two forts still presented a threat, but Butler got his troops ashore, and they cut the roads and lines of retreat, and on the 28th, the forts surrendered. Butler then got his troops up to New Orleans, which he finally occupied and garrisoned on the first of May.

———

Thus at the end of the disastrous month of April, the western Confederacy was in serious danger of being cut in half. Halleck had moved to Pittsburg Landing, where he concentrated a hundred thousand men. One of Halleck's other subordinates, General John Pope, succeeded in taking a Confederate fortress at Island No. 10 on the Mississippi, freeing further stretches of it, and the naval forces ranged here and there, interdicting supplies and making a nuisance of themselves. Staring disaster in the face, few Confederates could see how they might persevere. The Union appeared triumphant.

Then it all fell apart. Halleck spent a month reorganizing his army. He divided it into three wings, under Generals Thomas, Buell, and Pope. He made Grant his second-in-command, and gave him absolutely nothing to do. This became one of the low points of Grant's Civil War career, and he went off to drink and nurse his spirits. Thoroughly imbued with the spirit of eighteenth-century depot-style warfare, Halleck ignored the little army Beauregard could dispose against him, and began a ponderous advance on Corinth; it took him a month to make twenty miles. When he finally got there, instead of taking bold action, he divided his army up in packets and sent it hither and yon, with little positive effect.

The troops from New Orleans did no better. Farragut and Porter took their ships up to Baton Rouge, and then beyond, the sailors nervous all the way, fending off logs, running on sandbars, and generally feeling like fish out of salt water, but at least they did something. The soldiers, by contrast, dithered about, and let golden opportunities slip by. Butler got involved in a famous argument in New Orleans. His soldiers were constantly insulted by the female population of the city, so he issued what came to be known as the "woman order." In it he announced that any woman who insulted Federal troops would be held liable, and treated as if she were a prostitute soliciting trade. A howl of protest was heard all over the South, and there were calls for a price to be put on Butler's head. And not just the South; the London *Times,* which had printed the news of New Orleans' fall with mourning borders, waxed indignant at this slur upon the flower of Southern womanhood. Butler, a controversialist with the best of them, replied that the order was actually taken almost verbatim from the laws of the city of London. None of which did any good; Southern chivalry was outraged, and Butler seemed the archetype of the boorish Yankee. Which indeed he was. Leading citizens of the city spread the rumor that at dinner in their houses, Butler pocketed their silver spoons, and his own troops laughingly took to calling him "Spoons" Butler.

He was actually a pretty good military administrator, which was what New Orleans needed. He was also a terrible field commander, which was not what the Union needed on the Mississippi. So the golden days slipped away, while Butler and New Orleans sniped at each other. And while they did that, Halleck stood looking at his maps, dividers in hand, and mused upon the great campaigns of the past. And Grant sat in enforced idleness, feeling miserable. And the Union corps commanders wrote letters to friends in the government at Washington: "How I Would Do It Better" by An Aspiring General.

But little matter. General George Brinton McClellan had a plan; he, and he alone, would win the war and save the country.

Chapter 7

Spring in the East

MAJOR GENERAL George B. McClellan loved almost everything about soldiering. He delighted in the uniforms, the
traditions, the little military courtesies; his heart thrilled
when he saw himself at the head of ten thousand troops passing in
review. He even liked the paperwork, the returns, the reports, all the
minutiae of army life. If war could be waged in peace, McClellan would
have been a great soldier.

But there were parts of soldiering he did not like. There was always
that menacing vague presence, "the enemy," which assumed vast pro-
portions in the recesses of his mind. And even more annoying there
was President Lincoln, a simpleminded amateur who seemed to think
that just because McClellan commanded an army of well over 100,000
men, he ought to do something with it.

Admittedly, Lincoln was deferential enough, but he was also per-
sistent. Week after week, he asked what McClellan proposed to do,
and when McClellan proposed to do nothing, Lincoln kept suggesting
things that might, perhaps, possibly, if the general thought it wise, be
done. The general did not think it wise. Could not the president see
that the army was still untrained, still unequipped, still undermanned?
Did he not know that McClellan was dangerously outnumbered? Why
there, across in northern Virginia, sat an immense host of Confederates
under Joseph Johnston, 100,000 of them, no, 120,000, even more,
maybe 150,000! It would be gross folly to try to take the offensive
against such an army.

So McClellan convinced himself, so he assured Lincoln, and Lincoln,
poor man, could only tell himself the Young Napoleon must know

what he was doing, and put off the more importunate members of Congress and the cabinet. So as fall turned into winter, and winter into the early spring of 1862, the Army of the Potomac drilled and polished, held great reviews, and learned what real soldiering according to the gospel of George B. McClellan was all about.

Eventually, of course, something had to be done. The president, who thought with good reason that he had as much military sense as his generals, suggested a straightforward advance into northern Virginia. Yes, said McClellan, when I have the army trained well enough for it. Then, when the day finally arrived that even McClellan had to admit the army was sufficiently trained, he found an excuse not to go: he was vastly outnumbered, and a direct advance would be suicidal. But he came up with an alternative; instead of taking on Johnston directly, he would move the army down the Potomac by ship, to the little town of Urbanna at the mouth of the Rappahannock. Thus he would flank Johnston, and he would make a march toward Richmond. Forced to hurry back to defend his capital, Johnston would have to fight on ground of McClellan's choosing, and would be defeated.

So far so good. But then the wily Johnston retreated anyway, so the flanking move by Urbanna would be useless. Well, said Lincoln, if he is retreating, why not just advance and follow him up? Again McClellan dismissed this with contempt. He wanted to make the Napoleonic move, the gesture on the grand scale. He would take the army all the way to Fortress Monroe, at the bottom of Chesapeake Bay. Then he would advance directly on Richmond, up the peninsula formed by the York and James rivers. That was a distance of a mere sixty-some miles, as opposed to the hundred overland from Washington. More important, the route from Washington entailed crossing a number of difficult rivers, and was guarded by that huge Confederate army; there were, so McClellan assured the president and himself, no such difficulties in the Peninsula.

Lincoln doubted. In spite of his best attempts, he was slowly losing faith in his general. In mid-March, he demoted him from overall commander to command of the Army of the Potomac alone, and took into his own hands the coordination of the several forces in the eastern theater. Now he did not like the idea of taking the main army away from the capital, and leaving the direct route open to the enemy. McClellan insisted the capital was adequately protected anyway; not only did it have a garrison of about 45,000 troops, but General Banks had 23,000 more upriver at Harpers Ferry, guarding the mouth of the Shenandoah Valley, and General William S. Rosecrans, later replaced by John C. Frémont, had another few thousand in the mountains of western Virginia. All of these should be more than enough to calm the presidential fears. On March 17, McClellan began putting his troops aboard transports for the move down the bay to Fortress Monroe.

But while Washington fussed and fretted, what was happening across on the Confederate side? Here President Davis was busy worrying about his western theater—justly so—and doing far less for Virginia than McClellan thought he was. In fact, the "huge array" of Johnston's army turned out to be a mere 40,000 men! If one counted all the troops all over the war zone in Virginia, the Confederates could muster 75,000 men. McClellan alone had 155,000 in his army; the Washington garrison counted another 45,000, and Banks's and Frémont's troops, plus another 12,000 already garrisoning Fortress Monroe, amounted to 40,000 more. The truth was, the Federal forces had at their disposal a quarter of a million men; they outnumbered the Confederates three and half to one.

No one was more fully aware of the real state of affairs than President Davis and his generals, and they devoted themselves wholeheartedly to fostering McClellan's delusions. The coming campaign would have to be aimed at George McClellan's mind, for if it came simply to fighting bodies, the Union was going to win.

The first round was won for them by the United States Navy. McClellan had assumed, without ever bothering to ask, that the Navy would take his troops up the two rivers, and he would capture Yorktown by an amphibious operation. But there was a problem with that, and it arose from one of the great events of naval history.

———

At the beginning of the rebellion, the Confederates had seized the Federal navy yard at Norfolk; among their prizes was the hulk of the steam frigate *Merrimack*, which had been burned to the waterline and sunk at her moorings. The Confederates raised the ship, cleaned up the engines, and built a barn-like topside structure, turning it into a heavily armed and armored floating battery, patriotically renamed the CSS—for "Confederate States Ship"—*Virginia*. On March 8 the new vessel, under Captain Franklin Buchanan, sallied forth into the waters of Hampton Roads, and in two hours rendered obsolete practically every ship in every navy in the world.

The Federals knew the ship was there, and Flag Officer Louis M. Goldsborough had disposed of a substantial fleet, by pre–March 8 standards, to try to trap and destroy the *Virginia* when she came out. Instead, his own fleet was decimated. The *Virginia*'s first target was the fifty-gun *Congress,* whose solid shot bounced off the Confederate's armor plating. The *Congress* was swept by the Rebel fire, and the *Virginia* steamed ponderously on to ram and sink the *Cumberland,* which went down so fast it nearly took the *Virginia* with it. The *Cumberland*'s crew fought from deck to deck as the water rose about them, and the ship finally hit the shallow bottom, masts still standing and flag still flying, a splendid example but a sunken ship nonetheless. The *Congress* was then run aground in shallow water where the *Virginia* could not follow, but was destroyed by gunfire. One of the killed was her paymaster, McKean Buchanan, brother of the Confederate captain. Three other Union vessels, all big seagoing ships, ran aground trying to maneuver to attack the Rebel, and after unsuccessfully bombarding them at long range, the *Virginia* steamed triumphantly home to replenish and make minor repairs.

The next day, the 9th, the Confederates came out to finish the job. Something, however, had happened during the night. After dark a new vessel had joined the Union fleet, an ugly little thing named the *Monitor.* It was the brainchild of John Ericsson and was little more than a self-propelled barge with a large revolving turret on its flat deck. The turret had only two guns, but they were eleven-inch monsters, more than a match for the nine-and six-inch guns of the *Virginia.*

So, when the *Virginia* steamed confidently into Hampton Roads on the 9th, this odd-looking little craft cast off from behind the *Minnesota* and came out to fight. At first the Confederates thought it was some sort of anchor buoy loose in the bay, but they soon recognized it as one of the newfangled ships the Union was known to be building.

The battle between the two lasted for four hours and was, in the main, quite inconclusive; both could hurt, neither could destroy, the other. Eventually the *Monitor* was temporarily embarrassed by a hit on the tiny pilot house, and the *Virginia,* which had run aground, managed to escape while the Federal sailors were sorting themselves out. The only fact that was quite clearly demonstrated by this first ironclad duel in naval warfare was that the day of the wooden warship was over.

So the Navy regretfully told McClellan an amphibious operation was out, what with the *Virginia* still at large, and he would have to make his campaign without them.

Round two went to the Confederates as well, thanks to Major General John Magruder. In the old army he had been known as "Prince John," in part because of a predilection for the drama, and now he made full use of his offbeat talents. He had fewer than 20,000 men at hand with which to stop McClellan's advance up the Peninsula, but if he could hold on, he knew help would be on the way.

The Federals began to move on April 4. McClellan himself had reached Fortress Monroe on the 2nd, where he took command of the 50,000 men already there, with more arriving each day. His army was now divided up into corps, and the Civil War corps, about the size of a World War II division, tended to become the normal fighting unit of the war. Ironically, the corps structure had not been chosen by McClellan himself, but rather by Lincoln, who had insisted, quite correctly, that the army needed some order at that level. Eventually, McClellan had five corps, and a fighting strength of about 125,000 men, on the Peninsula.

But the Confederates had a better knowledge of the terrain, they had Magruder, who did better here than he ever did again, and above all they had those dark fears haunting the back of George McClellan's mind. Magruder held a position almost ten miles long, from Yorktown on the York River all the way across to the other shore of the Peninsula, on the James. For most of its length this line ran behind the little Warwick River, which was more of an obstacle than McClellan had thought it would be. Even so, the Rebel line was far too long for the troops available, so Magruder faked it. He had built gun embrasures all along the line, and manned them with heavy guns—"Quaker" guns, logs trimmed and set so that from a distance they looked like weapons. He marched his troops vigorously back and forth, and let the distant Federals count them here, then count the same men over again there. Totally flummoxed, McClellan decided he had no alternative but to open a regular siege: the lines were too heavy to carry by assault. Of course, the Federals, had they known it, or dared try, could have brushed the Confederates aside with ease—the Rebs were too busy laughing to have put up any real defense.

So for an entire month McClellan besieged an all but empty position. Meanwhile, events elsewhere turned the hollow Confederate defense into something altogether different. For as a diversionary measure, Stonewall Jackson went on the rampage in the Shenandoah Valley.

———

Thomas J. Jackson was decidedly an odd fish. What could you make of a man who was given to sucking lemons, and who often rode along with one arm stuck up in the air, in the belief that that improved his circulation? In the winter of 1861–62, he had returned to the Shenandoah, after his brief appearance at Bull Run, and had commanded the few soldiers, mostly militia, in the Valley for some months. Eventually he was reinforced by Confederate regular troops, his own Stonewall Brigade from the Manassas campaign. Still he did not have enough with which to accomplish anything, until necessity overrode common military sense.

That point was reached when McClellan went to the Peninsula, and the South desperately needed something to throw the Union war machine out of kilter. Jackson proved to be the man, and the Valley the place, to provide that something.

The Shenandoah Valley of Virginia is, in addition to being one of the most beautiful spots in America, peculiarly suited to military action. It is formed by the isolated Blue Ridge Mountains to the east, and then the main slopes of the Allegheny Mountains to the west, and it runs a little more than a hundred miles, from Staunton at its southern end, northeast to Harpers Ferry at its northern end. The top forty miles of it consist of the floor of the valley, through which runs the Shenandoah River; the bottom sixty miles is actually two valleys, those of the western and eastern forks of the river; confusingly, the western fork is known as the North Fork, and the eastern the South Fork. Between them is a ridgeline called Massanutten Mountain. The three lines of mountains that define the Valley, the Blue Ridge, Massanutten, and the Alleghenies, are all broken occasionally by passes that allow a force to move from one side to another, or even in and out of the whole Valley. The mountain slopes were heavily wooded, and especially to the west, access was difficult, but the Valley floors are spacious and well-farmed, and the area was considered by many as the breadbasket of the Confederacy. More immediately important, the whole arena was a perfect one for a daring commander who could inspire a small, fast-

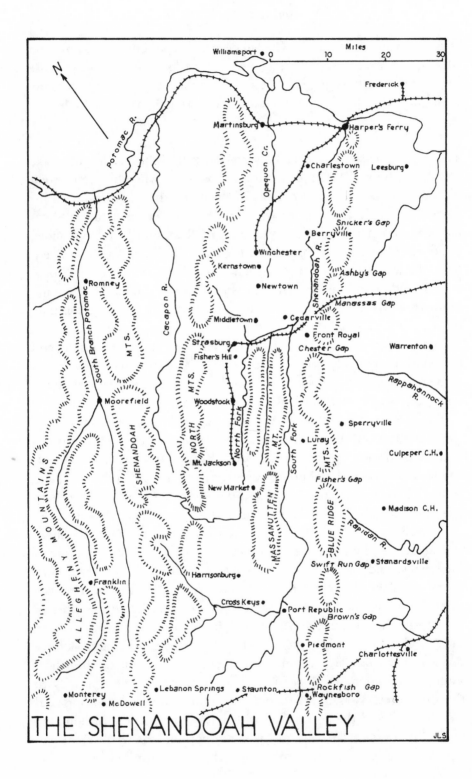

THE SHENANDOAH VALLEY

moving force against superior but unconcentrated numbers. The advantages of mobility, interior lines, and a unified command had not been so convincingly demonstrated since the young Napoleon's Italian campaign of 1796. Now the Civil War was about to get its Young Napoleon, too, but as it turned out, he was not George B. McClellan after all.

When he began, Jackson had about 10,000 men. Facing him was the Union V Corps commanded by General Nathaniel P. Banks, consisting of about 23,000 men in three divisions, plus some scattered Union forces in the western mountains, soon to be commanded by John C. Frémont. The War Department had told Banks to advance southward, clearing the northern end of the Valley, and then be prepared to detach troops to the Peninsula to assist McClellan. Banks moved south from Harpers Ferry to Winchester, and then started farther south on March 17, as the Army of the Potomac was boarding its transports for the trip down the bay.

The situation at that moment illustrates the importance of chance in the military command of the Civil War. Banks was known as "the bobbin boy of Massachusetts," a successful politician who had come up by hard work and his own ambition, and who had been strong for the Union cause; Frémont was a man of national stature, "the Pathfinder of the West," and Jackson was a humdrum West Point graduate who had gone off to teach at university. There was little reason to suppose any one would have done any better—or any worse—than the other two. Indeed, an assessment of their careers and talents to this date would have put Thomas J. Jackson a clear last.

Who now recognizes the names of Nathaniel P. Banks or even John C. Frémont?

The Valley campaign lasted three months, from mid-March to mid-June. As Banks pulled back northward, preparatory to dispatching some of his troops to Washington, Jackson moved to follow. On March 23 he attacked the Federals at Kernstown, a bungled battle in which he was repulsed. Jackson was furious over his tactical defeat, but even so he totally upset the overall Union concept. Instead of Banks moving to support McClellan, his troops were ordered to stay where they were; not only that, a couple of other divisions were held back from the Peninsula, and Irvin McDowell's command in northern Virginia was moved westward to concentrate against the audacious Confederate in the Valley. Deprived of the smallest portion of his overwhelming army,

McClellan began thinking even less offensively than he was already doing, so Jackson was succeeding strategically beyond his or Richmond's wildest hopes right from the start.

A whole series of Federal forces now tried to converge upon the artful dodger, but Old Jack was too fast and too wily for all of them. As Banks advanced slowly south up the Valley, toward an eventual junction with Frémont, Jackson hung about threatening everyone's flanks, cutting back and forth across Massanutten Mountain. Then he dashed off and fought Frémont's advance at McDowell on May 8; thinking to attack, he was himself attacked and barely fought off the Union onslaught. Having done so, he chased the Federals back into the western mountains, then turned again on Banks. On May 23, reinforced up to 16,000, he crushed a Federal outpost at Front Royal; on the 25th, he struck the now retreating Banks at Winchester. A furious assault sent the Federals reeling and then stampeded them to the north; Jackson's exhausted "foot cavalry" collapsed over their well-earned breakfast. The next day what was left of Banks's command crossed the Potomac and sought relief in Maryland.

The War Department in Washington now intervened, and set up an elaborate trap in which McDowell was to advance west, Frémont east, and a reinforced Banks south; between the three they should catch this gadfly somewhere. Again they failed. After gathering all the supplies he could transport, Jackson again moved south, and again, by skillful use of the roads, bridges, and terrain, he eluded the pursuit. At the end of the first week of June, he was at the south end of Massanutten Mountain, with Frémont to the west and the advance of McDowell's forces to the east. On the 8th and 9th, at Cross Keys and Port Republic, he turned on one and then the other, roughly handling both before slipping away yet again.

With that the Federals gave it up. The Valley campaign subsided, Washington decided to let Jackson alone; it even decided, albeit only temporarily, that administrators in the capital were not well suited to directing field operations. And Jackson, left alone, soon went off to help out in the Peninsula, having struck this distant but by no means insignificant blow at the equilibrium of General McClellan.

———

The Valley campaign did not achieve spectacular results in terms of enemy forces destroyed or smashing, bloody victories; indeed, it should have been but a mere footnote to the potentially far more significant operations taking place in the main theater on the Peninsula. It might be said that it bought the Confederacy time, but in fact it did not even do that; the time bought for the Confederacy was bought by Magruder and his theatricals, not by Jackson and his foot cavalry. But what it did do was upset Union plans and troop schedules, and in this way it furthered the profound malaise existing between McClellan and the government in Washington.

Lincoln had insisted that McClellan leave behind him enough troops to guarantee the security of the capital. McClellan insisted that he was doing so. But he was counting virtually every soldier he was not actually taking with him, while Lincoln was counting only those in the immediate area of Washington. Neither ever cleared up this simple misunderstanding. Thus when Jackson ran wild, and Washington held back troops slated for the Peninsula, both sides felt betrayed; Lincoln thought McClellan had misled him about what he would leave behind, McClellan thought the government was holding back men promised to him. He went beyond that; he began to see plots, possibly deliberate, to discredit and even destroy him: the Radical Republicans wanted him to fail, because he was weak on the slavery issue; the president was envious of him, and so was undermining his military strength. At first he had seen himself as the Noble Roman—"I am willing to save the Republic and perish by suicide to preserve its liberties"; now he began to see himself as the martyr; his letters to his wife were full of predictions of failure, and of himself sacrificed to the devious ambitions of the politicians. His memoirs remind one of the similar writings of French generals of 1940, self-serving and self-exculpatory, and totally at odds with reality. Whatever happened now, it would not be George McClellan's fault.

That was hardly the attitude with which to wage a vigorous campaign, and McClellan did not do so. On April 16, when General William F "Baldy" Smith pushed his brigade right into the middle of the Rebel line and found it all but empty, McClellan recalled him to his own line; didn't the man know this was supposed to be a siege?

By the end of April Joseph E. Johnston had got his army moved from northern Virginia down into the Peninsula, and the line was not as thin as it had been. McClellan scheduled a grand assault for May 5, but Johnston beat him to it, and started retreating on the 3rd. So the Federals lost the best month they were going to get.

They actually caught up with Johnston's rearguard, under the command of Major General James Longstreet, but accomplished little. The capable Longstreet gave them a bloody nose and got safely away. Both retreat and pursuit were difficult, with long trains bogged down on roads muddy from several days' rain, and both sides crawled along while Rebel cavalry under Brigadier General Jeb Stuart made a nuisance of itself to the Federals.

For two and half weeks the Union army plowed ponderously ahead, until by late May it was, in spite of itself, virtually at the gates of Richmond. It was a fascinating interlude, illustrating the adage that generals are among the most pacific of men. McClellan spent most of his time riding about looking at the scenery, and writing letters and telegrams back to Washington demanding more support so he could hope to fight on at least even terms. As has been mentioned, he was really a capable military administrator. He managed to move his headquarters as far up as White House, which is on the Pamunkey, the southern branch of the York River, and a mere twenty miles from Richmond. Meanwhile, with Yorktown lost, the Confederates abandoned Norfolk, and this allowed the Federal navy to move up the James as far as Drewry's Bluff, less than ten miles from the capital. There was thus a certain air of inevitability about the blue tide coming up the Peninsula, and the Confederates were rightly worried in the face of it.

None more so than Joseph E. Johnston. If McClellan's classical hero might have been Sulla, who saved Rome and then retired from a dictatorship, then Johnston's would have been Fabius Cunctator the Delayer, who wanted to defeat Hannibal by not fighting him. Johnston was a capable tactician, but he was a very cautious one; he was also almost perpetually at odds with Jefferson Davis over matters of promotion and precedence, and in spite of their constant close contact throughout the entire Civil War, the two did not work well in harness.

This was not really the place for caution. Johnston did not have a great deal of maneuvering room, with Richmond ever closer to his back, and he also did not have what he thought was necessary in the way of manpower. Johnston had about 60,000 troops in hand, outnumbered by the Federals at a ratio of about five to three in combat strength. Of course, McClellan, listening to his own intelligence people from the Pinkerton Agency, who apparently could not count, thought that he himself was now outnumbered by at least 200,000 Rebels. But then, Johnston did not know what McClellan thought; he only knew what he himself thought. And that was that he could not fight until the Federals made a big mistake and gave him an opportunity. So Joe Johnston twisted and turned, with McClellan to his front and Davis to his rear, and waited hopefully for something to turn up.

Something did. McClellan pushed his advance up the north bank of the Chickahominy River until he was within about six miles of Richmond. It was not an especially advantageous position, but it would have allowed him to link up with McDowell, advancing overland south toward the city. But in late May McClellan knew McDowell was not coming; he was going west to fight Jackson in the Valley. McClellan therefore considered shifting his base from White House on the York south to the much more accessible James River; as a preliminary to this, he had pushed one corps, IV, under Erasmus Keyes, south of the Chickahominy. Johnston decided to strike at and destroy this isolated segment of the Union army.

Johnston originally intended to attack the right end of McClellan's line north of the river, hoping to lever it away from McDowell's approach, but when he heard of McDowell's move westward, he decided instead to hit the isolated IV Corps. While he was getting organized, Keyes was reinforced by two divisions, under Generals Philip Kearny and Joseph Hooker, from Samuel Heintzelman's III Corps, so Johnston hit more than he intended when he attacked on May 31. Not only that, but his assault troops got all tangled up in their approach, and the attack went in late and disjointed. Fortunately for the Confederates, the Union troops were just as mixed up, and this Battle of Seven Pines, or Fair Oaks—like most Civil War battles, the two sides called it by different names—ended up being a nasty and messy little fight; neither side deployed all its available strength, nor brought to bear effectively what it did have on the field. About 40,000 men were engaged on each side, and the Confederates suffered about 6,000 casualties and the Union about 5,000.

There was one important result, though. At the height of the battle, Johnston was severely wounded. When it became apparent that he would be out of action for some months to come, Jefferson Davis looked about for a successor. On June 1, Robert E. Lee was appointed commanding general of the Army of Northern Virginia.

———

Lee's appointment to a field command was not greeted with the universal approbation a later generation associated with his name. Thought to be one of the first soldiers of the old army, an equal to Albert Sidney Johnston, he had not done much since secession. In western Virginia in the fall of 1861, he had not shone, and since then he had been down in the Carolinas, supervising coastal defenses. His penchant for fortification there had earned him the derisive nickname "King of Spades"; in March of 1862 he was recalled to Richmond as President Davis's military adviser, and he is largely credited with the idea for Jackson's diversion in the Valley. That of course was not well known at the time, so in Richmond there were those who harbored some misgivings about whether he could actually fight.

Ironically, General McClellan welcomed his new opponent. Lee, he wrote to Lincoln, would be *"too* cautious and weak under grave responsibility . . . wanting in moral firmness . . . and likely to be timid and irresolute in action." This at about the same time Lincoln was writing, "It is indispensable to *you* that you strike a blow. . . . *But you must act.*"

Lincoln did not add that if McClellan did not act, he would be acted upon. But that was the first thrust of Lee's thought. When he met his subordinate commanders, he immediately began considering how to gain the initiative; one of them remarked that they were heavily outnumbered, and Lee simply replied, "If you go to ciphering we are all whipped beforehand." So they would not go to ciphering; instead they would go to fight.

In preparation for that, Lee called in all the reinforcements he could get, including Jackson from the Valley. He was lucky to get a couple of weeks of rainy weather, which made the Peninsula wet and muddy, and made McClellan even less inclined to move than usual. The Federals busied themselves entrenching practically within sight of Richmond, and while they did so, Lee pulled together the threads of command, got to know his officers better, and made all ready. He needed to know as much as he could about his opponents, so on June 12 he sent out Stuart with a strong cavalry force on a reconnaisance of the northern end of the Federal position. Stuart and his thousand troopers were out three days, and instead of merely looking about, they rode around McClellan's entire army, breaking up some rail line, catching a few prisoners, and losing only one man in the process. The raid did little real damage, and even alerted McClellan, but it also undermined his fragile equilibrium even further, as well as making him and his army look at least slightly ridiculous—a bunch of Rebel yahoos riding rings around the largest and best-equipped army ever seen in North America.

That was but a sign of things to come. On June 26, Lee opened a series of strikes that is collectively known as the Seven Days' Battles.

After Seven Pines, McClellan had shifted most of his army south of the Chickahominy, but he left one corps, under the able Fitz John Porter, north of the river. Against these 30,000 men Lee now concentrated the bulk of his army, 60,000 strong. He left a mere 25,000 of his own to guard Richmond and face off all the rest of McClellan's army, and on the 26th, he struck. It was a beautiful plan, with Jackson coming down from the north on Porter's right flank, and the other Confederate corps falling on in succession, but it did not work. Jackson did not even reach the field until late afternoon, and all the others, A. P. Hill in the lead, were left to attack as the notion took them. So what should have been a lovely enveloping roll turned into a straight-up slogging fight known as the Battle of Mechanicsville, in which Porter's outnumbered bluecoats gave as good as they got—better, considering the disparity of numbers.

McClellan was totally at a loss what to do now. His other four corps had stood idle the entire day while Porter fought. Now McClellan decided he would shift his base south to the James River, but all he did was tell Porter to fall back a couple of miles from where he was. This Porter did during the night, but he was still more or less isolated, and the next day, the 27th, Lee hit him again at Gaines's Mill. Again Lee planned to roll up Porter's right, and again Jackson failed; A. P. Hill and then Longstreet attacked frontally, and for several hours maintained the contest alone. Jackson took the wrong road, got his columns scrambled up with others, backtracked, and did not attack until late afternoon. But by then Porter's men were finished, and they were pushed south across the river. Good artillery work and burned bridges enabled them to get away, but Lee got a respectable victory out of this one.

McClellan now implemented his decision to change his base to the James, and indeed, he went further than that: he threw the whole army into retreat. He started his move on the 28th, more or less splitting his army in two to do it. Lee spent the day trying to figure out what his enemy was up to. On the 29th he attacked again, this time hitting the three rear corps, II under Bull Sumner, VI under William B. Franklin, and III under Heintzelman, at Savage Station. Neither army commander exercised much control. Heintzelman's whole corps and part of Franklin's just wandered off, leaving Sumner to fend for himself; fortunately for them, Jackson took the day off to rest, leaving Prince John Magruder to do all the work, and Magruder's troops were not strong enough to do it. The Federals disengaged and got away.

Lee now enjoyed the unchallenged initiative, but his results had so far been disappointing. On the 30th, he caught the Union army again, around Frayser's Farm. He wanted to bag the whole lot, and to this end ordered attacks on both the south and north end of their line—really their retreating column. But again it could not be managed. Neither of his flanking columns got into position, and once more he had to settle for a series of ragged and uncoordinated frontal attacks. All he succeeded in doing was hastening the retreat.

This march south had been led by Porter, and he now took up a position overlooking the James, on Malvern Hill. During the evening the rest of the corps came in, and by morning, the Federals presented a solid front, well dug in and heavily supported by their excellent artillery. This would be a very tough nut to crack, but Lee was determined to have one last try at it. He ordered his artillery to clear the way, and early in the morning on the 1st of July, they opened a gunnery duel. But the Rebel batteries were not strong enough, and by afternoon they had been silenced by the Union guns. Lee gave up the idea of an attack, then saw movement among the Federal lines that he mistakenly took to be a retreat. So he ordered an infantry attack. Longstreet, D. H. Hill, and Jackson reluctantly sent their men in, piecemeal again, and to no avail. The attacks were sent reeling back with heavy casualties and tailed off as twilight came on.

The Seven Days was over. That night McClellan withdrew the army down to Harrison's Landing on the James, where it sat doing nothing for the next two months. For practical purposes the Peninsula campaign was over too, at a cost of about 30,000 casualties on either side. There was no more Southern criticism of Robert E. Lee as "the King of Spades"; as for George McClellan, that was rather a different matter.

———

Long before McClellan and Lee fought their climactic series of battles on the Peninsula, President Lincoln had realized that his new high command structure, with Washington trying to coordinate field operations in the eastern theater, was simply not working. Even with the short distances of Virginia and the telegraph, orders got mixed up, or were issued in response to situations too late to be of any use, and the whole idea was just a bad one. The Valley campaign graphically illustrated that the Union needed a field commander who could do what the War Department and the cabinet could not. So Lincoln created a second army, the Army of Virginia, composed of McDowell's, Banks's, and Frémont's corps, and he brought Major General John Pope out of the west to command it.

This was an odd choice. Pope had done well as one of Halleck's wing commanders. He had run a couple of useful actions on the Mississippi, notably the taking of Island No. 10, but had little else to recommend him in a purely military way. More important was that he was connected to important people in Washington, and he was a good solid Republican, and good solid Republican generals were hard to find. His appointment was received enthusiastically by the Radical Republican press, but far less so in the army itself. Pope was in fact junior to all three of his corps commanders, and Frémont resigned in a huff rather than serve under him. This may actually have been the greatest benefit of his appointment.

For whatever reason, here he was, arrived in Virginia to take up his new command. He got off on the wrong foot, issuing grandiloquent orders of the day pointing out that in the West they were used to victory, unlike these eastern soldiers, and that henceforth, "my headquarters will be in the saddle," prompting the troops to inquire sarcastically where his hindquarters might be.

Lincoln still felt the need of some overall direction. He now had two armies on his hands, Pope's in northern Virginia, and McClellan's sitting sulking in its tents down on the James. So he finally brought Henry Halleck east in Pope's wake, and made him general in chief of all Union military forces. At last the Union had a unified command structure, or at least it would have one if Halleck proved up to the job.

The first problem was what to do with McClellan, and Halleck solved that in a rather ingenious way. McCellan was too important politically to remove from command; therefore Halleck would remove the command from McClellan. He would draft off successive units from the Army of the Potomac, and add them to the Army of Virginia, and in the end McClellan would be an army commander without an army.

Meanwhile, on the Confederate side, Lee was busily scheming away. As soon as McClellan subsided after the Seven Days, Lee sent Jackson back north to face off what was now Pope's Army of Virginia. Lee himself did not dare leave McClellan's 100,000 men camped almost in the suburbs of Richmond, but gradually Lee worked out a plan. He fortified lines around the city, and the government brought in troops from the Carolinas to man them, thus gradually freeing Lee for field operations. McClellan cooperated by doing nothing, so Lee took a chance. Late in July he sent Ambrose Powell Hill with 12,000 men to reinforce Jackson, and early in August he moved out in that direction himself.

Jackson was already in motion. He had now recovered from the crankiness—in fact probably near-exhaustion—that had rendered him ineffective on the Peninsula, and he was again in top form, exercising independent command and trailing his coat in front of Pope's army. His advance bumped into Banks's corps, leading Pope's advance, at Cedar Mountain on August 9, and Banks, with a little luck and a little support, had his best day ever, giving the Rebels a nasty thump before the thing petered out.

Both sides now eyed each other warily for a week, a week in which Lee arrived, and with him the rest of the Army of Northern Virginia. Lee and Pope each now had about 55,000 men, but Pope could expect that he would soon be heavily reinforced, as practically the whole Army of the Potomac, four corps strong, was coming his way. Lee decided to act while he still had an even chance.

His plan was the epitome of boldness. In the face of an enemy who would substantially outnumber him within days or even hours, he split his army. Giving Jackson virtually half of it, he sent him on a long march northwest up the Rappahannock, then back east through the Bull Run Mountains, another of those isolated Virginia ridgelines. By marching around two sides of the triangle, Jackson cut Pope's communications to his rear, took his immense supply base at Manassas, and threatened his line of retreat back to Washington. Pope was totally confounded; he could not believe this was happening to him; indeed he refused to believe it until his telegraph lines went dead. McDowell, the corps commander in whom he placed most confidence, thought this presented a great opportunity, and urged Pope to attack his enemy while his forces were split. But Pope was not the man to seize what Lee dangled before him, and it was precisely on that condition of mind that Lee gambled. While Jackson's men gorged themselves on Yankee rations, and Lee marched hard to join up, Pope floundered about and ordered his corps commanders here, there, and everywhere.

On the afternoon of August 27, Jackson loaded up everything he could carry, burned what he could not, and set off to find a place to fight. He took up a position just west of the old Bull Run battlefield of last year, and his men settled down to gloat over their goodies and wait for someone, either Lee or Pope, to show up. While they slept with unwontedly full bellies, the Federals marched and counter-marched for miles, the troops shuffling along half asleep, and the staff officers going wild as orders from headquarters—"in the saddle"—sent them here, then there, then back to here again. Pope ordered up Porter's corps from McClellan's army, but did it in such a mixed-up fashion that Porter was not sure where he was supposed to go, and as he was not disposed to accept orders from John Pope anyway, he lolligagged along at a leisurely pace. And so it went.

Eventually, the reports Pope had received allowed him to construct a coherent picture of his situation. He decided that Jackson was march-ing west back over his earlier route, seeking to escape beyond the Bull Run Mountains. Longstreet, leading Lee's advance, was coming east to link up with him, but only for the purpose of helping him get away. Pope therefore ordered his forces, in effect, to pursue Jackson, concen-trating as they did so. At last he had it all together in his mind.

The only flaw in this was that the picture did not coincide with reality. On the morning of the 29th, several of Pope's units bumped into Jackson's men. A Union division led by John Reynolds, and then I Corps under Franz Sigel, who had replaced Frémont, hit the Rebels around the Henry House Hill, which had been the scene of heavy fighting back in 1861. Reinforced, eventually by Jesse Reno's IX Corps and Heintzelman's III Corps, the Federals slowly drove the Confeder-ates back until the latter were in a solid position along some rail cuts and around a hill feature called Stony Ridge or Sudley Mountain. Here they stuck, and held hard, through charge and countercharge. At last the impudent Rebels had been brought to bay. So thought Pope, and he called up his other corps, Porter off to the south, Franklin several miles east, and McDowell, who was within close supporting distance. Thus by nightfall, most of Pope's army was ready to crush Jackson.

Unfortunately, they were not ready to crush Lee as well. Longstreet, leading the advance, had made steady time, pushing aside the small forces of cavalry trying desperately to slow him down. Jackson was fully aware of this imminent assistance, and far from being caught, he had merely used his own force as bait for the trap, sucking Pope into a full-scale commitment. As Pope made ready to finish off Jackson, better than half the Army of Northern Virginia, all unknown, was in position to hit the Union left flank.

In fact, Lee decided not to do this. He would have preferred to maneuver even farther around, to the Union rear, and thus bag the entire army as it retreated. On the morning of the 30th, then, there was a hiatus as everyone made ready to move. But soon after noon, Pope surprised the Confederates, not by retreating as he should have, but by resuming his attack on Jackson. Totally unaware of Lee, he had ordered a pursuit of what he still took to be a retreating portion of the Confederate army. Porter's corps, now in the line in place of Sigel, hit Jackson's tired men so hard that he came within an inch of breaking through, and Old Jack was hard pressed to keep his position together. Indeed, if the Union attacks had been properly coordinated instead of piecemeal, the Rebels must have been broken.

Lee, now left with little choice, threw his divisions into line, and down they came on the Union left like the wrath of God. This was very close to what had happened at First Bull Run back in the fall, and the result was almost the same. The Confederates charged handsomely, and the Federals resisted manfully, both sides standing to their business with far greater finesse and firmness than they had done before. But eventually the pressure was too great, and the Union line bent back and back. Late in the afternoon, Lee sent Longstreet, five divisions strong, against Pope's left, southern, flank, and they drove the Federals up the slopes of Henry House Hill. Pope pulled troops over from his right flank, which enabled Jackson's weary troops to advance as well. By nightfall, the Union position was a horseshoe around that bloody hill, and Pope knew he was well beaten.

There was no panic this time, however. Pope ordered a withdrawal, and during the night his people carefully pulled out, destroying the bridges over Bull Run as they went.

Lee's pursuit over the next two days was laggard; his people were tired, hungry, and nearly fought out themselves. On September 1 Jackson caught a Union force at Chantilly, and though he had numerical superiority, he got very roughly handled. At that Lee quit, and turned back southward. The beaten Union army retreated to the Potomac,

humiliated and angry. Not so much at being beaten by Bobby Lee—
there was little disgrace in that—but rather at being poorly directed
by its own commanders. There was a great deal of complaint and bitter
commentary, most of it directed at John Pope.

The government in Washington reacted quickly to restore confidence, and they did so by relieving Pope and reappointing McClellan.
The latter put on full dress uniform and went out to meet the troops
as they marched, tired, dirty, and angry, back inside the lines at
Alexandria. News of his coming spread down the lines. Brigadier General John P. Hatch, in full view and hearing of General Pope, shouted
out to passing troops, "Boys, McClellan is in command of the army
again! Three cheers!" The soldiers responded with thunderous roars of
approval. Pope went off to Minnesota to fight the Sioux; he was little
heard from again, though for years Union veterans teasing each other
and recalling their war service used the phrase "as big a liar as John
Pope."

Chapter 8

Civil War Tactics and Strategy

ONE OF THE peculiarities of the Civil War that immediately strikes a student is the lack of decisive victory on the battlefield. Armies were thoroughly trounced—Pope's at Second Bull Run, Johnston and Beauregard's at Shiloh—and there would be further notable victories, such as Chancellorsville, Chickamauga, and others, yet almost never was an army actually destroyed in the field. One looks in vain for an Austerlitz, a Jena-Auerstadt, or a Waterloo.

This can hardly be blamed on the soldiers themselves. Even the most insensitive imagination is awed by the courage and endurance the soldiers displayed on both sides of the war. He is a rare person who can stand in the Cornfield at Antietam, or along the Sunken Road at Shiloh, without being almost overwhelmed by the courage and suffering so freely poured out there.

Some, but only some, of this inability to achieve victory can be blamed on the generals. There were some generals who were outright incompetents, others who made mistakes, either of commission or omission, and many who for one reason or another failed to seize opportunity when it was offered to them. Yet that is true in any war, generals being as human as the rest of us, and by and large it is probably safe to assert that no war in history has produced any better galaxy of generals than the American Civil War did. Napoleon's twenty-six marshals included a great many first-rate fighters, but not more than half a dozen really outstanding generals. On the Union side, Grant, Sherman, Sheridan, Thomas could easily have carried a baton in Napoleon's Grand Army, and so could many a corps commander, Sedgwick, Reynolds, Hancock, not to mention a host of commanders coming up the ladder toward the end of the war. On the Confederate side Lee and Jackson were virtually incomparable as tacticians, and their subordinates—Longstreet; the two Hills, Daniel Harvey and Ambrose Powell; Cleburne; the fabulous Jeb Stuart as a cavalryman—rank with any generals any other army or any other war has ever produced. Indeed at least part of the fascination of the Civil War for military buffs is watching genius and near-genius at work on the available material.

Why then the inability to achieve decisive victory in the field? Partly, of course, just because there were so many good commanders on either side; they tended to balance each other out. But it was not that alone. Even when Lee, for example, faced a very mediocre opponent, Burnside at Fredericksburg or Hooker at Chancellorsville, he could not destroy his victim. Only Grant managed that, at Fort Donelson and again at Vicksburg, but both of them were sieges where the defeated army had no place to go; and in the Appomattox campaign, when Lee's army was so worn down by siege and attrition that the operation was far from typical of the war.

The answer to this indecisiveness must therefore be sought elsewhere, in the operative military theories of the day, in the material conditions under which those theories were put into practice, in the available technology, and in the tactics that necessarily flowed from that technology. A brief examination of these may suggest why so many battles and campaigns were repetitious bloodlettings without immediately visible result.

To the extent that it was dominated by anything, the military theory of the era was essentially the product of the Napoleonic Wars, especially as their lessons had been distilled by the great Swiss thinker and writer Henri Baron Jomini. Serving as a staff officer in the French, and subsequently the Russian, armies, Jomini had worked out what he called the principles of war, and had published widely in the years after 1815. His ideas, and those of Napoleonic warfare generally, had been instilled into young American military minds by such great teachers as Dennis Hart Mahan at West Point. Henry Halleck, for example, was considered the most knowledgeable exponent of Jomini's ideas in America, and his proposals after Shiloh are full of ideas of "concentrating on strategic points," and other such stuff he got from Jomini.

Though Jomini's articulation of the principles of war was widely accepted, so that the idea of them is now commonplace, his attempt to derive practical rules by which one might fight and win wars was less successful. He himself had had plenty of practical experience, though more on the staff level than in the actual hurly-burly of combat, but his theories came out looking more like rules for chess than for war. He fell into disrepute in the late nineteenth and early twentieth centuries, though he has recently enjoyed something of a rehabilitation at the hands of American Civil War scholars.

The other major name for military theory in the period was Carl von Clausewitz, and he has since been accepted as the ultimate philosopher of war. His vogue, however, was yet to come, and few of the American officers of the Civil War would even have heard of him.

What Americans found themselves forced to do in the Civil War was adapt what they knew and what they had been taught of military history and military theory, and what their own common sense and experience taught them, to the conditions of the United States in the 1860s. Jomini, for instance, had said a good deal about lines of operation, but he had not said much about railroads for the simple reason that there were none when he had his experience of war. As late as 1859, France and Austria had fought a short war in Europe, and their generals, not knowing much about railroads, had done their best to ignore their existence; it was once said that this was "a war of 1859 fought by armies of 1809 using tactics of 1759." Americans, amateurs and civilian soldiers fighting a tremendous war, could not afford to play games as if they were European professionals isolated from day-to-day realities.

The overall grand strategy of either side was eminently straightforward, and has already been touched upon. For the Union, it was to reconquer and reoccupy the national territory, and restore the authority of the central government, and to do so while avoiding the foreign intervention that might well make such a task impossible. For the Confederacy it was simply to defend its claimed national territory until it achieved either victory on the battlefield, or foreign recognition, or failing those, simply to stay alive until the North sickened of the war and its costs, and recognized the impossibility of its own war aims.

To achieve these overall aims for either side—one obviously must inevitably be disappointed—was a matter of military strategy. The initiative here lay with the North; it must conquer the South, and thus it had the luxury, such as it was, of choosing how to go about it.

Neither side, of course, had the added luxury that students enjoy, of reflecting at leisure how best to achieve its ends. For the men involved, these things all had to be hammered out as they were happening, under the intense pressure not only of events but of divided counsels and ambitions as well.

The first Northern strategies brought mixed results. The policy of isolating the Confederacy from the outside world worked, at least to the extent that foreign intervention was avoided for the crucial first months of the war. The actual blockade was less effective than was hoped; more exports got out, and more supplies got in, than the Union would have liked, and the Confederacy proved more adept than had been suspected at producing the matériel it needed. The ground strategy of reoccupying territory was far less successful, for the simple reason that Confederate armies kept getting in the way. And even where they did not, in large stretches of central Tennessee, for example, the hostility of the population and its support of raiders and guerrillas meant that an inordinate proportion of Union strength had to be dissipated in guarding supply lines, railroad bridges, depots, and other military and support installations. Eventually the Union armies virtually gave up the hope of occupying territory, and resorted instead to a policy of large-scale raiding and destruction of the Confederate infrastructure, its economy, its manufacturing and transportation facilities, that enabled it to sustain the war. In this they struck not only at the Confederacy's ability to support the war in a material sense, but in a psychological sense as well. Memoirs of the period are replete with stories of Confederate women berating Union soldiers for making war on women, when they could not defeat Confederate armies, and the Union soldiers replying that it was the women, after all, who were keeping the war going: You wanted your men to go off and make war; this is what war is. If you now complain that you don't like it, you shouldn't have started it. Call your men home, and that will end it.

This was in effect an example of the ulterior strategy; the British theorist and historian Liddell Hart thought this was seldom effective in war, but it certainly worked in the later stages of the Civil War. It did so, of course, because the armies, to come back to the original point, were incapable of defeating each other decisively in the field.

Looked at from a Jomini-like theoretical construction, each army, or each of the several Union and Confederate armies, operated forward from a given base of operations. For example, in the Shiloh campaign

Johnston moved out from his base at Corinth, and Grant from his base at Fort Henry; Grant advanced much farther than Johnston did, but he had the Tennessee River as a logistics line, while Johnston had to march overland. Theoretically and ideally, as the armies approached each other, one should be able to maneuver onto the flank of the other, threatening the enemy's line of communications while preserving its own. If it did this, it could force the enemy to fight at a disadvantage; so fighting, the enemy would, or should, be defeated, and, driven off its line of supply and retreat back to its base, it could then be completely routed and captured or destroyed.

That was what was supposed to happen, but in practice it hardly ever did. Shiloh, to use it as an example again, was basically a meeting or encounter battle. Johnston wanted to flank Grant, and drive him away from his communications on the river, but he could not manage to maneuver his troops to do it. So the two just went at it, hammer and tongs. On the Peninsula in the Seven Days, Lee managed to lever McClellan away from his base at West Point on the York, but McCellan, thanks to the navy, was able to shift his base south to the James and set up shop all over again. Thus Lee's tactical ability to rough up McClellan was offset by the latter's strategic possibility of a shift of base.

The eastern theater, indeed, presented almost insuperable obstacles to decisive victory. These lay especially in the base line available to either side. Normally a base line would be roughly perpendicular to the line of operations—as a Jomini would envisage it—but in this area, the base line of either side was actually a concave curve: for the Confederacy from Richmond curving northwest up toward the mountains, and for the Union curving northwest to southeast roughly along the line of the Potomac and the shore of Chesapeake Bay. Thus if either army were maneuvered off its original line of operations, it was still likely to be pushed toward rather than away from another segment of its base line. No matter how hard an army tried, or even how successful in battle it might be, it thus became virtually impossible to drive an enemy into a position where he could be destroyed. This then accounts for the repetitive nature of the fighting in the east. Just as the Low Countries are the "cockpit of Europe," because geography has forced generals to fight the same battles over and over again, generation after generation, so northern Virginia became the cockpit of the Civil War; a fifty-mile-radius circle placed in the middle of the Richmond–Washington–Shenandoah Valley triangle takes in Bull Run, Antietam, Fredericksburg, and Chancellorsville, and the Wilderness, the vast majority of the great battles of that theater of the war.

On this larger strategic canvas, it was not only geography that impeded success; it was equally difficult to achieve coordination in the fourth dimension, time. The Union, with the burden of the offensive, repeatedly tried to bring about a concentration in time, so that all its armies in all their theaters would advance at the same moment, and thus overwhelm the Confederacy. Instead, they repeatedly advanced piecemeal, allowing the Confederates to shuffle troops from one theater to another and meet them in succession. In 1862, Halleck and Buell more or less moseyed along, each going his own way at his own pace. Lincoln, unable to achieve this coordination himself, appointed McClellan as his overall commander, and when McClellan failed in this regard, he eventually brought Halleck east to do the job. Halleck failed also, and Lincoln finally made Grant his commander in chief. It might have been expected that with those two mechanical marvels of the modern age, the railroad and the telegraph, to help them, achieving coordination and concentration would have become easier than it had been in the past, but such did not seem to be the case. Field commanders still reserved the right to go off on their own hook, in some unforeseen direction, or indeed not to go off at all. The indignant, hurt, frustrated, and angry exchanges between the War Department and some of the field commanders would almost be amusing in another context.

It is not only strategy that is difficult, however. If we move to the battlefield, we find the tactical problems even more daunting.

———

The tactical systems employed by both sides in the Civil War were a variation on, indeed almost the last variation on, the linear tactics of the eighteenth century. These had been evolved through the dynastic era, and were a response to the weapons technology of the period. Basically they had been developed to utilize the firepower of the flintlock-mechanism, muzzle-loading musket. Under this system, soldiers in their assorted units, battalions, or regiments, were formed up in long lines, three or four, or in the British case two, ranks deep, which enabled each army to bring as many muskets to bear on the enemy as possible. Two opposing lines would approach each other and exchange fire, ideally carefully controlled volleys, until one broke, or the other charged and closed with the bayonet. Commanders played games with this system literally for generations, for it changed little from about 1715 until about 1830. Frederick the Great, for example, developed the idea of the oblique attack, whereby his line came down on the enemy line at an angle and rolled it up. In the French Revolution the French experimented with the shock power of the column for breaking the line; this was something of a misnomer, for the "column" was really only a very thickened line.

One reason the linear system lasted so long was that there was little change in weaponry throughout the period. The flintlock musket was in universal use; it could be fired a couple of times a minute, depending upon the skill and practice of the soldier, but it was not really accurate beyond perhaps seventy-five yards. Indeed, in the eighteenth century such weapons were produced without sights; the soldier simply "presented" his piece and fired in the general direction of the enemy line. Anybody who got hit at a distance of more than about sixty yards was unlucky indeed.

This being the case, the whole course of a battle was capable of mathematical calculation. A line or column could charge home, by crossing that last fatal fifty yards at a run. While they were doing it, the opposing line could get off two or perhaps three volleys. If the attackers could get enough men through those volleys and across that fifty-yard-wide "killing zone" to close with the bayonet, they could, presumably, win the fight. Sometimes they could do it, as the British did at Minden, sometimes they could not, as at Fontenoy. Given the relative inadequacy of the weapons, what was most important was fire-and-march discipline, and keeping the men under control and in coherent formations so they could carry out the necessary maneuvers. Hence the obsession of commanders such as McClellan with drill for the army.

Unfortunately for the men of the Civil War, the technology changed just before the war began. In the 1840s the French army developed the minié ball, named after its inventor. This was essentially a soft-lead, shaped bullet that, upon the firing of the weapon, expanded into rifling grooves inside the barrel of the piece. Rifles, as opposed to smoothbore muskets, had been around for a long time, but they were expensive, slow to load, and prone to fouling. Now, with the new minié ball, every soldier could be armed with one. This rifled bullet had the effect of widening the killing zone in front of a line. Instead of taking effective fire at about 50 yards, the attacking force now came under it at 100 or even 150 or more yards. Under those circumstances, it became very difficult, and very costly, to carry an attack through to a successful conclusion.

The leaders of the Civil War did not quite know what to do about this. In the years before the war, the U.S. Army rewrote its tactical manual, and William J. Hardee, subsequently a Confederate corps commander, produced a new book, *Rifle and Light Infantry Tactics*. McClellan ordered several thousand copies of it for the Federal army, though it might have given someone pause to think that the other side wrote the book. Hardee's *Tactics* was the Bible of young officers learning their business in the war. But Hardee had not really known what to do about the new weapons, either; all he did in his book was shake out the formations a little bit, and try to increase the pace at which attackers moved. Neither proved very effective.

Indeed, in the conditions under which Civil War battles were fought, most officers were still necessarily more concerned with maintaining unit cohesion and control than with the danger of enemy fire. There are common instances of troops being stopped to reform their ranks and dress their lines while under enemy fire, which is, to say the least, a trying exercise.

In spite of the deadly nature of Civil War firepower, it was still necessary for armies to fight, of course. And they tried desperately to overcome their problems. In battle after battle, the attacker would attempt to outflank the defender; Chancellorsville is the outstanding example of this, practically in all military history. Often, of course, the terrain of a battle was so tangled or unknown that units got all mixed up. In the Wilderness some regiments launched attacks by compass bearing. An officer would pull out his pocket compass, take a line of sight, and lead his men forward until they bumped into something— officers led from the front in the Civil War, which is one reason so many of them were killed. But often there was nothing to do but launch a full-scale frontal attack, as on the second day at Shiloh or Chickamauga, or, in the classic setpiece occasion of the whole war, Pickett's charge at Gettysburg. Here, in the open, was war in all its gory glory, and those who saw it, or took part in it, never forgot it.

If they lived through it.

The force of the firepower, and the deficiencies of the tactical systems employed, explain why the battles were so bloody. Men wrote of whole trees being stripped by bullets, and even of trees being cut down by them, let alone by cannon fire, yet the men still stood up to it. They had to stand, of course, because it was almost impossible to load a muzzle-loading rifle lying down. Very soon in the war, wherever possible the troops dug trenches and threw up breastworks; and such fieldworks, if the defenders were given a little time for preparation, became all but impregnable to an attacker. When the Union army tried to take the Confederate position on Marye's Heights at Fredericksburg, there could have been few men below the level of corps command who did not recognize the impossibility of what they were trying to do. At Cold Harbor in 1864, the troops designated for the attack pinned little slips of paper with their names on them to their backs, so their bodies might be identified after the slaughter ended. That men should stand up and go forward in the face of such knowledge invites reflection upon the human condition.

Ironically, the muzzle-loading rifle of the Civil War era was not the latest word in firepower. Breech-loading weapons were becoming available, and not only that, but repeating rifles were also developed by now. These might have been put into general use, had it not been for the conservative attitude of military procurement people; their view was that to increase the firepower of the soldier would simply encourage him to waste ammunition, and would thus cause insurmountable supply problems. Nevertheless, a few Federal infantry units, mostly western ones, bought their own repeating weapons, and in the last stages of the war Federal cavalry was armed with repeating carbines, one reason why Sheridan's cavalry performed so well in the Appomattox campaign.

Given the increasing superiority of firepower over maneuver, and especially of defensive firepower from prepared positions, it was very difficult to win a battle, and usually as costly, or even more costly, for the attackers than for the defenders. Traditionally, of course, the offense is indeed more costly, but that is supposed to be offset by the fruits of victory; that is, the attacker suffers more heavily making his attack, but he then inflicts disproportionate casualties on his fleeing enemy. In the Civil War, however, the enemy seldom fled, except at First Bull Run and a few smaller battles. Even in such horrendous defeats as Chickamauga and Chancellorsville, the defeated side, the Federals in both cases, retained sufficient cohesion to draw off the field in good

order, or at least with a rearguard in adequate strength to discourage pursuit. This had to be coupled with the facts that the victor was often as exhausted by his victory as the loser was by defeat; the victor, in possession of the field, also got the task of cleaning up the debris— few Civil War commanders were ruthless enough to leave wounded to fend for themselves while they went off in pursuit of the enemy, even if they might have shortened the war by doing so; and finally, a retreating army, abandoning its wagons and trains and cluttering the roads as it went, could move much faster than an advancing one. So almost invariably, the loser got away with much of his army, to fight again another day.

Part of this may be attributed to the inadequacy of the cavalry arm of both sides through much of the war. Traditionally, cavalry served three purposes: reconnaissance and screening, which meant seeing what the enemy was doing while keeping him from seeing what you were doing; shock action at the climax of the battle; and pursuit. In this war, neither side could provide much in the way of shock; in the face of the minié rifle, the great cavalry charges, Austerlitz, Eylau, Waterloo, were all but a thing of the past. This left the other two functions, which were basically those of light cavalry. Both gray and blue riders performed screening and reconnaissance work, though for virtually the entire war, the Confederacy did it much better than the Union. But with a few exceptions, neither was very effective in pursuit, largely because the country was usually not open, and perhaps more because formed infantry, even beaten infantry, still could not be broken by cavalry. The weapons technology simply made it impossible. Throughout most of the war then, cavalry functioned largely as mounted infantry, moving on horseback, but usually fighting on foot. Acting in this way, both sides produced some effective cavalry leaders and actions, though the honors clearly went to the Confederacy, with Stuart and the man who was arguably the most talented light cavalry-mounted infantry leader in history, Nathan Bedford Forrest, "that devil Forrest" as he was habitually called by opposing commanders. This type of action was great for raiding rear areas, and annoying the enemy, and it could even have strategic ramifications, if supply routes were interdicted sufficiently to halt operations. But one looks almost in vain for the devastating pursuit, such as that after Ulm or Jena-Auerstadt, that transformed a battlefield victory into a crushing triumph.

It was ironic and unfortunate that these classic victories of the Na-

poleonic era, Austerlitz, Jena, Waterloo, were still fresh in men's minds. For they created the illusion that decisive victory *could* be achieved on the battlefield, and Civil War leaders, especially Robert E. Lee, sought again and again to emulate the Napoleonic victories, without really recognizing that the time for them was past. The battles of the Civil War thus have all the movement and flair of the earlier era, but in their actual results are really closer to the numbing horror of World War I, which in time was just about as far away from the Civil War as the Civil War was from Napoleon.

The other combat arm that merits at least passing consideration is artillery. This was pre-eminently an infantry war, in which artillery, like cavalry, played a supporting but not a starring role. At the beginning of the war, the United States Army possessed only about 4,200 cannon, and the vast majority of them were heavy pieces in coastal fortifications; only 167 were "field" artillery. The entire Union army employed about 7,900 cannon in the war, compared with more than 4,000,000 small arms, that is, individual weapons for individual soldiers. Numbers alone do not tell the tale, of course; firing shells, solid shot, or spraying grape and canister across a battlefield, the artillery, when properly employed, could be highly effective. Generally speaking, Union artillery was superior to Confederate; there was more of it, it was better supplied, and with some exceptions it was better handled. Malvern Hill in the Peninsula is usually considered its outstanding early triumph, but both sides performed occasional prodigies of fighting, such as the Confederate gunners on the first afternoon of Shiloh, or the Union artillery that shot the heart out of Pickett's charge at Gettysburg. Even in such notable cases, though, it still took infantry to finish the work at hand.

In studying the Civil War, then, one returns, again and again, to the men themselves. In part to the spirit and sense that motivated them to do what they did, but also in practical terms to see what they themselves learned and how they responded to field conditions. In the battles, they soon learned to dig, whenever they had a chance to do so. The attackers, of course, could not dig in; except in a siege, the two concepts were mutually exclusive. But the defenders learned very rapidly to take whatever cover they could find, a shallow ditch, a stone wall, a rail fence, a little fold in the ground, and to improve it as fast as they could. Bayonets were used far more frequently for scratching at the ground in the hope of creating cover, than they were for charging

the enemy. Senior officers sometimes discouraged this practice, in the belief that it inspired too defensive-minded an attitude in their men. But the men dug anyway; they might perceive themselves as mere instruments or victims of fate, but that did not mean they were fools, and they took whatever chance they could to lengthen the odds in their favor. Eventually this penchant for digging would transform the battlefield, and soon the face of war. By 1864 it was a rare, or a new, unit that did not seek to entrench whenever it stopped, and later in the war, in the operations around Atlanta or Petersburg, for example, trenches were a common and dominant feature of the battle terrain.

Another thing the men did, though this speaks less directly to tactics and strategy, was to develop an attitude that slowly altered the war. In 1861 and early 1862, under McClellan, the Army of the Potomac was punctiliously correct, and Confederate territory and property was handled with kid gloves, as it were. However, John Pope was cut from rougher, western, cloth. Under him the soldiers began to think that Confederates were indeed the enemy, rather than unfortunate civilians and erring cousins. If slaves of Confederates ran away to the Union lines, they would find shelter, such as it was; if they were not treated very kindly, at least they were not returned to their owners. Confederate chicken coops became fair game, and Confederate pigs legitimate targets. Pope did not encourage this, but he did not discourage it either. One early observer of the Union forces commented, "The problem with this army is that it doesn't hate enough." To its undying credit, it never did learn to hate very much. But it slowly learned to disregard the niceties.

By mid-1862, ideas were changing. Most of the fancy uniforms were gone now; on the one side changed for homespun butternut brown or dingy gray, on the other for shapeless but serviceable blue trousers and a simple dark blue fatigue jacket. Men were sloughing off the nonessentials. This war was proving to be a serious business, a far cry from what they had expected a year ago.

Chapter 9

The Year Ends Badly

B Y THE END of August of 1862, both Union and Confederacy were dissatisfied with their respective situations, and both, in their separate ways, decided to intensify the conflict. The war was already eating ever deeper into the fabric of society, and there were the inevitable divided counsels, those few on either side who would give it up as a bad job or lost cause, those few whose primary loyalty was in fact to the other point of view, and the many who thought the war must be prosecuted even more vigorously to bring it to a successful conclusion. These latter were of course now firmly in control.

In the North, recruiting was still proceeding satisfactorily on a voluntary basis; thirty-five new regiments joined the Army of the Potomac alone after Second Bull Run. But political leaders in Washington were increasingly conscious of internal dissension, and especially of the possibility of foreign intervention on the side of the Confederacy, and indeed the crisis posed by that latter threat was reached about this time. England or France or both might well accord full recognition to the South, and if they did, the war would be as good as lost.

It was a situation of extraordinary complexity; in Britain, the government professed to be friendly to the Union, but certainly acted as if it were not. Confederate vessels were equipped more or less openly, Confederate agents bought supplies to be shipped through the blockade, and the American ambassador, Charles Francis Adams, had his repeated protests casually if politely shrugged off. Ironically, the British middle and laboring classes, the ones actually hurt by the war and the shortages of cotton and other imports, tended to be strongly for the Union; it was the upper classes with their aristocratic ideas who felt akin to the Confederacy. But in mid-nineteenth-century England, they still exerted a totally disproportionate influence on national policy, and by now they openly discussed whether or not the time had come for intervention.

Not that they were in favor of slavery, but then all those strange Americans kept insisting the war was not about slavery: it was about some peculiar constitutional wrangle that only Americans seemed to understand. Indeed, if the war were openly about the abolition of slavery, then Britain might have to rethink its attitudes; after all, Britain had taken the lead, at great expense, in the suppression of the Atlantic slave trade at the start of the century, and had recently outlawed slavery in the British Empire. They might want to support their Confederate cousins, but not if they were overtly seen to be fighting to preserve human slavery.

As for Napoleon III, across the Channel, well, there was a man who would fish in any troubled waters. He was quite ready to recognize the Confederacy as soon as Britain would go along with him. Indeed, his readiness was one reason why Britain was a bit reluctant. Anyone who was going to dine with Napoleon III wanted to have a very long-handled spoon; Britain had gone to the Crimea with him, and had not enjoyed the experience. He might be able to charm Queen Victoria, but the man was really a trickster, variable as the wind, totally untrustworthy, and really not a gentleman, after all.

Abraham Lincoln was conscious of all this, but his mind moved in far deeper currents than Napoleon III's, or even Lord Palmerston's and Lord Russell's. In the middle of 1862 he was going through a very profound evolution in his view of the war and its causes. Before the war, and before his election, he had been capable of holding mutually contradictory views about slavery and the Union. In the great "House Divided" speech he had asserted that slavery and freedom were incompatible, and that, ultimately, the Union would endure and slavery would disappear. Yet in his election campaign, and after his assumption of the presidency, he repeatedly disavowed any intention of legislative action, or indeed any other kind, against slavery as it then existed in the South. When hostilities began, he still professed this view, and several times, he rescinded orders from commanders such as John C. Frémont and General David Hunter freeing slaves in areas under their control. Through the first year of the war he walked a tightrope between those Radical Republicans who insisted on war against slavery to the knife, and men such as McClellan, who insisted that the fight was not against slavery at all, and to say it was would fracture the war support in the North.

But Lincoln had now seen the war, almost at first hand. He had visited the hospitals, seen the wounded and the dying, knew the agony being inflicted on the country by this war, and as he walked the floor in the dark of the nights, he became more and more convinced that slavery must go. It was not simply a political problem, an inconvenience, a stumbling block to settlement. It was a moral evil, and a country that refused to acknowledge that had no right to claim to be what the United States claimed to be. Lincoln was a very wily politician, but he was also a man of profound intelligence, and the clarity of his thought shows through all of his writings. So, reluctantly and painfully, he reached the necessary conclusion: slavery must go.

Had it been possible to do so, he would have gotten rid of it by other means than war, and for some time he pushed legislative schemes for gradual, compensated emancipation; it was, after all, far easier and less costly to buy slaves' freedom than it was to free them by force, and throughout early 1862 he made efforts in this direction, largely without success. As late as the end of August, in response to an editorial by Horace Greeley in the *New York Tribune,* he still asserted that he was primarily interested in preserving the Union, and would do so by freeing all, any, or none of the slaves, whichever led most effectively to that larger aim. That was his public, and oft-proclaimed, position. But slowly, painfully, he came to agree with Greeley; the nation could not "put down the Rebellion and at the same time uphold its inciting cause. . . . " He was thus at last thrown back on emancipation, necessarily by force, as a means of stating once and for all, as clearly and unambiguously as possible, not only what the war was about, but what the United States was about.

Finally he took his thoughts to the cabinet, only to be rudely surprised. It was not that they disagreed with him on the overall principle, but they believed that the timing was impossibly bad. The Union, after all, looked as if it were losing the war. To announce emancipation of slavery under such conditions would be received very badly, at home and abroad; it would look like a last spiteful attempt to undermine the South by touching off a slave revolt. Lincoln held that spite was the farthest thing from his mind, but he accepted the argument. But then, if the Union should be granted a real victory, he would act.

The view from Richmond was different. When Jefferson Davis met his congressional colleagues, at the same time as Lincoln and Greeley were exchanging their views, he could point to the Confederacy's having survived its greatest peril. True, New Orleans had been lost, but the Federals had now stalled along the Mississippi, and above all, the threat to Richmond posed by the Peninsula campaign had been not merely averted, but crushed ignominiously. If that were not enough, Southern arms had gloriously trounced the enemy in northern Virginia as well. The South had but to persevere until its inevitable triumph.

But perseverance came at a price; the South had already brought in conscription for men from eighteen to thirty-five, and in September it raised the age to forty-five; there were enough exemptions that resisters immediately raised the cry that the whole effort made "a rich man's war but a poor man's fight." There was fierce opposition in Congress to Davis's attempts to create a centralized government, in part because Davis was not a very good political player, in part because opposition to a central government was what the whole Confederacy was about anyway.

Under the pressure of continued war, and in face of the stubborn intractibility of the Northern government—who would have thought they could fight?—the Confederacy began to rethink its defensive strategy. Let us, said some of the politicians, carry the war to the North. Let us liberate Kentucky, let us invade Maryland. We have shown they cannot beat us, but let us now place the weight of war on *them*.

Political fulminations do not often make for sound military advice, but it happened that the Confederate military leadership more or less agreed, at this juncture, with the men in Richmond. General Lee wished to retain the initiative he had so dramatically asserted at Second Bull Run. He needed to replenish his supplies, he wished to provide some relief for the fought-over territory of northern Virginia, and he even looked to the possibility that a successful raid into the North would bring the foreign recognition the Confederacy still hoped to attain. So he too thought that much might be gained by moving northward. Could he have sat in on conferences in Washington, he might have been even more hopeful.

General George McClellan, now back in command of the Federal troops in the East, and all that nonsense of the Army of Virginia done away with, was working diligently to rebuild his command; publicly he put on a good show, and said he hoped he could save Washington; but quietly he sent his wife away with the family heirlooms. His corps commanders spent their days trying to readjust to the reconstituted regime, something of a problem for them, as the McClellan clique felt it had a few scores to settle, and there were a great many recriminations about who had failed to support whom during the Second Manassas campaign.

Still, the Army of the Potomac was nothing if not resilient, and under the hand of the great organizer it began once again to look like a real army; the new regiments came in, more troops came back from exile on the Peninsula, and the poor infantry squared their shoulders and took heart yet once again.

Just in time. On September 4, with Stuart's cavalry screening it to the east, the Army of Northern Virginia crossed the Potomac and invaded the North. The bands played "Maryland, My Maryland" while the soldiers took up their march into new country. Lee detached Jackson and his corps to pick off the garrison upriver at Harpers Ferry, went himself to Frederick, and then sent Longstreet farther north toward the Pennsylvania line.

When the reports of these moves reached Washington, the government nearly panicked. McClellan performed his usual mathematical miracles, and decided he was faced by 120,000 men, and outnumbered; in fact, he had 85,000 men to Lee's 55,000. Halleck bombarded him with notes about the necessity of saving the capital, and under these pressures, McClellan gathered up his army and slowly began to move northwestward toward Lee. He reached Frederick on the 13th, to find to his relief that Lee was gone. The Confederates had slipped west, behind the Catoctin Mountains, a roll of low hills just past Frederick.

At Frederick, McClellan got a present. Until then he had received highly contradictory reports of the Rebels: they were starving, they were well-fed; they were ragged and scared, they were full of fight; they were few in numbers, they were as the leaves of the trees. Being McClellan, he was always disposed to believe the most painful of these stories, but now he got some hard intelligence. Two soldiers found, wrapped around a bunch of cigars, a copy of Lee's Special Order No. 191, written four days before, in which he had spelled out his entire plan of campaign and the dispositions of his army. McClellan was exultant, and he remarked to one of his officers that with this paper, "if I cannot whip Bobbie Lee, I will be content to go home." To President Lincoln he promised, "Will send trophies."

Lee soon knew that his plans were compromised, but with his army spread out from Harpers Ferry north to Hagerstown, there was not much he could do about it. He ordered his men to hold Turner's and Crampton's Gaps, the two most accessible passes through the Catoctins, recalled Longstreet, and urged Jackson to finish off Harpers Ferry as quickly as possible. The Federal garrison there, in an indefensible situation, surrendered on the morning of the 15th after a remarkably inept effort. Meanwhile, on the 14th, McClellan's advanced corps pushed its way through the gaps of the Catoctins. All the pieces were coming together for a major passage of arms.

Lee's first thought, once the mountain passes were lost, was to retreat back south, but when he heard from Jackson that Harpers Ferry had fallen, and that the first of Jackson's divisions was already on its way to join the main army, he decided to stand and fight. He chose his position around the little town of Sharpsburg, nine miles north of Harpers Ferry. His troops were placed in a roughly north-south line, a chord across several lazy bends of the Potomac, the southern end of the line along low heights fronting a shallow little stream called Antietam Creek. The position was reasonably strong, but Lee's troops were few, and the only line of either reinforcement or retreat was a small ford across the Potomac, called Boteler's Ford, near the southern end of the line. When he decided to fight, he had a mere 19,000 men in hand, and his entire strength, as his several detachments came in, was still only 40,000 men. McClellan had at least 90,000.

The Federals closed up toward the Confederates on the 15th, but McClellan did not act. On the 16th he still did not act, but spent the day instead making plans and letting his troops do some skirmishing to feel out the land. The Federals held the high ground east of Antietam Creek, and thus had good artillery positions, but they did not make too much use of them. Nor did McClellan make much of a plan. He seems to have intended attacks upon both flanks of the Confederate line, followed by a push through the center, but his orders were so uncertain that the timing, the major axis of the attack, the coordination, and all the other things a commander ought to do were left to someone else, or, as it happened, to no one. McClellan himself had not actually been present at one single battle in the Seven Days, and he might as well have not been present at Antietam. In fact, he was hardly even a spectator at his own battle; his headquarters was out of sight of the battlefield, and having spent the 16th thoroughly confusing his commanders about his intentions, he then left them to make the best of what they could on the day of the battle. Once again the corps commanders were left to fight their own, separate, struggles.

They did that with a will. At seven on the morning of the 17th, Fighting Joe Hooker's I Corps slammed into the Confederate left, held by some of Jackson's newly arrived men. Three divisions strong, the Federals came on in the classic American infantry formation—two up and one in support—and drove the Rebels through the North Woods and back around a little church called the Dunkard Church. But then Jeb Stuart hit them in the flank with artillery, and a brutal counterattack by John Bell Hood's Texans stopped them in their tracks. As I Corps melted away, General Joseph Mansfield led his new XII Corps up in support. With raw troops, Mansfield led from the front, and was immediately shot down, horse and rider, and carried off the field, to die the next day. The fight surged back and forth through a field of standing corn until the corn was all gone, replaced by the grim harvest of Union attack and Confederate counterattack, a dozen charges across that deadly field. Hooker was wounded soon after Mansfield; his corps passed to the senior division commander, George Meade, and while Meade tried to pull things together, and Mansfield's division commanders tried to press home, the Federal attack lost direction and force.

The focus shifted to the left. Bull Sumner now led the II Corps in. His first division, John Sedgwick's, he sent forward in column, without pausing for reconnaissance. The Confederates smashed it from three sides and drove it from the field with heavy losses, exposing the flank of Hooker's and Mansfield's attacks and regaining what they had earlier yielded. Sumner's other two divisions fared slightly better. They came on in echelon to the left, and hit very nearly the left center of Lee's whole line. The Condeferates here, D. H. Hill's men, held a little sunken path that came to be known as Bloody Lane, and the Federals repeatedly advanced against it over open ground, while gradually the dead and wounded on both sides piled up, and still the Rebels would not go back. Finally, the Federals got some guns up where they could sweep along the lane, and grudgingly the Confederates gave way, slowly at first and then in something of a rush. It was only mid-morning, and so ferocious had the attacks been that Lee had not one reserve formation left. His men were completely fought out, used up, mere handfuls of survivors left standing around the stripped poles that had held their colors. If only the thing were finished well now, George McClellan would hold the title deeds to the Army of Northern Virginia.

With the Confederate center broken at Bloody Lane, General William Franklin's VI Corps arrived on the scene, ready to go in and finish the affair. Instead, a shaken Sumner, reeling from his rough handling, asserted his seniority and told Franklin not to advance. At a loss, Franklin appealed to McClellan, who supported Sumner. The precious moments slipped by.

Meanwhile, at the southern end of the line, Ambrose Burnside was preparing to take his whole wing of the army across Antietam Creek. He thought he commanded Franklin, and that VI Corps was going to clear his flank for him, while he gave the immediate task of carrying the stone bridge across the creek to Jacob Cox's IX Corps. A little preliminary reconnaissance would have shown the Federals that the stream could be waded; instead they tried to storm the bridge, which, at right angles to the approaches and swept by fire, presented horrible difficulties to an attack. Two tries were blown away before a third rush carried it at about one in the afternoon.

While this was going on, other elements of IX Corps finally discovered how shallow the stream was, and began getting across, climbing the low height of the creek, and pressing back the thin Confederate line there. At last, by mid-afternoon, Burnside had his crossing secured, and his corps formed for a final push that would finish off the reeling enemy. The blue infantry wheeled to the right, faced northwest, and began pushing into Sharpsburg.

At this climactic moment, who should arrive but the troops of A. P. Hill, just come panting up the road from Harpers Ferry and Boteler's Ford. Totally unexpected, they crashed into Burnside's exposed left flank, and sent his men tumbling back to the banks of Antietam Creek, where they desperately hung on. The battle stabilized once again.

Stabilized and ended. Both sides were exhausted, men dead, wounded, lost, dazed; officers without their commands, commands without their officers. It had been a day of immense slaughter, the bloodiest single day of the entire war. Federal casualties were more than 12,000, Confederate nearly 14,000—15 percent of the Union army and a staggering 22 percent of the Confederate.

McClellan claimed a victory, but after that, he did nothing to exploit it. Indeed, on the 18th Lee sat in his reconstituted lines, as if daring McClellan to try again, but the Union commander did not accept the gauge. Instead, he left his opponent strictly alone, in spite of the arrival of fresh cavalry and two unused corps. That night, Lee put his trains on the road, and withdrew over his one thin line of retreat, Boteler's Ford. The next day, he was back in Virginia, and George McClellan had missed the best chance the Army of the Potomac would ever have to destroy the Army of Northern Virginia.

———

Lee, safely back in Virginia, was not disheartened by the results of his foray. He had never intended to remain in Maryland, though he would have exploited a clear victory had the opportunity offered. But for him it had been merely a raid, he had bought time for the Confederacy, and his army, much thinner though it now was, certainly did not feel it had suffered a defeat at Sharpsburg, or Antietam, as the North was calling it. Not only had they sustained themselves on the battlefield, they had captured or destroyed many supplies, and taken many prisoners at Harpers Ferry. All in all, it had not been a bad bit of work.

In this assessment, the Confederates neglected the effect of even a partial victory on the North. Northern commentators did not know that Lee was only raiding; they knew instead that he had at last been defeated and chased back into Virginia. Less than perfect though it was, this was still a victory, and hailed as such throughout the North.

Its most peculiar effect was on McClellan. As was now customary, he believed that he and he alone had saved the country. The country proved singularly ungrateful. Within a very short time, as men had enough perspective to examine the event, there were calls for his dismissal. Not only that, but Abraham Lincoln used the opportunity of Antietam to issue the Preliminary Emancipation Proclamation; two days later he suspended *habeas corpus,* a traditional legal protection of those who for one reason or another might oppose government policies; in this case, it was denied to anyone trying to prevent Federal recruiting. To McClellan, essentially a peace Democrat, this was using his own victory against him, and he was bitter in his denunciations of those in Washington who were trying to create a social revolution.

McClellan went so far as to canvass senior commanders in the Army of the Potomac; some, like Fitz John Porter, agreed with his views. Most did not. McClellan had proclaimed that the army would not stand for emancipation, and as the fall days went by, and the army drilled and did nothing, it became ever more obvious that a general so out of step with his political superiors could not last. Through October he and the War Department skirmished extensively, McClellan claiming he could not move until his broken-down cavalry was recovered, Stanton asking how his cavalry had broken down when it had been sitting in camp for five weeks, and so on. Few men ever got the better of Edwin Stanton in a telegraph duel. Finally, despairing of moving his commander, Lincoln removed him instead. On November 7, he was ordered to turn his command over to Ambrose E. Burnside.

McClellan found he was thoroughly out of step. Not only did the army accept emancipation—as one soldier wrote home, the army would accept *anything* that would help beat the Rebels—but the Union at large did as well. There was some sense that the proclamation was flawed by its application, for as the London *Times* sarcastically put it, Lincoln had freed the slaves where he had no power to do so, in the Confederacy, and had not done so where he did have the power, namely, in the North. As usual the British political classes misunderstood the situation. The proclamation was issued under Lincoln's war powers, against those areas in rebellion; he in fact had no legal means of freeing slaves in the North. Many ordinary Britons regarded emancipation as an extremely favorable step, and from that time on, there was less and less talk of intervention for the South. Far more important, men and women in the Union recognized first the necessity and then ultimately the justice of the move. In spite of emancipation, suspension of *habeas corpus,* and then the removal of McClellan, the Republicans handily survived the November elections. The country remained committed to the war effort—a good thing, for there was little to cheer about for the remainder of the year.

———

All through the summer and fall of 1862, Union commanders in the Mississippi area had failed to do anything significant, and golden opportunities had gone begging. Admiral Farragut, after taking New Orleans, had steamed up the river all the way to Vicksburg, and had actually bombarded that then ill-defended city for two months, from late May to late July. The troops that might have taken it for him were employed elsewhere, however, by General Butler patrolling the streets of New Orleans, or by General Halleck marching an inch a day toward

Corinth, Mississippi. Finally, Halleck went off to Washington. Upon his departure, the western theater was again split into two commands. Grant got the western part of it, including western Tennessee and the Mississippi River area, and his army was dispersed to garrison this already reclaimed territory. The eastern portion of the command went to Don Carlos Buell, and he was ordered to move east into northern Alabama, eventually to take Chattanooga; he started the move readily enough, but then found himself alone in the wilderness, his supply lines overstretched, and his rear areas and communications constantly cut up by guerrillas. As Buell was indisposed to live freely off the country, he was soon forced by this indirect pressure to give up any real offensive action. So the summer went by inconsequentially.

The Confederates too had their problems, and as usual in the west, they revolved around who commanded what. In the early summer, as Halleck had advanced upon Corinth, General Beauregard had conducted a very clever delaying action, and had retreated before the overwhelming Union forces with great skill. A clever retreat was not appreciated in Richmond, however, where Beauregard was already in disfavor after losing at Shiloh. So instead of being praised for what he accomplished, Beauregard was criticized for what he did not accomplish, and he responded by resigning his command, for reason, he said, of poor health. He was replaced by Braxton Bragg. Bragg was something of a stormy petrel, an intelligent, useful man, who was always hampered both by ill health and ill temper, one of those men who, giving of the best themselves, were never able to elicit the best from others. Indeed, his greatest defect was an almost complete inability to get along with his fellow commanders; to the detriment of the Confederacy, his greatest asset was his almost equally unconditional support by Jefferson Davis.

Placed in command in the west, Bragg went off to counter Buell's movement toward Chattanooga, which he did effectively by marching northward and invading Kentucky. Meanwhile, he left General John C. Pemberton to defend Vicksburg and the Mississippi River against Grant. This was a daunting task, made worse by the fact that Pemberton had little with which to work, received confused and contradictory orders from Bragg and from Richmond, and was further hampered by a divided command structure. Some of his troops were commanded by Sterling Price in Arkansas, but neither Price nor Pemberton was entirely sure who commanded what or whom. About the only clear instruction given Pemberton was, "Do not get shut up and besieged."

That was at least no immediate problem, as Grant found it extraordinarily difficult to get close enough to Vicksburg even to consider a siege. First of all, he had to worry about Confederate river rams being built on the Yazoo River; the Navy was alarmed about them, and Halleck kept pestering Grant to do something about it. Next, he had to chase Confederate forces under Earl Van Dorn, essentially Pemberton's field commander, around Corinth. Then, after Van Dorn had been beaten there but had managed to escape, Grant could at last turn his attention to Vicksburg. It still took him weeks to get Halleck's grudging permission to move, but finally he made his first bid on the Confederate stronghold.

Grant's plan was fairly straightforward. With 40,000 men he himself would advance south along the line of the Mississippi Central Railroad. Meanwhile, his second-in-command, General Sherman, would take another 32,000 men by boat down the Mississippi River itself to attack the city directly. Grant, on foot, started first, and by late November he had crossed the Tennessee line into Mississippi. He set up a major supply depot at Holly Springs and continued south. Sherman, organizing his river transport with the help of the navy, was not ready to leave Memphis until the third week of December.

Meanwhile, Pemberton had concentrated his scattered forces for the defense of Vicksburg, and eventually managed to pull together about 12,000 men around the city. That was not a major force, but Vicksburg, situated on a high bluff and surrounded by low-lying swamps and bayous, was an incredibly difficult target in its own right. Nature had done for it far more than the Confederates were able to do.

Pemberton gave to Van Dorn the task of holding up Grant, and this he performed admirably. Not strong enough to face Grant openly, he decided to hit his communications, and for this he cut loose with his own cavalry and that of Nathan Bedford Forrest. Maneuvering around Grant's army, he hit the supply depot at Holly Springs, and burned everything he could not carry off. Then his troopers went on a spree, tearing up about sixty miles of railroad track north of the depot, and leaving Grant to live in thin country without much hope of resupply.

Sherman fared even worse, on two counts. First, he got his troops down to Vicksburg all right, the Navy as always doing its excellent work, but then when he disembarked to move on the city, he found his approach blocked by strong Confederate fortifications at Chickasaw Bluffs, ten miles north of the city. Though Sherman outnumbered the defenders two and a half to one, the position was all but impregnable, well fortified and approach lines all channeled by the terrain and well covered by the enemy. He had a try anyway, which cost him 1,800 casualties to the Confederates' 200, a fair measure of the impossibility of the task.

His second problem was General John A. McClernand, an Illinois political general who, while all this was going on, had talked Halleck into giving him command of an expedition down the Mississippi. He arrived in the aftermath of Chickasaw Bluffs, took command of Sherman and his troops, and all on his own took them off to capture Fort Hindman at Arkansas Post, up the Arkansas River. Fort Hindman was almost completely useless in the larger scheme of things, but it was a lot easier to capture than Vicksburg.

Disappointed and disgusted, Grant then went back to Memphis, to think it all over before starting again.

———

Grant's failure to take Vicksburg was not the only difficulty besetting Union arms in the west by the end of the year. In eastern Tennessee and Kentucky, Buell and Bragg engaged in a tiring game of march and countermarch that finally ended on the bloody fields outside Murfreesboro, Tennessee.

Ordered by the War Department to march on Chattanooga, as part of Lincoln's oft-expressed wish to relieve the Unionists of east Tennessee, Buell had gotten as far as northern Alabama before being stymied by raids along his lines of communications. From there he felt compelled to move northward to Columbia and Nashville, to reopen his lines. But while he did this, Braxton Bragg stole a march on him. Bragg was able to move farther and faster through friendly country than Buell was through hostile, and the Confederate general reached Chattanooga in late July, as Buell was moving north through the central part of the state.

Bragg concluded that the best way to counter the Union moves was to seize the offensive, and he thought big. At Chattanooga he collected 30,000 men. To his northeast, at Knoxville, was General Edmund Kirby Smith with another 10,000. With these two forces operating in conjunction, and offering mutual support, Bragg proposed to cross all of Tennessee, invade Kentucky, occupy Louisville, and interdict Union traffic even on the Ohio River. He might even get as far as Cincinnati, in Ohio, thus carrying the war in the west to the heart of the Union. Alternatively, having wrenched Kentucky back into the Confederacy where it belonged, he might turn southwest and destroy Grant. Lee's army was at that time about to invade Maryland, and who could tell which of these blows might be the fatal one, or how many it would take to break the Federal war spirit? It was a daring conception, but it offered glittering rewards.

It all began well. Kirby Smith moved out of Knoxville in mid-August, and within a fortnight he had reached Lexington, Kentucky, making ten miles a day against almost no opposition. Bragg left Chattanooga at the end of August, and headed straight north across Tennessee. A hundred miles to his west, Buell was running for Nashville. Buell's subordinate, George H. Thomas, wanted to concentrate and fight at Murfreesboro, but Buell, conscious of his supply lines, kept going north. The two armies thus moved up their respective sides of an isosceles triangle, and by the middle of September, they were opposite each other, and only thirty miles apart, Bragg at Glasgow, Kentucky, with 30,000 men, and Buell at Bowling Green with 45,000. Bragg went a little farther north, as far as Munfordville, with Buell following him. There he offered battle, but Buell declined, so he moved out toward Louisville.

The North was now in an uproar. Militia were called out in the Lakes states, raw recruits were drilling and digging trenches all over the Midwest, the War Department was sending troops hither and yon, and telegraphing Buell every few hours to do something. It was chaos for a while. Unfortunately for the Confederates, things then began to fall apart. Kirby Smith might have joined with Bragg, but he was an independent commander, and his assessment was that Bragg really did not need his assistance, so he stayed around Lexington. And Bragg himself began to think he was out on a long limb. Starting out, he had received the usual assurances that Kentucky was just pining for a sight of Confederate gray, and that the entire state would welcome him with open arms. But when he got there, Kentuckians wanted to have nothing to do with him, and he found his army traveling in hostile country, which, as Buell could have told him, was a difficult thing to do.

The two armies finally bumped into each other as both were searching for water. Ironically, neither general had anything to do with the battle. Bragg was off installing a Confederate governor of Kentucky, and Buell did not realize his troops were fighting a battle until it was all over. Nevertheless, the Battle of Perryville became the main clash of the Civil War in the state of Kentucky, with 3,400 Confederate casualties and 4,200 Union, a fierce afternoon's work for the small parts of both armies that were engaged in it.

That was typical of this strange campaign in which neither general really wanted to fight. The armies marched great distances over Tennessee and Kentucky, foraging as they went and causing a flutter of fear or excitement. Once or twice, virtually by accident, they came together, and on some little rolling hills that otherwise were as peaceful as anything on earth, men screamed and struggled and killed each other for an afternoon. Then they buried their dead and picked up their wounded, or left them to the care of the local civilians, and moved on again as if nothing had really happened. And nothing really had, except for a few hundred young men and their families, whose lives were changed forever by a bullet shot by a man who would never know them, and who probably would have liked them had they met under different circumstances.

Bragg, realizing he was now outnumbered, took a long circuitous route back to Chattanooga, and Buell was quite delighted to let him go. By the end of November, the Union army was back in Nashville, the Confederate in Chattanooga, and everyone would have been happy to remain there. Neither Washington nor Richmond was that happy, however. The Confederate government, disappointed in its great hopes, appointed Joseph E. Johnston as overall commander in the west, and directed him to coordinate Pemberton, Bragg, and Kirby Smith, a belated attempt to bring order to its western command structure. Bragg, thoroughly at odds with his corps commanders, but retaining the confidence of Jefferson Davis, remained in field command. In Washington the War Department had already had enough of Don Carlos Buell; in fact, in the middle of the campaign it had sent orders to George H. Thomas, telling him to assume command. Thomas had refused, replying that Buell was planning to fight immediately, and that the campaign was going as well as could be expected. But when Buell let Bragg march away totally unhindered after Perryville, Washington's patience ran out. The Union army in Tennessee got a new commander, William S. Rosecrans. Since by now everyone knew Buell, and no one knew Rosecrans, the change was greeted with general enthusiasm.

Rosecrans was rather a peculiar character, even for a war full of them. He was a competent soldier, with a good eye for organization and administration. Unlike his opposite number, Bragg, he was friendly and loquacious, and often kept his staff up most of the night chatting about the affairs of the world. He was a Catholic, something of a rarity in the generals' ranks of those days, and he kept a spiritual adviser with him. But he was a little unstable, and given to excitement to the point of incoherence under stress. He had done reasonably well in detached subordinate commands; how he would fare as an independent commander, with the full weight of responsibility, remained to be seen.

It was now early December, and the winter rains were coming on. But neither side was quite willing to call a halt yet. Bragg sent cavalry forces off to harass the Union armies, Forrest to pester Grant and John Hunt Morgan—officially a brigadier general but in spirit closer to a cavalier of the English Civil War, at least to those who admired him— to bother Rosecrans. Halleck wanted Rosecrans to advance immediately against Bragg, but it took the new general several weeks to get his army properly organized and supplied, and then by Christmas he was ready to move out. On the 26th he moved southeast from Nashville, heading toward Bragg's army thirty miles away at Murfreesboro.

Bragg had moved up here with 38,000 men, in two corps under Polk and Hardee, and he proposed to give battle. Rosecrans, with 45,000 in three corps, Thomas, T. L. Crittenden, and Alexander McCook—the highest ranking of seventeen "Fighting McCooks" from Ohio, all brothers or first cousins—moved along the muddy roads through heavy rains, using his cavalry as flank guards, stalled by effective rearguard cavalry work by the Confederates, and not knowing exactly what he might bump into. On the night of the 30th, his troops bivouacked in the fields and scrub south of the Nashville Turnpike, about a mile west of a meandering stream called Stones River. He was only two miles from Murfreesboro, but in that two miles was Bragg's army, drawn up in battle line straddling the creek.

Expecting to be attacked on the 30th, Bragg had settled for a rather awkward position, accepting the stream cutting through his battle line for the advantage of holding low but dominant hills at the north, or right, end of his line. But as the Federals were slow, he changed his mind, and decided he would himself attack early on the morning of the 31st. To do this he reversed his order of battle, and moved two divisions of Hardee's corps from his right around to his left flank. One of the divisions was Patrick Cleburne's, among the hardest hitters of the Confederate army. Come dawn, these men and John P. McCown's division would flank and then roll up the Federal line.

Rosecrans planned to do pretty much the same thing: he was going to lead with his left, expecting to flank and roll up the Confederate line at its other end. Unfortunately for the Federals, the Confederate attack beat them to the punch. The Union units on the left flank were still receiving their orders and getting formed for their own attack when the storm hit the other end of the blue line.

This rapidly degenerated into a soldiers' battle. The terrain was covered with low cedar scrub, with clearings here and there in it. Nothing stopped infantry moving and firing, but it was very difficult for commanders to maintain any kind of control, or keep a clear picture of the progress of the battle. The Confederates drove hard, breaking up one regiment after another—one division was driven three miles before it re-formed—but these were seasoned soldiers now, and they simply stood to it, little knots in the scrub, here a company under a smart sergeant, there a gun section under a brigadier general. The Rebels kept on, and they drove hard, and they made ground; then they came to Sheridan's division of McCook, and he not only held them, he bought time with a nasty little counterattack before he too was pushed away. By late morning, the Union line was bent back into a horseshoe, but it was still full of fight. In mid-afternoon, Hardee fought out, Polk took up the attack, and hit what was now the Union left flank. By now, Bragg figured, his opponent was thoroughly mixed up, and this ought to finish him off. He was wrong. Hastily reorganized and re-deployed Union regiments shot the heart out of Polk's assault, and the battle sputtered out with the Confederates still not certain of their victory.

That night Rosecrans held a council of war: Should they fight on, or give it up and retreat? The most dramatic account of this, which is probably somewhat prejudiced, has Thomas deciding it by saying, "I know of no better place to die than right here." Whoever said what, they chose to stay. On the other side, Bragg thought he had already won his victory, so other than reporting the fact to Richmond, he did little.

Morning showed his error; the Federals were still there. Aside from some cavalry skirmishing, neither side accomplished much. On January 2, Bragg issued orders for an attack. Launched against strong Union artillery, it achieved little beyond heavy casualties for the attacking infantry. That night Bragg recognized facts; he set his army in retreat. As Rosecrans later summed up the affair, paraphrasing Shakespeare, "Bragg is a good dog, but Hold Fast is a better."

The dubious but hard-won victory was well received in the North, and especially in the Northwest, home of most of the soldiers. At that stage, the North desperately needed some good news, for the Army of the Potomac had just suffered another brutal defeat at the hands of Robert E. Lee.

———

The choice of Ambrose Burnside to replace McClellan in command of the Army of the Potomac was met with dismay, not least by Burnside himself, who protested his unfitness for the task. His chief recommendation seems to have been that Lincoln rather liked him, and was totally at a loss whom to turn to; Stanton is reputed to have told the President, "Well, you have made your choice of idiots; now you can expect news of a terrible disaster!" Burnside had done reasonably well in earlier, subordinate, commands, and most of the senior officers preferred him to the other likely choice, Joseph Hooker.

So Burnside it was, and the new general went forth to do battle with Lee and the Army of Northern Virginia. In November, when Burnside took over, Lee had about 85,000 men, as good as he was ever to do, and was encamped in a wide arc from Brandy Station on the Rappahannock north and west all the way to Winchester. He had now definitively organized his army into corps, with Jackson and Longstreet, both promoted to lieutenant general, as his corps commanders. Stuart commanded his cavalry, and had just celebrated the season by another ride around McClellan's army, one of the last nails in McClellan's coffin.

Burnside had 120,000 men, plus several thousand more detailed to guard Washington, which he could use if absolutely necessary. When he took over, the army was concentrated north of the Rappahannock, near the right end of Lee's positions.

The new general realized he had to act; that was why he was there. And McClellan's complaints to the contrary, the Army of the Potomac was in fine condition, well equipped and supplied, rested and reorganized, and lazing away the last of the good fall weather. Burnside decided he would feint to his right, toward Lee's center, then rapidly counter-march to his left and force a crossing of the Rappahannock at Fredericksburg. This would open the route to Richmond, and force Lee to scramble to defend the Confederate capital. Only one thing was needed: there must be pontoon bridges available, so the Fredericksburg crossing could proceed while the enemy was still at a disadvantage. Halleck, Lincoln, and Stanton were all a bit skeptical; few people so far had stolen a march on Lee. But since they could think of nothing better, they agreed.

All went according to plan at first. After marching back and forth, Burnside's leading corps, under Sumner, arrived at Falmouth on the north bank of the Rappahannock on November 17. But there were no pontoons there to meet them. It was raining; the river was rising. Sumner wanted to push across, secure the town, and grab the high ground behind it. Burnside grew cautious, and decided to wait. A week later, the pontoons finally arrived, on November 25.

Unfortunately, Longstreet had gotten there on the 21st, so the chance for an unopposed crossing was gone. There was still some small opportunity, though. To meet the threat, which had indeed surprised him, not by its direction but by its rapidity, Lee had split his army even wider apart than it was before, and Burnside might have moved back upstream and caught Jackson isolated from Longstreet. Instead, he chose to pursue his original objective of getting on toward Richmond.

So he continued to prepare for his crossing, and, to compound his difficulties, he lost more time waiting for more bridges to arrive. By the time they were there, so was Jackson, and thus, when he finally made his crossing, he faced the full strength of the Army of Northern Virginia.

The Rappahannock at Fredericksburg was about 250 yards wide. There were low hills on the north side of the river, suitable for the placing of batteries. The town of Fredericksburg, a substantial place, ran along the south bank for about a mile and a quarter, and extended in from the river perhaps half a mile. Running irregularly along behind and beyond it was a range of hills, called Marye's Heights right in back of the town itself. On these the Confederates took up their position, Longstreet on the left and Jackson, when he came in, on the right. Their line was almost eight miles long, with guns emplaced, rifle pits and trenches dug, interlocking lanes of fire, all that one could desire for a defensive battle.

Burnside had organized his army into three "grand divisions," under Sumner, Franklin, and Hooker. He intended that Sumner should attack on his right, through the town itself and against Longstreet, and Franklin on his left, downriver and against Jackson. Hooker was in reserve. The crossing began on the night of the 10th, and Franklin made it with little difficulty. Sumner ran into trouble, a Mississippi brigade determined to hold the town, and it was the night of the 12th before he finally cleared them out, got his bridges built, and his corps across. Burnside's orders for the 13th were, in effect, to take the heights.

Franklin opened at mid-morning with a furious assault by Meade's division that actually broke Jackson's first line. The Federals came storming up out of the river bottom as if there were no tomorrow, which indeed was all too true, and drove determinedly ahead. But the gray lines were just too strong, and too well defended, and by early afternoon, Franklin's corps was fought out. Jackson launched a short-lived counterattack, but the Federal guns from across the river shot it to pieces.

Meanwhile, Sumner organized his troops as they marched through the now burning town, and on the clear space between it and Marye's Heights, they formed up, regiment after regiment, colors uncased, lines dressed, musket barrels twinkling as the morning fog lifted off the river bottom, all the brilliant panoply of war. The Confederates in their trenches were unstinting in their admiration, and looked to their cartridge boxes. At last all was ready, and about eleven o'clock off they stepped, French's division, then Hancock's, then Howard's, then Sturgis's. In three hours the Confederates broke them all, and sent them in succession back the way they had come, those who could go back. The front below Marye's Heights gradually clogged with the dead, the wounded, the broken, the horrible wreckage of those fine divisions. Rebel guns grew too hot to touch, some ammunition ran out, and still there was no end of targets. Burnside ordered Franklin to try again, and Franklin ignored him; he then ordered Hooker to take up where Sumner left off, and Hooker did so, protesting as he went against a useless sacrifice of his corps. At the height of the battle, Lee turned to his staff and said, "It is well that war is so terrible, otherwise we might grow too fond of it," a remark usually taken as evidence of his humanity, but open to other interpretation.

By nightfall the battle subsided: the butcher's bill, 5,300 Confederate, 12,700 killed or wounded Federals. Burnside wanted to try again, but his generals refused to support him. Thus the disaster Stanton had predicted.

Part III

1863
GRAPPLING

Chapter 10

The War in the West

B Y THE BEGINNING of 1863, both North and South had reached the same conclusion: the war was a failure. Both bitterly denounced their respective leaders and politicians, both demanded more effort from their soldiers. One could suggest here a general rule, that modern war between even fairly equal opponents tends to become a war of attrition. Under such circumstances, it might appear reasonable that both sides should sit down and negotiate a peace settlement. The more normal course, however, is that both sides tend to intensify the conflict rather than back away from it, thus fulfilling Clausewitz's dictum that to the act of violence there can be no inherent limit, and that both sides will tend toward extremes. The American Civil War at the end of 1862 or the beginning of 1863 might therefore be compared to World War I at the end of 1915, or World War II in early 1942. In all three cases, at the stage mentioned, neither side had achieved a clear advantage; neither side was willing to make concessions in its war aims, and the war went on.

With the advantage of historical perspective, it is fairly easy to see this trend and to understand the reasons for it. But the Civil War suffered from the disadvantage of being the first of these great modern wars, so the leaders then, and even more particularly the critics of the leaders then, could not readily grasp what was happening, or why it was taking so long to attain a desired result. Indeed, they suffered from the additional handicap, already considered, of fighting this war while carrying the mental baggage of the Napoleonic Wars, which made it look as if they themselves ought to be able to achieve decisive results. From our own perspective again, the Napoleonic Wars look more attritional than they did to the Civil War generation, but the men of 1863 were more familiar with Austerlitz and Waterloo than they were with the wastage of a quarter century of war.

Thus as the third year of the war opened—a war that Lincoln initially thought might take ninety days, and that many Southerners thought would never happen at all—the belligerents had achieved a form of equilibrium. The Confederacy had not won foreign recognition, and had not won independence on the battlefield; it suffered marginally under the Union naval blockade, and there were substantial shortages, but it had made up for many of its pre-war economic deficiencies. It had resorted to conscription, but there were so many loopholes in the law that it was not unbearably burdensome as yet. In the Union, the war was far less intrusive, the Union being a far wealthier society than the Confederacy; conscription had not even been seriously considered to this point. Yet the federal government still had not made sufficient inroads upon the Confederacy to regard its war effort with any satisfaction. The Emancipation Proclamation of late 1862, however it was regarded by later generations, was not perceived as an earthshaker; the admission of the western counties of Virginia as the Union state of West Virginia in early 1863 was not a great recovery of territory to show for almost two years of strife. And the year had ended in failure on the battlefield. Stones River, or Murfreesboro, was a marginal victory at best, Fredericksburg was an outright disaster, and Vicksburg, free for the taking in early summer, was now becoming the Confederate Gibraltar of the West. Lincoln, somber but determined, summed it all up in his annual message to Congress in December of 1862: "While it has not pleased the Almighty to bless us with a return of peace, we can but press on, guided by the best light that He gives us, trusting that in His own good time, and wise way, all will yet be well."

———

Press on . . . Those words might have been the motto Ulysses S. Grant lived by. What to make of Grant? A small, often shabby, modest and unassuming man. If one looks at all the Union's commanders so far, Grant appears the least prepossessing. McClellan *looked* the part; so did Pope, and Frémont, and Fitz John Porter, and any number of others. And there were all those stories: Grant the failure in private life, Grant the drunk. But gradually Grant had made an impression on Lincoln. There was the famous story of a temperance delegation complaining to the president about Grant's drinking, and Lincoln's off-color reply, "I'd like to send some of his whiskey to my other generals," or the more trenchant observation that summed up the whole matter, "I can't spare that man—he fights."

And that was the nub of the matter. Grant fought. Not that he was a mere brute, or, as Wellington said of Napoleon, "a mere pounder after all." But Grant knew, as McClellan never would, that war is fighting, war is ultimately about killing. Grant, in spite of his subsequent reputation as the butcher of 1864, would never have said what Lee did at Fredericksburg, about the danger of becoming fond of war. He was never in the slightest danger of becoming fond of it. That was what made Grant, bored by civilian life and depressed by army life, the most tragic and probably the greatest general of the Civil War, or indeed of American history: he knew what it was all about. And knowing that, he did what had to be done.

———

What had to be done immediately was the taking of Vicksburg, and this was Grant's job in late 1862 and early 1863. By then, this otherwise insignificant town on a bluff overlooking the low country of the Mississippi had become the Confederacy's center of equilibrium, its last, largely symbolic, link with the western states, its last hold on the great waterway of the continent. Its geographic importance was greater than Verdun's in World War I, or Stalingrad's in World War II, but like them it came to be invested with meaning transcending its location. This was especially true for the Union, for it can be argued that the Confederate government, though aware of Vicksburg's importance, did far less than it should have to hold the area, that indeed, just as the Richmond authorities had done in early 1862, they now in 1863 left the western Confederacy to take care of itself until it was too late to do anything about it. One is left with the conclusion that if the capital of the Confederacy had remained in Montgomery, Alabama, instead of being moved to Richmond, it would have been a far different war.

So here was Grant, in late January of 1863, ready to have another try. What was he up against? First of all, the country itself. It had been a rainy season, and the rivers were high, and the low-lying countryside largely flooded. In much of the territory, it was hard to tell the difference between land and water anyway; in the old aphorism, it was all "too thin to plow, too thick to sail." Much of the Union operations depended upon the ability of the navy to operate on the waterways, but it was a strange setting for sailors. There were snags where huge old trees had been uprooted and caught in the currents, there were sandbars, there were shifting river channels. In many cases the ships, odd-looking contraptions with paddlewheels and with hay bales for armor, could not make a passage until sailors had gone ashore and cleared low-hanging branches off the trees, and what sailor could feel comfortable working his vessel in a spot where snakes might drop off the trees onto his head?

But it was just as bad for the soldiers, for much of their time "ashore" would be spent wading through bogs and backwaters. For a hundred miles up and down the river, the feeder streams twisted and turned, and overflowed their banks, and the infantry struggled and cursed and slept in the wet, and wagons could not move, and artillery might as well be forgotten. If the soldiers could not be moved by ship, they could barely move at all, so what passed for land approaches was just as bad as what was supposed to be water lanes.

The Confederates more or less controlled the Mississippi from Port Hudson, in southern Louisiana, up to Vicksburg itself, though Union vessels could run freely along most of that distance. The Confederates were more thoroughly in command for the twenty miles south of the city, down as far as Grand Gulf. Vicksburg itself sat on a bluff, so at least it was dry. Here as well sat John C. Pemberton, with something around 20,000 troops and instructions to hold the city indefinitely. For a few weeks his numbers made little difference; the Confederates needed only to sit there while the Federals floundered in the swamps. Unless Grant could conquer nature itself, Vicksburg had little to worry about.

For a while he could not conquer nature, but it was not for lack of trying. His first attempt, in December of 1862, had failed when the Rebels burned his supply bases behind him and Sherman was beaten at Chickasaw Bluffs. Sherman at least had the virtue, rare among field commanders, of writing an honest report: he told Washington, "I reached Vicksburg at the appointed time, landed, assaulted, and failed."

So Grant now knew he could not make an approach by land, relying on the Mississippi rail system for his supplies. He was just too vulnerable to Confederate raids for that. He had to operate south from Mem-

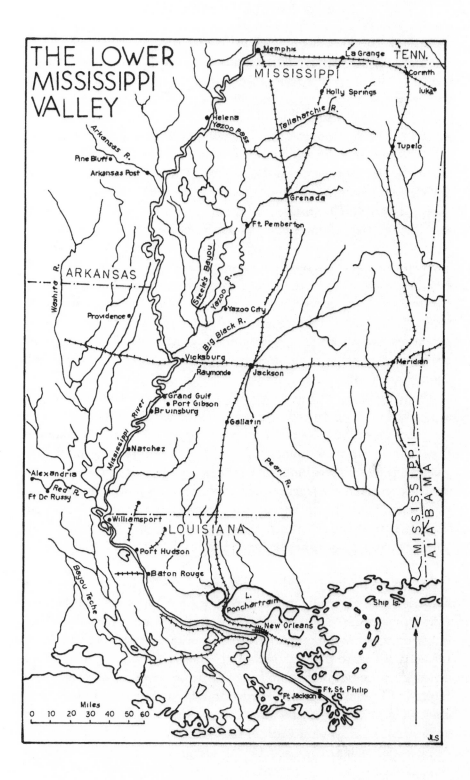

THE LOWER
MISSISSIPPI
VALLEY

Memphis • ———— La Grange TENN.
MISSISSIPPI
Corinth •
• Holly Springs Iuka •

• Helena
Yazoo Pass
Tallahatchie R.

Arkansas R.
Pine Bluff •
Arkansas Post • • Tupelo

• Grenada

Washita R.
ARKANSAS
• Ft. Pemberton

Steele's Bayou
Yazoo R.
Providence • • Yazoo City

Big Black R.
Vicksburg
Meridian •
Raymonde • Jackson

Mississippi River
• Grand Gulf
• Port Gibson
Bruinsburg
• Gallatin

• Natchez

Pearl R.
Alexandria •
• Red R.
Ft. De Russy

MISSISSIPPI
ALABAMA

• Williamsport
LOUISIANA

Bayou Teche
• Port Hudson

Baton Rouge

L.
Ponchartrain
Ship Is.

New Orleans
N

Ft. St. Philip
Ft. Jackson

Miles
0 10 20 30 40 50 60

JLS

phis along the Mississippi, and so he arrived at Sherman's camp on January 29, and took over operations the next day. The two generals talked it all over; they were developing an increasing confidence in each other, so they played with their maps, and argued, and crawled around the table looking from one angle and another. There was intense pressure from Washington to get moving, the latest manifestation being the disastrous diversion offered by John A. McClernand, and neither Grant nor Sherman was the type to sit idle and wait upon events anyway. Somehow there must be a way to get at Vicksburg.

So they tried. The irony of it lay in the fact that they were already at Milliken's Bend, a mere twenty miles from the city. Well, Vicksburg was on a large east-facing loop of the river; perhaps if they dug a canal across that loop, they could get ships and men and supplies below the city, and invest it from there. The troops were set to digging, and for two months they worked away, digging a mile-long ditch across the peninsula formed by the river's loop. After two months they had to give it up; the work was so flooded by sluggish water that it could not be made deep enough for the naval vessels to use it, and the whole effort went for nothing.

Then they tried an even more ambitious canal scheme. If they dug at Duckport, about halfway between Milliken's Bend and Vicksburg, they could get into Walnut Bayou, and from there into Roundaway Bayou, and from there into Bayou Vidal, and from there into the Mississippi. It was a three-mile dig, but they went at it with a will, and finally, they opened a way, and the muddy waters flowed through, and the Navy triumphantly sent a small steamer from the river into the bayous. But by now summer was coming on, and the waters were falling, so where the first canal failed for high water, the second failed for low water.

Meanwhile, they tried a different tack. General James B. McPherson's corps was ordered to try a route through Louisiana via Lake Providence. McPherson was to start forty miles north of Vicksburg, work his way down through Bayou Macon to the Tensas River, to the Washita, to the Red, and bring his men out on the Mississippi, away down below Natchez, after four hundred miles of swamp and mud. McPherson actually succeeded in making the trek, but the Federals were no better off below Natchez, where they were in control anyway, and on the west bank of the river.

That was four tries. Meanwhile, Washington kept suggesting a route down the east side of the river, so they looked there, too. Two thirds of the way back to Memphis, 325 miles north of Vicksburg, was Yazoo Pass. If they blew up the levee here, they could move into the Talla-hatchie River, from there to the Yazoo, and so on down behind the city. This was more promising than a land approach on this side, for riverboats were not as vulnerable to Confederate raiders as railroads were. It looked good; the levee was blown, the steamers floated through easily, and off they all went down the Tallahatchie. But the Confed-erates knew all about it, and Pemberton sent General William W. Loring north with a division to stop them. Loring built a fort, which he handsomely named Fort Pemberton, on the Yazoo, ninety miles from Vicksburg, and when the Federal gunboats showed up, he shot at them with everything he had, capering around, waving his one arm, and earning a nickname by shouting to his gunners, "Give 'em bliz-zards, boys, give 'em blizzards!" He was "Blizzards" Loring till the day he died. After a week the Federals gave it up and went back the way they had come.

Attempt number six was up Steele's Bayou. This started out as a possibility of supporting the Yazoo Pass expedition. Steele's Bayou entered the Yazoo a few miles above Vicksburg, and one could run north up it, and then work into Black Bayou, Deer Creek, the Sunflower River, and across to the Yazoo farther up. As the sailors of Porter's river fleet had a look at it, it seemed the most likely route of all, at least to Porter, who had some rather ill-formed idea that if he could get his ships far enough inland, they would eventually come out where they wanted to be, which was in back of Vicksburg. He was actually wrong in this, but since he did not know that, they decided to make a major effort of it. Porter took eleven ships and moved up the bayou. At the start it was deceptively easy, and the ships made good time, while Sherman marched along the banks with his infantry, trying to keep up. Once again the Confederates stole a march on them. The route soon deteriorated into snags and shallows, and the Rebels made it worse by felling trees into the water and sniping at the sailors. Sherman loaned Porter fifty pioneers for the lead ship, to cut a way with axes and saws, and they kept doggedly on. When they got to Rolling Fork, they ran into real trouble; the Federal gunboats were trying to push through swamp willows growing right out of the river. Then the Con-federates started felling trees behind the boats, so that they could not make any progress forward, and they could not go back either. Porter was suddenly in danger of losing his fleet to Confederate troops. He was saved at the last minute by the arrival of Sherman's infantry, moving by night through the swamps, with candles stuck in the barrels of their rifles. They arrived just in time to stop an advance of two or three thousand Confederates, and Porter had to admit he was not going to reach Vicksburg by this route. So, after three and a half months of mud, swamps, snakes, and swearing, the Federals were no nearer Vicksburg than when they had started.

Grant had other things in mind, however; he was not quite finished yet. Like his classical namesake, he was "fertile in invention," and he gradually evolved a totally new idea. To this point the Federal forces had been utterly stymied by their inability to approach Vicksburg through bad terrain, and at the same time keep open their supply lines back north. Indeed, in the larger sense it was slowly becoming apparent that the Union attempt to occupy and hold enemy territory was enormously wasteful of men, matériel, and effort. You could either concentrate and fight the enemy, or you could disperse your troops and try to hold his towns, roads, and bridges; the more territory you took, the more difficult it was to fight. Throughout the western theater, Federal commanders were constantly embarrassed and discomfited by Confederate raiders and guerrillas, ranging from such brilliant cavalry leaders as Nathan B. Forrest at the top, to men who were little more than brigands and murderers at the bottom. Maybe it was time to take these people on at their own game.

Grant was not alone in moving in this direction. In east Tennessee, the new general there, William S. Rosecrans, was considering the possibility of cavalry raids into Confederate country, and Grant's rear-area commander back in Memphis, General Stephen Hurlbut, also was developing an idea for raids against the Southern rail system. This concurrence led to three related actions. Hurlbut and Rosecrans mounted a raid under Colonel Abel D. Streight that struck through northern Mississippi and Alabama, confusing the Confederate command in that area. Streight's men, mounted on mules for the most part, did considerable damage before they were finally caught and captured by Forrest. Meanwhile, Colonel Benjamin Grierson led what became probably the most famous Union cavalry raid of the war. Grierson, a former music teacher, took three regiments, the 6th and 7th Illinois and 2nd Iowa Cavalry, and an artillery section, 1,700 men in all, and started south from La Grange, on the Tennessee-Mississippi line, on April 17. His mission was to burn, destroy, and wreck railroads and property, and to confuse the Confederates as to what was really going on.

This he did to a turn. Dropping detachments here and there, and traveling in several parallel columns, his men cut a swath through central Mississippi. There were numerous Confederate units in the area, but they were all sent here and there by contradictory orders and confusing reports, and Grierson actually did remarkably little fighting. Pemberton in Vicksburg had some thought that Grierson might well be heading south, for a junction with Union troops farther down the Mississippi, but he could not be sure of it, and the reports he was getting kept him futilely shuffling troops around, Confederates wearing out shoe leather and horses and growing increasingly frustrated. When they tried to ambush the blue cavalry, Grierson was warned by local Unionists and avoided the trap. The Confederates nearly caught him away down near the Louisiana line, but he broke through and led his tired troopers the last seventy-five miles to safety in Baton Rouge, in a little more than twenty-four hours. Altogether the raid lasted a fortnight and covered six hundred miles, and did a great deal of largely temporary damage, for a loss of three killed, seven wounded, and a dozen or so stragglers. Its most important effect at the moment, however, was that it totally absorbed the attentions of General John Pemberton when they should have been directed elsewhere.

That elsewhere, the third of the three developments, was west of the Mississippi, for there Grant was doing quite unusual things. He had conceived the idea of moving his army south of Vicksburg, crossing the Mississippi, and attacking Vicksburg from the rear. Having seven times failed in conventional approaches, he now thought this was the most promising avenue. He talked it over with his commanders. McClernand thought it could be done, but both Porter and Sherman, whose opinions he valued more, were skeptical. Much would depend upon Porter, for to make the plan work, he must run his ships downriver past the Vicksburg batteries; otherwise the Union army could not cross the river. Though dubious about the whole plan, Porter agreed to try. Next Grant had to get Halleck's approval in Washington, and pinning Old Brains down was as difficult as always. Finally Halleck agreed that Grant might use his own initiative, which, as every soldier knows, meant, I agree if it works, but it's your problem if it fails. That was enough for Grant.

He moved at the end of March. McPherson's XVII Corps and McClernand's XIII Corps started off south and west, while Sherman's XV Corps made noisy demonstrations upstream across from Vicksburg. The march was unopposed by the enemy, but far from easy. It led across an apparently endless series of bayous and swamps, and the troops built bridge after bridge, and corduroyed miles and miles of roads for the wagons and guns. It took a month to march from Duckport to Hard Times, only twenty-two miles as the crow flew, but more than fifty by the route the army was forced to follow. Yet by the end of April, there they were, south of Vicksburg. And there was the navy, ready to get them across the river.

Porter's forcing of the Vicksburg defenses became one of the naval set-pieces of the war, though in fact it turned out to be far more spectacular than dangerous. On the 16th of April the ships made ready; the gunboats were given extra armor in the form of hay bales and logs, and each vessel took alongside a barge loaded with coal, so it would not run out of fuel below the city. The ships got under way at full dark, at fifty-yard intervals, each echeloned on the quarter of its next-ahead, so that if one were disabled, it would not foul those following. Silently they steamed downriver, within range of the Confederate guns.

About eleven o'clock they were spotted, the Confederates touched off watchfires along the bank to light the scene, and the Rebel guns went into action, shifting targets as the ships came on, one after the other. The duel lasted for some time, and every vessel was hit, some repeatedly. The ironclad *Carondelet* turned a complete circle in the middle of the stream, caught in the currents and trying to avoid a collision, and a couple of the coal barges were lost. Below the city the transport *Henry Clay,* holed by a heavy cannonball, sank, but all her crew got off safely. In fact, when the Federal sailors answered to muster after the action, they found to their delight that not a single man had been killed. An exuberant Porter was now prepared to do anything Grant wanted.

Grant actually wanted a lot. One of his corps, Hurlbut's XVI, was detailed to go off south to collaborate with General Banks. Banks was expected to operate north from Baton Rouge against Port Hudson, thus turning the Confederates from the far south. Instead, he went off on his own, up the Red River, on another wasteful dispersion of effort. More to the point, Grant now wanted to cross the river, and as soon as his troops reached Hard Times, Porter began a bombardment of

Grand Gulf, on the Vicksburg side of the river. This turned out to be a tough little nut, and after a couple of days of futile shelling, Grant decided to move farther downstream. The Federals began crossing at Bruinsburg on April 30, and found the eastern shore empty. Within a day McPherson and McClernand both had their corps across, and Sherman was ordered to move south. By now, the water was falling, the roads were drying, and things were looking promising. On May 1, at Port Gibson, the Federals brushed aside the few thousand troops Pemberton had got south to dispute their passage. The Confederates abandoned Grand Gulf the next day, to avoid being trapped. In a week Sherman was across, and U. S. Grant had an army of 40,000 men within striking distance of Vicksburg, and in good marching and fighting country. Porter was pleased as punch with the role his ships had played; Sherman was still dubious—he thought they were out on a long limb—but now at least they had a clear shot at Vicksburg; they were done with swamps and bayous at last.

———

Ironically, at this point both sides were plagued as much by the inadequacies of their command structure as by anything else. Grant had expected Banks's cooperation from downriver, thinking to draw supplies from that direction, but Banks was off chasing up the Red. This left Grant with no clear logistic support, only the long tenuous lines back up the west side of the river, over the route he had come, and that was not really strong enough to sustain his field army. He was therefore in danger, not so much of running out of food for his troops, but of running out of those supplies, especially ammunition, that could not be commandeered from the countryside. Before he could move freely on Vicksburg, he had to decide what to do about this.

But the Confederates faced their difficulties as well. In November of 1862, President Davis had ordered General Joseph E. Johnston, returning to active duty after his wound at Seven Pines in the Peninsula, to take over the command of the western theater. Davis and Johnston did not get along, but Johnston was a senior commander, and Davis had no one else he could send in his place. Unfortunately, Johnston's orders and his command responsibility were equally vague, and he was not sure exactly what he was supposed to do, or whom he could order to do it. Most immediately, he was told that he commanded Pemberton, and he in turn told Pemberton not to get shut up in

Vicksburg, but if necessary to withdraw from the city rather than be trapped in it. Pemberton, however, received orders from Davis himself telling him how important it was that Vicksburg be held.

It may seem on the face of it as if these were silly confusions, readily capable of being resolved. Silly they may have been, but their resolution was another matter. The problem must be seen not in isolation, but against the shifting backdrop of a series of unfolding crises, constantly demanding attention, of action and reaction by either side, of uncertainty as to who was where and doing what. Was Grierson's Raid a serious matter, was Rosecrans on the move, did Grant really intend to move south, could the northern approaches to Vicksburg be held, what on earth was Banks up to, could troops be detached from the defense of Mobile, could Port Hudson be held, what did the western Confederate politicians demand, which of their demands could be met, which of their promises could be fulfilled? . . . and on and on and on, an almost endless sequence of possibilities and problems, none of them alleviated by the less than perfect harmony existing between Davis and Johnston. Had Davis had another Lee to send to the west, it might have been different. But he did not; there was only one Lee, and life has to be lived with what we have, not what we would like to have.

By the beginning of the second week of May, Grant had 41,000 men in three corps, Sherman, McPherson, and McClernand, across the river around Grand Gulf. Pemberton had about 32,000 around Vicksburg. Johnston was approaching Jackson, Mississippi, a rail junction forty miles due east of Vicksburg, destined to be the focus of Johnston's moves to cover Vicksburg. At that moment, there were only a thousand troops at Jackson, and Johnston could concentrate only about 6,000 altogether for the defense of the town. Still, he had to try. Both Johnston and Pemberton expected that Grant would move against Jackson, as it was the logical move if one were to try to isolate Vicksburg. If he did so, then perhaps Johnston could hold him while Pemberton moved south in behind him and cut his supply lines. Then, even though he had slightly superior numbers, the Union general would be caught between the two Confederate forces, his supplies depleted. Under these conditions, he might be defeated and the west saved for the Confederacy. Joe Johnston was not generally an optimist, but he had little choice this time; he had to hope for the best.

The key element in the whole campaign was supplies: who could keep his lines of communication open? Grant, disadvantaged by

Banks's failure to appear, decided now to change the basis of his operations. He could not expect to sustain his communications and still make progress. He was determined to make progress; therefore the communications must go. He called together his commanders and issued his orders. Sherman was told to bring forward a train of 120 wagons. The regiments would abandon all wagons and trains of their own; instead, each regiment would have two wagons which would carry spare ammunition; all pack animals would carry ammunition, nothing else. The troops would march with three days' rations in their packs; beyond that they must live off the country. This had not been tried before; cavalry raids, yes, but here was a whole army, 40,000 strong, setting out to face a determined enemy of unknown strength. They must either win, or they would be destroyed. Sherman doubted. On the face of it, it was an enormous risk, the boldest strategic decision of the war to this point. Grant's advance elements were already at Rocky Springs, sixteen miles from Grand Gulf and the same distance from Vicksburg. On the 11th of May, they started off into the void, and the supply line disappeared behind them.

For three days they marched northeast, heading toward Jackson. By the 14th, the gamble was paying off. McClernand's corps was astride the Jackson Railroad at Clinton, facing west against possible intervention by Pemberton. More important, Sherman and McPherson were both at Jackson. Johnston had arrived there the night before; apprised of the situation by the local commander, Brigadier General John Gregg, he ordered a delaying action while supplies were evacuated from the town. The Confederates held along a line of trenches west of Jackson for most of the morning, while the Federals came on in a heavy rain. But by noon the sky was clearing, and the Union buildup was just too strong, lapping around the flanks of the Rebel trenches. Johnston sent word to Gregg that most of the war matériel was safely away, and by mid-afternoon, the Federals were in full possession of the town. They then proceeded to wreck it, destroying especially all the railroad facilities so that there would be no subsequent threat from that direction.

Johnston now retreated to the northeast. Before he went he had ordered Pemberton to advance southeast against Grant's supply line. So on the 15th, as Johnston went away in one direction, Pemberton unenthusiastically advanced toward the Federal army, now full of fight and squarely, and securely, between the two Confederate forces. Having ruined Jackson, Grant now advanced west against Pemberton. The

145

latter now realized he was in serious trouble, and that Johnston's orders were badly out of date. On the 16th McClernand's corps caught up with him at Champion's Hill. McClernand sent a courier to Grant, asking what he ought to do, and Grant sent back the one word: Attack! Then he hurried McPherson's corps forward in support.

The Confederates had a decent position at Champion's Hill, but did not really want to fight. Neither did McClernand, and the result was a confused battle that, better handled by either side, might have significantly defeated the other. As it was, the Confederates were chased off their hill late in the afternoon, but most of them got away and headed for Vicksburg. Confederate losses were greater than Union, at nearly 4,000 casualties, and one Confederate division retreated away to the southwest, thus avoiding being trapped in the city. Pemberton was now down to 20,000 men, and by the night of the 18th, they were back in the Vicksburg defenses, with the Federal army closing in upon them.

Sherman soon occupied the heights to the north, and thus after two and a half weeks on the eastern side of the river, the Union force had its communications fully reopened, and resupply was readily possible. Grant had at last found the key to unlock Vicksburg, and with it the Mississippi River, or so it seemed for a moment. He was determined not to rest on his laurels, and on the 19th mounted a hasty attempt to force the city's lines, thinking to end the whole business in a hurry. The Confederates beat this off with ease. Nothing daunted, Grant decided to make a major assault on the 22nd, more thoroughly prepared and better coordinated than the first one.

At mid-morning on the 22nd, the Union troops advanced, Sherman's from the north side of the city, then McPherson's, then McClernand's. The Confederates were well dug in, with good fields of fire, and they easily repulsed the first charges. By early afternoon Grant was on the point of calling it off. Then he received messages from McClernand, saying he had two of the forts along the lines and with a little support could break through. Grant ordered the attacks continued. By late afternoon, he found that McClernand did not have the two forts at all; he had gotten troops temporarily into one, and had never got past the ditch of the other. At that, the attacks were finally called off, with 3,200 casualties, and Grant acknowledged that Vicksburg was too strong to be carried by a coup de main. There would have to be a regular siege.

Sieges are part of the standard repertoire of military history, and Vicksburg is among the most famous, at least on the North American continent. In terms of time or numbers involved, it hardly compared even with those of its own era, Sebastopol, Paris, Plevna in 1877, and was surpassed later in the Civil War by the siege of Petersburg. Nonetheless, perceived then and now as one of the turning points of the war, it captured the public imagination: Could the Confederates hold out until relieved? Could Grant break them? Could Johnston raise a relief force? Americans on both sides anxiously awaited the latest news from Vicksburg.

Those waiting for the news were far luckier than those making it, for it was a dull, grinding, bitter business of work, fatigue, casual danger, and, for those inside, gradual starvation. Grant, in the classic strategy used at least since Caesar besieged Alesia, shut the town up in a vise with one hand, and with the other maneuvered a field army to take care of Joe Johnston. With reinforcements—corps transferred from the east—he eventually commanded more than 70,000 men, enough to do both tasks with little danger. He extended his lines around Vicksburg until the whole town was covered, and his men dug and sapped and bombarded. Half of his army he put under Sherman, with orders to cover the eastern approaches in case the Confederates should manage a relief effort. With supply lines open along the river, and foraging parties scouring the country, the Union army settled down to see the matter through. At least they had plenty to eat.

That was hardly the case inside Vicksburg. The last order Pemberton had received from Johnston was that he should withdraw from the city if at all possible, and not let his army be trapped. Instead of obeying this as rapidly as he could, Pemberton called a council of war of his officers, and the vote was that they should dig in and hope for rescue. It was a valid option only if there were indeed reasonable hope that they could be rescued, so they soon found themselves trapped. The defenses, though, were formidable, as Grant found in his first two attempts to force them; in fact, the Union forces never did succeed in carrying the place by assault. They did not have to.

Instead Grant perforce let hunger do his work for him. Pemberton had 20,000 men, plus several thousand civilians and dependents, shut up inside an eight-mile-long perimeter, less than ten square miles, all of it subject to Union gunfire. It would have been highly unpleasant in the best of circumstances; but it was summer in Mississippi, and the heat and stench soon made it a fair approximation of Hell. The inhabitants quickly went to ground, living in caves in the bluffs over-looking the river, the only places more or less safe from random shell-fire. Southern men, who always prided themselves on their chivalrous treatment of ladies, found it difficult to preserve the amenities when a bucket behind a blanket represented the height of toilet facilities. Life soon concentrated around the search for food; cows disappeared, then horses, then mules; the garrison sickened, and men and women began to die; weakened constitutions could not stand the sicknesses that spread through the town, and delicacies such as mule tail soup did not do a great deal to maintain strength.

While Vicksburg went through its daily grind, Johnston sought to raise a force sufficient for its relief. Unfortunately for him, Braxton Bragg in east Tennessee was facing a Union advance double his strength, and Lee was in the process of invading Pennsylvania. There was no help from either quarter, and Johnston had to make do with whatever he could gather from Alabama and Mississippi. West of the big river, troops under General Kirby Smith made some moves toward Vicksburg, but these were treated with almost casual contempt by the Union troops over there, and by Porter's gunboats on the river. Johnston could draw little from farther south; Banks was finally besieging Port Hudson, so there was nothing much there to help. Finally, the hard-pressed Confederate general did gather a field force of about 30,000 men, and on June 28, he advanced westward from Jackson. He reached the Big Black River, a little more than halfway to Vicksburg, by the 1st of July. But instead of finding the vulnerable rear of Grant's army, he found Sherman concentrating almost 50,000 men to dispute his advance. The Union army was just too strong, and Johnston, always one to calculate the odds carefully, knew it. He hung about the Big Black for a couple of days, hoping for a miracle, but not expecting one.

What he got was news, on July 4, that Vicksburg had surrendered. He immediately retreated, and Sherman, reinforced to even greater strength, chased him back to and through Jackson.

All through June Grant's men had continued their approaches to the city; they had exploded a couple of mines, and everyone knew that eventually they would make an assault, and that when they did so, it would succeed. When the opposing pickets exchanged remarks, the

Rebels would ask, "When you all comin' to town?" and the Federals would reply, "We're gonna celebrate the Fourth there." The Vicksburg newspaper, printed on wallpaper and eagerly scanned by both sides, editorialized that before you could *cook* a rabbit, you had to *catch* it. Grant in fact had ordered preparations for an assault on the 6th, but fortunately for both sides, Pemberton recognized the game was up before that. On the 3rd he asked for terms; that afternoon the two generals, who had served together in the Mexican War, met between the lines. Grant had no terms to offer, only unconditional surrender, while Pemberton, grumbling at this lack of charity, demanded the honors of war. Negotiations threatened to break down over these niceties, but finally the Confederates agreed to surrender and be paroled. With rueful humor the last edition of the Vicksburg newspaper admitted that the Yanks had caught their rabbit. On July 4 the garrison marched out and stacked arms, whereupon the Union soldiers immediately opened their rations and the two sides sat down and began eating together, while Grant sent an aide off to the nearest telegraph point, at Cairo, Illinois, with a message to Washington beginning, "The enemy surrendered this morning. . . . "

The remainder of the river campaign went quickly. Sherman drove Johnston east, and Banks finally took Port Hudson on the 9th. From that point on, the Confederacy was cut in half, the rebellion in the states west of the river living on in a sort of semi-independent half-life. Men, even units and supplies, might slip back and forth across the river, but none of that meant much. Vicksburg effectively broke the back of the western Confederacy, and the war, however much was left of it, must now be fought and won or lost to the east. Indeed, there was a great deal left to it, as Robert E. Lee was even then demonstrating, but out in the western country, Vicksburg was recognized for the towering victory it was, and Lincoln could proudly write, in an often quoted phrase, "The Father of Waters again goes unvexed to the sea." Then he added, "Thanks to the great North-West for it . . . New-England, Empire, Keystone, and Jersey. . . . Thanks to all. For the great republic—for the principles it lives by, and keeps alive—for man's vast future,—thanks to all. . . . "

Chapter 11

Eastern Maneuvers

WHILE ULYSSES S. GRANT grappled with the complexities of approaching Vicksburg, Abraham Lincoln grappled with the problem of the Army of the Potomac, and more specifically, with the matter of its commander. Ideally, this should not have been the president's concern; ideally, this question should be resolved by Henry Halleck. But Halleck had already demonstrated that he was not the overall commander Lincoln had sought; he could administer, he could plan, he could write memorandums, but he was a better, and happier, military secretary than he was a general. For Lincoln, therefore, there was no one but himself to fill the command vacuum; he, after all, was the commander in chief, and until he could find a soldier who was capable of doing what had to be done, he must keep on with his search. It was a horribly expensive matter of trial and error, the price paid in time, money, and above all blood, but there was no way around it.

After Fredericksburg, the issue became ever more pressing. No one had any confidence in Ambrose Burnside, not his corps commanders, or his army, or the political men in Washington—indeed, not even Burnside himself; he knew he had risen beyond his capacity, and though he was loath to admit it, he was eventually content to go off as commander of the Department of the Ohio. So the difficulty lay not in getting rid of him, but rather in deciding who should replace him. By now the army had developed some very capable men, at one level or another, but it had also developed some vicious internal antagonisms and some long memories. John Pope, in the most celebrated example, had preferred charges against Fitz John Porter after Second Bull Run;

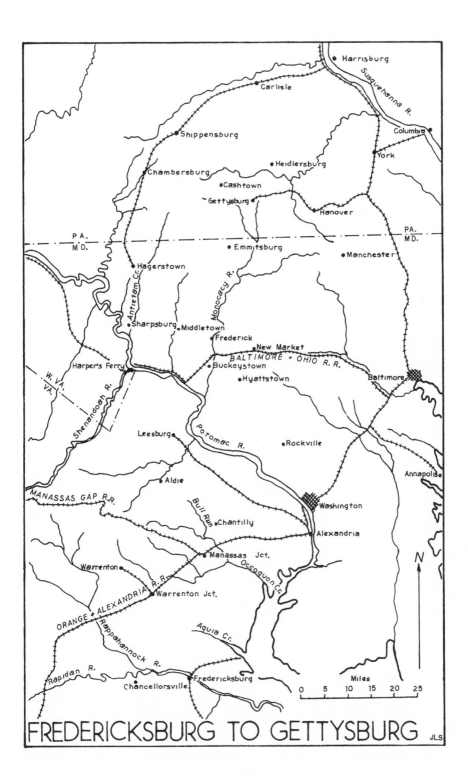

FREDERICKSBURG TO GETTYSBURG

JLS

Porter was relieved of his corps command after Antietam and court-martialed for disloyalty, disobedience, and misconduct in the face of the enemy. The trial was highly political, and it was not really aimed at Porter at all, but rather at his hero, George McClellan. Secretary Stanton, agreeing with Radical Republican pressure in Congress, stacked the court with anti-McClellan officers, and Porter was found guilty and dismissed from the service. The Army of the Potomac was becoming like the Royal Navy, where, as Voltaire remarked, "they shoot an admiral from time to time to encourage the others."

Finding a new commander, therefore, was a touchy proposition; not only the army itself, but the politicians in Washington all had axes to grind and scores to settle. Burnside, during his short and unhappy tenure, had divided his army into three "grand divisions," under Generals Franklin, Sumner, and Hooker, so these three were the chief candidates for the army command.

William B. Franklin was a classmate of Ulysses Grant; in fact, he was first in the class of 1843, while Grant was twenty-fifth. He had done well up to Fredericksburg, and had handled his Left Grand Division effectively there. But he had refused Burnside's order to renew the attack on Jackson, and Burnside subsequently wanted to court-martial him. Indeed, it was this quarrel that led to Burnside's dismissal, but he carried Franklin down with him. Though he was not tried, he was passed over for the higher command, and spent the rest of the war in sideshows.

Edwin Vose Sumner was the oldest corps commander in the U.S. Army. Nicknamed "Bull Head," usually shortened to "Bull," because a musket ball was once said to have bounced off his skull, Sumner had had an active career to this point. He had not shone in the Peninsula, but then few had; at Antietam he was criticized for deploying his troops improperly and for leading from the front, like a boy colonel instead of the old general he was. He was not really a contender now; quickly passed over, he asked to be relieved from his corps command. He was reassigned out west, and ironically and sadly, died before he got there.

Thus, almost by default, the command went to Fighting Joe Hooker. Another West Pointer, Hooker had done well in the Mexican War, then resigned in the fifties, and went to California, where he failed as a farmer. He returned to the army at the beginning of the war, and earned an odd reputation in the Peninsula. A newspaper correspondent filed a story under the heading "Fighting—Joe Hooker;" this was garbled over the telegraph wires and came out "Fighting Joe Hooker," and he was stuck with it. A loud, brash, intemperate man, Hooker had many friends and as many enemies. He was touted to replace McClellan after Antietam, but Lincoln chose Burnside instead. After Fredericksburg, Burnside wanted to fire Hooker, but it was his turn now. Secretary of the Treasury Salmon P. Chase liked him, and so did the Radical Republicans, though it was whispered about Washington that his chief claims were that he looked like a general ought to look, and that Chase knew he was not a political rival. When Lincoln appointed him, he did so with such misgivings that he wrote him a very stern cautionary letter, counseling good behavior, temperate speech, and above all the winning of victories.

To almost everyone's surprise, Hooker turned out to be a good administrator. The army had grown slack and sullen after Fredericksburg; soldiers always know when their officers are squabbling, for armies have few secrets. Morale was down, desertion was up, drill and dress were sloppy, field punishments were frequent and necessary, and it was obvious the Army of the Potomac had lost tone. Hooker took rapid and effective steps to restore order, authority, and confidence. He improved administration, rations, and delivery of equipment. Where McClellan had had thousands of men simply wandering off on extended leaves, Hooker instituted a rational furlough system. He made newspaper correspondents sign their dispatches, to stop irresponsible reporting. He cleaned up the army's rear areas, making one contribution to the vocabulary: "hooker" became a synonym for a prostitute because of his tolerance of them in the army's trains. Surprisingly quickly, the Army of the Potomac came out of its sulk and began to look like a real army once more.

Hooker also reorganized the army's command structure. The grand division system had not worked very well. He now divided the army up definitively into the corps structure first introduced, by Lincoln, for the Peninsula. Now there were seven infantry corps in the Army of the Potomac, and it was Hooker who formalized the practice of giving each corps a distinctive badge, furthering the concept of unit cohesion. Hooker's major contribution, however, was the creation of a separate Cavalry Corps. Up until this time the Union cavalry had been parceled out in driblets and used for odd jobs, one reason why it was always qualitatively inferior to its Confederate opponents. The horsemen were so happy with the new dispensation that they actually accomplished something. All winter Union lines had been harassed by the Confederate cavalry. Now, in March, Brigadier General William Averell took a whole cavalry division across the Rappahannock and chased off a Confederate cavalry division commanded by Fitzhugh Lee, Robert E. Lee's nephew. The Confederates were outnumbered, but even so, it was practically the first time in the war a Union horse soldier had seen gray backs, so it was a heartening event. So as spring warmed the ground in northern Virginia and the blossoms burst along the little rivers, the Army of the Potomac was ready once again to try its hand against its old, familiar foe.

———

The Army of Northern Virginia needed far less tinkering than its opponent. General Lee was perfectly happy with his command structure, and unlike the Federals, he enjoyed the unstinting confidence of his political masters. Where the Federal difficulty lay in its higher officers, the Confederate difficulty lay in the mundane matter of numbers and supply. The war was beginning to tell now, and as the Union war machine kept on growing with apparently undiminished vigor, the Confederacy was increasingly feeling the pinch. News that a Federal corps was loading aboard transports at the mouth of the Chesapeake forced President Davis and General Lee into a realignment, and Lee detached Longstreet and a corps of two whole divisions to guard the coast south along the Carolinas. This left only some 53,000 men in northern Virginia to face Hooker when he advanced with almost double that number.

If weak in numbers, the Confederates nevertheless enjoyed the advantage of good position. It was the same equation as had faced Burnside. Lee defended the line of the Rappahannock River, with his army still concentrated around Fredericksburg, and with strong patrols out and all the fords upstream well covered. Lee was considering an offensive in the Shenandoah Valley; he invariably thought in terms of the offensive, and seizing the initiative, and by now he had achieved such moral ascendancy over his opponents that neither he nor anyone in his army was unduly fazed by the Federals' numerical superiority. If the Confederates wanted to split their army, or send half of it off on a raid, they felt perfectly confident in doing so.

In late April, Hooker's cavalry began to move, and the bickerings of the patrols as they bumped into each other were a sure portent that something was up. Lee put his Shenandoah ideas to rest while he waited to see what was happening. Hooker had decided to leave two fifths of his army, under the able command of General John Sedgwick, in front of Fredericksburg, threatening a crossing there. Meanwhile he would move upstream with the stronger portion of his force, 53,000 men, carry the various fords, and come down on Lee's left flank. Sedgwick could force his way across at Fredericksburg as Lee necessarily moved to meet this threat, and the Confederates would be caught between Hooker's hammer and Sedgwick's anvil. Sending his cavalry out to cover and hide his moves, Hooker started his army in motion on April 27. Three corps, V under Meade, XI under Oliver O. Howard, and XII under Henry Slocum, marched by a long route northwest toward Kelly's Ford on the upper Rappahannock, which they forced on the 29th. Swinging south, they pushed across the Rapidan River as well, the south branch of the Rappahannock, at Germanna Ford, and then turned southeast, moving through Wilderness Tavern toward a little spot called Chancellorsville, an otherwise insignificant crossroads boasting one brick house. Meanwhile, on the afternoon of the 30th, Hooker began a second, closer, flanking move with Darius Couch's II Corps and Daniel Sickles's III, crossing the Rappahannock at United States ford, just below the point where the Rapidan and that river joined. While all this was in progress, Sedgwick pushed two corps across the river just below Fredericksburg, making as much noise and attracting as much attention as possible.

Lee was somewhat at a loss to figure out just what his enemy was up to, but it soon became clear that the Federals were attempting some sort of turning movement to his left. He pulled in a couple of divisions from his right, kept Stuart and his cavalry off at arm's length covering to the west. Nonetheless, by late afternoon of the 31st, Hooker had done his work well, and he had the better part of his army around Chancellorsville. Having done this much, he called it a day.

A lesser man than Lee, caught between two armies, each the strength of his own, might have retreated in a hurry. Lee thought only of which of his two enemies he could more profitably attack. He and Jackson looked over Sedgwick's position, and decided it was too strong, so they must take on Hooker. Lee left a mere 10,000 men, under Jubal Early, to face off Sedgwick, and marched with his remaining 43,000 west to meet the new threat. While they did so, Hooker lost the drive that had so far served him well. On the morning of May 1, his army had a leisurely breakfast, and slowly got organized to move east from Chancellorsville. This dawdling was fraught with consequences, for Chancellorsville was in a large patch of territory known generally as the Wilderness, scrub pine and stunted hardwoods all cut up with little lanes and meandering streams, sudden ditches and tangled second-growth copses. In it it was difficult to deploy and control infantry, and nearly impossible to handle guns or cavalry.

Early in the afternoon, as they began to get out of the Wilderness on its eastern edge, the advancing Federals ran into some of Jackson's divisions, Anderson, McLaws, and Rodes. Firefights sprung up in the clearings, and either side put in little charges where they could, or clung to clumps of cover. No one could be quite sure what was happening, but the Federals had the weight, and slowly, the Rebels gave ground. Indeed, on some of the roads leading east, the bluecoats marched blithely along, with nothing at all in front of them.

After two or three hours of this, Hooker was in substantial danger of winning a battle almost by default. But he simply could not believe his luck, and more important, he just could not figure out a picture of what was happening. Beset by doubts, he hesitated. Late in the afternoon he sent out orders to disengage, and fall back around Chancellorsville. His corps commanders were alternately incredulous and furious, but it made little difference; Hooker ordered them back, then, after their formations were all mixed up, changed his mind, and then changed it again. By dark the army took up defensive positions, throwing up abatises and breastworks in a long arc, stretching five and a half miles from the bank of the Rappahannock southwest toward Chancellorsville and then west along the Turnpike Road toward Wilderness Tavern. Meade was on the left, Howard's XI Corps on the right, the rest of the army bunched in the center.

The Rebels could hardly believe their luck, but as always, Lee was not disposed to rest content with that. As night came down, he and Jackson looked over their maps and tried to find an advantage. They knew that if Sedgwick moved strongly, Early must give way in their rear; if Hooker attacked vigorously from his left, they would be hard pressed to stop him. Thus there was little profit in a defensive battle. Yet to attack the Federals in even hastily prepared positions would be more costly than they could afford.

Then Stuart came in, to report that the Federal right flank, Howard's corps, hung in the air. At that far end of the Union line was . . . *nothing*.

Immediately Lee and Jackson made their plans; they would split the army yet again. Jackson would take the main force, 26,000 men, and by a long roundabout route of fourteen miles he would hit Howard's open flank. Meanwhile Lee, with a mere 17,000, must hold back the entire Federal army until Jackson could strike. Jackson's men started their march at sunrise on the morning of the 2nd.

The Federals watched them go. All morning the long gray columns filed off toward the southwest, and for much of that time, the Union army rested on its arms. Eventually General Dan Sickles got grudging permission to push out from the Union center with some troops, but the Rebels were already thinning out on his front, and all he succeeded in doing was further isolating Howard's corps.

Oliver Howard was a Maine man whose reputation, for some reason, was stronger than his record. He had lost an arm at Seven Pines, and he had commanded the XI Corps for less than a month. This corps was largely made up of German regiments, and had been under Franz Sigel until Howard's appointment. He did not particularly care for his new assignment, and his new corps did not particularly care for him, either. Ordered by Hooker to fortify his position, Howard thoroughly neglected his right flank, and throughout the midday, he simply refused to believe his officers' reports that a strong enemy force was marching past his line. Independently, his right-flank brigade refused its flank and put up some flimsy breastworks, but that was about all they could manage.

By mid-afternoon Jackson's men were in position, but in the scrub and tangle, it took them another two hours to get properly deployed perpendicular to the Union line. Finally, with a mere two hours of daylight remaining, they struck, 26,000 Rebels charging due east, rolling up an enemy line that faced due south. Howard's corps may not have been the best in the army, but it made no difference; the best men God ever made could not have stood to those odds. The Union regiments broke, piled up, tried to form, broke again, rallied, died, and broke again. For a full mile the Confederates drove them, with a bow wave of blue washing before their charge. But Bushbeck's brigade bought a half hour in well-placed rifle pits, and gradually, as the sun went down, the Confederates ran out of steam. Sickles's corps got back into its original line, and Hooker put troops together, and as twilight came, the drive flickered out. With little thanks to its commanders, the Army of the Potomac had lived to fight another day.

As the darkness settled, no one knew quite what was going on. Units wandered through the tangled battlefield, stray cavalry blundered here and there, officers tried to sort out their units. General Jackson and some of his staff rode forward to get some sense of the land; all unaware, they got beyond their own lines, and when they turned to come back, mounted shadows in the night, they were challenged, and fired upon. Wounded in the arm, Jackson was carried off the battlefield. Later his arm had to be amputated, and he then contracted pneumonia, from which he died on May 10.

On the morning of May 3, the Union army still possessed advantages, in spite of Jackson's brilliant maneuver. Its position was that of a long fishhook with the bend around Chancellorsville and the shank running back to the Rappahannock. But Reynolds's corps had come up in support, the Federals still had a two-to-one superiority, and the Confederate army was still split in two, almost beyond mutual supporting distance, and somewhat disarranged by Stuart replacing Jackson in command of half of it. Hooker might still seize the initiative if he chose.

But he did not choose. He remained essentially on the defensive, and when Stuart attacked, skillfully, fiercely, and at last with some artillery support, Hooker did little. When a cannonball struck his headquarters, he was stunned by concussion, and as the Confederates made some headway, he ordered the army to maintain itself as best it might. Meanwhile Lee, deciding that Hooker's position remained formidable, turned his attention to Sedgwick's belated advance. The latter had finally forced Early's men off their heights behind Fredericksburg, and was advancing cautiously toward Lee's army and its own colleagues, twelve miles away. On the 4th, then, Lee hurried to meet Sedgwick, leaving Stuart with a mere 25,000 men to watch Hooker's 75,000. Again the Confederates were nearly, but not quite, clear winners. Late on the afternoon of the 4th they hit Sedgwick, but he was a careful, competent fighter, and he threw up a defensive line and beat off their uncoordinated attacks, one after another, before withdrawing through Fredericksburg and across the river during the night. Hooker made no attempt whatever to help him. Lee, having chased Sedgwick back the way he had come, countermarched yet once more, preparing to destroy Hooker's army. But Hooker at last stirred himself, and his corps commanders conducted a skillful retreat under pressure, getting the army safely back on the north side of the river by May 6.

Chancellorsville, Robert E. Lee's "absolute masterpiece," demonstrated several points: First and most obvious, it demonstrated Lee's genius. Secondly, it showed the utter confidence and skill of his instrument, the Army of Northern Virginia. Here were master and men in perfect synchronization. Yet Confederate casualties were 13,000, a bill they could afford far less than the 17,000 Union losses. In terms of percentages, Confederate casualties were nearly twice those of their opponents. And most important of all, with every command advantage except size, the winners had not destroyed the losers. A week after the battle, the Army of the Potomac was as ready to fight as was the Army of Northern Virginia. Colonel Freemantle, a visiting observer from the British army, thought the Confederates were magnificent, "unbeatable"; demonstrating that point, Chancellorsville should also have caused more sober reflection.

———

While Chancellorsville was being fought, Grant was crossing the Mississippi below Vicksburg, so he had not yet developed the campaign that would free the river. In Richmond, then, there was no bad news from the west to offset the euphoria induced by Lee's great triumph. The Confederate capital was full of optimism, even if that feeling was restrained by the universal grief and mourning over the loss of the incomparable Stonewall. Surely now the North must recognize that the Confederacy was an established fact, and that its armies were invincible.

But the wretched Yankee hirelings refused to do any such thing. The two armies sat on their opposite sides of the river, and the pickets surreptiously traded coffee for tobacco, sending toy boats back and forth across the stream with their illicit cargoes. Lee reorganized his army; Longstreet came back from the Carolinas, and Richard Ewell, "Old Baldy" to his West Point classmates, got Jackson's old corps; Lee then created a third corps, and gave it to Ambrose Powell Hill, over the heads and the protests of men senior to him. Lee's problems were more in the area of supply than of command structure, and, as was his usual response to difficulties, he soon began to consider how he might best take the offensive.

On the Union side, there were plenty of supplies, and plenty of men, but the primary question remained: Who would or could command them? Though he tried to blame it on others, Hooker could hardly hide the fact that he had been whipped by Lee; indeed, the army generally believed that it was Hooker alone who had been defeated. The soldiers knew they had fought well, and that they had been mishandled. Letters home after Chancellorsville are full of remarks about what a waste the campaign had been, and what a shame it was that good men should die so that lesser men might learn their business. Such expressions were not confined to the soldiers, either. Though Lincoln was at first disposed to retain Hooker, largely for lack of a credible alternative, he was soon visited by several of the corps commanders, who told him frankly that Hooker must go. Go he would, if a suitable replacement could be found, but who might that be? Darius Couch told Lincoln that he did not want the job; John Reynolds said he would do it, but only on condition that he be given an absolutely free hand to direct the army as he saw fit. There was a surprising residual fondness for George McClellan, and only a small clique favored Hooker's retention, but Lincoln had had enough of the former, and so for the time being he was stuck with the latter.

This condition lasted for several weeks, until late June, when the ominous news came in: Lee was on the move again. The Confederates were faced with several problems, and some opportunities. Grant was now closing in on Vicksburg; in middle Tennessee, Rosecrans outnumbered Bragg almost two to one; and along the seaboard, the Federals were slowly tightening the blockade. General Longstreet, in discussions with Lee, suggested transferring troops from Virginia to Tennessee, and hitting Rosecrans in overwhelming force, which ought to result in dislocation of Union plans all along the line. Lee, however, remained preoccupied with his own theater of operations. He and Hooker faced each other across the Rappahannock still, Hooker now with about 115,000 men. Conscription and high-powered recruiting had brought Lee up to 76,000, the greatest strength he would ever enjoy. Hooker was too strong, and too numerous, to be attacked in his prepared positions. But if Lee were to launch a major offensive, all sorts of vistas opened up. The Army of Northern Virginia was badly in need of supplies, and the territory it held was exhausted by two years of heavy campaigning. Just across the Potomac lay the fat fields of Maryland, and a couple of days' march beyond that, the brimming barns and storehouses of Pennsylvania. An invasion of the Northern states would solve the army's supply difficulties; it would force Hooker out into the open to be fought and of course beaten; it would throw the North into a well-deserved panic, and it might indeed bring the war to a successful, glorious conclusion. It all depended upon achieving a victory, but at this stage, who could doubt that the Confederacy would win? Lee has been criticized for a narrowness of strategic view, but from the perspective of June of 1863, his plan was about as likely to work as Longstreet's idea, and he was more comfortable with it. He began sidling his units off upstream to the northwest.

Hooker soon discerned what was in the wind, and he proposed a couple of plans to Washington to upset Lee's intentions, but both were vetoed. He then demanded reinforcements, though he had earlier admitted he had all the troops he could handle. As the campaign began, the Union general and his superiors were thoroughly at odds with each other.

Yet Lee did not have it all his own way. He had ordered Stuart's large cavalry division to move out from its bivouacs around Brandy Station on June 10, but the day before, early in the morning of the 9th, General Alfred Pleasanton arrived with the Cavalry Corps of the Army of the Potomac, and for a whole day the two sides, each about 10,000 strong, whirled and charged at each other, sabers twinkling and carbines cracking, regiments and squadrons galloping and re-forming, until finally the Union horsemen drew off in good order, and Stuart, thoroughly humiliated by his surprise, was left to claim what he could of a victory. Brandy Station was the biggest cavalry battle in American history, though the casualties, 500 Confederate and about 900 Union, suggest how much less deadly a day of cavalry action was than infantry combat.

Brandy Station, all agreed, made the Union cavalry at last. More important immediately, it confirmed for Hooker that Lee was now on the move, and heading northwest. So he was, and over the next ten days, the long columns stretched out, Ewell's corps, then Longstreet, then finally Hill moving off as the Federals too began to slide to the north. Up the Rappahannock they went, then over the Blue Ridge and into the beautiful Shenandoah, where the farmwives came out with pails of milk and loaves of bread. At night they lay under the canopies of orchards, men wrapped in their threadbare blankets but comfortable in the June weather. And as they marched, they joked, and sang, and thought of home or, grimmer, how they were going to win this war once and for all. At mid-month, Ewell's corps crossed the Potomac not far from Antietam, and they kept on through Maryland and toward the Pennsylvania line, under strict march discipline now, but eyeing the barns and the fat cows in the fields, stared at by a people who had not yet seen war up close.

The North was in a near panic. By the third week of June, Lee's whole army was north of the Potomac, and half of it in Pennsylvania itself, while Hooker's advance was a good thirty miles southeast of Lee's rear guard. The Army of the Potomac was a poor instrument for a stern chase, dragging all its trains and impedimenta, so unless Lee turned east, there was not much hope there. The governors of Pennsylvania and New Jersey and New York called out the militia, who drilled and dug trenches around Harrisburg, and hoped the storm would pass them by; one hesitates to think what Lee's veterans would have done to state militia.

Hooker in fact was not doing badly. His army was well concentrated, and he had kept it between Lee and Washington, and by the 27th he had it around Frederick, Maryland, moving north toward Lee. Yet he was not a happy man, and he and Stanton and Halleck and Lincoln were all at odds. He began claiming that he was seriously outnumbered—as if he were possessed by the spirit of George McClellan—and the telegrams back and forth grew increasingly acrimonious. Finally, on the evening of the 27th, Hooker had had enough; he asked to be relieved. The War Department granted his request with practically indecent haste. A special courier was sent to find General George Meade, commander of V Corps. Awakened at three in the morning of the 28th, Meade stumbled out of his tent and asked, "Am I under arrest?" No, was the answer, you are in command of the Army of the Potomac.

Few generals who have served as prominently as George Meade have been as neglected by historians. A West Pointer who had spent almost all of his military career as an engineer, Meade had shown himself a steady, reliable performer through all of the Army of the Potomac's learning years, and he had gradually risen to corps level. Nonetheless, he was still relatively junior, and for him to be offered the army command, Couch had to be transferred out, and both John Sedgwick and Henry Slocum, as Meade's seniors, had to agree to serve under him; it says something for his reputation that they agreed to do so.

He inherited a thoroughly confused situation, with very little time to get it under control. On the 28th, Lee had his army in Pennsylvania, spread out in a long thin arc from Chambersburg in the west, north and east past Carlisle to York. Ewell was near the latter, and Longstreet and A. P. Hill near and around the former. Meade's army was about thirty miles south of them, around Frederick, Maryland. In the center of the rough circle that all the forces made was a little town called Gettysburg.

There was an added complication in all this, however, that vexed both sides. When he moved out, Lee had left Jeb Stuart to cover the rear and confuse the Federals. That job done, Stuart was given loose orders to rejoin Lee as he thought best. Stuart interpreted these as a license to go on another of his wide-ranging jaunts, and thus, as he had in the Peninsula, he rode around the Army of the Potomac. Crossing the Potomac River just above Washington, he rode north between Frederick and Baltimore. In the early stages of his march, he caught a few Federal wagon trains, but beyond that he did nothing much except get Union newspapers excited, and deprive Lee of desperately needed cavalry scouting. He did not rejoin until Lee had stumbled blindly into battle.

Meanwhile, as June became July, Lee decided to concentrate his forces around the little village of Cashtown, about halfway between Chambersburg and Gettysburg. Ewell pulled in from the north and east, and A. P. Hill moved his troops to the eastwards. Cashtown offered a good defensive position, and Lee had some thought that he might entice the Federals piecemeal into battle there. He was not sure exactly where they were, but they did not seem to be doing a great deal. On the 30th, some of A. P. Hill's troops moved toward Gettysburg, looking for a supply of shoes reported to be there. They bumped into two brigades of Union cavalry, under the able John Buford. After a sharp little fight, both sides recoiled. Buford went back toward Gettysburg. When the matter was reported to Hill, he, believing there could be no Federal infantry anywhere in the vicinity, ordered the march resumed in the morning. This is the genesis of the oft-quoted remark that Gettysburg was fought over a pair of shoes.

Hill was wrong, for Meade, though he was increasingly uncertain what was going on, was in fact keeping his army well together and moving it by stages up to the Pennsylvania line. As Buford fell back, reporting the presence of Confederate infantry and preparing to hold Gettysburg, Reynolds's I Corps, 10,000 of the best infantry in any army, was a mere six miles away, and the rest of the army only half a day's march behind it.

Buford had a cavalryman's eye for terrain and position; he had decided right away that Gettysburg must be held. The town was a pleasant little place, but its importance derived from the fact that several roads met there, and it was thus in a controlling position. The town itself was dominated by two low ridges, Seminary Ridge, so named for a Lutheran school located on it, to the west, and to the south a feature that looked like a fishhook or a reverse question mark, called Cemetery Ridge. The southern end of this was two isolated knobs, called Round Top and Little Round Top. It then ran north, more a gentle slope than a real ridge, for a couple of miles, before curving east just below the town, and then culminating in another more or less isolated rise called Culp's Hill. Between Seminary and Cemetery ridges, running south from the town, was the Emmitsburg Road, passing a peach orchard and a wheat field about two miles south-southwest of town, and the valley between the two ridges was a half mile to a mile wide. All in all, it was a peaceful spot, full of enchanting vistas, with just enough variation in the landscape to make it interesting, rich, rolling farm country where a man or a woman might live out a quiet and fulfilling life.

But on the morning of July 1, 1863, John Buford's troopers were deploying west of the town, past Seminary Ridge, and north of it up the Carlisle Road, getting ready to buy time with their carbines and their lives. Sure enough, about eight, Henry Heth's division of A. P. Hill's corps came marching east along the road, followed by Dorsey Pender's troops. The cavalry spoke up, and Heth's men deployed and started working their way forward. But Buford's men had breech-loading weapons, enormously multiplying their firepower, and it took the Confederates two whole hours to push them aside. When they did, they started toward Seminary Ridge, only to see infantry taking up position through the smoke and the trees. Push on, their officers cried, it's only a few militia. But it was not. As they got closer, and the rifles spoke up, the Rebels could see black slouch hats and frock coats: "Militia, hell! That's the Iron Brigade!" It was John Reynolds and I Corps of the Army of the Potomac.

These opening hours set the pattern of the battle. For once, for practically the first time in the war, it was the Confederates who reached each successive stage just a few minutes too late. Buford had appealed to Reynolds, and Reynolds to Howard's XI Corps and Sickles's III; so it went, Federal units heading for the sound of the guns, a magnet drawing ever more men into the growing fight. Reynolds's men shored up Buford's, and the fight spread along the north end of Seminary Ridge, and then lapped out the Carlisle Road as Ewell's men came down from the north. As Reynolds rode forward, deploying the 2nd Wisconsin, he was shot from his horse and killed instantly. Command went to his senior divisional officer, Abner Doubleday, and he managed to keep his troops going until the Confederate pressure mounted from the west and the north, and pushed the remains of I Corps, and Howard's XI, back through the town. Grudgingly the bluecoats fell back and up the low rise of Cemetery Ridge. As Ewell rode through the streets of Gettysburg, his aides heard a loud *whack!* and looked at him in alarm; Ewell quipped, "I'm better off than you; it don't hurt a bit to get shot in a wooden leg!"

Union command now devolved upon Howard, he of the infamous right flank at Chancellorsville, and he took up the position on Cemetery Ridge. Both I and XI Corps had already lost half their effectives, and the hill was clogged with men; but the artillery was in good shape, and gradually some order emerged. Then General Hancock appeared; commander of II Corps, he had been sent forward by Meade to take over the field. Howard was his senior, but few men argued with "Hancock the Superb" when his blood was up. He sent the remnants of the Iron Brigade east to hold Culp's Hill, and strengthened the positions around the top of Cemetery Ridge. In late afternoon one more push by Ewell's tired men might still have carried the day and broken the Union lines, but Ewell did not make it. Dusk brought Slocum's XII Corps, then Sickles's III—another 21,000 men—and whatever chance there had been was gone, while in the gathering dark the commanders took stock and the soldiers settled down for what little rest they could get.

In spite of its heavy casualties for those units engaged, the first day of Gettysburg was merely a preliminary to the next two, an encounter battle that turned into a sorting out of the battlefield. Over the night further Union units came in, and on the other side, Lee developed his view of how the battle should proceed. The Federal army was occupying the top portion of the fishhook of Cemetery Ridge, and extending down it for some distance. As Hancock's II Corps came up, he posted it south along the shank of the ridge, and then gradually that shank was extended by Sickles's III Corps, with George Sykes's V Corps, formerly Meade's own command, in reserve. The top of the ridge was held by John Newton, who succeeded Reynolds in command of I Corps, then

Howard, and then Henry Slocum around Culp's Hill and back down on the east side.

As Lee eyed the Union position from his own command post on Seminary Ridge, he decided on a classic approach. Over the next two days he employed essentially the same battle strategy as Marlborough had used at Blenheim, or Napoleon at Austerlitz: concentrate on the enemy's flanks until he had weakened his center by drawing off reserves, and then push right through that center to victory. Unfortunately for Lee, and for the Army of Northern Virginia, he was uncertain exactly what or how much he faced.

He had in addition command problems. First of all, he himself was not entirely well, and there is the sense that his hitherto sure touch was a bit off in the Gettysburg operation. Secondly, he was still poorly informed; Stuart did not appear in time to have any real effect on the battle, so Lee fought, as it were, in the dark. Perhaps most important of all, however, was the matter of personalities. Lee's three corps commanders, Longstreet, A. P. Hill, and Ewell, were all able men, and Longstreet at least was an exceptionally competent general, so much so that Lee once referred to him as "my wheel horse." But none of the three enjoyed the synchronicity of mind that Lee and Jackson had had. Lee's command style was a modest one; he preferred suggesting to ordering. With Jackson, who was if anything even more aggressive than Lee, this worked fine. But on the evening of the first day of Gettysburg, for example, Lee suggested Ewell make one more push, and Ewell decided not to do it. Longstreet, able as he was, had more caution in his makeup than either Lee or Jackson; he was often the anvil of the Army of North Virginia; he was a bit less successful as the hammer. Confederate apologists, who would never admit Lee might possibly have made a mistake, would subsequently blame Longstreet for the loss of Gettysburg, and ultimately even the loss of the war, but that ridiculous charge was a matter of post-war politics and finger-pointing.

On the morning of July 2, Lee intended to roll up the Federal flanks. Longstreet's corps would attack the southern end of their position, and when he was rolling, Ewell would then come in and crush the northern end. Lee wanted to start the battle early in the morning, but he did not get his orders issued until nearly noon, and then it took the usual while to sort out the troops detailed for the task. When they finally moved, after a couple of wrong turns, their approach march got all tangled up. Longstreet, who had wanted to stand on the defensive and let the Federals attack, was not happy. He tried to maneuver his divisions so they were out of sight of a small Federal signal station on Little Round Top, and with one thing and another, it was mid-afternoon before his guns opened up and his infantry went into the attack.

In one sense, the delay worked to the Confederate advantage, for while they were milling about, the Union commander facing them, Daniel Sickles of III Corps, advanced against orders and took up a position in a salient in the peach orchard along the Emmitsburg Road. He placed his two divisions at virtually right angles, one facing south, the other west, and it was this angle that Longstreet's gunners hit when they opened up.

Behind the flood of shot and shells came the Rebel infantry, John Bell Hood's Texans and Lafayette McLaws's Alabamians and Mississippians. Sickles's people, men who deserved a far better general than they had, fought hard but were utterly swept away, the entire corps ultimately destroyed.

Hearing the roar of the battle, Meade moved south along the ridge to see what was going on. Appalled at Sickles's position, but realizing it was too late to do anything about it, he began feeding Sykes's corps in to save the line. Sedgwick and VI Corps were just arriving, after a thirty-five-mile march, and these too were hustled along. But Hood's men were already climbing the slopes of the Little Round Top, and if they got there, they would flank the entire Union line.

On top of the rise was only that little signal station, and one man, Gouverneur K. Warren, chief engineer of the Army of the Potomac. Though Warren had no command status, he quickly saw what was necessary, and sent for help. The help was two of Sykes's brigades, and most immediately, Colonel Joshua Chamberlain and the 20th Maine. The Yankees won the race to the top by a few yards, just enough to throw together a firing line. Hood's men came on again and again, until, out of ammunition, Chamberlain ordered his men to fix bayonets. At the climactic moment, his thin line leaped up, yelling like madmen, and charged down the hill, springing from rock to rock, and driving the exhausted Rebels before them, saving the position and the day.

With the careful feeding in of reserves, Longstreet's attack was contained and finally sputtered out, leaving behind it a vast field of misery. On the northern end of the battle, Ewell had opened his attack when he heard Longstreet's guns, but in spite of several gallant attempts, he could not break the Union position there, and though Jubal Early's soldiers actually reached the top of Culp's Hill, they were quickly driven off. The day thus ended with the Union forces everywhere, at great cost, holding their positions.

During the night both commanders sought counsel as to what to do next. On the Federal side, the decision was to stay and fight it out, or at least to stand on the defensive and see what Lee might do. For the Confederates, the problem was a bit more complicated. Longstreet wanted to maneuver around the Federal left flank, and force them into the open and retreat. But Lee believed he was low on supplies, and wanted to finish off the job at hand. His view was that he had hit the left and the right, he knew he had used up Federal reserves, and therefore the center must be weak. He decided that Longstreet should co-ordinate a grand attack that would punch right through the Union position. Meanwhile, Stuart, arrived and under command at last, would maneuver far out around the Union right, ready to launch a pursuit once the Federals were broken and driven.

The 3rd was another beautiful, sunny, very hot summer day. All morning, while the sun climbed slowly in the sky, Longstreet mar-shaled his guns, 159 of them, along Seminary Ridge pointing east across the gentle valley. All morning long the Confederate brigades mustered and marched, men with tattered uniforms but bright records and even braver histories: George Pickett's Virginia division, with Kemper's, Garnett's, and Armistead's brigades, and Anderson's and Heth's divisions of Hill's corps, men of Georgia, Alabama, Mississippi, and North Carolina. Ironically, though the event has gone down in history as "Pickett's Charge," most of the men were not his and he did not in fact lead it; he formed the attacking units on Seminary Ridge, and led down into the valley, but his brigadiers, properly, were the ones to take it from there.

While all this was going on, and the Federal forces on Cemetery Ridge were adjusting and forming up their lines, Ewell tried again, and failed, to take Culp's Hill, in a fierce attack that has been over-shadowed by the events elsewhere. But by noon the armies were ready and waiting, and a curious hiatus came over the field. General John Gibbon, succeeding temporarily to II Corps command when Hancock was busy elsewhere, even had a little picnic with some of his officers, just at the point Longstreet had designated for the axis of the attack.

The Confederate guns opened up at one o'clock, with a tremendous crash, and for an hour they bombarded the Union lines, not very effectively, as much of their fire went over the ridge without doing any real damage to the troops in the front line. Nonetheless, it was an incredible noise, and unnerving enough to the recipients. The Union artillery replied with spirit, but after three quarters of an hour stopped to conserve ammunition and let the guns cool. By two, the Confederates were running low on ammunition themselves, and if the charge were to be launched, it had better be soon. Longstreet, despairing, gave the order. Colonel Freemantle, the British observer, remarked that he would not miss the sight for the world, and Longstreet answered, "I would like to have missed it very much!"

By brigades they came out of the trees and through the gun line, Pickett's men on the right, Anderson's on the left, row after row, brass and steel twinkling in the sun, the Rebel battle flags flapping bravely in the breeze. Some of the Virginians, relatively new to war, even had their bands there, to play them in. Down the little slope, while Longstreet watched, sick at heart. Pickett rode by, jauntily, Garnett buttoned up in his old overcoat, just out of hospital and too ill to march. In the open they paused to dress ranks and pick up their bearing, Archer's brigade providing the guide, its aiming point a clump of trees visible on Cemetery Ridge. The whole battlefield paused to watch; this was what war was supposed to be all about, and men would carry the proud memory of that scene with them for the rest of their lives.

At last they were all ready; the words of command rang out, and off they went. It was only a few hundred yards, farther for the right-hand regiments than for the left. Down the slope and across the Emmitsburg Road, losing alignment as they bunched or straggled to cross the road and the fences. The Union artillery spoke up, and the shells burst over them, and the lines thinned and wavered, and dressed again, and came on, leaving little trails of gray and red behind them. As they came up the other rise, the guns changed to canister and blew large holes in the ranks. The Rebels began to shake, and then to break into a run, screaming the Rebel yell as they came.

But they were aiming not at a weakened Federal center, but rather at Hancock's II Corps, some of the toughest soldiers in the entire army. The 8th Ohio lapped out around the Rebel left flank and poured in sweeping volleys, and three big Vermont regiments did the same from the Bloody Angle on their other side. Men went down in heaps; some started back. But the majority came on, and as the Union guns fell silent they hit the infantry line, where Webb's Pennsylvanians stood up to meet them with bayonets and rifle butts; Alonzo Cushing died as his battery fired its last shot in the faces of the charging Rebels and the whole dissolved into a huge welter of cursing and dying men.

For a moment it looked as if the charge might actually succeed, but only for a moment. Armistead, the leading brigadier, put his hat on his sword point, shouted "Boys, give 'em cold steel!" leaped a stone wall, and fell mortally wounded. A few hundred Confederates followed him, but they were hit in front by the Pennsylvanians, and on both flanks by Webb's supports, and it was just too much to ask of any soldiers. Sullenly they went back, pounded front and flank, until, from across the valley, the repulse was obvious. It was the crisis of the battle, and Meade and his men had won it. The broken regiments came straggling back up Seminary Ridge, men wounded and dragging comrades, weeping and exhausted, and Robert E. Lee rode out among them and said that it was all his fault.

Away out to the north, Stuart won his cavalry fight, but that made no difference; the battle of Gettysburg had been won and lost on Cemetery Ridge. More than 160,000 men had been engaged in the three days' fighting, 75,000 Confederates and 88,000 Federals, and Lee had casualties of 28,000 and Meade of 23,000. At last the Union had found a general who would at least try to utilize all the troops he had. But it still had not found one who would launch a relentless pursuit. On the 4th, Lee remained in position, inviting an attack which the Federals were too exhausted to make. It began to rain late in the afternoon, a hard soaking downpour, and under cover of it, Lee pulled out and headed back to Virginia. He might have been trapped against a flooded Potomac, but Meade let him go. Ten days after the battle, the great invasion of the North was over.

Chapter 12

The War Economies

THE ENTIRE Confederacy had been based on a succession of presuppositions. The North would not fight; Cotton was king; Europe would recognize the new nation and intervene; the South would prove invincible upon the field of battle; the Union would ultimately acknowledge the futility of the war; Northerners would not fight to end slavery. One after another these cherished shibboleths were proven false; the illusions were stripped away, and reality forced itself on Southern consciousness.

There were of course ups and downs, and this was hardly a straight linear progression. In late 1862 and early 1863 it did indeed look as if the South were militarily invincible, and as if the Union war effort were a failure. Fredericksburg and then Chancellorsville seemed to demonstrate the triumph of Southern valor, but then came, in a rush in July, Vicksburg and Gettysburg; Confederate morale took a downturn, and Union morale correspondingly improved. So the seesaw went back and forth, and good news for one side was bad for the other.

Few men had the length of view, in the middle of such an all-consuming struggle, to realize what all these victories and losses for either side really meant, which was, sadly, not much at all. Fredericksburg and Chancellorsville attested to the skill of Robert E. Lee and his army, or to the incompetence of his opponents. Gettysburg equally demonstrated the inability of the Confederacy to sustain an invasion, or a large-scale raid—they were never entirely certain which it had been—of the North. But none of the three had significantly altered the military balance, except to remove several thousand healthy young men from the rolls of either side. Even Vicksburg, the one battle of the four mentioned here that actually had some strategic significance, served essentially to strengthen an already established situation, the isolation of the western portion of the Confederacy. So in geostrategic or purely military terms, none of the four battles was as decisive as they each were dramatic. In the sense of morale, of course, Vicksburg and Gettysburg can now be recognized as significant turning points, the beginning of a long painful decline for the Confederacy, the sense for men in the North that yes, they would win if only they could stick to it long enough to do so. Since up to that time there had been almost as many doubters as there had been believers, in the morale sense they were extremely important battles.

What all this really shows is that the war was assuming a different character from that anticipated by those who first partook of it. Almost all wars do that, of course; in the case of the individual, few of the people who go off to war find that it is what they expected it to be, and in the collective sense, few states or peoples get out of war what they thought they would get when they entered it. The Civil War was thus hardly unique in this respect, but its effects were profound beyond all expectation. Not only was it the first modern war, a thing its participants could hardly have been expected to realize, but it also hastened the great transformation of American life. The war brought about the very triumph of "Northern," or "modern," values that the Southerners who seceded hoped to prevent. Many scholars for this reason have called the Civil War a second American Revolution.

None of this would have happened had the war been won or lost by the end of 1862—had it been possible, that is, to achieve the fondly anticipated and long-sought battlefield decision. Since it was not, more mundane factors became increasingly important. Staying power was not simply a matter of how many men were willing to fight and die, but to what extent their societies could sustain them while they did so. Could the Confederacy, while fighting for its life, build a sufficiently viable polity that it could maintain the struggle through to victory? Or could the North so mobilize its superior resources, and receive enough support from enough of its citizens, that it could successfully complete its self-imposed task of the destruction of the Confederacy? We now know, of course, the answer to both of these questions. But the men and women of 1863 could no more know the end of their endeavors than we can know the end of ours.

Scholars have differed mightily on the question of why the war took the course it did; they have, indeed, agreed upon little more than who won and who lost. Of all the areas of argument, none has been more fertile than that of the running of the Confederacy. Was it a noble effort that simply attempted a task beyond its strength, or was it a ramshackle hodgepodge of incompetent, selfish men, making the wrong decisions for the wrong reasons? The simple answer is, it was both. Like all human institutions, it had nobility and baseness in it.

In the classic example, or personification, take Jefferson Davis; few men had more nobility of mind or a higher character than did Jefferson Davis, and few could be more petty or small-minded than he. At least one authority has suggested that if Davis and Lincoln had changed places, the Confederacy would have won the war. But of course there was more right, and more wrong, with the Confederate government than the personality of its president.

One of its chief failings, oddly enough, was the lack of an organized party system. The idea of political parties, or "factions" as they were originally called, developed in England in the seventeenth and eighteenth centuries, and they were for a long time thought to be invidious. Southerners still tended to regard them in that light. In fact they were, and are, essential to the parliamentary or republican system. They focused ideas, and created currents of policy, and enabled men to function in cohesive, and coherent, groups. They offered the possibility of alternative courses of action based upon policies rather than upon mere personalities. Davis and his fellow politicians eschewed them, thinking themselves too high-minded to descend to party politics. The result was that Davis could never build a secure political base in his Congress or in his country, and his opposition could never offer a different course based on anything more substantial than personal likes or dislikes. Confederate politics became a welter of individuals, all shouting against the wind, pulling this way and that, and ultimately reduced to supporting or opposing Davis simply because he was Davis. Even his own vice president, Alexander Hamilton Stephens of Georgia, broke with the government, spent eighteen months of the war at home, and sat only rarely in the war cabinet through which Davis governed his country. This one example may be taken as more or less typical of the political confusion that reigned in Richmond.

Equally contentious were the relations between the central government of the Confederacy and its component states. Philosophically, of course, the entire basis of the Confederacy was the denial by individual states of a larger spirit of voluntary cooperation; in practice, therefore, developing a central Confederate government was an uphill struggle. The several state governors jealously guarded their own prerogatives, and repudiated the actions and authority of the Richmond government whenever it suited their own interests. Governor Zebulon Vance of North Carolina was especially insistent upon his state's rights, and in Georgia a triumvirate of politicians, Vice President Stephens, Governor Joseph Brown, and Davis's defeated rival for the presidency, Robert Toombs, spent practically the entire war feuding with the central government and opposing its policies. The separate states held back troops and supplies for their own use, refused to enforce laws passed by the central government, and went their own ways whenever it suited them. The effect of all this is a bit uncertain; some historians have argued that in looking to their own interests, the states were merely accomplishing for themselves many of the tasks the central government would have had to do, or try to do, anyway. But others have argued that this particularism was the chief failing of the Confederacy, and that it cost the South the war, that the theory of states' rights, carried to a destructive extreme, was what caused it to fail. One writer suggested that on the Confederacy's tombstone should be engraved, "Died of a Theory."

The southern part of the United States had always prided itself on the quality of national political figure it had produced, and it was something of a disappointment to find, when they were centered in Richmond rather than Washington, that Confederate politicians were such a mediocre lot. Idols when seen from afar, they were very much clay seen close up.

And if the aspirant national government failed to develop a workable political system, it failed even more miserably in its attempt to finance a war. Fiscally, the new government got afloat on a wave of local patriotism, which saw Southerners oversubscribe bond issues and make loans and outright donations. But Richmond refused to set up a high tariff on imports, because high tariffs initiated by the hated Yankees had been one of the things Southerners objected to in the old union. And in addition to denying itself that source of income, the government also failed to tax its citizens for the first two years of the war. Instead, Confederates established a taxation system analogous to their military one, and after assessing the national property, they assigned the respective states quotas, and left them to meet the demand. The states, rather than taxing, simply borrowed the money; in other words, as we are doing today, the Confederates passed their debts on to their children.

The central government did offer a number of bond issues, but except for the very early ones, they did not do well. The first was sold for specie, hard money; subsequent ones went for depreciated paper money, and eventually even for farm produce, as paper money became worthless and hard money disappeared. At one point the government was offering the very favorable rate of 8 percent return, compared with a mere 2.9 percent in the North, and still could find no subscribers, which meant, of course, that investors had no faith in the ultimate victory of the Confederacy.

Foreign loans, which the early Confederacy had optimistically expected, proved even more disappointing. The only substantial one was offered by a French banking firm, Erlanger and Company of Paris. Erlanger offered a loan against imports of Confederate cotton, and then issued bonds on the projected profit to be derived from the imports. Most of the bonds were bought by British investors—in the 1860s Britain had a great deal of surplus capital, and Britons could be got to invest in almost any get-rich-quick scheme. In this case, Erlanger substantially discounted the loan they gave the Confederacy, relatively little of the cotton reached Europe, the bonds fell very quickly, the investors lost almost all of their money, and the only people to profit by the entire transaction were—Erlanger and Company of Paris, a result that would surprise no one who knew anything about stocks and bonds at the time.

It was not until 1863 that the Confederate government made any serious attempt to tackle its revenue problems, and by then it was too late. In April it introduced a tax on naval stores and various agricultural products, a licensing tax on occupations, a sales tax of from 2½ to 8 percent, and an income tax that ranged from 1 percent on incomes of $1,000 to 15 percent on incomes of $10,000 or more. The government also introduced an agricultural tax in kind, and sent agents around to confiscate farmers' produce. As there was little ready coin in the country, the money taxes were fairly easy to evade, but the tax in kind was bitterly resented, and even when items were collected, they were so difficult to move that a great deal was wasted. Through the entire war, the Confederacy, according to estimates, paid for no more than 1 percent of its real expenses through taxation.

If politics and fiscal policies were both Confederate failures, the issue of production of goods and services, both for the actual waging of the war and for the sustenance of the population as a whole, is more problematical. For one thing, this covers such a wide spectrum of items that any generalization is bound to be wrong in many particulars, and students of the wartime economy have therefore found it very difficult to reach a broad consensus. The Confederacy obviously created a satisfactory munitions industry, and for most of the war produced, or imported, the supplies needed to keep its armies in the field. It was less successful in other war-related endeavors. For example, the naval side of the war has story after story of Confederate vessels destroyed when near completion, or burned to avoid capture, or breaking down in action. Given the weakness of pre-war Southern shipbuilding capacity, this is hardly surprising. A similar failure was in railroad building and maintenance; the unexpected success of the Southern railroad system for much of the war has already been considered, but by the end of it, the system was indeed collapsing. The Confederacy did not, could not, produce enough rails or rolling stock to replace wear and war wastage, and as the war progressed, the system became more rickety. There were more wrecks and more delays, and badly needed goods sat idle on sidings for days and weeks. Once the Union forces began their large-scale incursions into the heart of the Confederacy, they did damage that simply could not be repaired. By then, of course, the whole Confederacy was teetering toward collapse anyway.

How much derived from fundamental inadequacies, how much from the wastage of war itself, is a subject of considerable argument. The South possessed a great number of draft animals; but increasing numbers of these went for the war, impressed by supply officers from the army, first horses and then even mules and oxen. But a horse taken for the army meant one less to pull a plow, and therefore a diminution of the food crops that army, and also the civilian population, also needed. The government decreed that instead of planting cotton and tobacco, money-making export crops that could not be exported, planters should grow cereal crops instead. But there were still bread riots in the cities, notably Richmond in 1863, because poor working women could not afford to feed their families. Southern editors might attribute this unrest to "Northern hirelings" and "the lowest, base-born classes," but calling names did not lower the price of grain or put bread on the table. There were shortages of everything, both agricultural and manufactured goods. Needles were worth their weight in gold, Southern soldiers in captured Union supply depots were seen eating salt by the handful, and Confederates patriotically tried to convince themselves that a variety of drinks made from nuts or bark were the equivalent of coffee.

There was one shortage, however, even more troublesome, more crucial, and more intrusive than any of these others—the shortage of bodies. Southerners had rushed to arms in 1861, but within a year, most of those willing to go to war had already done so. The Confederacy had the same hierarchy of military service as the Union did, local militia, state troops, and national army, with limitations upon the uses to which each level might be put. Very quickly, even before Shiloh in the west or the Peninsula campaign in the east, Southerners began to lose their enthusiasm; what had looked like a lark in the spring of 1861 looked like something far more difficult in the spring of 1862. The Confederate Congress replied to this growing sentiment with the first conscription law in American history.

Officially, the law made eligible for conscription all white males between eighteen and thirty-five years of age, to be liable for three years' service. The law was actually meant less to conscript people than it was to encourage volunteering, and it was successful in the sense of achieving that. But there were several provisions that made the conscription act highly unpalatable; first of all, there was a large list of exemptions for various occupations, teachers, civil servants, industrial workers, and so on, and for certain pacifist religions. It was also possible to buy a substitute for fixed sums, which again meant that the poor had to go, while the rich might avoid service if they chose. And later an amendment offered exemption, or release from service, of planters or overseers with twenty slaves under their control. This naturally raised a howl of protest, that the slaveholders had caused the war, and now wanted other men to fight it for them. The government maintained that this provision was necessary for production purposes, as well as for preservation of internal order. Eventually thay had to give up both the slaveholding exemption and the substitutes, and to extend the age limits for eligibility. War service, or the avoidance of it, caused enormous bitterness, and one writer noted that by 1863 the South was full of women sitting around parlors saying to each other, "Why doesn't your brother go to war?"

Ironically, the presence of African slaves in the South seemed to

exacerbate the whole issue. Slaves used as laborers for military fortifications, and as agricultural workers, and in some cases industrial ones,
made a major contribution to the Confederate war economy. But they
were arguably as great a drain on it as a support to it, and the whole
Southern labor system broke down under the war itself. Slaves ran away,
they followed the Union armies as they invaded the South, they worked
slowly and unwillingly while their owners were away fighting. There
were of course the loyal house servants who identified with their rulers,
the stuff of subsequent romantic legend of the Old South, but the
existence of that hostile servile class presented Confederates with virtually insurmountable dilemmas. As the horizon darkened, the inevitable question arose: Should the slaves be used as soldiers? The mere
question itself illustrated how desperate the Confederacy finally was,
and how divorced from reality were its perceptions.

As the war went on, of course, increasing numbers of Southerners
were prepared to face reality; in other words, they became ever more
disillusioned with the war and its costs and sacrifices. Many had not
wanted secession, and certainly not war, in the first place. Thousands
of citizens from the South either fought openly for the Union, in what
have come to be called "orphan" units, or exercised covert antagonism,
or simply refused to support the cause of Southern independence. Western Virginia seceded from its parent state, and east Tennessee came
close to doing likewise. In Louisiana there was a strong Unionist movement as early as 1863. Still, all of these people, who may be considered
as passive Unionists, were less important than was the gradual erosion
of support among those who really had been in favor of secession and
Southern independence; these, after all, were the ones willing to fight
the war.

They were not ready to give up yet, but gradually they were being
worn down. Men were away, often killed or maimed, farms were
worked by women or not at all, shortages sapped the will to continue.
The Confederacy, in spite of maintaining itself militarily, simply did
not seem to be working well. The burden, as always, fell especially
heavily on the poorer classes, and every sizable town in the South was
filled with women and children who were in essence war refugees,
driven in from the country not by Union action—the Federals had not
yet developed their policy of penetrating raids—but simply by the
inability of society to wage war, and provide adequately for the families
of the soldiers doing the fighting. The Confederacy paid its private

soldiers eleven or thirteen dollars a month, almost nothing in the face of upward-spiraling prices and lack of commodities. States and localities attempted to provide relief for destitute military families, but women who were proud that their men were fighting for their rights resented being reduced to charity by that sacrifice. As 1863 limped toward 1864, more and more soldiers received letters that said, "Why don't you come home? The children are sick, I have no money, we can't keep the farm going, what are we fighting for anyway?" Faced with such complaints, men would stay for a while longer, through loyalty to their friends or their units, through pride or principle or simple stubbornness. They were a long way from ready to give up yet. Early elation had been replaced by dogged determination; but unless there was some substantial gain to show, that determination would ultimately give way in turn to despair.

The costs and sacrifices of the war lay far lighter upon the Union than upon the Confederacy. Not in the individual sense, of course; the Union soldier who lost a leg suffered every bit as much as the Confederate one; and the Union family whose son was killed mourned just as did their cousins in the South. And the wife of a working-class Union soldier may have had almost, but probably not quite, as hard a time as her Southern counterpart. But in terms of society at large, the Union managed to sustain its war effort and the associated costs far more readily than did the Confederacy. Writers, especially Southern ones, have often speculated that if the war had lain as heavily upon the North as it did upon the Confederacy, the North would have given up, a sort of retrospective apologia for the Confederacy's failure. Such an argument misses the point, however, which is that wars are fought not to see how much suffering can be endured, but to be won, and, to paraphrase George Patton, they are won not by enduring suffering yourself, but by inflicting suffering upon your opponent.

The picture of the North at war is indeed substantially different from the picture of the South. Though both sides were forced by the demands of the war to do much the same thing—both brought in conscription, both suspended normal civil procedures (such as habeas corpus), both increasingly centralized their governments, and on and on—the North had more resources to work with, and in truth it mobilized and utilized them more effectively in the long run.

President Lincoln, like his Confederate counterpart, faced opposition from a variety of sources. Much more successfully than Davis, however, Lincoln built a coalition of political support out of the party structure that still functioned in the North. Lincoln drew his support basically from moderate Republicans and from what were called "War Democrats," men who might be against him on party lines but were essentially committed to the war and the maintenance of the Union. This reduced the opposition to the two extremes: the Peace Democrats, known to their foes as "Copperheads" because they wore a copper penny in their lapels as an identifying badge, at one end of the spectrum; and the Radical Republicans at the other end. The former believed either that the war could not be won, or that it was not worth winning, and therefore wanted to give it up. They tended to be opposed particularly to emancipation, and generally to the increasingly vigorous prosecution of the war. After the Emancipation Proclamation, some of them went so far as to encourage soldiers to desert. They were strong especially in the Midwest, where the "butternut" southern counties of Ohio, Indiana, and Illinois were populated largely by people with Southern connections. In Indiana, Oliver P. Morton, the Republican governor and one of the strongest supporters of the war, ran his state for two years with no legislature, resorting to one political trick after another to keep his war effort going.

Almost more troublesome to Lincoln than the Peace Democrats were those extreme members of his own party known as the Radical Republicans. They were talented, influential, intolerant, and very astute politically. They had supporters within the gate, as it were, in the persons of Chase and Stanton in the cabinet itself, but their greatest power lay in Congress, where Galusha Grow was the Speaker of the House, and Senators Charles Sumner and Benjamin Wade of Massachusetts, and Zachariah Chandler of Michigan, all were important committee members. Their most powerful instrument was the earlier-mentioned Committee on the Conduct of the War, set up to inquire into early military disasters, and dedicated thenceforth to getting rid of "soft" generals, notably George McClellan, and promoting its own faithful, who unfortunately included a number of incompetents, such as Frémont, Ben Butler, and Fighting Joe Hooker. With them, military skill was far less important than being correct on the great political questions of the day, especially abolition. They drew their strength largely from New England, and over the course of the war, much of the North grew to resent bitterly what it saw as New England's dominance of the war effort and policy. The Radical Republicans would have been a Committee of Public Safety if they could have managed it, and like Robespierre, they were willing to kill men to make them free. Lincoln found them very uncomfortable allies, but he could not do without them, and as the war intensified, he found himself perforce adopting some of their views. Washington politics, and state politics as well, given that the states were obviously more important then than they are now, were thus a constant Scylla and Charybdis act, with Lincoln and his gubernatorial counterparts trying to preserve their support in the middle. Still, in comparison to the fog in Richmond, they did very well.

It was the same with paying for the war. Union finances remained remarkably sound, though there were temporary embarrassments as a result of military reverses. In fact, after a poor start, the war forced the federal government into modernizing its financial and banking system, and getting rid of the antiquated banking practices that were a legacy of the Jacksonian era. Before the war began, the federal government cost about 2 percent of the gross national product; during the war that cost rose to 15 percent. At first these expenses were covered by short-term borrowing, but in late 1861 Congress brought in an income tax, to be collected starting in 1863, and of course they immediately began bond issues. The crisis also necessitated the introduction of paper money on a national level, though before the war the government had insisted that all its business be transacted in hard currency. The advent of the greenbacks was in fact a disguised blessing, for in 1860 there had been more than seven thousand different banks circulating their own paper money throughout the country, and no one could be sure what a note was worth, as many of those seven thousand had gone bankrupt in the depression of the late fifties. By 1865 the United States was well on the way to a national banking system, a necessary precursor to the enormous national expansion of the next generation. In the matter of money, as in many other things, the flood of war swept away the deadwood.

In mid-1862, Congress introduced a heavy-handed revenue act that imposed taxes on almost every imaginable product or service, and Congress also hiked the import duties to protect American manufacturers. Americans were taxed as they never had been before, though not of course as they have been in the last fifty years. All of this was considered at the time to be enormously intrusive on the life of the citizen, but the war was used as its own excuse for these changes, and it developed its own momentum. The bond issues, for example, gave the one family out of every four who subscribed to them a personal financial stake in winning the war: if it was lost, those bonds would never be redeemed.

The respective success or failure of the two competing governments is graphically illustrated by the inflation rate. Money is notorious for its lack of patriotism, so here was an honest yardstick of how well either side did. In the Union, wartime inflation, from 1861 to 1865, was about 80 percent, the same as in World War I and slightly higher than in World War II. In the Confederacy the wartime inflation was more than 9,000 percent.

Economic historians have differed on the effect of the war on production in the North. Some point out that if a yardstick several generations long is employed, the decade of the sixties actually shows a drop in production, compared with those before and after it. Others counter that this is misleading, because for the war years, the productive performance of only the Union is counted, against that for the entire United States in the preceding and succeeding decades; in other words, during the war, the Union was producing almost as much as the entire country before or after the war.

One of the reasons for this is that war, as much as necessity, is the mother of inventions. It happened that many of the technological advances that transformed industry and agriculture in the nineteenth century, gadgets such as sewing machines for both clothes and shoes, mechanical reapers and harvesters, and machines for canning and preserving food, had all been developed just before the war. Then the sudden demand of the war itself brought these machines and processes to the fore. Ironically, this demand existed at the same time as there was a labor shortage, because so many men went into the armed services, so during the war years there was an increase in mechanization, and in the level of production in the North, and at the same time a decrease in the skill and aptitude of workers. Far more children were brought into the workforce, the percentage of unskilled foreign-born workers increased, and women's share went from a fifth to nearly a third of the manufacturing population. And this in turn was reflected in a fall in income for the Northern worker. His, or her, wages went up but did not keep pace with the inflation rate of the war years, so while many manufacturers made large amounts of money, they did it at the expense of the working class. Thus in spite of a graduated income tax, there was the time-honored phenomenon of the rich getting richer, while the poor and middle classes not only got to fight the war, they got to pay for it as well. It truly was a modern war.

One of its unintended effects was to free up a great deal of capital, through war production, profits, and investment, and also, because of the absence from the national government of those conservative Southerners whose presence would have resisted this trend, in allowing far freer play to those capital forces. The legislative foundations of the Gilded Age and the great postwar boom period and western expansion were laid during the war years. In 1862, for example, Congress passed the Homestead Act; the Morrill Act, which provided for land-grant colleges in the western territories; and the Pacific Railroad Act, which culminated after the war in the completion of the transcontinental railroad. While thousands of young men were fighting the war, thousands of others were still able to move into manufacturing jobs, or to move west and take up new land. The economic and geographic horizons continued to broaden even as the military situation remained uncertain.

One of the reasons for that uncertainty, aside from the continued skill and tenacity displayed by the Confederacy, was the matter of manpower. Just like its opponent, the Union found that men were less willing to volunteer for war once they had some idea of what it was like. Given their greater manpower pool, it took the North a year longer than the South to reach this stage, but by 1863 the issue was becoming acute. Indeed, in late 1862 volunteering had slowed so significantly that the federal government resorted to a draft of the state militias for a nine-month period, which was a thinly disguised form of conscription. This was but a stopgap measure, however, and in the next year, in March, Congress passed the Enrollment Act, making every white male between twenty and forty-five liable for conscription.

As usual, the act was full of loopholes for various categories of men, and it also allowed the purchase of substitutes. By the time the war was over, 46,000 men had been drafted, and 118,000 had hired substitutes to go in their places. The two figures together were less than 10 percent of the total in the Union armies, and the draft has therefore been considered a failure. The fact was, however, just as in the Confederacy, that the conscription acts were designed less for their ostensible purpose than they were designed to stimulate volunteering. Any state that could fulfill its quota by volunteering did not have to draft men, so the relatively small proportion of draftees in fact testified to the success of the policy in its hidden intent.

This subtlety was lost on many men, and the four draft calls by the president, the first in July of 1863 and three more in 1864, produced a great deal of bitterness, as well as real violence. The worst reaction came with the draft riots in New York City in July 1863.

The largest city of the North was always peculiarly volatile, and especially so in 1863. It was packed with immigrants and native working-class people who resented the poor conditions under which they lived and labored, and the anti-foreign sentiment that was a feature of the daily lives of the entire populace. Besides that, both the city and the state were firmly in Democratic hands, and Governor Horatio Seymour was bitterly opposed to President Lincoln. When the president issued his draft call, Seymour challenged its constitutionality, almost openly urging resistance. And when the names of the first draftees, drawn on Saturday, July 11, were published in the newspapers the next day, mobs quickly gathered and began parading up and down the streets of the poorer sections. For three days they were out of control, and the city cowered under their rampage. The rioters caused a million and a half dollars' worth of property damage, and worse, they burned a black orphanage and lynched a number of unfortunate blacks caught in the wrong place. The city and state authorities responded weakly, and it was not until the arrival of Federal troops that the mob was suppressed. The soldiers came right from the battlefield at Gettysburg; men who had recently been shot at by Longstreet's Rebels had little sympathy for New York rioters. The soldiers opened fire on the mob, killing some hundreds, but quickly solving the problem. Under their iron blue hand, order was soon restored.

New York in the summer of 1863 was only the most famous of numerous riots throughout the North, at this draft call and others, and the outbursts illustrate once again the fragility of the coalition Lincoln and the Republicans had built to support the war. There was one more opposing force as well, outside the spectrum of legitimate opposition, and it is best seen in the odd person of Clement L. Vallandigham.

An Ohio lawyer and congressman, Vallandigham was bitterly opposed to the war, which he believed was, among other evil things, an abolitionist conspiracy. He was also an outspoken foe of President Lincoln, and when he was maneuvered out of his congressional seat by the War Democrats of his own party in 1862, he began a campaign to win the governorship of Ohio. He stumped the state, speaking against the war, against conscription, and against Lincoln. All of this was legitimate, but Vallandigham was a born plotter, one of those typical men of his day who sought refuge from the advance of modernity in secret societies, lodge meetings, hidden messages, and silly handshakes. He was thought incorrectly to be a member of the Knights of the Golden Circle, the pre-war, largely Southern, secret society dedicated to the annexation of Mexico and the creation of a great slave-holding empire around the Caribbean. This group had numbers of cells, "Castles," in the border and Great Lakes states, and no one knew—then or now—how many members it had, or how great a threat it was, or if it was indeed a threat at all. It was certainly real to some extent, but probably more so in the mind of Edwin M. Stanton than in objective reality. To the government, anyway, Copperheads, Knights of the Golden Circle, and Clement Vallandigham were all of a piece—they were traitors.

Into this volatile mix enter Ambrose Burnside, appointed commander of the Department of the Ohio after leaving the Army of the Potomac. Burnside, concerned over possible sedition, issued Order No. 38, making it a crime to speak against the war effort or express sympathy for the Confederate cause. On April 30, 1863, Vallandigham made a speech calculated to get himself arrested, and five days later, Burnside obliged him. Denied the right of habeas corpus, Vallandigham was tried by a military court and sentenced to two years' imprisonment. Burnside happily thought he had done a good bit of work.

In fact, he had created a teapot tempest. Vallandigham may well have been a nuisance, a gadfly, and possibly a fool, but none of those was really illegal. What was illegal was seizing a civilian and trying him by military court when martial law had not been proclaimed, and the government was in a fair way to making Vallandigham the political martyr he so desperately wanted to be. To keep the man prisoner would be bad, and to release him might be even worse. Fortunately, there was Lincoln with his wry sense of humor, and he solved the dilemma. Vallandigham dearly loved the Confederacy—perfect; President Lincoln commuted his sentence from imprisonment to banishment. Two and a half weeks after his military trial, Vallandigham was delivered

185

under a flag of truce to the Confederate lines in Tennessee, and turned over by the amused Yankees to the bemused Rebels.

The Democrats professed to be enraged by all this, and in Ohio they nominated their exiled hero for the governorship. He himself soon found the Confederacy no more to his taste than the Union, left for Bermuda, and from there went to Canada, where he took up residence in Windsor, Ontario, across the river from Detroit, to carry on his absentee political campaign. Most of the country thought it hilarious, however, that a man who professed to be so opposed to life in the Union as it then was should be so anxious to return to it. He was defeated for the governorship by more than 100,000 votes, and in 1864 returned to Ohio in disguise. From then on the government left him alone, but his fangs were drawn, and for the rest of the war he was more of an embarrassment to his friends than to his enemies.

So many things were happening in the America of the 1860s that the times would have been difficult enough even without the war, as men and women strove to adjust to demographic, economic, techno-logical, and societal change. The war, of course, submerged all those things under the more immediate issue of the Union and its survival or disruption. But they kept burbling up to the surface; the immigrant ships kept coming into the American ports, families gave up farms and moved west to take up new land, or were drawn into the cities growing up along New England's rivers, to the mills and the shoe factories; poor men rioted against the draft in Wisconsin and New York. It was all of a piece; the country was changing, and what men at the time saw as desperation—what at the time was indeed desperation—was also the ferment of a great new nation being born, a nation that could fight an immense war, and still grow by leaps and bounds while doing it. It was exciting—but it was not easy.

Chapter 13

The War in Equilibrium

BUOYED BY THE twin victories of Gettysburg and Vicksburg, the Union might hope for great things in the remainder of 1863. Grant was cleaning up the Mississippi Valley, Banks from New Orleans was taking the few residual Confederate footholds on the river, Rosecrans was preparing to advance in Tennessee, and Lee had been chased, or allowed to escape, back to Virginia. On all fronts, then, the Union appeared ascendant. But like so many previous hopes and predictions, this one too was doomed to disappointment.

President Lincoln was not entirely certain of George Meade yet. His new commander had done well in a very difficult situation at Gettysburg; he had moved quickly to take over his new responsibilities, he had concentrated his forces well, and he had done his best to use all of them; he seemed to have the support of his corps commanders, in itself a novelty in the Army of the Potomac; above all, he had managed to win a battle. But after doing so, he let the beaten enemy escape unhindered across the Potomac; he seemed to be infected by the army's deadly we've-done-enough-for-one-day disease, and as he moved his troops south, he kept demanding more reinforcements. So Lincoln might well wonder, Was this man going to be just another McClellan?

In fact, Meade was doing pretty well. Lee, upon crossing the Potomac, had moved south up the Shenandoah Valley, a *via dolorosa* in which his tattered army seeped dead, wounded, and most ominously, deserters. The Army of Northern Virginia had been beaten at last, and beaten badly, and every man and officer knew it. It was as good an army as the world would ever see, and it knew that, too, and it was therefore smart enough to know when it had been whipped in a fair fight, and it was not happy. As Lee moved through the always sympathetic valley, the army slowly pulled itself back together, but it would not again be the force that had marched north less than a month earlier.

Meade too moved south, but he took a more direct route, crossing the Potomac to the east of Lee's crossing and marching down along the east side of the Blue Ridge Mountains. For once, for practically the first time in the war, the Federals marched faster by a better route than their opponents did. There was opportunity in this, and Meade tried to seize it. He sent III Corps through Manassas Gap to try to catch the retreating Confederates. This had been Dan Sickles's corps at Gettysburg, the men Sickles had pushed out into The Wheat Field and The Peach Orchard; Sickles had paid with his leg for that move, and the corps was now commanded by Major General William H. French. French had done well with brigades and divisions hitherto, but he soon proved out of his depth handling a corps. He dawdled through the gap, taking forever to push aside some Rebel skirmishers, and by the time Meade got the army through to support him, Lee had his whole force in battle line around Front Royal. Meade prepared to attack, but Lee slipped off on the night of July 23–24. Lee then crossed the Blue Ridge through the next two gaps to the south, and a couple of days later the armies faced each other back on their old ground on either side of the Rappahannock.

They sat there for the month of August, adjusting both armies: furloughs, detachments, new recruits coming in, training, drilling, shaking down, convalescents coming back, officers shuffling about, all the sort of thing armies and other institutions have to do simply to function. The Confederates sent Longstreet and his whole corps off to Tennessee, to see what might be done there. Meade looked at his maps, and tried to figure out what he should do.

His problem was the same old one faced by his predecessors: how to maneuver so as to force Lee into battle on terms favorable to Meade's own army. The Union had a numerical superiority of about five to three—it fluctuated through the summer—but Lee had the advantage of position. By September, Meade had decided to repeat Hooker's Chancellorsville maneuver, and was on the point of moving to do so, when news came in of disaster in Tennessee; Meade was thus forced to detach two corps and send them west. The news of this immediately reached Lee, of course, and even though he was still substantially out-numbered, he decided to move.

On October 9, Lee started west and north, intending to get between the Army of the Potomac and Washington. But Meade moved rapidly north with him, and once more, did so by a more direct route. After Meade's men had marched about forty miles, and Lee's nearer seventy-five, both armies faced each other again up around the old Bull Run area. But not much came of it. Stuart got in a scrape with his cavalry, and had to hide all night in the middle of the Union army. The biggest fight came at Bristoe Station. Gouverneur Warren, commanding the Union rear guard, set a neat trap for the Confederate advance, and destroyed two Confederate brigades, nearly 2,000 men, for a loss of less than 600 Federals. Seeing his plan thwarted, Lee then moved back south, with cavalry bickering all the way, and by early November he was in a position south of the Rappahannock, off which Meade ma-neuvered him, and then he settled behind the Rapidan River.

Meade now reverted to his earlier idea, of flanking Lee out of posi-tion. To this end he moved his army suddenly sideways, to the east, his left, and attempted a crossing of the river at Germanna and Ely's Fords. Meade worked all this out very carefully, and issued detailed orders more in the British than the American style, the whole move carefully and minutely timed. Again it went wrong. The fords were high, the river proved wider than the engineers had calculated, and there were insufficient pontoons to bridge it; time was lost in impro-visation. Then, once across the river, the leading corps, French's again, took the wrong road and marched off crossways. By the time the Fed-erals got sorted out, Lee had received word of their moves, and he quickly countered them, taking up a strong position along a little creek known as Mine Run. Meade came up against this on the 28th, and prepared a heavy attack. He proposed to put Warren's II Corps in on his left, against the Confederate right flank, and then, when that attack developed, Sedgwick's VI Corps would go in on the Confederate left.

The attack was set for the morning of the 30th, but during the 29th Lee got A. P. Hill's corps up and dug in on his right, and the next morning, when Warren looked things over, he decided to postpone the attack. Meade came over to have a look, and agreed with him, wisely, as there was not a better eye for a position in either army than Gou-verneur Warren's. As Sedgwick's assault depended on Warren's, the Federals gave it all up as a bad job.

Lee, aggressive as ever, planned in his turn to attack, expecting to turn the Federal left flank and roll it up against the river. But Meade was too wily for that, and when the Rebels moved out, they found their enemy gone. Meade had pulled back across the Rapidan, and by the first of December, the armies were back in their former positions, settling down for the winter, soldiers building huts and trading for dainties between the picket lines, officers getting ready for furloughs, to go home to see the family, or at least to Washington to see friends in Congress and the War Department.

The whole season in the east after Gettysburg illustrated the balance between the two sides. The Army of the Potomac was numerically stronger, and better supplied and equipped than the Army of Northern Virginia, and George Meade was a good deal better than the commanders who had preceded him. But Lee himself still offset whatever quantitative deficiencies the Confederates labored under, and so the two armies maneuvered skillfully back and forth, without either one being able to gain an advantage sufficient to risk a full-scale battle. The operations here were like the middle game in chess between two equally matched opponents.

But there were several other factors off the immediate chessboard, and those would inevitably, if slowly, have an effect. The most immediate one was President Lincoln's dissatisfaction with Meade. As the months after Gettysburg went by, and nothing was accomplished, Halleck and Meade went through the usual hectoring exchange, Meade wanting more men and supplies, Washington wanting more action. Slowly, but far less slowly than he had with McClellan, Lincoln came to the conclusion that Meade was not quite what he wanted. He was a little too prone to see difficulties, a little too cautious. Lincoln needed a field commander with a bit more drive. In fact, he was giving way here to rising expectations. A year ago, he would have been perfectly happy to find a man who could march an army anywhere in the same state with Robert E. Lee.

———

While Meade and Lee chased each other fruitlessly around northern Virginia, the war in the Mississippi Valley was winding down. The last Confederate holding on the river, Port Hudson, about 125 miles south of Vicksburg, surrendered on July 9, after a siege that was smaller but even more brutal than Vicksburg's. Conducted by Nathaniel

Banks's Army of the Gulf, it cost the Federals 3,000 casualties and netted more than 5,500 Confederate prisoners. Union forces in the west were now free to reorganize, pull themselves back into shape, and get ready for further operations. This took much of the remainder of the summer, and while they did this, the focus of the war shifted eastwards. From the standpoints of both Washington and Richmond, the "west" was no longer the Mississippi Valley, but rather Tennessee and Kentucky, and in this theater, a quite bizarre series of events occurred.

Both governments let their view be overshadowed by what was happening elsewhere, and both relied on men who were military perfectionists. Generals Rosecrans for the Union, and Bragg for the Confederacy, were in fact well suited to each other. Each wanted his army in the best shape he could manage, and neither liked to fight. They had met each other at Stones River, or Murfreesboro, over the New Year of 1863, and it was an experience no one could want to repeat. So for six months they were quite content to live at peace, or as near it as they could get while each was being badgered by his respective government to do something. As a sop to their capitals, they indulged in widespread, large-scale cavalry raids. On the Confederate side Joe Wheeler, Nathan Bedford Forrest, and John Hunt Morgan all rode about the countryside, accomplishing little; Morgan led his troopers all the way to Cincinnati in Ohio, spreading alarm and excitement, but was eventually run to ground and captured without his achieving anything. For the Union Rosecrans sent out several parties to raid Bragg's communications and lost them with no profit.

The only real point of these forays was to allow the respective commanders to look active, but neither Washington nor Richmond was really deceived. Rosecrans and Stanton and Halleck engaged in an acrimonious exchange of telegrams, which ended with Rosecrans insisting he would advance when he was able and ready, and not a minute before, and Stanton protesting against "the expense to which you put the government for telegrams."

If relations among the Union leadership were bad enough, they were worse among the Confederates. Braxton Bragg retained the confidence of Jefferson Davis, but he had lost that of his corps and division commanders. Bragg was broken down in health, unhappy, a constant nagger and worrier, and anyway not a man to inspire warm-hearted support from his juniors. Led by Leonidas Polk, in peacetime an Episcopal bishop who would have been happy as a Renaissance cardinal, the senior officers of the Army of Tennessee had practically mutinied against their commander, to the point that President Davis himself was forced to intervene. Unfortunately, instead of sweeping away both the commander and his disloyal subordinates, Davis was determined to keep all of them, and did so, to the ultimate detriment of the Confederate cause. As spring came across the hills of Tennessee, Bragg's army was not a happy place to serve.

Matters went from bad to worse. Several of Bragg's units were detached to aid in the defense of Vicksburg; meanwhile, fearing exactly that, Washington was ordering Rosecrans to advance, and giving him a deadline for doing so. Finally, long after the threatened date had come and gone, Rosecrans moved. After such a long wait, he did so with surprising speed, skill, and agility. His army, 65,000 strong, lay around Murfreesboro; Bragg with 44,000 was twenty miles to the south, in two corps, Polk on the left at Shelbyville, and Hardee on the right at Wartrace. On June 26 Rosecrans advanced, in five corps, and noisily threatened Bragg's left while maneuvering around his right. Bragg took the bait, prepared to fight on Polk's front, and then was levered out of position by the news of Union troops on his right. In heavy rain that turned the roads to quagmires, he retreated fifteen miles to Tullahoma. Rosecrans then advanced to Manchester, and sent his cavalry to take the crossings of the Elk River, which would cut off Bragg's retreat. Forrest's cavalry won that race, however, and Bragg, with his line of retreat secure, took advantage of it, and fell back again. There was now no good defensive position this side of the Tennessee River, thirty miles southeast, so Bragg went all the way back there, rain falling all the time and troops cursing all the way. By the end of the first week of July, Rosecrans had cleared all of central Tennessee, and done so practically without fighting. He was so pleased that he sat down, well short of the Tennessee River, and spent another six weeks reorganizing his army.

The fact that Bragg did not want to fight made Rosecrans's maneuver look only a little less brilliant than it actually was. In fact, it was a strategic success of considerable magnitude; with Bragg forced back across the Tennessee, and clinging to Chattanooga, all sorts of possibilities opened up to the Union forces. From this area, they could move into Alabama and cut the South again, by operating through that state to Mobile; alternatively, they could drive toward Atlanta in Georgia, now become virtually the rail hub of the Confederacy; or they might move northeast against Knoxville to clear east Tennessee, less reward-ing strategically, but dear to President Lincoln's heart. Rosecrans's suc-cess was completely overshadowed in the popular mind by the bloody events of Vicksburg and Gettysburg, which took place concurrently with it, but he had accomplished a major advance. That was lost on neither Washington or Richmond. In the former, the government urged, demanded, that he move forward and capitalize on what had so far been gained. In the latter, the authorities at last acknowledged that something drastic must be done to recoup Confederate fortunes west of the mountains.

It was high time that this area received some major attention. By now, July of 1863, things looked parlous indeed for the whole western Confederacy. Most of it, indeed, was now gone. With Union troops firmly in control of the Mississippi Valley, Texas, Arkansas, and most of Louisiana could be written off, and soldiers from these states would not go home again until the war was over, if they were lucky enough to live that long. Kentucky was now secure for the Union, and west and central Tennessee were occupied by Federal forces; this left the Confederacy the Gulf Coast and Atlantic Coast states, from Mississippi to Virginia. Even that was deceptive, however, for Florida was thinly populated, and many of the Atlantic ports and coastal islands were already occupied, while the major ports remaining in Confederate hands were closely blockaded. Ever so slowly, the Union was strangling the Confederacy, and if this trend were to be reversed, it would have to be done soon. Given the face-off in the east, the best, perhaps the only, place to do it was around Chattanooga.

This in turn presented Jefferson Davis with a dilemma, one largely of his own devising: the command problem. He still trusted Braxton Bragg, even after the general had given up central Tennessee without a fight, but Davis was practically the only one who felt that way. Bragg's subordinates, Polk and Hardee, were even more disgruntled than they had been four months ago, and they had then been on the verge of mutiny. But Davis's problem was not simply that he liked Bragg; it was also that he could not find anyone suitable to replace him even if he wanted to do so. Neither Polk nor Hardee was entirely trustworthy, nor capable of commanding a full army; Hardee at least seemed to recognize that, though Polk did not. He was quite sure that a man who could be a bishop could be an army commander too. If Davis could not find an in-house successor in whom he had confidence, he might have looked farther afield. But the pickings there were also lean. Officially, Joseph E. Johnston was still in command of the Confederate Department of the West, but he and Davis cordially disliked each other, and Johnston was just another retreater. If Davis had to have a commander who would not fight, he might as well have one he liked. Then there was Pierre Gustave Toutant Beauregard, off commanding the Carolina coast area, but he had already failed in the West, and been relieved of command there a year ago, so he was another senior general Davis did not like.

That left Robert E. Lee. After Gettysburg, Lee had offered to submit his resignation if it were thought desirable that he should do so. The mere fact of that was an example of Lee's superiority of character over practically every other major figure in the whole history of the Confederacy; almost every other man, from Davis on down, accounted for mistakes by blaming them on someone else. It was of course unthinkable that Lee's offer should be accepted. For practical purposes, he *was* the Army of Northern Virginia, an identification that would grow ever stronger as times got worse. Davis did consider, however, the possibility of sending Lee west at least temporarily, in an attempt to retrieve the situation in Tennessee. The two discussed it, but Lee was not really willing to go. His identification with his army, and his state, was as strong as its identification with him, and he really preferred not to leave his home ground. That was indeed probably the greatest shortcoming of the master tactician: either Lee could not see, or he chose not to see, the larger strategic difficulty of the Confederacy, that he might win his own war in the east, and still see his country destroyed from the west.

Yet Davis had to do something about the crisis. He was beset not only by the problems of military command, and dealing with prickly personalities; compared to the soldiers with all their faults, the civilian politicians were even worse. The Western Concentration Block, led by Senator Louis T. Wigfall of Texas, one of Davis's most virulent enemies, bombarded the Confederate executive with plans and suggestions for western operations. Wigfall and his supporters were hand in glove with both Johnston and Beauregard, and they vigorously pushed elaborate and unrealistic plans that the ebullient Beauregard pulled out of the air. The Louisianan was a more or less competent field commander, but when he put pen to paper, his imagination soared. Now he thought Johnston could be reinforced and Rosecrans crushed, after which the

victorious Confederate armies of the west could march to the Mississippi and destroy Grant and the Union armies there. It was all the kind
of cloud castle with which Confederate strategists were increasingly
often defying reality. Still, something had to be done. . . .

Out of all this came a scaled-down strategic concept. There was one
man in high position in the Army of Northern Virginia who would
go west to see what might be accomplished. Lee talked the situation
over with General Longstreet, and Old Pete expressed his willingness
to be detached, with his corps, to be added temporarily to the Army
of Tennessee. Just as Rosecrans again lurched into action, advancing
toward Chattanooga in mid-August, the Confederates reached a decision: Johnston must send 9,000 men from Alabama and Mississippi to
reinforce Bragg, and Longstreet and two divisions of the Army of
Northern Virginia would also move to Chattanooga. That was as much
as the Western Concentration advocates were going to get, and it had
better do the job.

The Confederates were nearly too late. Rosecrans began his advance
on Chattanooga on August 16. Again he had five corps, McCook,
Granger, Thomas, and Crittenden, and Stanley's Cavalry Corps. As he
had at Tullahoma, he advanced on a broad front, cleverly deceiving
Bragg as to the real weight and direction of his move. It looked as if
he were heading for crossings of the Tennessee River upstream from
Chattanooga, but in fact, while Crittenden noisily demonstrated upstream, Sheridan's division of McCook reached the river downstream,
at Caperton's Ferry, quickly seized a crossing, and got over the river.
This was far more dangerous than the other flank, for it threatened
Bragg's line of supply and retreat back into Georgia. To put pressure
on that line, the Western and Atlantic Railroad, Rosecrans would have
to push his troops across two mountain lines, Racoon Mountain and
Lookout Mountain, and the tangled country east of them and south of
Chattanooga, but there was not a great deal of Confederate strength to
stop them, and Bragg found himself in serious difficulties right from
the start.

He responded with his usual move: he retreated. Not that there was
much else he could have done, in these circumstances, but giving up
Chattanooga, apparently without a fight, did not look good, and did
little to improve morale and relations in his command. But as Federal
troops pushed east over the mountains, Bragg welcomed in his new
reinforcements, the troops from Johnston, and he eagerly awaited the

arrival of Longstreet and his nine brigades. These had to take a round-about route that strained Confederate rail capacity to its limits, for concurrent with Rosecrans's move, Burnside had advanced in east Tennessee, and had taken Knoxville, cutting the direct rail link between Chattanooga and Virginia. Longstreet's men rode the rails all the way down through the Carolinas, across to Atlanta, and from there up to Chattanooga. While they did so, Bragg looked for a place to fight.

The situation finally held some promise for the Confederate army. Bragg had his own troops more or less concentrated, and he was well served by his cavalry, screening in a wide arc in front of him to the westward. The Union forces were rather spread out, Crittenden's XX Corps occupying Chattanooga, but Thomas with the XIV Corps pushing across Lookout Mountain, a good fifteen miles from Crittenden, and not in direct communication with him, and McCook also pushing over the mountain, but another twenty miles from Thomas, and again not within direct supporting distance. Thomas, working his way through Stevens' Gap on Lookout, pushed his advanced division, under Major General James S. Negley, about eight miles ahead, across the next hill line, Missionary Ridge, through a hollow know as McLemore's Cove, and into Dug Gap of Pigeon Mountain. Bragg decided to snap up this isolated unit, and began concentrating two corps, plus part of Polk's corps as well, to do it. The plan fell apart when Crittenden began to advance south from Chattanooga, whereupon the Confederate corps commanders took matters into their own hands, maneuvered independently, and let Negley get away. Bragg was furious, but as he usually seemed to be in that state, no one paid much attention. Now he had to look once again for a place to trap the Federals; they were through the worst of the mountains now, and developing lateral communications through McLemore's Cove. Still, something might be done, and Bragg massed his army along a sluggish, dull stream known as Chickamauga Creek, an Indian name sometimes translated as "the river of death."

For one of the few times in the entire war, the Confederates achieved battlefield superiority in numbers. Bragg managed to amass 62,000 men, about three quarters of them infantry, which he disposed in six corps, two of cavalry and four of infantry, the latter averaging about 8,000 men each. Longstreet's corps of 6,000, led by John Bell Hood's division, began arriving from Virginia on the early morning of the battle, and had to stumble around in the dark trying to find its positions for the morning assault.

Rosecrans had managed to delude himself that the Confederates were in headlong retreat, and Bragg helped him by spreading rumors to that effect. But gradually the Union general realized that such was not the case, and he moved, a little too slowly, to concentrate his forces. Crittenden continued marching south from Chattanooga, moving, although he did not know it, across the right front of Bragg's dispositions. The reason for this ignorance was that Rosecrans expected an attack, if it came, from the south, and he therefore had most of his weak cavalry force out scouting in that direction, and thus could not penetrate the Confederate cavalry screen to his east. On the eve of battle then, his forces were deployed from north to south: Crittenden, Thomas, and McCook, with Mitchell's cavalry trailing off from there. Granger's reserve corps was back in Chattanooga, starting south but out of supporting distance, and the three infantry corps that constituted Rosecrans's main body were still not entirely linked up. This would be all right if Bragg were doing what Rosecrans wanted him to be doing.

He was not. Bragg planned, on the morning of September 18, to attack Crittenden's left flank, and cut him off from Granger and Chattanooga, and at the same time to push troops in on Crittenden's right, blocking Thomas and McCook to the south. If he succeeded, he would gobble up Crittenden's corps, and then have the other two Union forces isolated and at his mercy.

Unfortunately for him, the plan did not work. It was a little too sophisticated for the coordination possible over winding roads and dirt tracks, and through swamps, and the Confederates spent almost the entire day trying to make their approaches and get in position. Rosecrans, seeing all the dust they raised, finally twigged to what was happening, and ordered Thomas and McCook to march north as fast as they could. With slightly better roads to move on than the Rebels, Thomas got his corps moved north, and during the night of September 18–19, took up positions in back of and on either side of Crittenden. By dawn of the 19th, the Federals still did not know that half the Confederate army was west of Chickamauga Creek and about to hit them, and Bragg did not know he was about to hit two Union corps instead of one. He planned for the day to do what he had planned to do the day before.

Unlike Gettysburg, with its clear vistas and excellent observation sites, the battlefield of Chickamauga is a confusing welter of winding trails and tangled thickets. The Union forces were generally disposed in a north-south line along a little rise that parallels and is just west of Lafayette Road. Behind their center was a horseshoe-shaped hill called Snodgrass Hill, and that more or less covered the road that ran back to and across the much more dominant Missionary Ridge. Chickamauga Creek meandered along, anywhere from a mile to three miles east of the Lafayette Road; the ground between the two was cut up in a few fields along the road, running down into low ground, swamp, and tangles of woods and alders. Early on the morning of the 19th, Thomas, believing that the Confederates had one brigade across on his side of the stream, ordered a division forward to push it back. This developed into a full-scale fight that gradually drew in most of Thomas's corps, and elements from Crittenden's as well. While this was going on, McCook got his people up on the southern end of the battlefield and moved them into position there.

By the day's end, Rosecrans had done marginally better than Bragg had, which is to say, he had a slightly clearer picture of what was going on than his opponent. Bragg's troops had spent the day in heavy but piecemeal fighting, and though almost his entire army had been engaged at one point or another, he did not know it. When Longstreet arrived late in the evening, Bragg told him that he had had fairly heavy skirmishing that day, but was planning to envelop the enemy's left early the next morning. On the other side, Thomas's men, when not engaged in fighting for their lives, had thrown up log breastworks at several places along their line, had been reinforced from their right, and were as ready as they could be for the storm they now knew was coming at them.

Finally, on the 20th, Bragg's army was at last ready for the battle its commander had wanted to launch for three or four days. Or at least most of it was ready. Polk decided to have a leisurely breakfast and read the newspapers before he got his people going, thus causing a significant gap in the timing of Bragg's succession of attacks. Nonetheless, the Confederates hit hard against Thomas's left, northern flank, gradually bending it back. Both sides fought tenaciously, little charges and countercharges across the few open fields, and regiments standing up to volley at each other at close range. With Forrest's cavalry out on the flank, Breckinridge of Walker's corps began to lap around the

Union flank. Patrick Cleburne, one of the best divisional commanders in the entire Confederacy, smashed into the bend of Thomas's line, and it began to wilt under the pressure. With Thomas calling for reinforcements, the battle spread south along the line, and by late morning, was in full cry. Bragg, thwarted in his hope of a successful turning and rolling up of the enemy line, now launched a series of what became bloody frontal assaults, and the carnage was unbelievable, whole units reduced to a few men, trees stripped of leaves and limbs, dead everywhere and wounded leaving a bloody trail behind them. By noon the Federals were still holding their general line, and the Confederates continued pressing on with foolhardy bravery.

At this point the battle fell apart. Rosecrans, from his headquarters in the rear of the battle line, had handled himself well up to now. He continued shuffling units about in response to the calls from his corps commanders. About noon he was moving Sheridan and Davis's divisions of McCook north to reinforce Thomas, when he noticed what appeared to be a gap in his center. He sent a staff officer with orders to General Thomas J. Wood to fill the gap, to "close up and support Reynolds." Now it happened that, unseen by headquarters, there was another division, Brannan's, between Wood and Reynolds, so the only way the order could be obeyed was for Wood to pull his troops out of line, march them behind Brannan, and form on Reynolds. Wood might have pointed this out, but earlier in the day, he had been publicly yelled at by Rosecrans, always intemperate in language and virtually incoherent in a battle, for not obeying orders quickly enough. Determined not to let it happen again, come what may, and thinking that after all the army commander knew more than he did, Wood formed his division and took it out of the line.

He thus left a quarter-mile gap wide open in the Union position, and into it charged two full divisions, McLaws's and Hood's, of Longstreet's corps. Firing as they came, shrieking and yelling, they bore right through the Union line like a gray tidal wave. They turned Brannan's flank, they smashed aside Sheridan's and Davis's divisions, they lapped up toward Rosecrans's headquarters, they crushed everything in front of them; they looked as though they could go all the way to Chattanooga and the Tennessee River without pausing for breath.

Here if ever in the history of battle was heaven-sent opportunity for one side, disaster for the other. Or so it should have been, and nearly was. On came the triumphant Confederates, and hundreds of Union soldiers ran before them; from privates to generals, they took off for parts north and west, and some, most notably William S. Rosecrans, carried off in the flood with several other generals, did not stop until they were back in Chattanooga. All of that was perfectly normal, and only to be expected. What was not expected was how many men did not run. Brannan's people, and Reynolds's beyond them, pulled back their flank and ended up on the southern slopes of Snodgrass Hill; hundreds of stragglers joined in with wandering regiments, and threw together a firing line, and far sooner than it might have done, the Union army was reacting to the pressure. Thomas, apprised of the collapse in his rear, came across and threw in a few more regiments. Far to the north, Granger, whose corps had not even been in the battle, hastened a few units south onto the field. By mid-afternoon, what might have been utter shambles was a viable position, bent back upon itself, around Snodgrass Hill, with George H. Thomas, ever after called "The Rock of Chickamauga," sitting calmly in the middle of it, sending troops here and there, getting ammunition distributed, and organizing his battle. Time and again the Rebels came charging up the hill, to be met with rifles, bayonets, and in some cases rifle butts and rocks. Try as they might, they could not break through the charmed circle. When blessed dusk came down on the hill, the bluecoats were still there, and both sides were glad to give up fighting.

Essentially a soldier's battle, Chickamauga was a brutal and costly one, and the casualty figures belie the appearance of Confederate victory. As mentioned, this was one of the few battles in which the Confederates outnumbered the Federals, and the casualty figures, given the tactical advantage handed to Bragg by the famous "muddled order," were surprising. Union losses were 16,200, and Confederate 18,500, twenty-eight percent of either side. Few armies could stand up to that kind of wear, but the Union could stand it better than the Confederacy.

Ironically, even with Rosecrans pushed back into Chattanooga and besieged there, which he was in the immediate aftermath of the battle, the Confederates were far from elated by their victory. Theoretically, Chickamauga should have erased the dismay over Gettysburg and Vicksburg, but it seemed to have more the opposite effect. Daniel Harvey Hill, who led a corps there, said that Chickamauga was recognized as the beginning of the end by the Confederate soldier, that the man in the ranks realized that if they could not win a clear-cut victory under those conditions, they could not do it at all.

One other result of the battle was a housecleaning of higher officers. Hill was so loud in his criticism of Bragg that it cost him a promotion, and Bragg removed Polk from command and ordered a court-martial for him—an order Davis later canceled—and got rid of a couple of other corps commanders as well. This among the victors. On the other side, Rosecrans tried to blame his defeat on his corps commanders, too; Thomas was obviously untouchable, but he preferred charges against Crittenden and McCook, and he also removed Negley from his command. All three were subsequently acquitted of the charges.

———

While the commanders engaged in this game of beggar-my-neighbor, the troops tried to survive. Rosecrans had now completely surrendered the initiative, and let himself get shut up in Chattanooga with an army of 40,000 men. Except for the city itself, he had surrendered the entire south bank of the Tennessee River. Bragg, following up his victory, closely invested the town, and occupied the commanding heights, the abrupt end of Lookout Mountain to the southwest and Missionary Ridge to the east and south. These were enormously formidable positions, just from geography alone, and there seemed little Rosecrans could do about it.

One reason he could do little was because his army soon went hungry. The Confederates controlled the river on either side of the city, and land transport was either broken by Rebel cavalry, or just collapsed under the fall weather and the strain of feeding so many inactive and immobile mouths. There was one single line operating from central Tennessee, and the soldiers were quickly on short rations.

Yet the Union had learned nothing if not how to cope with defeat and crisis. Within a week of Chickamauga, two corps were on the way from the Army of the Potomac as reinforcements for Tennessee, and men were also moving east from Memphis and Vicksburg. The War Department also turned its attention to the command situation. In mid-October it consolidated the whole trans-Appalachian area, except for New Orleans, into one giant Military Division of the Mississippi, and gave the command to Grant. Under him were to be the Army of the Tennessee, commanded by William T. Sherman, consisting of the troops not shut up in Chattanooga, and the Army of the Cumberland, made up of those who were. To command it, Grant could have Rosecrans or Thomas; whom did he want? He chose Thomas; when the order appointing the new commander was read out to the troops in Chattanooga, they broke ranks and cheered like madmen.

Soon after this, Grant himself appeared in Chattanooga to confer with Thomas. Could the city be held? Of course, replied Thomas, known even from his student days at West Point for his imperturbability. The chief problem was supplies, and Grant left to set about organizing them, as well as the relief of the city. The supply problem was resolved by the end of October. Cleverly seizing bridgeheads on the south bank of the river, the Union forces reopened a railroad route that ran almost to the city, and this "Cracker-barrel line" brought enough into the city to keep the garrison there going.

Meanwhile, Grant moved more and more troops toward Chattanooga, and by the third week of November he was ready for operations. He had Sherman push across the river above the city, and Hooker below. With them on either side of Thomas, he was ready for a major fight. His idea was that Sherman should attack first, roll up the Confederate right, and then as Thomas came on, the Confederates would be pushed south off their ridgelines.

While all this was going on, Bragg had remained essentially quiescent. He had not bothered Chattanooga, being content to invest it closely, and he seems to have spent most of his time writing letters of complaint about his subordinates. There was one additional distraction. In east Tennessee, Ambrose Burnside had begun to advance at last, and early in November, Bragg sent Longstreet and his corps, as well as Wheeler's cavalry, off to help slow down the Federals there. So he had managed to surrender the initiative, weaken his army, and cause disaffection among his commanders all at once. The Confederacy was going to pay a high price for President Davis's support of Braxton Bragg.

Sherman's move and proposed attack were delayed by heavy rains, washed-out bridges, and the general difficulty of the country. On November 23, then, Grant ordered Thomas to launch a small-scale attack, a reconnaissance in force, against some of the outlying positions of Missionary Ridge, just to see how many Confederates were there and what might be going on. This was carried out quite handily, taking a hill called Orchard Knob, and had the desired effect; it made Bragg cancel further reinforcements for Longstreet up against Burnside. It also set the stage for the next two days, which provided as dramatic fighting, in as grand a scene, as anything in the entire war, or indeed in the whole range of military history.

Grant's plan for the 24th was that Sherman should attack Missionary Ridge from the north, while Hooker fought his way past Lookout Mountain at the other end of the battle line. Then Thomas would move forward in the center, and the whole Confederate position could be driven. Sherman's men did manage to take some ground, but did not make as much progress as hoped, being delayed by their approach march and by confusions about the lie of the terrain. But on the other flank, Hooker's men surpassed themselves and all expectations as well.

Lookout Mountain offers one of the most spectacular vistas in the eastern United States. The long north-south ridge ends in a plateau, about 1,100 feet in the air, which drops off abruptly to the Tennessee River. The plateau overlooks the river's Moccasin Bend, as well as the city of Chattanooga. Both from the top and from the bottom it looks impregnable. The Confederates had got some guns up to the top, and had posted two brigades along the slopes of the mountain, digging trenches and rifle pits in among the tumbled boulders and fallen trees. The position was in fact, however, quite deceptive; in profile the slope was a sort of lazy S, the upper curve being concave and the lower convex. What that meant in practice was that guns posted on the top could not be brought to bear on the too-steep slope, and men posted in the middle did not have much of a field of fire; not only were there lots of obstructions, but the slope of the hill provided an attacker with a good deal of sheltered ground.

This was what Fighting Joe Hooker's infantry found when they came up against it. Hooker's orders for the day were to push around the base of the mountain and get behind, east of it, ready to advance south toward the Confederate communications. His troops did that, pushing past the Confederate brigade posted at the base of the mountain. Then they turned hard right, and started climbing the slopes. By late morning they were fighting around Craven's Farm, a white house that was one of the few marks on the side of the mountain discernible from Chattanooga. No one at either headquarters could figure out exactly what was going on; the top of the mountain was shrouded in low cloud, its tendrils drifting down the slopes, and gradually the cloud and battle smoke totally obscured the view. Inside that smoke men fought and climbed, and panted and puffed, and tried to form lines, and little groups rushed here and there, running from cover to cover, while the fight swirled around and over the Craven farm. When it finally ended about mid-afternoon, the Rebels had gone, driven back out of reach, and the exhausted bluecoats sat down to catch their breath and try to figure out where they were.

With the main position on the slope lost, the plateau at the top could not be held, and the Confederates pulled out during the night. The next morning a group of the 8th Kentucky Infantry climbed to the top and hoisted the Stars and Stripes on the edge of the cliff, and Lookout Mountain became "The Battle Above the Clouds." Hooker's men had done the all-but-impossible, and even today, hikers who walk the trail with no one trying to stop them are proud of making the top.

Yet even that was not the most spectacular event of the whole. The next day, the 25th, Grant continued with his general plan for the battle. Accordingly, Sherman launched a heavy assault on the end of the Missionary Ridge position. This was a semidetached spur named Tunnel Hill, and it was now held by Cleburne's division of Hardee's corps. They were every bit as determined to hold it as Sherman's men were to take it, and they had good defensive positions. For more than five hours the two sides slugged away at each other, with the Federals paying heavily for every little bit of ground they gained. By mid-afternoon they were pretty well fought out, and though they did get Tunnel Hill eventually, they could not cross the saddle that anchored it to the main ridgeline.

Hooker was equally held up on the right flank, more by terrain than by Confederates, but by about three o'clock the battle was clearly losing momentum. At that point Grant decided to probe the Confederate center.

Here, along two and a half miles of ridge, Breckinridge's corps had dug three lines of trenches, one at the bottom, one halfway up, and one at the top. It looked better than it was, for none was complete, and they were not within really effective supporting distance of each other—and Breckinridge was not strong enough to hold them anyway. Grant asked Thomas to see if he could carry the first line, at the bottom of the ridge, and Thomas sent out four of his divisions to try. The troops formed up and soon after three-thirty they advanced in good order and swept up to and over the first line. The Confederates, after a not-too-spirited defense, went back up to the second line, and from there opened a distant but annoying plunging fire on the bluecoats below them. The Federal company and regimental officers realized they could not stay where they were; it was either go forward or go back, and their blood was up now, so quite independently they started forward. The story, perhaps apocryphal, is that Sheridan pulled out a bottle of whiskey, drained the last of it, lobbed it up and hill, and yelled out, "Here's how! Let's go! Follow me!"—and up they went, yelling, shouting, encouraging each other on, swarming up the hill. Back on Orchard Knob, Grant turned to Thomas and asked archly, "By whose orders are those men going up there?" and Old Tom opined, "By their own, I guess."

Up they went, and over the second line, while the discomfited Confederates again fired their broken volleys and fled up the hill. There was not much to stop the Federals now, except the hill itself, and on they went, racing to the top. No one knows who reached the top first, though several regiments subsequently claimed that they had done so, but they burst almost simultaneously onto the crest of the ridge and immediately began spreading left and right, new parties getting up all the time. Little knots of Confederates fought bravely, or turned and ran, or surrendered in the confusion, and all control of the battle had long been lost.

The whole feat, again an absolutely remarkable one even when one understands the nature of the terrain and the difficulties of defense, took but an hour, from the troops moving off until they reached the crest and broke the last Confederate line, one of those perfectly glorious moments in which men transcend what they are supposed to be capable of doing. The Federals were so happy, so elated, and so disorganized that they hardly knew what to do next. Only Sheridan, running here and there along the top, had sufficient presence of mind to try to organize a pursuit, and his division did bag about 2,000 prisoners, though many other Confederates escaped, hustled and humiliated.

Among them were not only General Breckinridge, whose corps was practically destroyed, but Braxton Bragg as well. Thus the Confederate Army of Tennessee lost Chattanooga and lost its pride. The remains of the army limped back into Georgia, bitter in its shame, while its generals blamed each other for their failures, and the hard-won laurels of Chickamauga withered under the bludgeons of November.

Part IV

DYING

Chapter 14

Problems of Command and Strategy

T HE END OF 1863 brought entire satisfaction to neither side, nor could it have been said to have brought much to many people in either country. Scarcely a home, North or South, did not now feel the full burden of the war, and few men believed it could have gone on this long, with as little tangible result. After two years of solid fighting, and nearly three of war, where now were the fanciful visions of glory, of the elegant fanfare of war as chivalry, as a modern tournament out of Sir Walter Scott, all blushing maidens and uniformed gallants? The blushing maidens were running farms or plantations, or nursing amputees, and had long learned not to blush. And all too many of the young heroes were lying face down in the thickets of Virginia, or languishing in prison camps, or sitting staring at the wall from wheelchairs. If people could see the end product, they would seldom go to war as enthusiastically as they do.

The war cared nothing for all this. War, like the famous illustration of Hobbes's *Leviathan,* consumes all it comes in contact with, treasure, resources, above all bodies. Even the most sophisticated of maneuvers, carried out by a Turenne or a Frederick the Great or a MacArthur, still ends the same, with charred machines and dead bodies. And the war became its own justification; the very fact of its horrible nature meant no one could quit now. To stop short of victory would be to betray all those who had already suffered. The Union must continue until the South was defeated; the South must persevere to victory. The question was not, Should we continue? but rather, *How* should we continue?

———

In the Confederate capital, it was obvious that the options were narrowing. There was no longer hope of foreign intervention, of, say, the Royal Navy contemptuously brushing aside the Union's blockade to deliver recognition, money, and supplies to the Rebel cause. Nor was there, now, much realistic hope of straightforward military victory. The Mississippi, and with it the entire western Confederacy, were gone, the invasion of Pennsylvania had failed, and the victory of Chickamauga had turned to ashes in the disgraceful rout—it was little less than that—of Chattanooga. There were food riots in Richmond, and everywhere the chorus of complaint rose to the skies.

It is ironic that President Davis, who died revered as the embodiment of the Lost Cause, was so thoroughly vilified while he was actually functioning as the Confederacy's president. Southerners, especially their politicians, laid a great deal of their dissatisfaction at the president's door. Much of this was unfair; there were simply weaknesses in Southern society that made it incapable of meeting the challenge it assumed, of asserting its independence, both systemic weaknesses and those of resources. Yet part of the problem was indeed Davis himself.

Personally he could be a charming man, as long as he got his own way. But he took any disagreement over policy as an affront to Davis the man, so he tended to see what might have been reasonable and legitimate policy questions as personal antagonism. And indeed, unless one were a member of the charmed circle around the president, he was easy to dislike. His cabinet meetings were unstructured, long digressive ramblings that seldom reached any decision. He could not bring himself to delegate authority, especially in the military sphere, and thus trying to do too much, he left much undone. Above all, he was argumentative; when his field commanders dared to disagree with him, he sent them long, carefully reasoned legal briefs, which proved with irrefutable logic that they, and reality, were wrong, and that he, Jefferson Davis, was not only right, but that there could not possibly be any other conclusion than the one he himself had drawn. A reader of these missives might well suspect that winning his point was more important to Davis than winning the war; in more homely idiom, he could not see the forest for the trees, or, he threw the baby out with the bathwater.

All of this might have been tolerable had the South possessed half a dozen Robert E. Lees, for Davis and his chief field commander remained remarkably sympathetic and mutually respectful. But it did not. It had Lee in Virginia, but he wanted to remain there. The other men who enjoyed Davis's confidence, such as Polk and Bragg, were lesser men altogether; and other senior generals, such as Beauregard and Joe Johnston, were not in the president's camp or his good graces either.

This must surely be one of the more notable failures of the Confederacy: its inability to evolve excellent senior commanders. By and large the Confederacy ended the war with those army commanders it had at the beginning. Some of course died, most particularly Albert Sidney Johnston and Stonewall Jackson, but it remains difficult to avoid the suspicion that giving more responsibility to more junior men, to figures such as Nathan Bedford Forrest and Patrick Cleburne, or perhaps Edmund Kirby Smith or Richard Taylor, for example, would have served the Confederate cause well. Instead such men were left in corps command, or put in positions where their talents, no matter how remarkable, were of marginal use to a state fighting for its life. This kind of narrow-mindedness on Davis's part, and selfishness and insistence on seniority within the officer corps, was a luxury the South could not afford.

They were far from beaten yet, however. There were shortages, there was conscription, much territory had been lost, but those who were left must fight all the harder. By now the Confederacy was losing whatever strategic initiatives it had possessed; it looked now like a matter of doggedly hanging on until the North tired of the effort. If the cost of winning could be raised prohibitively high for the Union, then it might give up. In 1864 there was to be a presidential election in the North; unless there were some startling success for Lincoln and his crew of Black Republicans, they might be turned out. The Confederacy could hope to win in the election booth what it had not been able to win immediately on the field of battle. So it was the same old story: Tighten your belt, and your grip, and hang on.

————

And for the Union as well, it was a matter of not giving up. In his annual message to Congress at the end of 1863, President Lincoln remarked, "It is easy to see that, under the sharp discipline of civil war, the nation is beginning a new life." A few weeks earlier, in November, speaking at the dedication of a national military cemetery at Gettysburg, he had called for a renewed devotion to "a new birth of freedom," so that "government of the people, by the people, for the people, shall not perish from the earth." Those noble phrases, and the ideal they embodied, must be sustained at whatever cost. But it remained difficult to see what the cost might be, or how long the Union would have to pay it.

An immediate problem was the Union command situation, and at last, after his many tries, Lincoln found the right answer in the right man. It was of course the man he could not spare, because "he fights." After the stunning victories around Chattanooga, General Grant had been busy over the turn of the year neatening up his department, securing the Union hold in east Tennessee, for example, and undertaking operations against Joe Johnston in northern Mississippi. In early March, promoted to the newly revived grade of lieutenant general, the first to hold it since George Washington, Grant was ordered east to the capital.

Washingtonians, who were used to sounding trumpets, hardly knew what to make of Grant, a small, compact man in shabby clothes, who did not seem to have a great deal to say for himself. But it was far more important that he and Lincoln hit it off, and they seem to have gotten along well from the start. At their first formal meeting, Lincoln tendered his general the thanks of the country, and Grant replied that he had done his best, and would continue to do so. He was now placed in command of all the Union armies in the field, and he decided, after a mere week in Washington, that he would have to remain in the east. His original intention had been to return west and direct operations from there, but a week around the capital showed him that the political pulling and hauling here was so great that only the general-in-chief could resist it.

The day after his visit with Lincoln, he went out to look at the Army of the Potomac and meet George Meade, whom he had known, in passing, during the Mexican War. This was a potentially touchy proposition, in part because Meade's army had recently been reorganized yet again, melting its several corps down into three, and there were assorted senior officers on the lookout for new postings. But Meade himself, in an expression of sentiment rare enough in this war to deserve recording, told Grant that he recognized Grant might want his own man in command of this nearest army, and that he, Meade, was quite willing to step aside for the good of the cause. Grant replied that he was happy to retain the Pennsylvanian in command, and that, though he would probably take the field with the army, he would still prefer to work through parallel headquarters.

This ultimately worked better than it might have been expected to do, though by the closing stages of the war, under the pressure of making immediate decisions, Grant virtually usurped Meade's role. Basically the arrangement worked as well as it did because both men were conscious of their larger mission, and especially because Meade was such a gentleman. As Grant later wrote, "Men who wait to be selected, and not those who seek" offered the most effective service.

After his quick visit, Grant returned to the west to bring about a command reorganization there, and to mature his plans for the campaign that would soon open. Sherman was now to command the Military Division of the Mississippi; he and Grant had already reached substantial understanding on how the war should be conducted from this stage on. There has been some discussion among historians as to who developed what plan when, but the two principals never argued about it; they enjoyed a very real synchronicity of minds, and had a clear picture of what they wanted to do.

Thus when Grant returned to Washington at the end of the month, and discussed his situation with President Lincoln, he had already worked out his main line of advance. The president had himself produced a plan, for a waterborne end-run around Lee's army, and he propounded it with great detail and equal diffidence. He admitted that he really was not a soldier, and that he had no desire to be one, but the generals he had had in the past seemed incapable of action on their own, and so totally unconscious of the political pressures upon the government, that he had been forced essentially to be his own general-in-chief. Grant listened politely, assured the president that he would indeed act, and went away, keeping his own counsel.

Ulysses S. Grant now commanded some 550,000 men in a whole welter of commands. It was impossible both to administer this number and to direct it operationally, so he retained Henry Halleck as his chief of staff, at last finding the position for which Old Brains was actually suited. Grant's war strategy called for two main offensives, and a number of supplementary operations. First of all, he recognized that the character of the war had changed; it was a fight to the finish, and it could be won only by destroying the Confederate will to fight. That in turn could be accomplished either by depriving the Confederacy of the resources with which to sustain the struggle, which was desirable, or by killing Confederates, which was lamentable but necessary. To this end he told Meade: Your object is Robert Lee's army; you go where he goes; fight him and destroy him. He told Sherman the same thing: Destroy Johnston's army.

In practice this meant for Meade an advance straight ahead, or as near as might be, toward Richmond, and bringing Lee to battle. For Sherman it meant advancing from Chattanooga southeast toward Atlanta. Joe Johnston, now in Bragg's place, was in the way, and he too was to be brought to bay, fought, and destroyed.

Supplementary operations were designed to assist these main thrusts, and these were extremely important, for on them, and their success or failure, rests much of Grant's reputation. Taken in their bare outlines, the two main thrusts of Grant's operation looked like little more than a recipe for butchery. There was, however, more to it than that. Grant intended that Sherman's advance should be supported by a land move against Mobile. In southern Louisiana, around New Orleans, General Nathaniel Banks commanded a substantial force. Unfortunately, Banks was already committed to another operation, and thereby hangs a tale.

The American Civil War meant that the United States was in no position to enforce the famous Monroe Doctrine, which had stated that European intervention in the western hemisphere would meet American disapprobation and, if necessary, resistance. Therefore when Mexico went bankrupt, as it periodically did during the nineteenth century, and defaulted on payment of its bonds to European investors, Emperor Napoleon III of France decided to take over the country and establish there a colonial empire. To rule it he found an out-of-work archduke, Maximilian of Austria, and this unfortunate and his lovely and ambitious wife, Carlotta, were soon sitting uneasily in Mexico City, supported by a French army and unmindful of Voltaire's famous dictum that you can do anything with bayonets except sit on them. Because of all this, the Washington government intensely desired to assert a Federal presence in the state of Texas, and over the winter of 1863–64 developed the idea of an expedition up the Red River from New Orleans, penetrating into western Louisiana and ultimately, it was expected, into the Lone Star State itself. This entire area was already cut off from the Confederacy, of course, and was known in Confederate quarters as "Kirby Smithdom," after the able general who commanded it in splendid isolation. Both Grant and Sherman thought this was a useless diversion of effort, and even General Banks, to give him his due, was against it. But it looked good in Washington; Halleck, musing over Jomini, thought it was a sound idea, and there were numerous politicians and speculators who were all too well aware that the Red River area was bursting with cotton, just begging to be confiscated and sold.

So when Grant wanted Banks and his army available to move against Mobile, in support of Sherman's move on Atlanta, he was told that Banks was busy elsewhere, but never mind, the expedition should be successfully completed in time for a campaign to the eastwards. Unfortunately, that estimate left out of consideration the competence of Kirby Smith, and his able subordinate Richard Taylor, and the incompetence in field command of Nathaniel P. Banks.

The other two subsidiary moves Grant intended were in support of Meade's operations. On the Army of the Potomac's strategic right flank, General Franz Sigel, commanding the Department of West Virginia, would advance south up the Shenandoah Valley, and thus cover that standard avenue from which emanated so many threats to Washington. And on the strategic left flank, there was General Benjamin Butler's Army of the James, two corps strong, located down at the mouth of the Chesapeake. Grant directed that this force, of 33,000 men, should advance up the James River and threaten Richmond from the east and rear while Meade advanced overland across the old Virginia battlefields. In this way Lee's army, and Richmond and all it contained, should be caught between two pincers, one or the other of which, if not both, should score a striking success.

All five of these operations, two directed against Joe Johnston's army and the area supporting it, and three directed against Lee's army and the area supporting it, provided the Union at last with a coherent strategy that should achieve several things. There was concentration both in time and in place, with separate Federal armies operating in such a way as to deprive the Confederacy of the ability to defeat them in detail. And there was as well what might be called a logic of objectives, with the Union aiming both at the main Confederate armies, but also at the main areas from which those armies derived their sustenance. Not since early 1862, with the campaigns that ended with the Seven Days and Shiloh, had the Union produced an overall strategy that was so potentially rewarding, and if everyone did his part, the result would be the final destruction of the rebellion.

The flaw is of course immediately apparent: the command personalities. Grant in the east with Meade under him, Sherman in Tennessee, were men who could deliver. But Commissary Banks, Spoons Butler, and Sigel? The retention of these three in field command defies military sense, for all three had proven inept at best, and downright incompetent at worst, when entrusted with actual operations. Whatever their administrative skills—and all three did indeed possess talents in that area—it was courting disaster to retain them in positions that called for so much responsibility, and contained in them not only the seeds of local failure, but the possibility as well of dislocating the entire overall concept. Unfortunately, all three had political capital to be employed on their own behalf. Butler had strongly identified with the Radical Republicans, and when he was removed from command in New Orleans in December of 1862, he was almost immediately reappointed to command of the Army of the James down at Fortress Monroe. He could be relieved only at Lincoln's peril. This did not become an issue, however, as Grant for some reason rather liked him, and was content to have him remain in the field. Banks was in the same boat, a former Speaker of the House of Representatives, and a former governor of Massachusetts. With those credentials, it hardly mattered if his military record was as lackluster as it was; indeed, he received the official Thanks of Congress for his reduction of Port Hudson after the fall of Vicksburg, an unnecessarily costly operation that he had handled with notable ineptness. Sigel was in a slightly different situation, but his importance derived from the fact of his influence among the German-born immigrants who had so strongly supported the Union cause; for many of them the rallying cry had been "I fights mit Sigel!" After many defeats, their fellow soldiers had often jokingly changed that to "I runs mit Sigel!" but the fact remained that he was important politically, and he happened to be in the wrong command at the wrong time.

———

The potential for all this to go awry is best illustrated by the fate of the infamous Red River expedition, not even part of Grant's overall plan, but a previously decided operation that was supposed to be completed in time for Banks to move east against Mobile in conjunction with Sherman's drive toward Atlanta.

On paper the campaign looked as if it ought not to cause too many problems. Kirby Smith was located at Shreveport, in the the northwest corner of Louisiana; he had about 30,000 men under his command, and his base had become an important supply depot for the western

Confederacy, and the main link with Texas. Banks, Sherman, and General Frederick Steele, who commanded the Union Department of Arkansas, were all ordered to cooperate against him, and they agreed that Banks would command the main force, of some 17,000 men, who would move up the bayou system from New Orleans to Alexandria. There they would meet 10,000 more contributed by Sherman, and commanded by Brigadier General Andrew J. Smith; these would come up the Red River, convoyed by Admiral David Porter, of Vicksburg fame. Finally, Steele was to march 15,000 men south from Arkansas, to link up with the others as opportune. In the event, Steele got started so late the campaign was ended before he took any part in it, so that left Banks with 27,000, more or less concentrated, to deal with Kirby Smith's 30,000 more or less scattered.

The real problem lay less with the Confederates than with Union timing, and especially with the rapid falling of the river levels, for as the Federal flotilla advanced upriver, the water got more and more shallow. Porter and Smith reached Alexandria on March 19, but Banks was a week late, and it took yet another week to get the ships past the rapids just upstream from the town. Meanwhile, Confederate General Richard Taylor, commanding Kirby Smith's field forces along the river, retreated upstream, creating as much delay as he could with his cavalry.

The two armies bumped into each other on April 8 at Sabine Cross Roads, and Banks got badly beaten up, having about 2,500 of his men taken prisoner. He then took up a position at Pleasant Hill, and when the Confederates attacked the next day, they were repulsed in turn, suffering considerably. At the end of the day Kirby Smith arrived and ordered a retreat for the next morning. When day came, however, he found to his delight that Banks had beaten him to it, and was going back himself. Meanwhile Porter and a shipborne contingent had pushed on upriver, only to be stopped finally by obstructions in the river and Confederate field artillery, who found stalled riverboats a juicy target.

The combined Federal forces thus fell back again, to Alexandria, Porter losing a couple of ships to harassing fire on the way. When they got there, they ran into real trouble. The river had fallen to a depth of three feet, and Porter's boats drew seven. He was faced with the possibility of having to abandon his ships, or burn them, and retreat overland with the army units.

The navy was saved from such humiliation by the timely intervention of Colonel Joseph Bailey. A lumberman in civilian life, Bailey said they could dam the river, build up a head of water, and then blow the dam and float the boats through on the flood. It took about a week to do this, but it worked; the water built up behind the dam, the riverboats were brought down, the dam was successfully exploded, and the boats went triumphantly off downstream on the artificial crest of floodwater.

Meanwhile, Taylor had been busily sniping away at boats, Banks's troops, and anything else that looked like it was wearing blue, and his cavalry and light artillery made a thorough nuisance of themselves along the flanks of the Federal retreat. Taylor thought he might try to bag the entire expedition, but Kirby Smith disagreed, and the two fell into an angry correspondence that permanently soured their relations and the western Confederate command structure. The same happened on the Union side; a number of officers resigned in disgust or were relieved, charges flew back and forth, Porter and Banks exchanged bitter notes, and the whole sorry affair collapsed in finger-pointing. Kirby Smith had burned sixty million dollars' worth of cotton rather than see it fall into Yankee hands, and Banks was relieved of command in May, his military career at last over. All the whole expedition really did was throw off stride Grant's coordination of his western offensives.

———

Nonetheless, in spite of this dislocation of the overall plan on one of its margins, the Union still possessed a substantial superiority of men and matériel, and Grant was prepared to utilize it to the fullest possible extent. Among the more than half a million men the Union had under arms, literally thousands were either training, or in garrison, or on leave, or doing useful duty in secondary theaters of operations, for example along the Atlantic coast supporting the blockade. But that generalization is true of the Confederacy as well as the Union; in any organization, military or civilian, it is always amazing how few people actually do the work for which the organization is intended, and how many provide the support or backup services.

There was another problem to be faced as well, one this time of organization rather than of strategy. At some point in 1864, enlistments were going to expire for many of the three-year volunteers of 1861, the men who had formed the backbone of all the Union armies since the real fighting began. It was in the face of this threat that the

Union had resorted to conscription, and it was a threat not faced by the Confederacy, as it had had the wisdom or foresight to enlist and conscript men for the duration. But in the North, there was a very real possibility that so many men might leave the army as to make it almost impossible to pursue the war.

In the spring of 1864, then, the government undertook vigorous measures to get soldiers to re-enlist. It offered bounties of four hundred dollars, plus whatever bounty the separate states might offer in addition. It conferred on these men the title "veteran volunteers" and gave them a little chevron to wear as a mark of distinction. It offered thirty-day furloughs. Most important, in view of unit cohesion, it decreed that in any regiment where three quarters of the men re-enlisted, it would keep the formation together, designating it a veteran regiment. In spite of all these inducements and a great deal of patriotic oratory, less than half the men, about 136,000, signed up again. A great many of them obviously thought they had done their bit, and it was time for others to make the same sacrifices. Oliver Wendell Holmes, for instance, left the army in July of 1864. He felt guilty about doing so for the rest of his life, though after three serious wounds he was probably not really fit for service anyway.

One of the most interesting questions connected with the whole manpower issue was that of enlisting blacks. Here, on both sides of the line, was a quite contentious source of bodies. In the Confederacy, few could bring themselves to face the issue, and it hardly seemed feasible to ask black men to fight in support of a system that was based on keeping them in servitude. Yet Patrick Cleburne thought it might be done, and in the dying days of the war, the Confederate Congress tried to do it. More important, and less fraught with contradiction, was the widespread use of blacks as support personnel and laborers on fortifications. Ironically, slave-owners often protested vehemently against the drafting of their slaves for military labor; in this as in so many other things, they refused to face the facts of the day.

The issue in the North was less complicated but no less contentious. In the early stages of the war, in spite of attempts by individual blacks, and by the few acknowledged black leaders, to get black men into uniform, there was general agreement that this was a white man's war. The North, after all, though less systemically racist than the South, was hardly less racist in its individual attitudes. Yet blacks were casually recruited into the navy, and a few free blacks managed to get into the army. Then as the Union armies found themselves a haven for more and more blacks fleeing from servitude, or liberated by Federal progress around the fringes of the Confederacy, the regulations, and after them the attitudes, began to shift. General David Hunter began recruiting blacks as early as the spring of 1862 in his Department of the South, and when enlistments lagged, he began conscripting them, both moves that President Lincoln officially disapproved. Actually, many were eager to serve, believing, as Frederick Douglass said in an often-quoted passage, "Once let the black man get upon his person the brass letters U.S. . . . and a musket on his shoulder . . . and there is no power on earth which can deny that he has earned the right to citizenship in the United States." Not only did blacks believe it, but many whites feared exactly that.

Still, as in other wars before and since, any blood would do; gradually black enlistment gathered strength in the North, and finally there were 300,000 black soldiers in 166 regiments of United States Colored Troops. They were officered almost exclusively by whites, for some time they were paid at lower pay scales, and they were most often used as labor and support troops. Under the stress of combat conditions, however, these inequities slowly went by the board, and black units gradually won acceptance by fellow combat soldiers. Sharing the opportunity to die is, after all, one of society's great equalizers.

In practice, this particular opportunity was long denied the blacks, and less than half of the regiments saw actual fighting, all of it of course in the later part of the war. The first black unit in combat was the 79th U.S. Colored Infantry, which fought at Island Mounds, Missouri, in October of 1862. One of the most famous black actions was the ill-fated assault by the 54th Massachusetts on Battery Wagner, outside Charleston, South Carolina, on July 18, 1863, in which the regiment lost 272 out of 650 men. The event came hard upon the New York draft riots, and led President Lincoln to ask publicly who deserved better of the republic, the black man who fought to preserve it or the white man who rioted to destroy it?

Southerners less sophisticated or thoughtful than General Cleburne often responded with a visceral hatred to black soldiers, refusing to exchange those unfortunate enough to be taken prisoner, maltreating them and their white officers, who were regarded as traitors to the race. The most notorious example of this was the taking of Fort Pillow on the Mississippi River north of Memphis. It was invested and stormed by Nathan Bedford Forrest's troops on April 12, 1864, and in the general confusion that followed the collapse of the defense, a large number of the black contingent of the garrison was killed. Union charges that it was a blatant massacre were denied by Confederates, who insisted it was but an incident of war, and there has been argument about it ever since, though the weight of evidence does indeed suggest a massacre.

———

All of these various issues, the federal election, the manpower problem, troop retention, the role of black soldiers, would of course become unimportant if the Union could win the war in the spring and summer of 1864. And if it could not, then they might become very important indeed. In the Confederacy as well as in the North men could count and read a calendar, and thinking persons knew that the war was approaching a crisis. The resolution of that crisis was going to depend very largely upon the armies facing each other in northern Georgia and northern Virginia.

As the blossoms burst across the hills of Tennessee and Georgia, William Tecumseh Sherman gathered his forces for the great advance. He had three armies under his command, his old favorite and former command, the Army of the Tennessee, now commanded by James B. McPherson, 24,000 strong; the Army of the Ohio, 13,500 men, formerly Burnside's force around Knoxville, and now under John M. Schofield; and finally the boss of the shield, George H. Thomas's Army of the Cumberland, 61,000 strong. All told there were nearly 90,000 soldiers, as good as any men in the world and commanded by officers who would have made Napoleon's marshals think twice.

Facing them was Joseph E. Johnston, who had replaced the unfortunate Bragg after the defeat at Chattanooga. Johnston's Army of Tennessee contained about 50,000 men, growing to 60,000 early in the campaign; it was divided into corps commanded by Hardee, Polk, and John Bell Hood, with Joe Wheeler as its cavalry commander. On paper Sherman vastly outnumbered Johnston, but the Union army had been hard hit by reorganization and the re-enlistment furloughs, and would take a while to work up to full stride. More important than the disparity in numbers was the fact that the Confederate Army of Tennessee was still not a happy army; morale remained down, the officer cadre was still unsettled, and there was a poor-relation feeling about the whole thing. About to fight for its life and the life of the Confederacy, it was going to have to do better than it had done in the past.

Meanwhile, across the mountains, there was brewing one of the great passages of arms in all military history. For his greatest challenge, Robert E. Lee commanded 64,000 men in the still superb Army of Northern Virginia. Jeb Stuart was in charge of Lee's cavalry corps, and Longstreet, Richard Ewell, and Ambrose Powell Hill each led a corps of infantry. The Army of Northern Virginia might not be quite what it had been this time last year, but it still thought it could lick all the forces of Heaven and Hell combined, and on its record, it was certainly entitled to such an opinion of itself.

It needed such confidence, for north of the Rapidan River lay the Federal forces in daunting numbers. Under his direct control, Grant had George Meade's Army of the Potomac, now disposed in three corps, II under Hancock, V under Warren, and VI under Sedgwick. Ambrose Burnside commanded a separate IX Corps under Grant himself, an awkward arrangement, soon set aside, necessitated by Burnside's seniority. Grant had brought Philip Sheridan east to command his cavalry, now reorganized into a separate corps and ready for some serious action. Altogether the Federal forces totaled 118,000 men, outnumbering the Confederates nearly two to one.

At midnight on May 3, 1864, the Army of the Potomac quietly marched eastward toward the fords across the Rapidan, crossed to the southern bank, and began passing through the Wilderness.

Chapter 15

The Killing Season

MAY IS A beautiful month in Virginia; the trees and shrubs are in bloom, the roads are dry, the weather is generally pleasant, with the stifling summer heat yet to come. The thickets and meadows are alive with insects, birds, and small furry creatures; the earth swells with life.

On the night of May 3–4, there were other sounds as well: the clink of harness and equipment, muffled commands, the sound of hooves, heavy breathing, and the steady tramp of infantry. The Army of the Potomac was on the move, heading south. Ulysses Grant had wanted a quick march, and he had ordered that all unnecessary baggage be left behind; he even marched without a large portion of his artillery. Still, this was an army that always moved at a stately pace, and that liked its creature comforts; even stripped down for action, it had sixty miles of wagon trains in its rear.

The army moved in two large columns. On the eastern flank, Hancock's II Corps led the way across Ely's Ford of the Rapidan, moving southeast toward Chancellorsville. To the west, Warren's V Corps crossed at Germanna Ford, and paralleled Hancock's march. General Meade had split the cavalry corps, and there was a division leading each column, and supposedly scouting to the south and west. They were not doing much good, for as the troops moved into the tangles of the vast area known as the Wilderness, scouting was almost impossible. The roads were little tracks, poorly mapped, often leading to nothing more than abandoned clearings or poor, isolated farmhouses where they trailed off into nothing. The cluttered second-growth forest grew right down to the sides of the roads, and often arched over them,

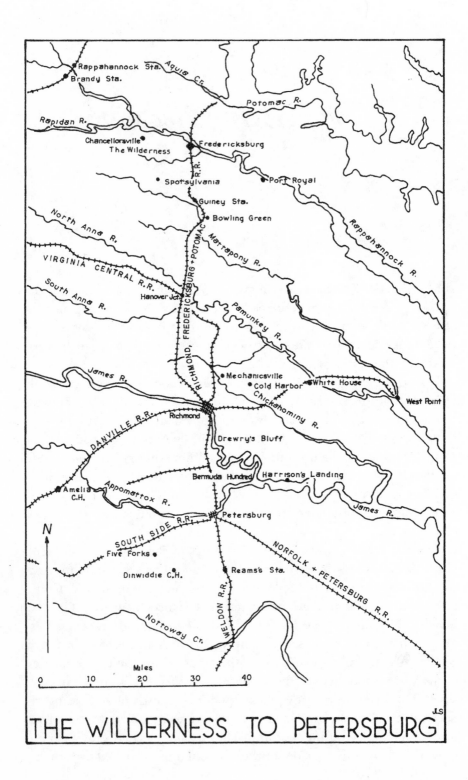

Rappahannock Sta.
Brandy Sta.
Aquia Cr.
Potomac R.
Rapidan R.
Chancellorsville
The Wilderness
Fredericksburg
Port Royal
Rappahannock R.
R.R.
Spotsylvania
Guiney Sta.
Bowling Green
North Anna R.
Marrapony R.
VIRGINIA CENTRAL R.R.
South Anna R.
Hanover Jct.
Pamunkey R.
RICHMOND, FREDERICKSBURG + POTOMAC
James R.
Mechanicsville
Cold Harbor
White House
West Point
Chickahominy R.
DANVILLE R.R.
Richmond
Drewry's Bluff
Bermuda Hundred
Harrison's Landing
Amelia C.H.
Appomattox R.
James R.
Petersburg
N
SOUTH SIDE R.R.
NORFOLK + PETERSBURG R.R.
Five Forks
Dinwiddie C.H.
Reams's Sta.
WELDON R.R.
Nottoway Cr.
Miles
0   10   20   30   40

THE WILDERNESS TO PETERSBURG

JLS

so the troops moved in an all-encompassing blackness that turned slowly to dappled shadow as the sun rose to their left. It was eerie, disturbing country, the atmosphere made even heavier as the troops occasionally came across some pathetic remnant of the fighting in the area the year before, rusted rifles, rotten leather equipment, piles of bones.

By mid-afternoon of the 4th, they were all tangled up. Grant had wanted to march through and get out on the southern side of the tangle in one day, but his trains were so mixed up and falling so far behind the infantry that he ordered a halt. With several hours' daylight left, II Corps bivouacked around Chancellorsville, and Warren's men stopped and took up positions around Old Wilderness Tavern, about five miles west. It was a less than auspicious beginning for a lightning campaign.

As always Robert E. Lee knew what was going on, but he was not in a very good position to do much about it. His army was spread out over a front of more than forty miles, the dispersion made necessary by the Confederates' scarcity of rations. His right flank was covered by Stuart's cavalry, over near Fredericksburg and east of the Federal advance, but on his left, Longstreet's corps was away back around Mechanicsburg, out of easy supporting distance. He had, of course, been thinking of taking the offensive himself, but had been at least slightly lulled by the mistaken assessment that the Federal force was only half the size it actually was. When his patrols brought in the news that the Yanks were on the march, he moved to counter. He sent off orders to Longstreet to bring up his I Corps, and he sent Ewell's II Corps moving northeast to intercept Warren, and A. P. Hill's in support, aiming for Hancock. The Confederates were outnumbered, but they were used to that. Lee thought that if he could catch the Federals while they were still stuck in the Wilderness, his troops' better cross-country skills and superior knowledge of the terrain would offset the numbers problem.

On the morning of the 5th, then, as Griffin's division of Warren's corps moved south, it bumped into Ewell's advance moving east. Neither force knew what it was facing, and the battle quickly grew in size, as more and more units marched to the sound of the guns on either side, and degenerated, as all order and cohesion collapsed in the tangled country. Lee actually did not want a full-scale battle until Longstreet should be able to come in, and Meade and Grant were uncertain exactly what they were facing anyway. While the generals tried to figure out what was going on, and retain some control of their armies, the soldiers took to fighting.

It was a terrible battle; units could barely form, the underbrush was quickly smothered in the low-lying smoke of thousands of rifles, regiments blundered into each other, fired at shadowy forms in the fog, thought they were in line, suddenly to find their flanks were in mid-air, friends fired on each other, and foes backed into each other. Officers tried to advance by compass bearing, only to look over their shoulders and find that what they thought was a regiment had dwindled to a color guard; the rest had wandered off into the brush. In the gloom men grunted and shoved and fired their rifles and died.

Afterwards, it was possible to make some kind of sense out of the affair. Warren had got his corps into line, and Sedgwick, following him with his VI Corps, had fallen in on his right, northern flank. Together they had about 35,000 men. Ewell faced them off with half that number, and the two sides gradually stabilized west of Old Wilderness Tavern, on either side of the Orange Court House Turnpike. Through the morning Hancock had moved his II Corps to the west, falling in on Warren's left flank, but his men had bumped into A. P. Hill's corps, and together they had simply extended the battle line farther to the south. With its five big divisions, Hancock's corps outnumbered A. P. Hill by even more of a margin than Warren did Ewell, but the Confederates again held their own, and a little better. Both sides tried to dig in, as neither was sure who was attacking and who was defending. By nightfall, after a terrible day of charge and countercharge, the soldiers on both sides were exhausted and fought to a frazzle.

Yet for both, it seemed that help was on the way. Longstreet was coming near now, so Lee ordered an attack for early morning of the 6th. A. P. Hill was to lead off from the Confederate right, and the plan was to turn the Federal flank and roll them up back against the river. But on the blue side, Grant had Burnside's big IX Corps south of the Rapidan, and he ordered it to move across the back of the Union position, fall in with Hancock, and to attack A. P. Hill at dawn. Sedgwick and Warren would both attack, almost simultaneously, in support. In other words, both commanders were planning to do the same thing at the same time at the same place: hit the enemy's southern flank and roll him up to the river.

The result was an even worse day, if that were humanly possible, than the day before. Ewell held Warren and Sedgwick with no gain and heavy losses, but Hancock crashed into Hill's front and flank, and the Rebels broke under the strain. They gave way slowly, and then with increasing speed as the collapse spread. Disaster stared the Army of Northern Virginia in the face, and Robert E. Lee himself rode among his retreating men and asked them to stand and do the impossible.

But then, up the road at a steady pace came Longstreet's corps, the men of Chickamauga and a hundred other hard-fought fields. They casually brushed through their retreating comrades, who took time to catch their breath and rally. Anderson's division of Longstreet's advance crashed into Birney's division, leading Hancock's assault, caught it past the crest, and sent it reeling back on its supports. By late morning Old Pete's men had stabilized the battle once again. Neither side could get far enough south to flank the other, and once more there was a straightforward, stand-up fight, no quarter asked and little given. The trees were stripped by the bullets and shells, hundreds of men went down, the leaves and brush caught fire, and the wounded screamed in agony and were burned alive where they lay.

Lee still had a trick up his sleeve. He sent his aide, Moxley Sorrel, to gather some of Longstreet's brigades and try a wide envelopment. It took most of the mid-day to get these men together, and to march by little-known tracks around the Union left, but they finally managed it, and they hit Hancock's flank late in the afternoon. For a few moments it looked like Chancellorsville all over again. But this was Hancock the Superb, one of the finest combat leaders of one of the finest corps in the Union army. He personally rallied and placed his men, and they dug in, taking what bits of cover they could, little knots of resistance here and there, and they finally broke the momentum of Sorrel's drive. As welcome dusk came down, the two armies virtually collapsed on their respective lines.

Thus ended the Battle of the Wilderness, two days of shockingly bitter fighting. Neither Grant and Meade on the one side, nor Lee on the other, had been able to master the terrain, though Lee had done marginally better in that respect. But both had been ready to fight it out to the finish, and it was as if the two armies had been infected with that same berserk quality. The casualties had been enormous. On the Confederate side no one knew how many they had lost in the horrible tangle, but returns showed a bill of between 7,500 and 11,000. Longstreet himself was wounded, along with several other generals; he turned his corps over to R. H. Anderson. A. P. Hill went off sick, giving his corps to Jubal Early. On the Federal side losses were even worse, and the more careful returns kept there showed a loss of 17,500 men. More significant than the actual numbers were two things. The Union casualty rate was about 17 percent, the Confederate between 12, if the lower figure of losses was accepted, and 18, if the higher figure was taken. The Union figure was higher, of course, especially if one applied losses solely to the troops actively engaged, for Burnside's corps did little fighting in the two days. So one important consideration was the scale of the fighting, and the willingness of the armies, or at least of their commanders, to accept losses of such magnitude. Perhaps one should suggest less "willingness" than inability to accomplish results without incurring almost prohibitive costs. The second factor is, of course, that the Union could afford these losses, heavy as they were, and perhaps disproportionately so, better than the Confederacy could. It came back to the old equation—that if this war were ultimately reduced to a matter of attrition, the Union was going to win it. Or as Lee had remarked so long ago, "If you go to ciphering, we are whipped beforehand."

Maybe so, but it did not appear as if they had been whipped this time. Once again the Army of Northern Virginia, by better luck and marginally superior tactical handling, had stopped the Army of the Potomac. On the 7th, the two sides stayed where they were, each holding its lines and waiting to see if the other might try a move. The long day wore on, as the soldiers tried to get a little rest, a little food, and to do what they could for the tragic wreckage of the previous days' fighting, always a grisly task, and now made more so by the fires that had run through the battle lines.

As the day passed, Grant looked at his maps and talked things over with Meade and his senior commanders. But he had already decided upon his next move, and he issued orders to the corps commanders. The army would leapfrog, by corps, to its left, in a southerly direction. March orders to and through Meade's headquarters desired that Warren should lead off, followed by Sedgwick, pass behind Hancock, and move on the next road junction, south of the Wilderness, a place called Spotsylvania Court House. Grant wanted to keep the pressure on Lee, partly for its own sake, partly because he received reports through the day that Butler with the Army of the James was advancing, and had reached City Point on the way to Richmond. Grant wanted if possible to prevent Lee from detaching any troops to stop this other move.

So after dark Warren's men quietly pulled out of the line, and started east. They were not happy; it looked to them as if they had been beaten again, and as if they were on their way back to Washington; just the way it always was, you advance, you fight, you get beat, you go back and think it all over, and then you start again from the beginning. These men had learned in a hard school the patience that long endureth, but they were far from happy about it.

Then a remarkable thing happened. As the heads of the columns made their way out of the Wilderness, they were met by guides who took up the trail; then at one crossroads there sat a little clump of mounted officers, among them George Meade and General Grant himself. Silently the officers waved them on, to the roads turning not back to the Rapidan fords and safety and Washington, but south, deeper into the enemy's territory. Suddenly, as they realized where they were going, the men began cheering, a deep spontaneous roar that caught from regiment to regiment and echoed back down the long blue columns. Hancock's men took it up, and Sedgwick's and Burnside's, the whole army carried forward on a deep welling tide of exultation. If ever there was a moment of apotheosis for the Army of the Potomac, it was that one, when all those men, so long hard-used and abused, eagerly turned their backs on safety and salvation, and went forward to suffering, destruction, and quite probable death.

The Confederates, hearing the widespread cheering, thought it presaged a night attack, and fired volleys in the dark. It really meant more than that: it meant the death knell of the Confederacy.

———

With Grant moving south, Lee must move as well. Stuart's cavalry was out there, bickering with some Union horsemen, but that was not going to be enough to hold them. Lee quickly sent out his orders, and off they went. He had hoped to destroy the Union army in the Wilderness, and had not managed to do it. The next important position was the road junction around Spotsylvania Court House; he could see that just as readily as Grant, and he told his people to get there first. As usual, they had to cover only the chord of the circle while the Federals had to march along the arc, and since the Confederates were the faster marchers anyway—no sixty miles of trains for this army—they were soon on the roads and hastening southeast. But the larger significance of all this was not immediately apparent: for almost the first time in the war, Lee was responding to the Union strategic moves rather than the other way round. Less than a week into the campaign, Grant had wrested the initiative from Robert Lee.

The Federals almost won the race. General James H. Wilson, one of the "boy general" horsemen who were remaking the Union cavalry arm in their own image, got his division to Spotsylvania in the early hours of May 8, and he held the position for most of the morning against growing Confederate strength. But Anderson, now commanding Longstreet's corps, got his foot soldiers in front of Warren's advance, and before the infantry could force their way through, Wilson's troopers were finally pushed off their ground. As the Rebel infantry swarmed around the little road junction and immediately began digging, it was apparent that there was going to be another big fight.

In fact, it need not have been so. Hancock's II Corps in its advance swung a little to the westward, and at one point, he was in danger of marching across the Confederate route and getting behind the whole Spotsylvania position. But this was good luck, not good management, and once more the tangled roads and tracks of northern Virginia played the Federals false. After blundering around a while, totally unaware of how much good they might be doing, the bluecoats pulled back, and all unknowingly lost a great opportunity to flank Lee's army.

In part this was a failure of cavalry to obtain the intelligence the army needed, and that in turn stemmed from a personality clash and a doctrinal difference between Meade and Sheridan. Like most foot soldiers, Meade thought cavalry was a bit of a nuisance, generally more trouble than it was worth, and that was the way he used it: to provide headquarters guards, to do a bit of screening, and not much else. Sheridan, a feisty little Irishman from the bottom of his West Point class, had taken over the Army of the Potomac's cavalry corps on condition he be given a free hand to do something with it, and so far his condition had not been fulfilled. Now he and Meade fell to quarreling over this, and went to Grant about it. Grant's response was, Well, if you think you can do something, go ahead and do it.

Within hours, Sheridan's troopers were saddling up, drawing rations and ammunition, and moving out, three divisions of horsemen, 10,000 men, a column thirteen miles long. They were looking for a fight; this was not to be one of those wild will-o'-the wisp rides that covered a lot of ground but garnered only headlines. Sheridan's intent was quite clear: he was going to whip Jeb Stuart, and anything else that got in the way was purely incidental. The column advanced at a steady walk.

With 10,000 Federals between him and Richmond, Lee had to do something about it, and he detached Stuart's cavalry to catch Sheridan. Stuart, however, had a mere 4,500 men. He soon caught up with the Union rear guard, and dropped one brigade to harass them; with the rest of his force he sped ahead cross-country, hoping to catch the advance and halt it. There was a good bit of skirmishing between flanking parties, but the main Federal force rode stolidly on, taking time to wreck bridges, tear up the odd bit of rail line, and generally raising the devil as they passed by.

They had almost reached Richmond before Stuart and his hurrying followers got in front of them, and the two forces met at a place called Yellow Tavern, a mere six miles north of the Confederate capital. Here Stuart deployed his force across the road, and about noon the Federals came on in strength against him. The two sides fought for the whole afternoon, carbines, pistols, and sabers, and as the day went on, a series of charges by General George Custer's Michigan brigade began to press Stuart's left flank. Stuart himself rode over to shore up his line, and in one of the exchanges, a passing Union private got off a pistol shot at him. The bullet took Stuart in the stomach, a fatal wound in those days before antiseptic. The Confederates were driven off the field, and Stuart was carried into Richmond, where he died the next evening at his brother-in-law's home.

Sheridan then went on around the capital, bivouacked on the southeast side of it, and linked up with Butler's Army of the James. He stayed there for week, and then took his command back the way it had come, joining up with Meade and Grant on the 24th. He and his troopers were very pleased with themselves, and Lee, who lamented that he had lost his right arm with Jackson, said he had now lost his eyes with Stuart, another of the South's paladins gone forever.

———

By the time Stuart died, so had a good many other men, for as the Union cavalry rode south, Grant attacked the Confederate position at Spotsylvania Court House, and the result was some of the most desperate fighting in a war filled with desperation. As usual, the position was a bit uncertain, for the armies were still in the Wilderness, Spotsylvania Court House being a little hamlet toward the southeastern extremity of the area. The Confederates dug a long trench line, extending roughly north from the hamlet for about a mile and a half, then bending abruptly west for another couple of miles. Early held the eastern side, Ewell the angle, and Anderson the western side of the position. Hancock had blundered past this left, western, flank without realizing exactly where he was. Meanwhile, Warren and Sedgwick had come up on Hancock's left, and began feeling out Anderson's line, trying to figure out just what they were up against. The growth was tangled, entrenchments could be seen through the trees, but it was difficult to get the lie of the land. When "Good Uncle John," as his troops called Sedgwick, went forward to get a look, one of his soldiers said, "You better keep down; there's snipers up there." Sedgwick replied jokingly, "Nonsense, they couldn't hit an elephant from here," and dropped, struck below the eye by a rifle bullet, dead before he hit the ground. Horatio Wright took over his VI Corps.

That was on the 9th. On the next day, Warren launched a heavy attack against Anderson late in the afternoon. Warren himself put on full-dress uniform and led from the front, a target for all to see, and it was a wonder he escaped. The Confederates, well dug in and with artillery support, drove his troops off. Later that afternoon Wright followed with a carefully planned attack on the angle of the Confederate position, known to them in homely terms as the "the mule shoe," from its rounded shape. Led by Colonel Emory Upton, twelve Federal regiments swept over the position, and momentarily occupied it, only to be driven back out for failure of their supports to come up.

On the 11th, Grant and Meade shuffled their units about a little, allowing Lee to think they were going to retreat. But they were not done yet. They were merely organizing a large-scale repeat of Upton's attack, and this time they were going to do it right. Hancock was going to hit the mule shoe with four whole divisions of his II Corps, and as soon as he did so, Burnside would attack from the east and Wright from the west, and they would go right over the Rebels.

So they thought. Actually, Lee was thinning out his line while they were preparing, getting ready for an attack of his own. Just to be on the safe side, he began his troops digging a fallback position across the base of the mule shoe. Many of his guns were moved out, but when the pickets heard heavy movement to their front during the night of the 11th–12th, the Confederates began bringing their artillery back.

They were thus caught on one foot at daybreak of the 12th, when

Hancock launched his attack. The Confederate pickets heard a deep-throated cheer, and out of the early morning rain came 20,000 men, huge deep columns like something from the Napoleonic Wars. They came right up to and over the ditch and escarpment and burst into the mule shoe in a tidal wave of blue. Confederate regiments were swept away like chaff, and the entire Stonewall Brigade, what was left of it by now, was hustled off as prisoners to the rear, with hardly time to fire a shot. The Army of Northern Virginia was torn asunder, its life hanging by a thread.

But the Rebels rallied; John B. Gordon's division of Anderson stuck at the fallback line, and he quickly organized a counterattack. The Federals in their dense masses were momentarily confused by the ease of their success, milling about with their units mixed up. Gordon threw together a line and back they went, literally to do or die. Robert Lee himself brought up supports, and for the second time in a week he rode among his men, his sword drawn, arm uplifted, intending to lead the charge himself. The soldiers screamed, "General Lee to the rear! General Lee to the rear!" and he replied, "We must take that position," and again they cried, "General Lee to the rear! We'll take it, we'll take it!" and went forward yelling, swearing, crying, a furious burst of energy and emotion that transcended humanity. With fire and bayonets and butts they pushed and shoved the Federals back, to the firing step, to the parapet, and out of the mule shoe and into its outer ditch.

Yet the Federals were as determined as their foes, and they stuck on the outer side of the entrenchment, and would not go farther. After an hour and a half, by a mere six in the morning, they were still there, when Wright's VI Corps attacked on their right. His people too got as far as the parapet, and there the two sides remained, locked in battle. Men clawed at the bank with their bayonets and hands, trying to fire through it. Others from both sides jumped up onto the top and fired down into the enemy, fed a succession of loaded weapons by their friends until they were shot. Each side went up and over for a few minutes, here and there, before being shot down or driven back, and this went on for hours, men going temporarily crazy in their frenzy.

Historians say this cannot be done, that men cannot stand on slippery piles of dead and wounded in the wet and mud and continue to fight, that human beings cannot behave and endure as these men behaved and endured. Yet the evidence is clear enough, from hundreds of eyewitness survivors and contemporary photographs. The fighting here went on for twenty hours, Hancock finally contained and fought out, Wright exhausted, and a later attack on the eastern flank by Burnside turned back after some little success. By midnight Lee had finally got his line redug across the mouth of the mule shoe, and his people, what was left of them, went sullen and exhausted back to the new position. By the end of the day the mule shoe had a new name, and has been known ever since then as The Bloody Angle, the article capitalized as in The Cornfield at Antietam, or The Peach Orchard at Gettysburg, or The Sunken Road at Shiloh.

Appellations such as that are dearly bought; Spotsylvania Court House cost both armies a heavy price in dead and wounded. On the two days of the 10th and 12th, the Federals lost another 11,000 men. Lee could not even manage a correct count of his losses; his army was too exhausted to file proper returns.

On both sides, behind the lines, people were shocked and appalled by the stories coming out of the Wilderness. Yet Grant had telegraphed Washington on the 11th: "We have now ended the 6th day of very hard fighting. . . . Our losses have been heavy as well as those of the enemy. I . . . purpose to fight it out on this line if it takes all summer." Lincoln had wanted a man who fought, and that was what he got.

Reports indicated that Sheridan was cutting up Confederate communications and destroying their stores and rations, that Butler's cavalry was operating down around Petersburg, threatening the southern approaches to Richmond, and Grant saw little reason to alter his original strategy. It was costly, but it was working. Confederate prisoners were downhearted, and there were rumors of substantial desertions in their ranks.

Grant thus issued orders for another leapfrog to the south, and at dark on the 13th Warren set off, moving behind the army from its right to its left flank. Wright followed on a wider swing several hours later. This night the Confederates got lucky; it poured all night, the roads turned to glue, the creeks rose, and the Federals, trying to march cross-country, floundered around in the wet, cursing and stumbling and wading. This gave Lee just enough time to extend his right flank to the south, a precious day gained and lost by the heavy rain.

For the Federals, things went from bad to worse. Grant received word that Butler had let himself get beaten at Drewry's Bluff, by a scratch force gathered under Beauregard, and he was thus stalled. Even worse, over in the Shenandoah Valley, Sigel also got beaten, by a gaggle of Confederates that included 247 ever-glorious cadets from Virginia Military Institute, and he retreated hastily north down the Valley. Instead of having the balanced campaign he wanted, Grant was now going to have to do it all alone, and that significantly altered the picture of the overall strategy. On the 18th, Grant shifted back to the north, and hit The Bloody Angle hard with Wright, Hancock, and Burnside. Again there was bitter fighting, but the Confederates had been well dug in and ready, and there were substantial losses but no real gain.

While all this was in train, both sides were reinforced. Grant got units sent out from the Washington garrison forces, large regiments of so-called heavy artillery that had already served for a couple of years without seeing any fighting, and were now suddenly transformed into infantry. At full strength and burdened with all their parade-ground impedimenta, these units got the usual joking welcome from the old-timers; a full-strength regiment of 900 men would be teased with, "What division is that?" As they have since the days of Alexander the Great, the old-timers shouted out, "You'll be sorry!" "Wait till you see what's waiting for you," and suchlike pleasantries. But they soon shook down, littering their line of march with discarded junk, and their bulk was sorely needed and welcome; in this campaign, any blood would do. They showed they could fight, vigorously if not too skillfully, when Lee sent Ewell out to try to flank the Federal army to its north on the 19th. Ewell's whole corps, a mere 6,000 men now, bumped into some new Federal units, and was lucky to get back safe into its own lines. Lee for his part got units from both the James River front and from the Shenandoah, altogether 8,000 or 9,000 men. A. P. Hill also soon rejoined him, though he was still not well, and took over his old corps from Jubal Early.

What Grant really wanted to do was get Lee out in the open; if he could meet him clear of the Wilderness, or when the Confederates had not had a chance to dig in, he thought he could win a stand-up battle. Disappointed by the Army of the James and by the results in the Shenandoah, he had little choice but to keep going.

Once again the Army of the Potomac moved south. Grant sent Hancock all the way to the North Anna River, about twenty miles south of Spotsylvania, and halfway to Richmond. His idea was that with Hancock in this threatening position, Lee would have to move against him, and then Grant could in turn follow with the rest of his army, and catch Lee between the two forces. As usual, the plan failed. Lee pulled out his corps, got them on the roads south, and ended up strongly dug in on the North Anna, his advance squabbling with Hancock's over the river crossings. Grant then hurried the rest of his army down to support Hancock, fearing the isolated II Corps might be overwhelmed. Lee had taken up an extremely strong position, similar to that at Spotsylvania Court House, but this time with the angle resting on the river so it could not be overwhelmed. It was a good thing the Confederates were so well disposed, for Lee went down with a bad attack of the runs, and for a week was in no condition to direct a battle. Grant spent several days trying to figure out how to force a favorable battle, and in the end decided to move yet again.

He was also modifying his original plan with respect to General Butler and the Army of the James. As that force was now thoroughly boxed in, he ordered that a corps-strength detachment under W. F. Smith be sent up the Pamunkey River to White House, to link up with his own advance. This arrived on May 30. Meanwhile, he sideslipped the Army of the Potomac again, marching southeast from the North Anna confrontation down that stream and down the Pamunkey, of which it is the northern branch. Wright and Hancock led off, followed by Warren and Burnside. The move meant that once again they had halved the distance to Richmond.

But once again, they had failed to bring Lee to battle on favorable terms. He quickly retreated, and got his men between the Federals and Richmond by a matter of a few hours. This led to some preliminary fighting around Mechanicsville—shades of the Seven Days—and an oddly named little crossroads in the middle of nowhere called Cold Harbor, oddly named as it was at least five miles from any water big enough to float a boat. Sheridan had actually reached this place first, with two divisions of cavalry, and he held it for some time, waiting for the infantry to arrive. On June 1 his troopers, armed with repeating carbines, held off a serious attack from the Confederates for the whole day. Then, when Wright's VI Corps and Smith's XVIII Corps arrived, they all went over to the offensive. By then the Confederates had dug in again, and all they got for their pains were 2,600 casualties.

So here they were, back to the same old business, both sides consolidating, and both digging. Lee really wanted to catch the Union forces strung out and in the open, and at this first try he had almost, but not quite, succeeded. For two days both armies dug furiously, while the rearward corps closed up, and they extended their lines somewhat to the south from the original Cold Harbor position. Grant badly wanted an early assault, realizing that the sooner he did it the better, but Hancock's men came in completely exhausted after marching all night through scorching heat. An attack scheduled for dawn of the 2nd had to be postponed until evening, and then, after several days of killing sun, the skies opened and the rain poured down. Grant again postponed the assault, till the early morning of the 3rd.

By then Lee had all of his army in hand, and they had dug effectively on a front of more than five miles. Their works were covered by some swamps and rough patches, and most important, each segment of the line supported its flanking portions, so that almost anywhere the Federals might attack, they would face frontal fire and angling, enfilading fire at the same time. By now both armies knew all there was to know about field fortifications and how to site artillery cover, and with the possible exception of the new Union garrison regiments, there was not a soldier in either army would keep his bayonet in preference to his shovel. By the morning of June 3, Lee had created as good a killing trap as it was possible to do.

Nonetheless Grant determined to assault it, and did so early in the morning with Hancock, Wright, and Smith, while Warren and Burnside covered the northern flank. The orders were for a full-scale assault, and not much more. There had been little preliminary reconnaissance, and not much attention was paid to who would do what when; just form your troops and give the command, Forward, March! The troops themselves, far from stupid and with a well-developed eye for the strength of a position, knew what all that meant. In the leading assault columns the veterans, as has been mentioned earlier, pinned little slips of paper to their backs, with their names on them, so friends could identify their bodies after it was over.

The real battle lasted little more than an hour. The Federals came on gallantly, driving in the Confederate pickets. Then as they neared the main line, thousands of Rebels jumped to their feet, and a sheet of flame burst in the faces of the Union infantry. Men went down in heaps; others stumbled blindly about until they were shot down in their turn. The leading Union regiments were simply blown away in sheer butchery. Here and there they managed to reach the breastworks. A couple of Hancock's regiments actually made it to the top of the parapet; Colonel MacMahon of the 164th New York died planting his regiment's color on the top of the breastwork, but the successes were few and totally isolated. Wright's men made fourteen determined rushes, and could not reach Anderson's line. They could not carry it, and would not or could not go back. By mid-morning the remnants of his leading divisions were clinging grimly to scooped-out holes within yards of the Rebel line. Smith's corps included several of the big new heavy-artillery regiments, and as they tried to advance, they were simply shot to pieces. They pressed on bravely, only to add more bodies to the wreckage.

Cold Harbor was the worst battle of a campaign full of them. It was later charged that Grant the butcher had "thrown away twenty thousand men in ten minutes"; that was not quite the case. Union losses were about 7,000, and it took about thirty minutes. But the accusation was not totally unfounded. The attack had been casually prepared and poorly orchestrated, and neither Grant nor Meade nor their staffs had done their work properly; if they had, they would have easily seen the folly of the attack. Being tired, confused, and impatient is still a lot more bearable than being dead, and Grant later admitted that Cold Harbor was the one battle he really regretted in his campaign.

It was also the last in what came to be called the Overland Campaign. In one month of fighting, the Army of the Potomac had advanced sixty miles, roughly two miles a day, at a cost of nearly 2,000 men a day. This was an expensive but by no means a small achievement. Northern newspapers might castigate Grant as a bull-headed butcher, but there was far more to it than that. A more discerning eye would have seen that Robert Lee, the consummate master of maneuver, had been repeatedly forced to respond to Grant's initiative. The Peace Democrats loudly pointed out that after all this squalor and waste, Grant was only where McClellan had been at the beginning of his 1862 Peninsula Campaign, and that was true too, but what they forgot was that McClellan, when he finally got around to fighting, could not do it. Federal losses had been substantially heavier than Confederate, the price of retaining the initiative and of repeated attacks, but however tragic they were, the Union could afford its losses better than the Confederacy could. It may occasionally, if the other side chooses, be possible to win a war without much fighting. The Confederacy was not that kind of opponent.

Grant now moved again, a move he had been working out in his mind for several days. He very carefully and cleverly organized a shift south from the lines around Cold Harbor, all the way to the James. He decided to operate against Petersburg, the rail junction twenty miles south of Richmond. Almost all of the Confederate capital's supplies moved through that city, and if it could be taken, then Lee must fight in the open, or the capital must fall, or both. The preparation for the march, across country from the Chickahominy to the James, the sites of the Seven Days' Battles, was very precisely worked out. Lee let himself be lulled into thinking this was just another leapfrog to the immediate south, and on the 13th of June, the Confederates found the Union lines around Cold Harbor empty.

As Lee's men marched to their right, they found swarms of Union cavalry covering the country, and by the time Lee realized what was happening, Federal units were crossing the James, and Beauregard was screaming for the return of his troops, because he was under increasing pressure around Petersburg.

In the third week of June, the Army of the Potomac lost its best opportunity to win the war then and there. In four days of very confused fighting on the outskirts of Petersburg, Beauregard, that often maligned Confederate stormy petrel, fought a brilliant delaying action. He was immensely helped by poor staff work on the Union side, and a hard-learned reluctance to mount a determined assault against dug-in Rebels. By a hair's breadth, the Federals failed to take the city before Lee got his troops down there. The truth was, the Army of the Potomac was virtually exhausted. On June 22, Hancock's famous II Corps was handily beaten up by a far inferior Confederate force, and after that, Grant decided on a siege. He would entrench around the city, and operate against its communications. It looked like the best he could do. He had immobilized Robert Lee and whittled away his army. Now he would hold him in a death grip while others elsewhere continued the war of movement. So ended the most bitter seven weeks of fighting ever seen on the North American continent.

Chapter 16

The Atlanta Campaign

FROM CHATTANOOGA to Atlanta is a matter of some one hundred miles. For General William T. Sherman, now Ulysses Grant's chief lieutenant in the west, that hundred miles was the be-all and end-all of his existence. A rail line connected the two cities, and the Confederate Army of Tennessee drew its sustenance up that line, enabling it to maintain a precarious hold on northern Georgia. If the Federal forces could move down the line, and take Atlanta, then as now a hub of transportation and commerce, they would be well along in their aim of cutting the Confederacy in half a second time.

This was easier said than done. Sherman had plenty of troops, nearly 90,000 men in three armies, but his supplies were a bit tenuous, and the weather was bad in the late winter and early spring of 1864. He was also, according to Grant's overall conception, supposed to have had assistance from Nathaniel P. Banks, in the form of some of the troops who had been sent off to aid that general in his Red River expedition, and also in the sense of Banks moving east to threaten Mobile, Alabama, and distract the Confederates as to the primary aim of Federal strategy. Instead, Banks had managed to get stuck up the Red River, and he kept the troops there with him.

It was fortunate for the Confederacy that the Union was beset by difficulties of its own devising, for Confederate stock in this area was pretty low. Braxton Bragg was gone at last; even Jefferson Davis had finally to acknowledge that he had no more credibility as commander of the Army of Tennessee. Davis removed him in November of 1863, after the Chattanooga debacle, but he kicked him upstairs, moving him to Richmond, appointing him as Military Adviser to the President,

240

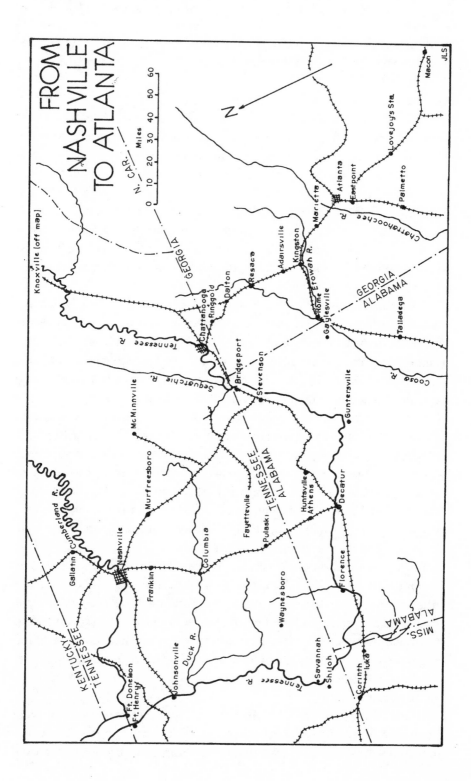

FROM NASHVILLE TO ATLANTA

JLS

and in name at least, making him a virtual general-in-chief of the Confederacy. In fact it was a paper position in which Bragg did very little at all.

As its new commander the Army of Tennessee got Joseph Johnston; Davis and Johnston, of course, vigorously disliked each other, but Johnston was a senior general, and he had the support of the western Confederate politicians. He was considered an astute and careful strategist, but as he had demonstrated before, he was a man who wanted everything to be perfect before he took the initiative, and in war such conditions seldom pertain. In appointing him to command, Davis made it clear that he expected Johnston to take the offensive, recover recent losses, and re-establish the Confederate position in east Tennessee. As soon as he took up his command, Johnston immediately disregarded all such expectations.

That was only sensible, as they were quite unrealistic anyway. Davis's repeated response to the west had been that if he could not solve the problem, he would change the man tasked with attending to it; hence the succession of Albert Sidney Johnstons, Joe Johnstons, Beauregards, Pembertons, Braggs, Kirby Smiths, and on and on, all of them asked to make bricks with no straw, none of them able to do it.

So in December of 1863 Johnston had taken up his new command, about 50,000 men scratching out a bare subsistence in the hardscrabble hills of Georgia along Rocky Face Ridge, some twenty miles southeast of Chattanooga. It was not a good winter. The internal bickering in the upper officer levels of the army went on apace, and the men went hungry. Yet these were decent troops, in spite of what they had done or failed to do at Chattanooga, good soldiers hard used, and they were ready to fight yet, as would soon be shown.

Rocky Face was the most eastern of several ridgelines, and about the last one that straddled the railroad from Chattanooga to Atlanta. The hills generally ran north and south, and paralleled the rail line, so that if Rocky Face were lost, the next really good defensive position would be away down near Cassville, forty miles south, and halfway to Atlanta. There were possibilities for maneuver in all of this, but Sherman, outnumbering Johnston almost two to one, was in a better situation to profit by them.

Grant's instructions to Sherman were also more realistic than were Davis's to Johnston. Sherman was to follow and if possible destroy Johnston's army, and beyond that, to get into the interior of Georgia and do as much damage as possible. In this Sherman's mission paralleled that of Grant and Meade in Virginia; both intended to operate against the enemy army as their primary objective, but both had the secondary mission of moving against a major center. This meant that the opponent would be deprived of a certain degree of flexibility; Lee could not cut completely loose against the Army of the Potomac, indulging in, say, another end-run wide-flanking maneuver because, with Richmond at his back, he dared not try the kind of move against Grant and Meade that he had successfully employed against John Pope. Similarly Johnston, with Atlanta to defend, had only limited freedom of maneuver with respect to Sherman. Davis would have liked Johnston to move on Chattanooga, or even Knoxville, but faced with the Federal superiority, this was simply impracticable.

The Union strategy of course had its own dangers, chief among them the possibility that the field commander might be so distracted by the physical prize that he neglected the primary mission, destruction of the opposing army. This would carry one back to the eighteenth-century war of posts, where the aim was to amass counters to be used at the bargaining table, rather than to defeat the enemy in the field. Grant managed to avoid this, and even though he operated against Richmond, he always did so in such a way that Lee was forced to conform to his moves; thus when he finally brought Petersburg under siege, he also brought Lee's army to the same condition, and in this way managed to deprive it of its greatest asset, its mobility. Sherman, not entirely through his own fault, was less successful in this regard. Less his fault because Johnston, not nearly as aggressive a commander as Lee, was disposed to fall back toward Atlanta anyway, but even taking that into account, Sherman became preoccupied with the city. Unable to catch and defeat Johnston in the field, he increasingly looked to Atlanta as an objective in its own right. Ultimately the political advantages of having done so made this a correct decision, but it was a near-run thing, and for a while, it looked as if Sherman had gotten his priorities thoroughly mixed. In May of 1864, all this was still to be decided; by late summer, it looked as if the Union were on the verge of losing the war.

———

Sherman's three armies began to move on May 7. They were somewhat misnamed, for McPherson's Army of the Tennessee and Schofield's

Army of the Ohio, at 24,000 and 13,500 respectively, were really oversized corps. Only Thomas's Army of the Cumberland at 61,000 was truly of army size. Nonetheless, the command structure was a workable one, Sherman and his three subordinates understood each other and got along reasonably well, and this was in aggregate a fine army, as good as any on the continent, which meant at the moment as good as or better than any in the world. Though there were a few wandering eastern regiments, the army was made up mostly of westerners, men from Illinois, Ohio, and Indiana, with Michigan, Wisconsin, Iowa, and Kentucky thrown in as well. They prided themselves on their free and easy manners, their long, loping marching stride, their slouch hats, and the absence of the military punctilio they associated with the eastern armies of the Republic. Big, rawboned men from the farms, canal boats, and lumber camps of what was then the west, they were fiercely independent and conscious of their tough reputation. And rightly so.

Yet the Southerners they faced, if there were fewer of them, were no less determined than they were. The poor settlements of northern Georgia did not look like much to Yankees from the prosperous Midwest states, but they were home to these men, Georgians, Alabamians, Mississippians, and they would fight and die to save them. Poorly dressed, roughly shod, their wives and children often existing on little more than charity, these men were no strangers to sacrifice, and they did not have to be educated or even literate to know that the climax of the war was upon them. They were prepared to give it all they had; if that was not a great deal in physical resources, heart and courage would have to make up the difference, and they had all of that that anyone could possibly ask or expect. In the days of mythology this contest, like the one taking place concurrently in Virginia, would have excited the interest of the gods.

With his comfortable numerical superiority, Sherman planned to press and then envelop the Confederates. Schofield's Army of the Ohio, the smallest of his three, would act essentially as his left flank guard, and Thomas's Army of the Cumberland, the largest, as the main force, moving down the railroad directly against the Confederates. Meanwhile, Sherman's favorite, the Army of the Tennessee, his own former command, now under the able James McPherson, would function as the maneuver arm on the right flank; using the hills and ridges to the west, McPherson would attempt to get past Johnston's left flank and cut off his line of retreat. The whole army was occasionally forced to move beyond mutual supporting distance, but given its strength, and considering Johnston's tendency to be less than a bold commander, there seemed to be little risk in this.

Johnston's problem was not that he was afraid to fight; his problem went deeper than that. It was that he could never find just the right opportunity. The position was always wrong, the lines of retreat too uncertain, the supports too distant—a general who always thinks there is a better position just a few miles back is not going to be very aggressive, and Joe Johnston was just such a general. He was as strongly entrenched on Rocky Face Ridge as he could well expect to be. He had Joe Wheeler's cavalry out scouting both his flanks, though it would not be able to accomplish much, as it was very heavily outnumbered by the Union horsemen. But his infantry positions were strong along the ridge, held by troops of Hardee's and John B. Hood's corps. Thomas levered his outposts off Tunnel Hill on May 7, and the next day the Federals attacked Rocky Face itself. This was supposed to be merely a pinning attack, that is, something to hold the Confederates in place while other, more important things were going on elsewhere, but they gave it a good try. In fact, they gave it three tries, and at one point the 33rd New Jersey even got onto the crest for a few minutes before being pushed back off. They tried again on the 9th, less seriously, and Johnston was able to report to Richmond that he was successfully holding his position.

Just as Johnston was feeling fairly satisfied with his situation, who should appear but McPherson, pushing through Snake Creek Gap, ten miles south of the Confederate positions on Rocky Face and a mere five miles from their line of retreat at Resaca. Indeed, McPherson approached Resaca itself, and the rail line there, but he found it held in some strength, or so he thought; thus, instead of forcing his way in and taking the town, which should have been well within his capacity, he fell back to Snake Creek Gap.

As soon as he heard this news, Johnston retreated. He left Rocky Face and hustled his divisions back to Resaca, where he took up another defensive line north and west of the town, with Hood on his right, Hardee in the center, and reinforcements, Polk's corps, on the left. Thomas and Schofield followed him down the rail line, and on the 14th there was heavy fighting as the Federals tried, again unsuccessfully, to assault the Confederate lines. That day and the 15th, through more desultory skirmishing, Johnston held his lines, and even mounted a nasty counterattack on Hood's front.

But Sherman had enough men to spare for this kind of work, and as he fought at Resaca, he sent some cavalry and an infantry division from Thomas south again, toward Rome, twenty-five miles southwest of Resaca. When Johnston heard of this, even though he was holding his own on the immediate battlefield, he had no choice but to go back once more. His troops hastily packed up and decamped for Cassville.

Here he stopped again, and waited for Sherman's advance to catch up. When his scouts brought in word that Schofield, leading the Union advance, was somewhat isolated, he thought to trap and destroy him, with Polk in front and Hood striking the Federal flank. But Hood got his orders mixed up, and faced the wrong way, and by the time it was all sorted out, the other Union forces were closing up on Schofield. So now the missed opportunities were about equal on both sides—Sherman had said to McPherson at Resaca, "Well, Mac, you just missed the chance of a lifetime"—but the difference was still that Sherman had advanced more than halfway to Atlanta, and Johnston had still significantly failed to stop him, or even to slow him down.

Nor was he through yet. He consulted his corps commanders about fighting at Cassville; they, however, conscious as he was that the Etowah River was only a few miles back, recommended retreating again, to Allatoona Pass, where surely they could put up a good fight. Off they went again.

None of this was happening in a vacuum. Sherman had his cavalry out, burning, disrupting, and destroying supplies anywhere he could find them. His troops wrecked large amounts of rolling stock and mills at Rome, and generally raised hell through the countryside. The interior of Georgia was not naturally prosperous, but a fair amount of Confederate war industry had been relocated to the towns there in the course of the war. Atlanta itself, a town of only about eight thousand before the war, was now inhabited by about twenty thousand people; a lot of them were war refugees, but many were there because of railroad works, iron foundries, and other industries essential to the Southern war effort. If Sherman were not stopped, and soon, he was capable of doing real damage.

Johnston was as aware of all this as the next man. Unfortunately he was also aware of the reality of his situation. Southern editorial writers might slay entire armies with the stroke of a pen, and, as one wag sarcastically remarked, politicians could perform biblical feats, and overwhelm enemies with the jawbone of an ass, but all of that was a little more difficult to accomplish in northern Georgia, where the enemies actually were. As he went back yet again, Johnston was ever more conscious of the chorus of criticism rising behind him. Surely he would fight—if only he could find the right spot to do it.

He thought he had that at Allatoona. About five miles below Cassville, it gave him a good range of hills for his line, with the Etowah River in front of him. If Sherman tried to force that position, he would face a very difficult prospect indeed, and it seemed he had little choice, for the rail line ran right through it, and so far, the Federal forces had had to utilize the rails for supplying their army. Unfortunately for Johnston, Sherman agreed perfectly with that assessment, so he decided once again upon a wide maneuver. He gave his troops three days' rest, while filling his wagons with everything they could carry, and then, like his mentor Grant at Vicksburg, he cut loose from the rail line. Instead of following Johnston and banging his head against the Etowah-Allatoona line, he headed off southwest, crossed the Etowah unopposed around Kingston, west of Johnston, and moved toward Dallas. Flanked again, Johnston shifted his army out of its prepared positions to meet the new threat, and hastily dug in around Dallas and New Hope Church.

Here Sherman developed his line on May 26, but instead of attacking him, the wily Federal simply used his numbers to slide east, back toward the rail line at Big Shanty. The frustrated Confederates, tired of apparently useless digging and sick of marching back and forth—especially more back than forth—moved to conform once again. After several days, by the first of June, they were back straddling the rail line. Then it began to rain.

The rain fell for a week, and rain meant trouble. Sherman was now out on a very long, thin limb, that one rail line leading all the way down, not only from Chattanooga, but in fact from his main supply depot away back in Nashville, a distance of some 250 miles. This entire distance was vulnerable to Confederate raiders, and there were numerous parties of them operating in the general area. The Federals used the first weeks of June, and the arrival of reinforcements, to strengthen their lines of communication, bring up supplies, and get ready for a further push.

Even so, there was only so much Sherman could do, and only so far he could maneuver away from the rail line. Mathematics kept intruding. It was a well-tested military fact, for example, that the largest army that could reasonably subsist in any given area on its own, in the days before mechanical transport, was about 20,000 men. This was the size of a Roman double consular army, the standard field army of the Roman Empire. If more than that number was gathered in a single area, they could not feed themselves on the countryside, and the limits of animal-drawn transport were such that they could not be fed effectively by wagon train. There had of course been armies much larger than 20,000 men before, but they had been kept together only by careful manipulation of conditions. For example, the eighteenth century developed the depot system, with stocks of supplies pre-positioned for armies operating out of their bases. When Wellington came up out of the Peninsula in 1812–13, he had 80,000 men, but he marched them in four separate detachments by four separate routes. Napoleon's army usually marched in a corps organization, and the standard corps was about 20,000. In his later years a sort of gigantism overtook Napoleon, but so did military disaster. Sherman, in 1864, was able to operate away from the rail line for a week or so, as he did in flanking Johnston's Allatoona position, but this was a risky proposition, and it strained his wagon transport to the limit. Thus when he was blocked around Dallas and New Hope Church, the logical thing to do was to sidle back east to the rail line. Indeed, he was lucky here, for had his army been caught by the week of rain when it was still out to the west, it would have been a very hungry army by the time the roads dried up and the wagons could work again. Northern Georgia's dirt roads quickly turned to mud under a week's rain and heavy wagon traffic.

But now he put his rear areas in better shape, and prepared to move again. There was some heavy preliminary sparring, both sides working on their lines and trying to outflank and outdig each other, and Johnston gradually took up a solid position anchored on a high, abrupt ridge known as Kennesaw Mountain. By late June, with the weather still wet, the Confederates were thoroughly dug in on a front of more than five miles, north and west of Marietta. Even this so-called lull had its daily fights and losses. On June 14, Johnston, Hardee, and Polk were looking over a position at Pine Mountain, when a Federal battery opened up on them. Polk, who had come up to give his colleagues copies of a religious tract entitled "Balm for the Weary and Wounded," was hit by a three-inch solid shot and killed instantly, his body torn apart. Blizzards Loring took over his corps command.

By the third week of June Sherman was again ready to act, and indeed had to do so. He now had McPherson and Thomas facing the Kennesaw Mountain position, and Schofield extending to his right, to the southwest. But Schofield had gone as far as his transport would allow him to move, under the road and weather conditions of the moment, and still had not forced Johnston to give up his lines. There was little left to do but try an attack, and this Sherman did, on the morning of the 27th.

It lasted only about four hours, which was enough to demonstrate that the task was impossible. The Confederates were well dug in, the slope itself was formidable, and the Federal assaults were uncoordinated and unsophisticated, a standard example of Civil War butchery. The Union regiments lost any number of officers, leading from the front, including Dan McCook of the Fighting McCooks, who had led his brigade off by reciting Macauley's "Horatius at the Bridge," from the *Lays of Ancient Rome:* "Then how can man die better, than facing fearful odds / For the ashes of his fathers, and the temples of his gods." And they also lost more than 2,000 casualties. The Confederates, actually outnumbering the attacking units, suffered only about 450 casualties, a measure of the one-sided nature of the battle.

One of Sherman's reasons for attacking was psychological; he thought his men were sick of marching, and wanted a fight to finish things off. If that were indeed the case, Kennesaw Mountain quickly disabused both army and commander of such a silly notion. So now it was back to marching again. The rainy spell had ended just before the battle was fought, and the roads were drying quickly in the Georgia sun. It was possible to move once more. The Federals began sidling to the right again, moving out past Johnston's flank.

In Richmond, and in Confederate newspapers generally, it was difficult to see why Johnston must fall back yet again, even after having won so clear-cut a tactical victory. But neither Richmond nor all those editors were trying to stop an invading army with an army less than half the invader's size, and Johnston, having skillfully preserved his force thus far, went back once more. He decided to hold the line of the Chattahoochee River, a mere six miles from Atlanta. Oddly enough, he took up his position this time on the north side of the river, though as it was well bridged behind him, this was not as dangerous as it might have looked.

Nonetheless, it was enough to surprise Sherman, and it worked to the Federal advantage. The Yankees advanced on several diverging axes, hitting the river along a stretch of nearly thirty miles. Johnston could patrol that distance, but had no hope of holding it, and his own lines were soon compromised on both ends by cavalry forcing crossings both upstream and down. Schofield got across in some force on the 9th of July, and Johnston went back again, to a southern tributary of the Chattahoochee known as Peachtree Creek. Now he was only three miles from Atlanta.

By this time President Davis, and virtually everyone else, was seriously alarmed. Apparently this general intended to retreat forever; he lost battles and he retreated; he won battles and he retreated; he did not fight battles, and he still retreated. Davis sent his chief military adviser, Braxton Bragg, out to see if Johnston ever intended to fight. Given the history of the Army of Tennessee, it might have been considered a poor choice of emissaries.

By now that army was engaged in its usual game of letter writing on the matter of "Why the commander is incompetent and guess who would do a better job?" The chief contender for the top command this time was John Bell Hood, commander of one of the army's three infantry corps, and known throughout the Confederacy as "the gallant Hood of Texas." Tall, blond, full-bearded, a first-class combat leader, Hood was one of the Confederacy's darlings, an esteem he fully deserved. Badly wounded in an arm at Gettysburg, he lost a leg at Chickamauga. Convalescing in Richmond, he had become a faithful familiar of President Davis, and wooed and won the famous Richmond belle Sally Buchanan Campbell Preston, known to her friends as "Buck." Mary Chesnut knew Sally did not love him, but he was a wounded hero, and what could a young girl do?

Hood was not quite the straightforward simple soldier he presented himself as being; he shamelessly used his connections with Davis to undermine Johnston, and repeatedly recommended Johnston's replacement, even for making moves that Hood himself had advised. In mid-July he got his wish, and he replaced Johnston on the 17th. Sherman was delighted: here was a man who would make mistakes.

Both Hood's orders and his temperament dictated that he should fight, and he immediately moved to do so. On the 20th, as Thomas's Army of the Cumberland began forcing Peachtree Creek, Hood struck. His divisions came on in echelon, so the battle spread from right to left along the creek line, and everywhere the Federals stolidly turned back the oncoming Confederates. Hood failed to control his units' movements carefully, and at one point, he took Patrick Cleburne's division, the best in Hardee's corps, and sent it off on a tangent when it might have been more effective left where it was. None of this was particularly fatal, or indeed not to be expected; this was Hood's first battle as anything more than a corps commander, and it was reasonable that it might take him a while to get used to the job. Unfortunately, the Confederacy did not have a wide margin to allow for on-the-job training. By mid-afternoon, the battle was over, and the Federals were firmly south of Peachtree Creek, and another defensive position was lost to the Confederates. Sherman's corps immediately began extending around to the east of the city, cutting the rail line through which reinforcements from Virginia might reach their opponents, and after Peachtree Creek, Atlanta was closely invested on the northern and eastern sides.

Closely invested but far from taken. The overcrowded little city was now ringed with formidable trench lines, and using them, Hood was able to conserve his forces and face Sherman with some hope of local equality. The two sides were now on the verge of a siege.

For a month the two armies poked and prodded, looking for a weakness that might be exploited. Atlanta, unlike Vicksburg before it, was not on a river, so Sherman did not have the luxury of completely surrounding and cutting off the city; even his large army was not sufficient for that. Sherman was actually taken somewhat by surprise at this development. As the Confederates moved back into their entrenchments, he thought that they were beginning a withdrawal from the city, and he was far from pleased to find that Hood intended to stay and fight it out. On July 22nd, as he was moving his forces farther to the eastward, Hood hit him from the south, along the rail line that led from Decatur to Atlanta. Hardee's infantry and Wheeler's cavalry hit McPherson, whose flank was exposed to the south, and threatened to roll up his army. Fortunately, there were plenty of Federal troops around, and they quickly stabilized the line.

It cost them McPherson, though. Caught out in the open and summoned to surrender, he tried to make a run for it, and was shot through the lungs by a Confederate private. Sherman, who had refused McPherson leave to go get married, wept like a child when the body of his friend was finally recovered. John A. Logan, a War Democrat politician who made a very successful combat soldier, temporarily took over the Army of the Tennessee. Later, Sherman gave the command to Oliver Howard, who was a West Pointer, while Logan was only a politician, another example of the West Point Protective Association at work, even though Logan was almost undeniably a better field commander.

This Battle of Atlanta, as it came to be called, demonstrated that Hood simply lacked the muscle to break up the Federal moves, and after it, Sherman gradually strengthened his grip on the city. Balked in his hope of taking Atlanta almost on the run, Sherman now resorted to a series of cavalry raids, while Hood, equally stymied in his intention of defeating the Federals in the open, sought the same remedy. Neither had much success. Sherman sent General George Stoneman and his cavalry off to cut the rail lines down near Macon, supported by McCook's cavalry as well. Stoneman separated his forces, got himself trapped and surrounded, and his command was broken up and captured, McCook managed to tear up some railroad stock and line, but the Confederates coalesced against him too, and he had to fight his way back to his own lines, losing several hundred troopers in the process, for only momentary gain. Meanwhile, Hood was sending his cavalry out against Sherman's supply lines, but their success was equally marginal. All of these operations demonstrated little more than the fact that cavalry by itself was insufficient to operate against any real opposition, and all the raids provided little more than nuisance value. Closer to home, Sherman began extending to his right, westwards, and moved McPherson's Army of the Tennessee, now under Howard, from one end of his line to the other. Hood tried to attack this extension around Ezra Church on July 28, and his advance, led by Stephen D. Lee's corps, ran into Howard's leading elements. These were XV Corps, with Logan back in command of it, and Logan gave the Confederates a sharp rap, amply demonstrating that if, as a political general, he could not have an army under Sherman, there was not much he did not know about handling a corps.

For nearly a month after that, there was costly bickering to no real effect. By now every man in both armies fully understood the advantages of fighting from behind field entrenchments, as well as the disadvantages of trying to storm them. No matter how tired the soldiers might be after a march, the first thing they did upon stopping was scratch out a line of works, with picks and shovels, or bayonets and mess tins if necessary. They quickly threw up a parapet in front of their ditch, braced it with logs if they could find any, and propped up a "head log," with a firing slit beneath it. The men were rapidly becoming moles, quick to defend, nicely calculating the odds if called upon to attack. Now they were thorough professionals, willing to take the necessary chances of war, but doing everything in their power to lengthen the odds in their favor. This made for a very messy battlefield, dirt and junk everywhere, and over all the stench of human waste and dead bodies in the Georgia summer heat. And it was distressing to senior commanders, who then as now liked their troops to think offensively, but the troops were smart enough to realize that thinking offensively wasted lives, and as it was their lives that were being wasted, they clung tenaciously to their own views of how to make war, whatever the generals might think or want.

For the troops, it was a matter of simple survival, life or death, which was after all pretty elemental. For the generals, there were other considerations. By mid-summer, the whole war appeared to hang in the balance. Grant, after an enormously costly campaign, was apparently stalled around Petersburg; on the surface, he appeared little farther ahead, at infinitely higher cost, than McClellan had been on the Peninsula more than two years ago. And now, it appeared as if Sherman too were stalled, unable to put the cap on a campaign which, though it had begun auspiciously, looked now like degenerating into another stalemate. The casualty lists were appalling. And there was a presidential election coming up; to Confederates and Union men alike, it began to look as if this war might be won or lost in the election booth.

Chapter 17

The Folks at Home

MILITARY HISTORIANS naturally enough concentrate upon military matters, and especially upon operations; after all, the battle is the payoff, as has been said so often. Increasingly, however, historians recognize that battle history is only the visible tip of the iceberg; it may well be the most exciting part of the story, but it is far from the whole thing. Even within an army or navy, in the middle of a war, relatively few men are involved in actual fighting at any given moment or for any length of time. In World War II, for example, the United States Army developed a strength of nearly nine million men, but only about two million of them were in ground combat forces; it produced a mere eighty-nine divisions, less than Japan, and some of them did not go into combat until the beginning of 1945, when the war against Germany was nearing its end. The naval historian Edward L. Beach has estimated that the entire combat experience of the entire United States Navy, if lumped together, would span only a few hours.

Such modern comparisons are of course somewhat invalidated by the ever more complex nature of warfare and the perpetually increasing substructure needed to sustain twentieth-century armies. The proportion of infantrymen in a Civil War army was far greater than in a modern army, but nevertheless, most men in most armies spend most of their time doing something other than fighting. And of course what is true by circumstance for armies is true by definition for the civilian society behind them. It has become increasingly apparent in contemporary society that, to sustain military operations, a state needs the support or at least passive acquiescence of its citizens. Frederick the Great might have thought a good war was one the civilian population remained ignorant of, but that was in eighteenth-century Prussia. That sort of view does not work today, certainly in the United States, as the government discovered with the Vietnam War, or even in the former Soviet Union, as its leaders found out with Afghanistan. An army may be the point of a nation's spear, but without societal support, that spear has no shaft.

In 1864, Abraham Lincoln and his government were seriously concerned that that shaft might be broken in their hands.

Ironically, this was a problem unique to the North. Jefferson Davis had been elected for a one-time, six-year term. He did not have to run for re-election during the course of the Civil War, though it is interesting to speculate on what might have happened—probably nothing—had he been forced to do so. But Lincoln was required to go to the people and ask for their support for his policies. In the summer of 1864 astute observers thought, and many hoped, that he would be repudiated.

"Lincoln's war," as the Democratic newspapers called it, certainly seemed unpopular enough. Hardly anyone could even remember the early days, when the president-elect had opined that they'd manage somehow, when he had called for 75,000 volunteers for three months' service. Thoughts of those days now seemed so naive, so innocent, so stupid. After three years the fancy uniforms were all gone, replaced by serviceable work clothes; the young heroes were old before their time, hollow-cheeked men of twenty-five who had seen their friends die horrible deaths, and all too many of the belles of Boston and Baltimore were widows before they had the chance to become mothers.

'Sixty-two and '63 had been bad enough, so incredibly worse than anyone had expected, but '64 was proving an absolute nightmare. Day after day after day the papers printed the horrible casualty lists from Virginia, and the trains came home with the wounded, the blind, the maimed. Sometimes it seemed as if the entire North were either in mourning or a vast hospital. And yet, ". . . I purpose to fight it out on this line if it takes all summer . . . ," and Julia Ward Howe, touring the camps of the Army of the Potomac, had seen the glory of the coming of the Lord. In July, the president issued a call for another 500,000 volunteers. Those who saw him around Washington noted how aged and stooped he looked, as though the entire country were carried on his shoulders. Physically, he was not well, though few knew that; mentally, far more than most, he felt the cost of the war:

Dear Madam [he wrote to Mrs. Bixby],—

I have been shown in the files of the War Department a statement from the Adjutant General of Massachusetts, that you are the mother of five sons who have died gloriously on the field of battle.

I feel how weak and fruitless must be any words of mine which should attempt to beguile you from the grief of a loss so overwhelming. But I cannot refrain from tendering to you the consolation that may be found in the thanks of the Republic they died to save.

I pray that our Heavenly Father may assuage the anguish of your bereavement, and leave you only the cherished memory of the loved and lost, and the solemn pride that must be yours, to have laid so costly a sacrifice upon the altar of Freedom.

So many had laid such sacrifices upon the altar of freedom, and in this fall of 1864 the people were to decide, Was it worth it? Was it worth the lives and hopes of those who had already gone, and the unknown numbers yet to be demanded? No! cried the Democrats; the war is a failure! Throw the rascals out! And Yes! cried the Republicans; yes unto the last breath. But the people must decide; in the last analysis, that was what the war was all about.

It was certainly an open question in mid-summer of 1864, and the fact that we now know what the people decided obscures the degree of uncertainty that then existed. With the war apparently bogged down in costly stalemate, anti-administration hopes ran high throughout the North. In spite of all the government's efforts to quash opposition, there was widespread disaffection. The draft was universally unpopular, the exemptions and substitutes it allowed even worse. The laboring classes were suffering from inflation, losing status and position even in a time of full employment. The country resented the new taxes, resented the impositions and inconveniences of a wartime economy, tired of the war news, sickened of the butchery. Throughout the North, men asked whether it was not time to stop throwing good money after bad, to stop wasting more lives, to make peace and be done with it. The

South had proven itself unconquerable on the field of battle; why not simply recognize what could not be denied, and get on with life?

———

In Northern disarray lay Southern hope. Thinking men in the Confederacy had by now come close to the conclusion that this war was no longer winnable by military means alone; they had long given up hope of some magic foreign intervention, a great loan heralded by the arrival of a British fleet to break the blockade, for example. Their own resources seemed increasingly inadequate to the demands of their task. But they knew—the papers made no secret of it—how rampant in the North was opposition to the war. They had their friends, and their contacts, and they did their best to cultivate the situation.

In this they were unwittingly assisted by one of the most difficult of Lincoln's wartime associates, Horace Greeley, the extremely powerful editor of the *New York Tribune*. The newspapers of the 1860s were the equivalent of today's television journalism, and no more nor less responsible than it. In the days of the written word, Greeley was a power in the land. Unfortunately, he did not know from one day to the next what he wanted to do with that power, and he blew in every direction, like the spring breezes. In the summer of 1864 he was blowing in the direction of peace, and he wrote Lincoln that there were Confederate commissioners in Canada, right across the border, ready to treat for peace, if only the president would receive them. Lincoln correctly assessed the Confederates as agents there to stir up trouble, rather than legitimate emissaries, so with his usual adroitness, he called their, and Greeley's, bluff. Did they have credentials, and peace proposals, in writing, and would Greeley vouch for them? Greeley folded, but nonetheless Lincoln sent his able young secretary, John Hay, to New York to meet the editor, and the two then went on to Niagara Falls, only to find, as Lincoln believed from the start, that it was a sham.

About the same time there was a second unofficial meeting, this time between Davis and two Union men, a journalist and a minister-turned-soldier. From this, widely publicized, it became apparent that the Union government would accept nothing short of reunification and emancipation, while the Confederate government would accept nothing short of independence. In other words, they were still stuck on two, or three, irreconcilabilities. There were those who thought that if Lincoln waffled on the principle of emancipation, he might win the other point, of reunion. He himself did not think so, and as a political matter, he believed that to give up emancipation, in the hope of winning over the Peace Democrats, would cost him the anti-slavery Republicans anyway. If he would not sacrifice his principles for some gain, he would certainly not do it for none.

One sees here, of course, the evolution of Lincoln as the war went on: from his early insistence that the war was not about slavery; to his painful recognition that it was; to his commitment to emancipation as a useful expedient; to his profound conviction that emancipation was a Good, and slavery was an Evil; this latter to the point where he was willing to stand or fall on it, even that his nation should stand or fall on it. All of these were agonizing transitions, for the president personally, and for the country as a whole. The latter is illustrated in the letters of soldiers, early ones saying they would desert rather than fight for the slaves, later ones acknowledging the changing character of the war, and of their own views of the issues.

Confederates missed much of this evolution; they remained convinced that the war was a Black Republican hoax worked upon Northerners, and that the voters of the North would repudiate Lincoln and his gang, and would resoundingly record their unwillingness to die to free the black man. They readily obtained Northern newspapers, and like all people everywhere, they drew from them what they chose to do. If Greeley editorialized that Lincoln could not possibly win reelection, they believed him and quoted him; if Greeley wrote that the war must continue, they ignored him. In a sense they were exiles from their own country, and as all exiles do, they developed an inaccurate view, fixed at some pre-exile moment, of what they had left behind.

President Davis might indeed have done more than he did to capitalize on dissent in the enemy camp, but Davis was not very good at the minutiae and million little deals and connivances of everyday politics. He would far rather lecture men on first principles than engage in the handshake, slap-on-the-back, nudge-and-wink kind of politics that was unavoidable in the modern state. He could not woo Northern voters with his humanity, because to the world at large, he appeared not to have any. In fact, that was grossly untrue; Davis's problem was not his lack of human feeling, but rather his total inability to share and show it beyond his small circle of intimates. At the end of April, Davis's young son fell off a balcony of the presidential mansion in Richmond and died; racked by grief, the president manfully continued his duties, trying to pretend nothing had happened. One journalist who observed him closely, though, wrote that he had "the face of a corpse and the form of a skeleton." It was the apparently awkward and ungainly Lincoln, not the austere Davis, who slowly impressed by his humanity and ultimately awed by his principles. One measure of the course of the war was the way Lincoln grew in office, and Davis shrunk.

That again is the view of hindsight. In 1864 the Democrats thought they could beat Lincoln, and many Republicans agreed with them. A good many of the latter, indeed, went so far as to suggest that the Republicans should rid themselves of Lincoln, and that they would have a better chance at winning the election if they replaced him with, say, Salmon P. Chase or John C. Frémont, or perhaps General Ben Butler. Chase was the Radical Republicans' first choice, a cabinet member and an ardent abolitionist, and a devious and determined political climber. He, however, tipped his hand too soon, and in spite of substantial support within Congress itself, his campaign to replace the man he had sworn to serve loyally fizzled. Frémont, unemployed since his military defeats in 1862, was a fallback choice for some, but he was always too willing to be used by somebody—by anybody, it seemed— and though he gained endorsement from some splinter groups, he represented no real threat. Neither did Spoons Butler, and thus when the Republicans met in convention in June in Baltimore, Lincoln handily won his party's nomination for re-election, though a number of cracks had to be papered over to do the job. The Republicans nominated as vice president a man who was actually a War Democrat, Andrew Johnson of Tennessee, and they decided to call themselves the National Union Party to broaden their appeal.

They certainly needed to cover themselves as best they could, for the game was there for the Democrats to win, if only they could develop a combination to do it. That was the real rub. It was all well and good to cry, "The war is a failure!" but what did they offer as an alternative? They did not really know. They had some vague ideas that if they stopped the war, somehow all would be well again; the country might be reunited, and everyone could agree that the late unpleasantness had just not happened. It was far from a positive program, and even that was achieved only by diligently ignoring a great many facts, most notably that the war *had* happened, and that the Confederacy still insisted upon its independence.

Their dilemma was underscored by their search for a candidate. Who would possibly be the Democratic standard-bearer against Lincoln? Since they were going to repudiate the war, it would look best if they had a war hero to do it. The extreme Peace Democrats did not want even that, and they did their best to nominate Horatio Seymour of New York, one of the most difficult anti-war state governors with whom Lincoln had to contend. There was, however, a more charismatic figure, and he let it be known he was available: George Brinton McClellan. The man who had once been willing to "become dictator to save the country, and perish by suicide to preserve its liberties," was now willing to become the Democratic presidential candidate.

There was one small problem. McClellan wanted to win the war, and then negotiate on the basis of some pre-war situation; the Peace Democrats wanted to end the war, and then open negotiations, and they managed to write a plank to that effect into the party platform when they met in Chicago at the end of August. McClellan, when he accepted their nomination, did so in a convoluted letter that he rewrote several times, and ended up by emphasizing his priority rather than the platform sequence. This was more than a crack that could be papered over; it was a potential chasm, and the nomination of a Peace Democrat, George Pendleton of Ohio, for vice president did little to disguise it. The Republicans gleefully ridiculed the Democrats as "wanting both peace and war—peace with the Confederacy, war against the United States government," and they were not far from wrong. McClellan, to do him credit, quickly felt the false position he was in, and spent most of the campaign trying to square the circle.

It would all be up to the voters then, and what did they think about it? Few could tell for sure. The nineteenth century was blessed with the absence of our contemporary polling establishment, so how things were going depended very largely upon what men were saying around the cracker barrel in the store at the crossroads, or in the barbershop, or after church on Sunday. For the Republicans, things did not look good. The country was not happy.

The news from the front offered few consolations. Grant was stuck down around Petersburg in Virginia; Democrats could point out that their man had got that far two whole years ago, and with a lot fewer casualties than it had cost Grant. Of course, what their man had done after he got there was another matter, but in a political debate, a lot gets skipped over. Then Sherman was lost God alone knew where down in Georgia someplace, perpetually advancing on Atlanta but never getting there. In July, Confederate forces under Jubal Early swept up out of the Shenandoah Valley once again and raided within sight of Washington itself. Lincoln told people he hoped neither the capital nor Baltimore would be sacked, hardly the remark of a victorious and confident commander in chief.

But what did people *really* think, in the middle of that summer as they went about their daily lives? Could the war be won, could they stay the course, was it worth the effort? Now one looks back at the overriding issue, and because it occupies all our attention, we think it must have occupied all their attention, too. For some, of course, it did; for soldiers, or the families of soldiers, the war was all-consuming, literally a matter of life and death and survival of the family unit. Yet the soldier, who after all wanted to live, might as well vote to end the war as to continue it. And his father at home, who wanted to see his son grow old, might think the best way to ensure that was to vote for a party dedicated to stopping the war immediately. Mothers and wives, who might be thought to have an equal stake in the war, were of course not allowed to vote—though anyone who has ever had a mother or a wife will realize that saying they had no vote is not the same as saying they had no influence.

Most observers were pretty sure the military men, or those connected with them, would in fact vote Republican, but what of the rest of the country, all the millions of people who just needed to get on with their day-to-day lives? They might well not support a war to which they could see no end, and in which they could see little profit. These were the people to whom the Democrats appealed. The war is a failure, the war is a waste; "this bloody and expensive war" was a stock phrase of Democratic editorials and oratory. Lincoln and his gang had suspended civil rights, imposed burdensome taxes, wrecked the country, and for what? To free the slaves? To keep South Carolina in a union it wanted to leave? Surely the country deserved better than these abolitionists, fanatics, political charlatans and backwoods yokels. Surely the country deserved George B. McClellan and peace and prosperity.

In July and August it looked not only as if that was what the country deserved, but also as if that was what it wanted. The reports Lincoln received from his political managers did not look good. They would almost certainly lose many of the state governments, much of Congress, and they would probably lose the White House too. People were so tired of war and death and destruction; peace was worth almost any price.

The electoral campaign was balm for the Confederacy, and it spent a great deal of money to support the Democratic effort. Every anti-war headline and editorial in the North was greeted with jubilation in the South, and in Richmond they made a very simple equation: If the Democrats won the election, the Confederacy won the war. That was all there was to it. From the heights of pre-election rhetoric, Confederates could see victory just down the road. Confederate morale rose to levels it had not seen since before Gettysburg and Vicksburg.

Abraham Lincoln agreed with them. In early August Admiral Farragut took his ships into Mobile Bay, closing off completely one of the last few ports in the Confederacy, but even that was not enough to alter the political balance. Lincoln shuffled his cabinet; he got rid of Chase, he got rid of the Radical Blairs, thought to have too much influence over him. His political people damned the Democrats as traitors to the cause and the nation, hinted darkly of Copperhead plots, warned that the opposition was only encouraging the Confederacy to fight longer and harder. All in vain. All paled before the siren song of peace. By late August Lincoln was sure he was going to lose.

On the 23rd he wrote his famous little memorandum, which he took into cabinet, had signed, and then tucked away for further reference:

> This morning, as for some days past, it seems exceedingly probable that this Administration will not be re-elected. Then it will be my duty to so co-operate with the President elect, as to save the Union between the election and the inauguration; as he will have secured his election on such ground that he cannot possibly save it afterwards.

Thus Abraham Lincoln toward the end of the summer. Unless something very dramatic happened to change not only the course of the war, but the public perception of the course of the war, Lincoln was going to lose the election, and if he did, the Union was going to lose the war and all that it represented. Bowed down with care and anguish, the president paced the floor in the dead of the summer nights.

Chapter 18

Trampling Out the Vintage . . .

T HE INTIMATE relationship between the military course of the war and the contemporaneous political situation was well understood by all parties. President Lincoln, Generals Grant and Sherman, and all the other senior Union commanders knew that somehow they must achieve some success sufficient to convince voters, less of the justice of the Union's cause—they already believed in that— than of the fact that the cause was winnable. On the other side, President Davis and his generals and supporters knew that if they could only hang on until after the election, and while doing so deny the Union that significant success, then they might well triumph in the end. For the Confederacy, the Northern election was the last bulwark of their hopes, the last of those fallback positions from which they might still persevere. It all came down, then, to those tired thousands in blue and gray, and their willingness to buy time or ground with their lives, their willingness to suffer for their friends or their families or their principles or whatever motivated them to risk their lives. But then, that was what it had always been anyway.

———

General Grant's shift of operations south to the Petersburg area was conducted with skill approaching brilliance, but once the Army of the Potomac was facing the entrenchments of this little southern city, things rapidly fell apart. The initial assaults on the town were bungled, and the very real opportunity of taking it in mid-June was frittered away, by poor planning, poor coordination, poor staff work, and simple carelessness and stupidity. It was a pity that having fought so hard and come so far, at such a heavy price, the Union forces fell just short of success. But that seemed of a piece with the history of this army: it was fated to deserve more than it ever achieved.

The Army of Northern Virginia, on the other hand, deserved everything it did achieve, and achieved far more than anyone had any right to expect of it. It was not only a great army—they both were—but it was a lucky army as well, while its opponent was not. The student seeking rational explanations for history may decry the role of luck, but most soldiers believe in it. Napoleon certainly did, and he was a man of some considerable experience in this area.

Robert E. Lee arrived at Petersburg on the morning of June 18, and that afternoon the first elements of A. P. Hill's corps started filing into the trenches around the town. That was the end of Grant's opportunities for carrying the city by a coup de main; he was now stuck with the necessity of besieging the place, with no real prospect of a quick end to the struggle. Few men could see that the fight for the town would last nine months, a blindness which was undoubtedly a blessing.

The simple truth was that both armies were sadly run down, exhausted by the marching and fighting of May and June, and significantly losing tone as they went. Casualties among the officers had been heavy, and among the men frightful, about 55,000 for the Army of the Potomac and something close to perhaps 40,000 for the Army of Northern Virginia. The Union army was shedding veterans and replacing them with regiments that were new to combat, or indeed even new to soldiering. The veterans resented the new men, and the conscripts, and contradictorily, the fact that they themselves were still in the war and that there were not more of the very men they resented. Clear logic should not be expected of men who had been marching and fighting and seeing their friends die for three years. On the Confederate side, there was no relief for old soldiers; they stayed until they were killed, wounded, or gave up and deserted; theirs was a Hobson's choice indeed. The Confederacy, which had already run out of almost everything else, was running out of bodies as well.

Operations went on, a bewildering, bungling sequence of battles and misery as one side or the other sought to break the stalemate. The numbers, and the initiative, lay with the Army of the Potomac; that very fact was a measure of Grant's success against Lee, ever the most aggressive and offensive-minded of generals. But the fortifications and the interior lines were with the Confederates, and try as he might,

Grant could not find a way through or around the impasse.

The geographical situation was as complex as the sequence of battles. Petersburg is twenty miles south of Richmond, and its major importance derived from the fact that of the five railroads which fed the capital from the south and west, three funneled through this city. Thus if the Union could capture the town, or so seriously interdict those railroads as to make them useless, Richmond might well become untenable. There was a second geographical factor of great significance, and that was the lie of the rivers in the area. Richmond is on the James, and from that city the river flows south in a straight line for five miles to Drewry's Bluff; it then goes into a series of lazy bends for several miles, passing New Market and Malvern Hill of 1862 fame, before becoming a substantial estuary at Bermuda Hundred, where Ben Butler let himself get shut up at the start of this campaign. Petersburg itself is on the Appomattox River, about seven miles west of where the Appomattox joins the James estuary. The Confederates developed a long system of defenses that traced the James, then jumped overland from its bends to the Appomattox and on around south of Petersburg. They could not of course hold the entire line from Richmond past Petersburg, a distance of perhaps thirty miles, but they did not have to do that. They had to hold Petersburg itself, keeping the Union forces away from the railroads, and a line north of the city until the James River did their work for them.

Grant and Meade operated against this system in three locations. There were some efforts to force the Confederate lines north of the James River, but these were largely secondary to the more serious assaults south of it, directed against Petersburg itself. And thirdly, Grant attempted to develop cavalry raids that ranged farther afield than the immediate Petersburg area, with the thought of cutting those vital railroads at a greater distance than the Confederates could counter. The Civil War has often been called the first railroad war, and the siege of Petersburg graphically illustrates how important rail traffic had become in a few short years.

On the larger scale of the entire eastern theater, Lee, deprived locally of the initiative as he was by Grant's grip, sought to regain it by having recourse to the old strategy of 1862. Then, the Confederates had been forced to fight McClellan on the Peninsula, and distracted their enemies by unleashing General Jackson in the Shenandoah Valley, providing a distant threat to the security of Washington. Now Lee tried the same thing, with Jubal Early playing Jackson's part. The results were quite catastrophically different from anything anyone, especially the Confederates, might have expected.

———

The raiding portion of Grant's strategy developed even before the siege of Petersburg was fully engaged. As he was moving across from Cold Harbor to the James, Grant set Sheridan in motion with two full divisions of his cavalry corps. These were ordered in a long arc north and west of Richmond, their ultimate aim to join in with General David Hunter, supposed to be advancing east out of the Shenandoah Valley. The two forces were to meet at Charlottesville, fifty miles from the Confederate capital, and from there tear up portions of the important Virginia Central Railroad, another of those crucial lines feeding Richmond.

This did not work. Not only did Hunter get himself beat at Lynchburg, but Sheridan's troopers, after a leisurely ride, got caught by Wade Hampton's and Fitzhugh Lee's cavalry divisions, and in a confused melee around Trevilian Station on the 11th and 12th of June, the Federals definitely got the worst of it. Sheridan gave up his assigned mission and headed back the way he had come. By the time he rejoined the Army of the Potomac, Grant had shifted bases from Cold Harbor to the James, and failed in his opening moves to get Petersburg on the run.

Grant now began his strategy of inching out to the west and south, trying to extend beyond the area the Confederates could cover. In the third week of June he sent Birney's II Corps—Hancock, never really recovered from Gettysburg, had given up the command—to cut the Weldon Railroad, and Horatio Wright's VI Corps beyond it toward the Jerusalem Plank Road. These two units moved out independently. Lee countered with A. P. Hill's corps, and Hill managed to find the uncovered gap between the two Federal outfits, slammed into their flank, took about 1,600 prisoners, and inflicted another 1,300 casualties. Though the Federals did manage to hold positions along the plank road, they had received a nasty little shock; obviously the Army of Northern Virginia was a long way from done yet.

So it went. When Grant sent James Wilson and two cavalry divisions south and west to tear up railroad, Lee countered with four cavalry and one infantry divisions. The discomfited blue troopers lost 1,500 men, their wagon trains, and a dozen guns, and all they got in return was a few days' interruption of the Southside Railroad. By early July the armies were settling in to the siege of Petersburg.

———

Next came one of the oddest incidents of the war. Both sides now agreed that to send men against prepared field positions was virtually suicidal; the odds so heavily favored the defenders, fighting from behind breastworks, catching the attackers in the open in a crossfire, that relatively few men could hold off many times their number. There was no way through, and judging by events so far, no way around either.

But maybe there was a way under. Mining is one of the standard scenarios in siege warfare, and it happened that in the Union army there was a regiment of coal miners, the 48th Pennsylvania. When Lieutenant Colonel Henry Pleasants, himself a mining engineer in civilian life, heard one of his sergeants say, "We ought to dig a mine under them," he took the suggestion up the line. Burnside, his corps commander, was keen, Grant less so, but for lack of any better alternative, he agreed to the idea.

Pleasants's men set to work with an ingenuity and enthusiasm that amazed those who preferred to live their lives above ground. Eager little moles, they dug and planned, took sights and measurements, squinted and figured; for the month of July the front in Burnsides's area looked like a deranged anthill. Eventually they produced a tunnel more than 500 feet long, with a gallery at the end that ran perpendicular to it, seventy-five feet long, and twenty feet deep under the Confederate trenches. Into this they carried 320 kegs of powder, four tons in all, and by the end of July they were ready to blow the whole thing sky high.

So far so good. From here on everything went wrong. Burnside had one division of black troops in his corps, commanded by Brigadier General Edward Fererro; he selected it for the assault, and the troops were carefully rehearsed for their attack. Then Meade said it would be politically unwise to use blacks in this unconventional way, because it would look, should the attack fail, as if they were being sacrificed. Burnside saw the matter falling apart, lost interest in it, and had his other division commanders draw straws to see who got the nod. General James Ledlie drew the short straw. He did nothing in the way of preparation.

Thus when the mine went off with a spectacular roar early on the morning of July 30, the Federals totally failed to exploit their stunning surprise. The mine created a crater 170 feet long, sixty or seventy feet wide, and thirty feet deep, and killed several hundred Confederates who were in the wrong place. But when the assaulting Union regiments finally cleared their own entrenchments, instead of charging across the open spaces on either side of the crater, they charged into it. With the crater clogged with bluecoats, Burnside then ordered forward Fererro's division in support, and by mid-morning there were several thousand men packed into the crater and trying to claw their way up the crumbling, smoking sides to get out.

The Confederates reacted with admirable speed, and were soon lining the crater shooting down into the clogged mass of Federals, who could go neither forward nor back. In spite of some attempts to exploit on either side of the hole, the affair turned into a straightforward butchery. While Fererro and Ledlie sat behind their own lines sharing a companionable bottle of rum, their divisions were cut to pieces, and by the late afternoon, the entire sorry mess was over, at a cost of almost 4,000 casualties, a full quarter of the men engaged. Ledlie was dismissed in disgrace, Fererro managed to get off, and Burnside was allowed to resign, none of which was of any import to all those poor dead soldiers.

The little battles, and the constant wastage, kept on. At the end of July, as The Crater battle was being fought, Grant attacked north of the James at Deep Bottom Run; no gain. He tried again two weeks later; no gain. In late August there were further attempts to extend to the south and west, and the armies fought at Globe Tavern, and a few days later at Reams' Station. In September Lee riposted with a raid by Wade Hampton against, of all things, a Federal cattle pen; Hampton's cowboys came back into their own lines herding 2,500 beef cattle, a welcome addition to the short rations of the Confederate troops.

At the end of September they fought at New Market Heights, north of the James, and a day later at Poplar Spring Church back on the south side, a week later at Darbytown, and three weeks after that at Hatcher's Run, all just names now, forgotten little hamlets and dusty crossroads where good young men died, a steady dripping of lives and blood, a wearing away of the flesh of both armies. The men got dirty, and tired, and raw, and drunk when they could manage it, and cursed their sergeants, and their officers, and their fate, and day after day, week after weary week, the armies ground away at each other while the leaves turned orange and the days rolled inexorably on toward the election.

———

Meanwhile, Lee tried to work the old magic; he played the Valley card again. It was two long years now since the glory days of the first Valley campaign, and Stonewall Jackson lying in his grave for one of them. But it might still work. He gave the task to Jubal Early, a black-browed, profane, bitter fighter, and Early set off with his corps in mid-June, a measure both of Lee's confidence in his ability to hold Grant with few men, and of his unconquerable determination to regain the initiative in the campaign.

Early arrived in the Shenandoah Valley just in time to assist in the defeat of General David Hunter's force at Lynchburg, and as Hunter fell back to the westward, into the mountains, Early assumed command of all the Valley forces, about 14,000 men, reorganized them into two infantry corps of two divisions each, and a cavalry division of four brigades, and set out northward down the Valley. Simply put, his mission was to raise hell, and Old Jube thought he was just the man for it. He intended to do nothing less than strike at Washington itself.

By the first of July the Rebels were swarming around Winchester, twenty miles from the Potomac. An alarmed Franz Sigel began concentrating his forces at Maryland Heights, on the south side of the river across from Harpers Ferry. He was too strong for Early to take on, so the wily Confederate slipped around him, crossed the river, and swooped into Maryland. By July 9 he was in Frederick, levying a requisition of $200,000 on the town. Meanwhile his cavalry troopers swept over the country, taking contributions and scaring Maryland silly.

Grant and Meade had not paid a great deal of attention to this problem, until they got word that the Confederates were across the Potomac; then they had to react. In the second week of July, while Early moved toward the capital, Grant detached Horatio Wright and VI Corps and sent them north to bolster Washington's defenses. While they were on the way, Early brushed aside a scratch force of Federal troops commanded by Lew Wallace, threatened Baltimore with his cavalry, and moved closer to Washington. Garrison troops and hastily mustered civil servants dug trenches and manned the city's fortifications, and a near panic spread throughout the North.

Early camped in Silver Spring on the night of July 10–11, but even as he did so, Wright's veteran troops were filing off the steamers at the city docks, and marching through the town to take up their positions. Here were men long past scaring, and they were alternately determined to chase off the Rebs, and amused by all the silly civilians in the capital. As they took up their positions, President Lincoln himself went out to have a look at the enemy; he stood, conspicuously tall, by one of the earthworks, only to be told by a regimental officer, "Get down from there! You'll get your head shot off, you damned fool!" The president obediently got down; the whole episode made the kind of story he loved to tell on himself.

The Confederates actually considered an assault, but upon learning of the arrival of heavy Federal reinforcements, they decided to retreat. By the 14th they were back across the Potomac and heading up the Valley again. Wright pursued for some distance, but then Grant decided the crisis was over, and recalled him to the Petersburg front.

Early, however, was not yet finished. Just because he had been chased did not mean he had been caught, and for a couple of weeks he led a merry dance around the Valley, while Federal troops from four separate departments tried ineffectually to coordinate their movements and get him in a trap. For Grant it was all a bother; he and Washington got into a squabble about what should be done. Grant wanted to give the area command to General Franklin, but President Lincoln demurred: Franklin had not supported Burnside away back at Fredericksburg, and he was still paying for it. Grant then suggested Meade himself. While the War Department chewed this over, Early came out of his hole, rampaged around Maryland, and sent his troopers north over the Pennsylvania line. There they burned Chambersburg, when the town could not raise a ransom, in retaliation for Federal ravages in the Valley. Lincoln then put Henry Halleck in charge of coordinating the Federal forces, and Halleck managed to get as tangled up as he usually did when faced with field operations. Finally Grant bit the bullet. All right, he said, I will send up Phil Sheridan, and we shall put a stop to this once and for all.

After a slow start in the war, Philip Henry Sheridan had proved the epitome of Aristophanes' "bandy-legged little captain full of guts." Short, stocky, graceless, fiery, he had proved a peerless combat leader. Now he was given a new area command, styled the Middle Department, and told to destroy Early. For a good five weeks the two sides eyed each other warily and maneuvered back and forth without much result. Then, when Early became overconfident, Sheridan caught him in a poor position at Winchester on September 19 and slammed into him front and flank. As the Federals enjoyed a superiority of at least two to one, they had everything in their favor. The Confederates were pushed back fighting through the town, and then collapsed when hit again on their flank. Sheridan lost 5,000 casualties to Early's 4,000, but the Rebel army could not afford the losses, and the Federals could.

Early never really recovered from this rude shock. He retreated south, and got beat again at Fisher's Hill on the 22nd, and was then chased right out of the Valley. Sheridan now fell back toward Winchester, ravaging the territory as he went. But Early came back yet again, reinforced, and on October 19 he caught the Federal army at Cedar Creek; he was pushing it back from position to position when Sheridan, who had been twenty miles away at Winchester, arrived on his lathered horse, gave new direction to the troops, who were already rallying, and completely turned the tide for the day. "Sheridan's Ride" was written into the schoolbooks, and his horse, Rienzi, was eventually stuffed and placed in the Smithsonian Institution. Even so, it was not the famous ride for which Sheridan in the Valley was best remembered. It was the destruction of what many considered, or still consider, the most beautiful territory in the entire continent.

———

There was one way to stop the Confederate threats from the Shenandoah Valley, and that was to destroy the Valley itself. Here again we see at work the peculiar military balances of this war, or of warfare at this stage. Sherman could not completely, permanently, destroy the army ranged against him, so he would have to deprive it of its sustenance, by making war upon the infrastructure that supported that army. Grant could not beat Lee in the open field, nor Lee Grant; therefore the field maneuvers descended into a war of posts, a war against supplies and supply lines. Sheridan might beat Early, but he could never catch him and wipe him out, so the next best thing was to deny him the possibility of rapid movement and resupply by wasting the country through which he moved. There was in fact good historical precedent for this; it was actually warfare as practiced in the late seventeenth century, typified by such things as Turenne's ravaging of the Palatinate during Louis XIV's wars. The eighteenth century, with its more cosmopolitan and urbane—and generally less destructive—ideas, would have been

271

shocked by this, and the twentieth century, which gassed soldiers and bombed civilians, would have shrugged it off. In the nineteenth century, it seemed a necessity to its Union practitioners, and a shame and outrage to those Southerners upon whom it was visited. But as Sherman wrote to Halleck, "If the people raise a howl against my barbarity and cruelty, I will answer that war is war, and not popularity-seeking. If they want peace, they and their relatives must stop the war."

Phil Sheridan could burn a barn and turn a phrase with the best of them. Told by Grant to clean out the Valley, he replied, "I shall leave them only their eyes to weep with," and his troopers set to work with a will. They ran off the stock, they burned the barns, they trampled the standing crops; they broke down bridges and girdled fruit trees; they carried off wagons and burned farm implements. At first there was some little attempt to provide sustenance for civilians, and to leave dwellings alone, but this sort of violence inevitably begat more of it. When Confederate guerrillas caught and hanged some Union soldiers, the bluecoats responded by burning ever more, and hanging Rebels whom they earlier might have imprisoned. The Federal passage through the Valley was marked by the trails of smoke rising up lazily into the sky, in an orgy of destruction that eventually became known simply as "The Burning." Sheridan wrote Halleck, "I will soon commence on Loudoun County, and let them know there is a God in Israel." When he was finished, he wrote to Grant that "a crow would need to carry rations to cross the Shenandoah Valley." The ravaging of the Valley may arguably have shortened the war; it unarguably embittered the peace.

———

That summer there was another turn of the screw in a different quarter. For some time little had been heard from the navy, which might well, as in Britain, be considered "the silent service." Yet the blockade had continued doing its slow, insidious, and deadly work. There has been considerable argument among historians as to the effectiveness of this policy, and its contribution to the overall victory, and opinion has swayed back and forth. At one time it was thought that the blockade had virtually won the war; then scholars, who after all make their reputations by attacking established views rather than supporting them, decided that the blockade had actually accomplished relatively little. They pointed out that it was not wholly effective, and that the

Confederacy never did run out of supplies and necessary imports. In other words, in a sort of all-or-nothing argument, since the blockade alone did not win the war, it must have made no significant contribution to it.

In fact, the impact was enormous, and it grew steadily worse for the Confederacy, until by 1864, shortages were really beginning to hurt. The South had, as noted earlier, about 3,500 miles of coastline and some 180 ports and points of access, so stopping them up was extraordinarily difficult. In 1861 only one vessel out of every nine sailing to or from Confederate ports was intercepted. But by 1862 it was one in seven, and by 1864 it was one in three. In itself, that might mean only a one-third cut in imports or exports, but in actuality it meant a great deal more than that. For even if some foreign merchants, notably British and a few French, were attracted to the profits of blockade-running, far more sober and legitimate merchants were deterred by the risks. About eight hundred ships ran the blockade in 1861, but in 1860 there had been six thousand ships entering or clearing Southern ports, so the very fact of the blockade, let alone its real effectiveness, diminished Confederate trade by about four fifths. If one adds to that the further losses of items that would have been sold or traded in the southern states by the northern ones, the diminution becomes ever greater. Between the blockade itself, and Union diplomatic efforts in France and especially in Britain, Confederate foreign trade and assistance was practically cut off.

The blockade was a slow, grinding business of Union soldiers occupying the sea islands and coastal barriers of Georgia and the Carolinas, of raids and boat expeditions and fevers and little sudden ambushes. For example, New Bern, in North Carolina, is thirty miles from the open ocean, but it was occupied by Ambrose Burnside's troops in March of 1862, and was in Federal hands for the rest of the war. On shipboard it was a stultifying routine of coaling, standing watches in all kinds of weathers, heat prostration in the boiler rooms and sunstroke on deck, of the pitch bubbling out of the deck seams or the rain coming down in sheets, while the ships steered back and forth, back and forth, across the entrances to Charleston or Wilmington or Mobile. Week after weary week went by in the ugly monitors or the stripped-down steam frigates and sloops. Occasionally a blockade-runner was caught, or a ship burst into flame, or ran aground, or the Rebels came out and traded shots. The Federals tried to take Charleston and failed, and they besieged it for several months, tried again, and failed again. The ships' officers took to drink, or reading classical history, and the war went on in a dull, soul-destroying routine, under which nothing ever seemed to happen but no one could ever dare relax.

It was a thankless, apparently unrewarding task. All it was doing was strangling the Confederacy. There were women in Carolina sewing with needles carved from bone, and coffee was a luxury drink available only to the privileged few. And always, off the few remaining ports, there were those hated topmasts just visible over the horizon, the despised enemy, the dirty Yankee, and where now was King Cotton, and who dared make war on him?

In the summer of 1864, Admiral Farragut finally closed down Mobile Bay, the Confederacy's last major port in the Gulf of Mexico. This had been a thorn in the Federal side ever since the war began. Alabama has of course only a short coastline, about forty miles of it, and most of that taken up by the large indentation of Mobile Bay. In Confederate hands the area was a standing affront to the U.S. Navy, and it was only fifty miles from Pensacola, never surrendered and the headquarters of the West Gulf blockading squadron. Before the war, Mobile had been the chief cotton-shipping port of the South; after the fall of New Orleans, its importance increased dramatically.

Yet the Union was slow to do anything about it; other matters kept getting in the way; the Mississippi River campaign took up most of 1862 and 1863, by the time Port Hudson was finally captured; then in early 1864 there were the Red River expedition and the attack on Charleston over in South Carolina, both of them failures. So it took Admiral Farragut a long time to get Mobile to the top of the list of priorities.

The local terrain and defenses were peculiar. Mobile itself sits at the top of a twenty-five-mile-long shallow bay. The bay is protected by sandbars, and there was only one deepwater entrance. This was guarded by two forts, Morgan and Gaines, the former on a long sandbar extending from the eastern shore of the mainland, the latter on the end of Dauphin Island, basically another low bar. Into the channel from Fort Gaines the Confederates had strung a line of underwater obstacles to which they had fixed mines, known in those days as "torpedoes," constructed with contact fuses so they would explode if a ship bumped into them. There was only about 150 yards of clear water between the end of this line and the guns of Fort Morgan.

Beyond that, the Confederates had constructed a small fleet of local vessels for inshore work, and were also building, away up the Alabama River at Selma, a large iron ram, the *Tennessee.* They hoped the *Tennessee* would have the same effect the *Virginia* had had in Hampton Roads when it first appeared: any Union ship that got past the torpedoes and the forts should be rammed and sunk by the new monster warship.

Farragut knew about this, and he raced to get his squadron ready before the *Tennessee* was completed and sent downriver. But he had to have ironclad monitors himself; he could not do the job with wooden oceangoing ships alone. In July he got four of the ugly ironclads, and he got troops to mount a land attack once he was inside the bay. He decided to take his wooden ships in, two by two, lashed alongside each other so one could carry the other through if either was disabled; they would go in past the torpedoes. His monitors would take on Fort Morgan, their heavy guns and small silhouettes the best counter he had to the fort's guns.

The attack took place on August 5, the fleet coming in on a rising tide. The steam frigate *Brooklyn* led the port column, as it had a heavier bow armament than Farragut's flagship, the *Hartford,* which came next in line. Stripped of their topgallants and all padded and armored, the ships were a far cry from the delicate, balanced beauty of a sailing vessel at sea, but they were all business. The monitor *Tecumseh* led the other line in. As the line swept past Fort Morgan, the *Tennessee* appeared ahead, and the *Tecumseh* steered straight for the Confederate ship. Before the two could engage, the Federal monitor ran across a torpedo, which exploded under the keel and tore out the bottom; the *Tecumseh* went down in seconds, taking most of her crew with her.

Meanwhile the *Brooklyn* too ran into trouble. As she neared the channel entrance, lookouts reported objects in the water ahead; the captain ordered the engines into reverse, swinging the ship across the entrance channel and fouling the whole line. Astern, in the *Hartford,* old Farragut, lashed to the rigging and looking like some ancient mariner, demanded to know what was going on. "Torpedoes! torpedoes!" came the answer, and Farragut roared out, "Damn the torpedoes—full speed ahead!" The *Hartford* surged into the lead, and the rest of the line, including the *Brooklyn,* followed in her wake. Down in the boiler room they heard the primers snap off the water-rotted mines as the ship ran over them.

The *Tennessee* ran down the Union line, firing clumsily as she went but doing little damage. Three hours after they had weighed anchor, the Union fleet stopped, well up the bay, and Farragut sent the hands to breakfast. The Confederates then played into his hands. Confederate Admiral Franklin Buchanan, the same who had commanded the *Virginia,* might have kept the *Tennessee* safe under the guns of Fort Morgan, a semiperpetual threat to the Federal ships. Instead he chose to come out and fight to a finish. Informed of his coming, Farragut chortled, "I didn't think old Buck was such a fool."

For a while the *Tennessee* did well. Several times rammed by the Union frigates, she was so heavily constructed that she did more damage to them than they to her; in the confusion the *Hartford* was rammed by another Union ship, and for a while there was a wild melee. But Union gunnery took its toll, and the *Tennessee* slowly had her gunports jammed and her stack riddled, so there was no draft for her engines; the rudder was struck, and after about an hour the *Tennessee* was little more than a stationary hulk. Her captain climbed out in the open and waved a white flag, and that was the end of her.

It was the end of Mobile as well, for the last of the forts, Morgan, surrendered to the army by the end of the month. The city itself was not occupied until the war was virtually over—and then only with considerable loss—but with the forts gone, and the approaches blocked, it was no longer of any utility to the Rebels, or anyone else. The Confederacy no longer had a major port on the Gulf of Mexico.

———

Not only was the Confederacy deprived of one of its last major ports; by now it had almost nothing left of its navy either. Southern shipbuilding efforts during the war were quite remarkable, considering what they had to work with, but they were usually ineffective, and a substantial number of warships never managed to get launched, or were destroyed or broke down almost immediately after being put into service. That bald statement dismisses a great deal of effort and heartbreaking work on the part of the Confederacy's navy and its able head, Stephen R. Mallory; during the war they produced some sixty warships, ironclads and rams, as well as a host of improvised vessels from gunboats to tugs to premature attempts at a couple of submarines.

More exciting, if in the long run no more significant, were the Confederate efforts in the direction of oceangoing commerce raiders and cruisers, as well as a few privateers. There were a mere seven of the former, and only one of them was homegrown. Early in 1861 Captain Raphael Semmes converted a New Orleans-to-Cuba packet into the commerce raider *Sumter,* and got past the blockading squadron at the mouth of the Mississippi. He took several prizes before he was trapped in Gibraltar in January of 1862, where he sold the ship for lack of anything better to do.

It turned out that it was easier to buy ships in Britain than to build them in the Confederacy; British shipbuilders and agents were delighted to be of service. At one time they even began building armored rams for the Confederacy, and gave it up only when the American minister, Charles Francis Adams, threatened the British government with a declaration of war. He did so, of course, in the most polite way: "I am ignorant of the precise legal niceties, but it is superfluous of me to point out to your lordship that if those ships are allowed to sail, it means war."

Those, however, were purpose-designed warships, and easy to spot. It was harder to prevent the sailing of ostensibly commercial vessels that once at sea might readily be converted into armed commerce-raiders; it was especially difficult to prevent that when Her Majesty's government shrugged off protests, and appeared much more favorably disposed to the Confederacy than to the Union. In this way, a number of ships did get to sea, and became a major nuisance. Wisely, the Federal navy refused to be distracted from the primary mission of blockade, but Rebel commerce-destroyers did a great deal of damage around the edges.

Three cruisers particularly achieved fame or notoriety. In the spring of 1862 a British steamer named the *Oreto* emerged from her cocoon as the CSS *Florida.* She made several cruises, taking a great number of prizes, before she was finally cornered in Bahia in Brazil. There the USS *Wachusett,* under Commander Napoleon Collins, rammed her and opened fire in a blatant disregard of Brazilian sovereignty and international law. The *Florida* was taken by a prize crew to Hampton Roads, and when a court awarded her to Brazil, to be returned to the Confederacy, she was rammed again and sunk—accidentally, of course—by an army transport steamer. Collins was court-martialed and dismissed from the service, but Secretary of the Navy Gideon Welles set the verdict aside and reinstated him.

The most famous of these cruisers was the *Alabama,* built by John Lairds at Liverpool and allowed to sail with the open connivance of

British authorities. She lasted almost two years, under the command of the aforementioned Raphael Semmes, and took a great many prizes all over the Atlantic and Caribbean before she was finally trapped in Cherbourg by the USS *Kearsarge.* Semmes might have waited it out, or tried to flee in heavy weather, but instead he chose to fight, and on June 19, 1864, in full if distant view of crowds of spectators on the French coast as well as a sight-seeing British yacht, the *Alabama* was sunk in a little more than an hour. It was one of the most famous, and just about the last, single-ship engagements of the century.

None of the other cruisers, the *Georgia,* the *Tallahassee,* or the *Rappahannock,* was as successful as the last of them, the infamous *Shenandoah.* Commissioned late in 1864, she rounded the Cape of Good Hope, visited Australia, and then sailed for the North Pacific and the Arctic, where in the space of a few weeks she virtually destroyed the American whaling fleet. It was especially tragic, for almost all of her work was done after the war had already ended. When her commander finally heard the news, in August of 1865, he disguised the ship and got her back to Liverpool, where the British virtuously seized her and turned her over to the Americans.

These cruisers had little effect on the overall course of the war, but they did make one enormous contribution: they assisted in the demise of the American merchant fleet. Shipowners fled to foreign flags and cheaper crews, and the war, plus concurrent technological change, struck American merchant shipping a blow from which it never really recovered.

There was one other footnote. In 1872 an international tribunal found the British government culpable in the matter of allowing the Confederacy to obtain ships, and awarded the United States government a settlement of fifteen and a half million dollars in gold.

––––––

With Farragut in Mobile Bay, Grant down around Petersburg, Sheridan containing Jubal Early in the Shenandoah, and Sherman closing in on Atlanta, an objective observer might have concluded that the Union was definitely gaining the upper hand, and that the war was at last beginning to proceed satisfactorily. Objective observers were few and far between, however, and the Democratic papers still trumpeted their cry of the war as failure. They were full of Grant the drunken butcher, Sherman the insane, Early as a new Stonewall, and Lee as invincible as ever. In spite of all that had been accomplished at such great cost since the turn of the year, that decisive success still eluded the Union leaders, and by late August, it still looked as though the election, and therefore the war, would be lost.

Down around Atlanta, John Bell Hood had done his considerable best to fend off Sherman's grab for the city. After the sharp little fight at Ezra Church, west of Atlanta, on July 28, the two armies had sat sullenly eyeing each other. Each was now dug in firmly, and daring, inviting, hoping, for an attack by the other. Sherman's raids had failed to dislodge the Confederates, and resulted only in loss to his own cavalry. An attempt to rescue the prisoners held under inhuman conditions at Andersonville had collapsed ignominiously. And Hood's efforts at breaking the Union supply line up along the railroad to Tennessee had also failed. With a company of Federal infantry at every bridge and trestle, and gangs of soldiers who could rebuild rail line faster than the Confederates could tear it up, Sherman's logistics were about as secure as they were likely to get. So it appeared as if they were at an impasse, and for a month they were.

But Sherman was always impatient when tied to a rail line. After a month he decided to replay the gambit Grant had used at Vicksburg. Atlanta was fed by two rail lines, the Montgomery and Atlanta from the southwest, and the Macon from the south. The two joined at Eastpoint, about five miles south of the city. If Sherman could break those lines, Atlanta must fall. Come what may, he decided he was going to do it. For three weeks, his three armies had sat around Ezra Church, facing off the Confederates. Now, with their rations on their backs, and otherwise stripped down for action, they started to move again. On the night of August 26th the Federals slipped westwards, out past the Confederate lines, and began stretching out again. Thomas's big Army of the Cumberland crossed the Sandtown Road on the 27th, heading for Mount Gilead Church. Schofield and Howard fanned out to either side, a broad front of blue soldiers heading generally south.

When Confederate pickets reported the lines in front of them emptying out, Hood was at a loss. He could not figure out just what was going on, so he assumed it must be what he wanted it to be. He reported to Richmond that Sherman had given up his attempt on Atlanta, and was retreating northward. He then scheduled a great victory ball in Atlanta itself.

The momentary taste of sweet victory turned to bile when the telegraph line from Montgomery went dead. On the 28th the Federals were across the first rail line, tearing up the track and destroying everything they could get their hands on, parties ranging up and down the line making a mess of it. That was bad enough, but three days later they had swung east and hit the Macon Railroad. Schofield, the inner element of the wheeling movement, broke it at Rough and Ready, below Eastpoint, then Thomas was across it, then Howard. By now, of course, Hood knew he was in trouble. When the first rail line went on the 28th, he had canceled the big victory ball and instead sent Hardee's corps hustling south to protect the Macon line. Then he himself followed with the rest of his field force. Hardee and Stephen D. Lee attacked Sherman at Jonesboro on the 31st, and failed to dislodge Howard's men. Stephen Lee then managed to evade the rest of the Federals and get his troops back into Atlanta, where they could do no good, and while he did that, Sherman attacked and failed to bag Hardee.

Hood finally pulled the scattered elements of his command together around Lovejoy's Station, a bit farther south on the Macon Railroad. There he took up a very strong position and hoped Sherman would attack him. Sherman was too smart this time to take the bait. Besides, he had other, more important, prizes to attend to. Early on the morning of September 2, troops of Henry Slocum's XX Corps of the Army of the Cumberland marched into the city of Atlanta and raised the Stars and Stripes.

Sherman immediately telegraphed the good news to Washington, "Atlanta is ours, and fairly won." The country went wild. Before Petersburg, the Army of the Potomac fired a hundred-gun salute. All over the North, salutes were fired, bands paraded, towns burned bonfires, and windows were illuminated for the great news. But the most important victories, said Clausewitz, are those won over the mind of your adversaries. Here is George B. McClellan, erstwhile commander of the Army of the Potomac, and now in the fall of 1864 accepting the Democratic nomination for the presidency of the United States: If I agreed to peace before reunion, "I could not look in the face of my gallant comrades of the Army and Navy, who have survived so many bloody battles, and tell them that their labors, and the sacrifice of so many of our slain and wounded brethren had been in vain." Now the whole war, and the election along with it, looked different.

Chapter 19

... Where the Grapes of Wrath Are Stored

S UMMER SLID into fall, the apples reddened on the trees, and the grain ripened in the long fields of the Midwest. In spite of burgeoning industrialism, men and women still lived their lives in tune with the ageless rhythm of the seasons, more conscious of the flocking of birds and the habits of animals than the sound of train whistles. Cities rise and fall, but farms go on forever. On the blockade stations along the Atlantic and Gulf coasts, sailors rigged for the hurricane season; down around Petersburg, the water standing in the trenches after a rain stayed colder; even in the hills near Atlanta, men thought of fall coming. And of what was to come with it.

One of the things to come with it was the Northern presidential election, held this year on November 8. It was an anxious time; a week before the election, Secretary of State Seward warned the mayor of New York that Southern agents were gathered in Canada, preparing to come south and set fire to New York City on election day. On the 6th a hundred men were arrested in Chicago, many of them heavily armed; reports said they were planning to release Confederate prisoners held near the city, seize it, stuff ballot boxes and burn the place down. Why they would have wanted to stuff the ballot boxes and then burn the city was unanswered, but men were keyed to too high a pitch to think entirely rationally, and the wildest stories found willing believers.

On a more practical level, the Republicans were determined to do all they could, legally and occasionally illegally, to win the election; both sides urged their followers, as the quip has it, to "vote early and vote often." The fall of Atlanta, though it was perceived as cutting a good deal of the ground from under the Democrats' "The war is a

281

failure" campaign, still did not make the election a sure thing or even approach it. One measure the Republicans chose, wisely as it turned out, was to allow and encourage voting by the soldiers themselves. The government hoped that its fighting men would support the war effort, rather than repudiate it. Soldiers from some states that required their physical presence were furloughed so they could go home to vote. Other states sent commissioners to their regiments in the field to record the soldiers' ballots there.

The result was gratifying beyond the Republicans' wildest hopes. Here were the men doing the actual fighting and dying, asked to vote in support of a government, in effect a war, that would make them continue to fight and die—and they did so resoundingly. These men were not fooled by the Democrats' hedging on the great question of the day, and they knew better than any others that when Jeff Davis said independence was a precondition to peace, he and those who followed him meant exactly that. Of the soldier votes that were tabulated separately, 119,754 out of 154,045 were for Lincoln—78 percent for the war. There is no reason to believe those who went home voted any differently from those still in the field; thus Lincoln carried the army by three to one.

The military vote may have made the difference between victory and defeat in New York and Connecticut, and possibly in Indiana as well, and it was far more favorable to the Republicans than was the vote in the country as a whole. Nonetheless, even without it, Lincoln still would have won the election, with 2,206,938 votes to McClellan's 1,803,787; he got roughly 55 percent of the popular vote, and the electoral college, when it got around to meeting, gave him a lopsided 212 votes to 21 for his opponent.

The meaning of all this was simple enough: the Union would see it through. And by now few men could doubt that the Union, having expressed the will to fight on to victory, had sufficient strength to do so. In 1863 the visiting British officer, Colonel Freemantle, had concluded that the South was simply unconquerable. Now, a year later, the New York correspondent of the London *Times* reported exactly the opposite; it was the North that was invincible, with the strength and spirit of a free people quite unprecedented in human history. As one disgruntled Democrat put it, there was a revolution occurring in the United States, and no one knew where it might end, but it would have to run its course.

Jefferson Davis put the best face he could on the news, but like most thinking men in the Confederacy, he knew what it all meant. Over the coming winter, Confederates would talk less of ultimate victory, and more of suffering God's will to be done, of fighting the good fight with honor, and of bearing that which must be borne.

———

It was war to the knife now. Sheridan had torn the heart out of the Shenandoah Valley, and Grant and Meade held on to the siege of Petersburg with a death grip. The Union, knowing the Confederacy was short of bodies, had now refused to exchange prisoners, and in Southern camps Federal prisoners were practically starving to death; part of that was poor administration, part of it was criminal neglect— one third of the 32,000 Federal prisoners at Andersonville died in the last year of the war, and its commandant, Captain Henry Wirz, was tried and executed. Many Southerners argued that as they themselves were being starved by the Union blockade, they could hardly be expected to feed their prisoners. For the Union, the policy was painful, but it was also another example of the intensification of the war, and another means of bringing yet greater pressure upon the enemy, even if unfortunate Federal soldiers bore some of the burden of it.

How to bring it to an end? How to tighten the vise that much further until the Confederacy finally cracked? What would make those people give up? William T. Sherman, his forces concentrated in and around Atlanta, thought he had an answer.

Though Sherman's advance to Atlanta had eventually succeeded in taking the city, it had still been only a partial success. Grant's initial orders had given Sherman the Army of Tennessee as his primary objective, and damage to Georgia as an only secondary aim. Sherman had actually failed to destroy the army facing him, and it now hovered in the wings, John Bell Hood waiting for the Federals to make a move and a mistake. The month of September went by quietly, while Sherman tried to decide what to do, and get Grant's permission to do it, and on the other side, Jefferson Davis came south to commiserate with Hood. The president and his general finally chose to operate against Sherman's communications. Hood's army would slide westward into Alabama, and from there move perhaps northeast against Chattanooga or even due north well into Kentucky, heading for Nashville. With a little luck, they might lever Sherman out of Atlanta; if he had to abandon that and move back the way he had come, Southern morale might well rebound as quickly as it had plummeted with Atlanta's fall. It was a long shot, a bit of a counsel of desperation, but these were desperate times.

Sherman too was concerned about that tenuous supply line, and through the month he sent detachments back up the railroad, thinning out his field army but presenting a strong cordon facing southwest against Confederate raiders. But that was a half-baked response, and he was hatching a larger idea. Georgia was actually pretty good country, and past Atlanta it was largely untouched by the war. Sherman believed he could feed his army on the move; instead of chasing Hood about, a potentially futile effort, why not cut loose and march from Atlanta to the sea, perhaps to Savannah, tearing up rail lines and generally raising the devil as he went? By a process of trial and error, the Union leaders had learned that while they might not be able to destroy Confederate armies in open battle, they might, by a policy of destructive raids, weaken the entire infrastructure of the Confederate economy and society, make the Rebels feel the full brunt of the war, and perhaps ultimately cause them to collapse. It was what the British theorist of war Liddell Hart called "the indirect approach" carried to extremes, the mid–nineteenth century's equivalent of the strategic-bombing theory of World War II. If you can't beat the enemy in the field, perhaps you can beat him behind it. In total war, with the entirety of a society committed to its effort, perhaps the economy and civilian population, or at least civilians' determination to maintain the war, would prove the soft underbelly of the enemy.

Even before he was committed to march through Georgia, Sherman began to dispose his troops in such a way as to make any option feasible. In late September he sent George Thomas back to Nashville, to take command of all the troops from there to Atlanta, while he himself stayed in the latter city, keeping 60,000 men with him ready to move. Grant dragged his feet; he would have preferred that Sherman destroy Hood rather than march off into the unknown, but Sherman's view was that Thomas had sufficient strength to handle the Confederate field army, and that he himself could do more good, and more damage, by operating independently. He summed up his view in a letter to Grant: "Until we can repopulate Georgia, it is useless for us to occupy it; but the utter destruction of its roads, houses, and people will cripple their

military resources. I can make this march, and make Georgia howl."
This was written in early September. Two weeks later the issue was
still up in the air, when Hood made his move.

Marching rapidly northeast, with cavalry raiding parties out, the
Army of Tennessee hit Sherman's rail line around Allatoona. The line
was held by John M. Corse's division, and when Samuel French's Confederates attacked, there was some of the hardest fighting seen by western soldiers in the entire war. It also inspired some highly dramatic
mythologizing; Sherman, bringing up reliefs, could see the fighting
from away back on Kennesaw Mountain, and managed to signal the
Federals that help was on the way, in a terse message that was written
into American hymnbooks as "Hold the fort for I am coming." There
were 1,500 casualties out of the 4,000 men engaged, but French finally
drew off, and Corse was able to signal to Sherman, "I am short a
cheekbone and an ear, but am able to whip all hell yet."

Nor did Hood's tearing up of track benefit him a great deal, what
with Sherman's efficient railroad troops quickly rebuilding in Hood's
wake. Indeed, the effect of Hood's moves was simply to make Sherman
even more convinced that it was futile to chase a smaller and highly
mobile army around the backwoods of Georgia. He simply could not
catch Hood, and Thomas was perfectly capable of containing him.
When Sherman had marched halfway back to Chattanooga, Hood simply skipped off into northern Alabama again by mid-October. At this
point, however, Grant and the authorities in Washington finally agreed
with Sherman, and gave permission for him to abandon his useless
chase, and start instead for the sea. A bemused Hood was left hanging
in mid-air in northern Alabama, while the Federal troops in front of
him began mysteriously to thin out.

Hood still intended to march north and invade Tennessee, and that
was what he set about doing. It took him three weeks to gather sufficient supplies around a base at Florence, and to pull in his scattered
cavalry, but on November 19 he started north. Thomas, who had let
himself be somewhat lulled by the last couple of weeks of inactivity,
had left his forward units under Schofield widely scattered, and now
had to rush to concentrate. The result was a race for Columbia, Tennessee, and the crossings of the Duck River, Schofield moving north
from Decatur, Alabama, while Hood marched slightly east of north
from Florence. Schofield won, and concentrated his forces south of the

river, holding the crossings around the town. But he could not fight there, as Hood's cavalry ranged up- and downstream, and levered him off his position.

The next stage was quite peculiar, as both armies moved north, the Federals going up the road from Columbia toward Franklin, while the Confederates moved parallel to and past them, trying to get across their line of retreat. They actually succeeded in doing so; Benjamin F. Cheatham's Confederate corps got onto the Columbia Pike, and then gave it up and went into bivouac, not realizing they had the whole of Schofield's army trapped to the south of them. During a long, tense night, the Federals quietly moved past the weary, sleeping enemy, and got away to Franklin.

The denouement of this particular mix-up was tragic. Hood was furious at his corps commanders, though he himself had not given them any real direction. Now he pushed his pursuit hard, and late on the afternoon of the 30th of November he caught the fleeing Federals. Or so he thought. In fact, Schofield's men had reached the little town of Franklin early on that morning, and though tired from their marching, they spent the day digging and entrenching. By the time Hood got there they had a firm position, both flanks anchored on the Harpeth River, all neatly dug in, fields of fire across open ground, and they wanted nothing more than for the Rebels to attack.

Hood obliged them. He was sick and tired of complaining soldiers and corps commanders who did not do as he thought they should. He threw his corps into line, Cheatham on the left, A. P. Stewart on the right, and ordered an attack. There was no artillery preparation, no cover for two miles, and the Federals were well dug in. Even so, the Confederates nearly broke through. They overran two advanced Union brigades, and as these retreated to the main line, while their comrades held their fire to let them get in, the Confederates came on so quickly that they too broke over and through the main line of works. For a half an hour it was hard work, Confederates flooding into the gap, Union regiments, heads down and shoulders hunched, launching bayonet charges into the swirling mass. Slowly the breach contracted, and the Confederates went back. Still they refused to give way, and Hood flung charge after charge at the Union line. Not until dark at about nine in the evening did they finally give it up. By then the Army of Tennessee was ruined, a full quarter of those engaged casualties, thirty-two colors lost and five generals dead, including States Rights Gist and that incomparable combat leader Patrick Cleburne. Except for that one break in the line, Franklin was little more than an execution, the Confederate losses proportionately three times those incurred by the Federals at Cold Harbor.

During the night Schofield retreated across the Harpeth, and the next day his tired but happy troops marched into Nashville. Oddly enough, Hood followed them with his defeated army; he thought that if he retreated after Franklin, the troops would desert in droves and the army collapse. So he advanced instead, and on December 2 he laid Nashville under siege. This was a strange situation, Hood with some 30,000 starvelings blockading Thomas's 50,000 men. Hood knew he could not take the city, but he thought that Thomas would attack him, and he believed that if he chose good ground, and fought an effective defensive battle, the Federals might well be broken. Given Hood's, and most generals', penchant for the offensive, his reasoning is testimony to the power of the defensive in the later stages of the war.

For two weeks, Slow Trot Thomas refused to oblige. In fact, Old Tom—he seemed to have more nicknames than most generals of his day—spent more time fighting with Washington than he did with Hood. Nashville under siege was a major embarrassment to Grant and the administration, and a whole series of telegrams urged Thomas to go out and fight. He steadfastly replied that he would, when he was ready, and please stop bothering him. Thomas never liked to be rushed, though unlike Buell or Rosecrans, when he did move he would do so effectively. Grant threatened to remove him from command, to which Thomas replied that he was free to do so. The two men, both phlegmatic in temperament, were in fact less sympathetic than they might have been; perhaps they were too much alike, for Grant seemed to get on better with the mercurial Sherman or the fiery Sheridan than he did with Thomas or the stolid Meade.

Finally, Grant did order Thomas's relief, and he sent John A. Logan out to take command. Thomas attacked on December 15, before Logan arrived. The result was a two-day battle and the virtual destruction of the Army of Tennessee.

The Confederates had lacked sufficient troops to match the Federal lines around Nashville, and Hood had thus been forced to settle for a position along a range of hills to the southeast of the city. He relied on Nathan Bedford Forrest's cavalry to cover the rest of his front, but early in December he sent Forrest off toward Murfreesboro, where he got into a fight and got whipped. When the time came for the battle, then, Hood had the three corps of A. P. Stewart on his left, S. D. Lee in the center, and Cheatham on his right, a position a little over four miles in length. Thomas moved out with a diversionary attack on Cheatham's right-flank end of the line, and then, when Hood's attention was fully engaged, he hit the other end, Stewart, with Wood's and A. J. Smith's two full corps, while maneuvering Schofield's corps around the Confederate flank. To extend the pressure farther, he had several thousand cavalry, often fighting dismounted, out beyond Schofield.

For a while the Confederates held their own, but as the pressure built up, Stewart's men slowly bent back. With heavy Union infantry attacks on their front, and the horsemen lapping past their flanks, there was nothing they could do but retreat. About mid-afternoon, after several hours, they broke altogether, and went streaming off to the rear. Hood was not yet done, however, and he managed to stop the rout and cobble together a new line as an early dusk came on.

At that point he should have given it up and thrown the whole army into retreat, but instead he decided to stay and see the matter through. He spent the night marching his troops back and forth, as if they were not sufficiently tired already, and rearranging his corps. By the next morning, he had slid Stewart and Lee sideways, and moved Cheatham's whole corps over to the left flank; his position now looked like a long C on its side, with both flanks refused and the open end facing to the south. Even more important, he was backed up against a feature called the Brentwood Hills, and he had but one road, the turnpike south to Franklin, open as a possible line of retreat.

Thomas spent most of the morning of the 16th closing up to the new Confederate position, then he attacked shortly after noon, repeating exactly the tactics of yesterday. The result was exactly the same, too. For a while the Confederates held, but then they broke. Late in the afternoon, with Federal infantry hitting both their front and flank, and blue cavalry seeping around in back of them, Cheatham's corps collapsed. A horde, a herd, of broken Rebels fled for the hills and that one road south. To add to their misery, but to aid in their escape, the skies opened up and it began to pour. Wagons, guns, broken-down horses clogged the roads, Union cavalry was all over the hills and snapping at the stragglers, and the Army of Tennessee dissolved in defeat, disgust, and despair.

Hood put the best face he could upon it. He reported that his losses were actually quite small, but in fact he had given up 4,500 men just as prisoners. No one knows how many killed or wounded there were, as many regiments never recovered, and never even submitted returns. The sad remnants of the once-proud Army of Tennessee limped back across their name state, and eventually took refuge in Mississippi. The soldiers knew full well what had happened to them, and one of their poets added a new verse to the famous "Yellow Rose of Texas" song:

Oh, now I'm goin' southwards, for my heart is full of woe;
I'm going back to Georgia, to see my Uncle Joe.
You may talk about your Beauregard, and sing of Bobby Lee,
But the Gallant Hood of Texas raised Hell in Tennessee.

A month after the battle of Nashville, John Bell Hood submitted his resignation, and Jefferson Davis accepted it. As for George H. Thomas, the Rock of Chickamauga was also henceforth known as the Hammer of Nashville.

———

". . . make Georgia howl . . ." What, while all this was going on in Tennessee, of William Tecumseh Sherman? While Thomas was ably performing his half of the task, and finally defeating Confederate forces in the field, what was the rest of Sherman's army doing? It was, in fact, validating his idea of waging destructive war, cutting a swath across the Confederacy that illustrated the hollowness of its claims to viability. "Sherman's March" became one of the standard pieces of the Civil War, one of the few things heard of even by those who know almost nothing about the war as a whole.

When Grant had explained his concept of the war to President Lincoln, the latter had replied, in his homely way, "As I understand this, you propose to hold him by the leg while Sherman skins him." Though they did not yet know it, by late 1864 the Union commanders were embarking on the final stages of that process. The Army of the Potomac still held Robert E. Lee, the Army of Northern Virginia, Petersburg—and ultimately Richmond—in a vise-like hold that was substantially underappreciated but absolutely vital to the prosecution of Federal strategy. Lee could no longer move, and his ability to do so had been the factor discomfiting the Federal war effort for two years. With that factor removed from the equation, Union armies were now free to range

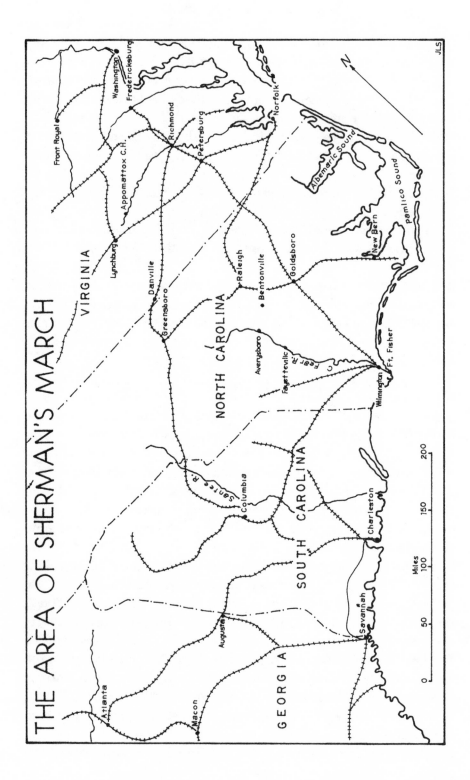

THE AREA OF SHERMAN'S MARCH

through the Confederacy, and this was what they were doing, most spectacularly, at this particular juncture, in Georgia.

By the middle of November, Sherman had collected an army of 62,000 men, 55,000 infantry, 5,000 cavalry, and 2,000 artillery with 64 guns. He organized the army into two wings, a right wing, composed of the Army of the Tennessee under Oliver O. Howard, and a left wing, which he himself usually accompanied, the Army of Georgia, under Henry Slocum. His cavalry was formed into a division under Judson Kilpatrick, the Lothario of the Union army, whom Sherman characterized as "a hell of a damned fool, but I want just that sort of man." Assured by Thomas that Hood was no real threat, Sherman had gathered twenty days' rations for his men and animals, and on the 15th he burned Atlanta, according to the Confederates and their subsequent partisans, or anything there of military value, according to Federal accounts. To protests of the mayor he had replied, "You might as well appeal against the thunderbolt as against these terrible hardships of war." He had, or the war in his mind had, taken on the magnitude of a force of nature. What was now happening was as if one of those destructive tornadoes were sweeping across Georgia. Sixty thousand strong, Sherman's army set out to make Georgia howl.

There was not much to stop them. Joe Wheeler had some cavalry, and there was some militia, and a few Georgia state troops, and some scattered regiments of regulars here and there, but they were never more than about 15,000 men, and nothing near that in any one place. The Confederacy sent down a bevy of out-of-work generals, of which they had a surplus, but could not find many troops. If words could have stopped the Federals, they would never have set foot past Atlanta. In an age of high-blown oratory and prose, Southern editors wrote and Southern ministers preached about Union desperadoes with their boots on the throats of Southern womanhood, and screamed, "Men of the South, Arise!" But the men who might once have answered that call were bleaching their bones in the thickets of Chickamauga, or filling shallow graves in northern Virginia, and they would never rise on this earth again. The Union army marched across a country whose white inhabitants consisted of only women, old men, and children.

The soldiers could be careless of their enemy, and ultimately almost contemptuous, but Sherman's strategy was careful. He advanced with his two wings, four corps, strung out, and cavalry on either flank, on a front from twenty to fifty miles wide, and he maneuvered so the

Confederates could never be sure where he was going. It looked by times as if he might be heading for Macon to the south, or Augusta to the east, or Savannah to the southeast. And even if all the Confederate forces in the state had finally figured out what he was up to, and concentrated, they would still have been only the size of one of his four corps.

There were a few little fights, mostly of cavalry out on the flanks or well in advance of the main body, but essentially the army rolled on unimpeded, practically on holiday. March discipline was loose, and got looser as they went. Sherman's original orders were that the troops should destroy any property of military use, and "forage liberally on the country." Each day each unit sent out a party of foragers to find food and destroy matériel, and the troops put an increasingly liberal interpretation on what was of military value.

They tore up railroads wherever they found them, stacked the ties, set them afire, and laid the rails across the bonfire. When the iron softened, they grabbed the ends of the rails, and bent them into giant hairpins. They burned bridges and broke culverts. They burned public buildings and military stores, they carried off draft animals. They burned barns, and they burned crops; after all, in total war everything is of military value. Gradually, of course, as armies do, just like every other society, they spewed out a hard core of stragglers, "bummers," who liked burning and scaring, and they ravaged the land, robbing houses, insulting civilians, enjoying destruction for its own sake. Sherman and his officers rode with a loose rein, and Kilpatrick seems actually to have encouraged wanton wrecking. It all depended upon one's perspective, of course. To the Union soldiers, the war had been forced upon them by these people, and it served them right to find out what war was all about. Women who complained were told, "Call your men home and stop the war, if you don't like it." To the Georgian women and civilians, it was the worst kind of cowardly, backhanded way to win, making war on those helpless to resist. Yet to the slaves of Georgia, it was Liberation, the Jubilee, Kingdom Come, and black men whom Georgians thought were trusting, loving dependents, surprised their owners by showing the Yankee raiders where the stores were hidden. Many a little black child in later years would remember that Freedom was "blue shirts and brass buttons."

In less than four weeks, Sherman's army marched 250 miles, and cut a path up to sixty miles wide across the heart of Georgia. They did an estimated hundred million dollars' worth of damage, and they wrecked the state's capacity to carry on the war. They had less than 2,200 casualties, and when they arrived outside Savannah on December 10, the Confederacy was cut in half yet again.

At Savannah, General William Hardee of the Confederate army actually had some troops, 10,000 of them, and as the city was one of the few the South still had, he intended to fight for it, at least as long as he could do so. It was well fortified, and might stand a siege. Sherman summoned it to surrender and was refused. He then opened communications with the naval squadron blockading the port—"Have you taken Savannah yet?" "No, but we will in a minute"—got supplies that had been sent to it in expectation of his arrival, and set to work. Within a week he had taken one of the outer forts, and was moving to cut off Confederate retreat out of the city to the north. Hardee, seeing himself about to be trapped, and realizing his men were more important than his position, threw together a rickety pontoon bridge across the Savannah River, and on the night of December 20 he pulled out, escaping into South Carolina. The Union troops marched in the next day, and Sherman triumphantly reported to President Lincoln: "I beg to present you as a Christmas gift, the city of Savannah with 150 guns and plenty of ammunition, and also about 25,000 bales of cotton."

South Carolina was next on his list.

Thus ended 1864.

Part V

1865:
ENDING

Chapter 20

The Death Grip

IN JANUARY of 1865 Mary Boykin Chesnut wrote in her diary of a holiday gathering she had attended, "Mrs. McCord and Mrs. Goodwyn had lost each a son, and Mrs. McCord her only one. Some had lost their husbands, brothers, sons. . . . The besoms of destruction had swept over every family there."

The truth was, the Confederacy was now marching steadfastly toward an early grave. The year just ended had been one of almost unrelieved disaster for it. At New Year's of 1864, one might still hope to salvage victory from the crisis; Vicksburg and Gettysburg could be balanced by Chickamauga. But now, there was no offsetting triumph. Lee's army was crippled by the losses of the spring campaign, and grimly starving within the Petersburg lines; Hood's army had been smashed beyond repair by the Hammer of Nashville; Sheridan had devastated the Shenandoah, Sherman had burned and wasted his way through Georgia, and Farragut had stormed into Mobile Bay. What successes could the Confederacy pit against these Union victories? Very few; the frustration of Banks's Red River campaign, away out in the West, in a part of the Confederacy where no one even bothered to send letters anymore. And the temporary defeat of a Union expedition to take Wilmington, North Carolina, the South's last real port, already closely blockaded and carefully watched.

Useless little victories, useless little men: Joe Johnston for dictator! Alexander Stephens for peace! Senator Wigfall for Senator Wigfall! The Confederacy was drowning in a sea of defeat, of failure political, economic and military, and of recrimination. If only Davis had done this, if only Hood had done that, if only Stonewall had not died, if only . . . if only . . .

President Davis himself spent the holiday season at home. He had been sick in the week before Christmas, and rumors of his impending death had spread through Richmond and much of the Confederacy. But he recovered to spend Christmas with his family, and to attend church. On New Year's he was at church again, and wrote letters to his distant sister, "Another year has gone and the new one brings to us no cessation of our bitter trials." He of all people was conscious of the desperate situation that faced his Confederacy, and whatever his shortcomings as a leader, he deserved far better than the hatred of lesser men who spent their time blaming him for their own and their nation's shortcomings.

By now the Confederacy was all but past saving, though not yet ready to admit it. The Union victories on the battlefield, and the re-election of President Lincoln in November, had virtually sealed its fate. Confederates responded to their ever more parlous situation by making a curious mental adjustment. They had gone from thinking the Yankees would never fight to thinking they could last them out; now they moved, many of them, to the comforts and consolations of religion. It was of course a religious age, when men and women still devoutly, and profoundly, believed in an immanent God who was personally interested in their being and behavior. Now their God appeared more and more as He was in the Old Testament, God the Judge, a God who had weighed the Confederacy and found it wanting. Now they must suffer for their sins of pride and foolishness; a few, a very few and seldom openly, came to the conclusion that the Almighty would not support a society founded upon the principle of human slavery. More recognized this as a time of trial and tribulation, something to be borne as a burden from on high, and they determined to meet their fate as brave soldiers and Christian men and women. The only alternative was to make peace now, and though thousands had already done so, in those areas under Union occupation, and many thousands of others were perhaps ready to do so if given a chance, as a society, as a nation, the Confederacy was still not ready to give it all up. The cup would have to be drained to its dregs.

Ironically, the men and women of both sides believed in and appealed to the same God, and when Abraham Lincoln took his oath of office for his second term in March of 1865, he made much the same kind of reference to the Almighty as was now current in Confederate pulpits. In his second inaugural address he stated, "Fondly do we hope, fervently do we pray, that this mighty scourge of war may speedily pass away. Yet, if God wills that it continue until all the wealth piled by the bondsman's two hundred and fifty years of unrequited toil shall be sunk, and until every drop of blood drawn with the lash shall be paid by another drawn with the sword, as was said three thousand years ago, so still must be said, 'The judgements of the Lord are true and righteous altogether.' "

Indeed, unless there were now some divine intervention, the end of the war, and Northern victory and Southern defeat, was a foregone conclusion. The number of Confederates who could still see victory in the future was ever smaller; desertions from the army were up, inflation was skyrocketing, resources ever scarcer. But men fought on, for their refusal to admit they had been mistaken, for their comrades, for their sense of themselves, for their pride, or stubbornness, or their honor. It was an age very strong on honor; thousands of young men would die for it yet.

Confederate options were increasingly narrow. They had few courses left to them, and their military forces could do little except respond, however inadequately, to the moves of their Union opponents. The reins were now firmly in the hands of Ulysses Simpson Grant.

By and large, Grant's conduct of the campaign of 1864 had justified the confidence Lincoln placed in him. Early on he had attempted to achieve the strategic coordination in time and place that had eluded his predecessors. In this he had been only partly successful. Banks's abortive Red River operation had thrown off schedule both Sherman's advance toward Atlanta and the projected moves against Mobile in Alabama. Sigel's failure in the Valley caused distraction, and Butler's inept handling of the Bermuda Hundred campaign had taken much of the finesse out of the overland campaign of 1864 in northern Virginia. Yet Grant had recovered from these setbacks; Sherman had finally taken Atlanta, without Banks or his men, and Farragut had broken into Mobile Bay. In the East, albeit at immensely increased cost, Grant and Meade had crippled Lee's army and driven steadily south, ultimately past Richmond to bring Petersburg under siege. And they had held the Confederates there while Sheridan destroyed the Shenandoah and Sherman marched unimpeded through Georgia to Savannah. So the tale of Southern disasters, repeated here, became a tale of Federal victories that vindicated Grant's overall vision of how the war should proceed. It was a question now of tightening the noose.

Or perhaps not; some on both sides hoped that further suffering might be avoided, and once again, there was a little cautious diplomatic sparring. Francis P. Blair, the septuagenarian newspaper editor who was one of the great backroom powers of American politics, still thought he might engineer a compromise peace, and in January of 1865, with Lincoln's unofficial blessing, he visited Richmond to talk to President Davis. Blair's scheme was an odd one. He would avoid any more American bloodshed by getting the Union and the Confederacy to sign a truce, and then act jointly to expel Maximilian and the French from Mexico, presumably on the assumption that Americans killing Frenchmen would be less costly and painful than Americans killing Americans. This shared experience would then bring the two sides back together, and a compromise could be worked out.

Although Davis still insisted on talking of "our two countries" while Lincoln talked of "our common country," Blair nonetheless did manage to get agreement on a meeting, and the Confederacy sent three commissioners who met quietly with President Lincoln at Hampton Roads in early February. But there were the same old sticking points, Lincoln insisting upon reunion and emancipation, and the Confederates insisting on independence. By now, of course, things had changed from the last time there were any explorations, and the major change was that the Union was patently winning the war. If Lincoln had not made concessions when he appeared to be losing, he was certainly not going to make them now, and the conference came to naught.

That was pretty much what the few people who knew about it expected anyway, so once again the issue was thrown back to the battlefield. Blair's initiative, and the subsequent Hampton Roads Conference, was perhaps the last thin chance to end the war short of total military victory or defeat. Seen in that light, one might say the Confederate leaders threw away one opportunity to avoid an enormous amount of additional suffering. Davis, however, was true to his character: believing himself right, he would make no concession whatsoever, come what may and cost what it might.

––––

The cost was growing ever worse. For the soldiers, sitting around their campfires at night singing that saddest of Civil War songs, "Tenting

Tonight," or huddling in the Petersburg lines dreaming of real food, the war stretched away, an infinity of waste and want, a vista as bleak as the battlefields over which they watched, enveloped in fog, mist, horrible odors, and misery. Young men grown old, they longed for the end of war as they longed for home, and warmth, and the normal comforts of life. Even as they realized, and most did, that this was the greatest experience they would ever have, they ached for it to be over. An all-pervasive war-weariness lay over the combatants and their countries like a wet blanket.

No one sensed this more than General Grant; indeed, one of his qualities, like that of his opponent across the lines, was his ability to empathize with the ordinary man and to understand what he was feeling. Generals Grant and Lee were both highly extraordinary men, Lee an aristocrat to the manor born, and Grant the epitome, the achetype, of the ordinary man, and no small part of the genius of each was their ability to know what their men thought, and how they felt. Leading men, especially leading them to possible death, is far more a matter of sympathy and shared feeling than it is a matter of business management, a lesson Americans have periodically forgotten at great cost.

General Lee knew his men were suffering, and he knew they were receiving despairing letters from home, when the mail got through at all, and there was very little he could do about it. Just as Lincoln's larger humanity had outweighed Davis's cooler rationalism, Grant's strategic vision, plus the resources to back it, had overcome Lee's tactical genius. By early 1865, there was very little that Robert E. Lee could do to alter the fate of his country. He was a master of mobile warfare, and he could not move.

Little was accomplished around Petersburg by either side over the winter. In December, Gouverneur Warren's V Corps of the Army of the Potomac tore up forty miles of track of the Weldon Railroad, the easternmost of Petersburg's still open rail lines, and the Confederates pulled their belts in yet another notch. There was a steady seepage of desertion as hungry men in gray and butternut gave it up and and left for home, or slipped across the lines to surrender to the Federal pickets. Lee had to send units off to help defend Wilmington, and to cover South Carolina from the impending storm, but there was not much he could do about any of these things. In January the Richmond Congress, fed up and angry as always at Davis, created the post of commander in chief of the Confederate armies, and automatically appointed Lee to the office. If ever there were a hollow honor, that was it; Lee could do nothing about the Confederacy beyond Virginia even if he was thoroughly disposed to do so, which he was not. He shuffled a few officers around in the Richmond offices, and this slightly improved the army's supply situation, but there were few supplies anyway, so it did not make much difference.

In early February Grant sent a strong force raiding along the Boydton Plank Road, which led into Petersburg from the southwest. Reports indicated that the Confederates were running wagon trains along that road, and bringing in substantial supplies. Federal infantry fought off a halfhearted attempt to stop them, and the blue cavalry rode here and there, but they found surprisingly little. The hard truth was that there was simply not much to find. Unless and until the Federals could reach the Southside Railroad, running into Petersburg from almost due west, they had about played out their hand here. The Southside gave the Confederates just enough to keep them alive and not much more, but it was beyond Federal reach, especially in winter, when the roads were mud and the rainwater lay oozing on the land.

This meant that all the Confederates could do was wait it out; the Federals could do a little more, in a preparatory sort of way. They had supplies, they had reinforcements, and they spent the first few months of 1865 turning conscripts into soldiers, and getting ready for what they knew was coming. Horatio Wright brought VI Corps back from the Shenandoah Valley in December of 1864; over the opening months of the new year, the regiments filled up once more, the soldiers did their drill and took their turns in the lines surrounding Petersburg, and the waiting game went on.

Lee finally concocted a scheme, full of desperation, but one that seemed the only choice to him. Somehow he must regain the initiative, and for him, that meant the ability to maneuver. He decided to launch a surprise attack on the Federal lines, hoping to break them and throw them completely off balance. That done, he would leave a much smaller force behind to guard his lines and protect Richmond, and march the greater part of his army off to the south. Somewhere in the Carolinas, he would effect a junction with Joseph Johnston, commanding there. The two together would fall on Sherman and destroy him, and then march back north and destroy Grant in turn.

At the time he developed this idea, Lee commanded about 57,000 men in the Army of Northern Virginia; Johnston had perhaps 20,000 men. Grant had 125,000 with Meade in the Army of the Potomac, and Sherman had more than 60,000 in his army. The numbers alone suggest the futility of Lee's plans, but he could see no other choice; unless he did *something,* the end was inevitable. He set the first part of his plan, the attack on the Union lines, for late March.

———

While the Confederacy was slowly withering, and Davis and Lee were casting about for some means of escape from fate, the South had enjoyed one last short-lived success, albeit a defensive one. That was courtesy of General Benjamin Franklin Butler. Who else? one might almost ask.

Butler had managed to survive the Bermuda Hundred fiasco; there, Grant had given him the Army of the James and ordered him to advance on Richmond while Grant and Meade were fighting Lee's army in northern Virginia. Butler had managed instead to get himself halted and then virtually besieged; his 40,000 men were stopped at first by a scratch force of a few hundred Confederates under George Pickett, of Gettysburg fame. Once Butler stalled, the Rebels sent down General Beauregard to take command, and he built up a force that kept Butler where he was until the whole operation was subsumed by Grant's move against Petersburg.

In spite of this glaring failure, Butler retained his strong congressional support, and neither Grant nor Lincoln could afford to be rid of him—this was still before the fall election. But they could at least get him out of sight, and Grant ordered him to command an expedition being prepared to take Fort Fisher and capture Wilmington, North Carolina.

By this time, Wilmington was the South's only remaining major port, and it was a blockade runner's heaven. Reached by two widely separated openings in the outer banks, it was difficult to blockade properly. The Federals had thought to occupy the city ever since 1862, but it was well defended by a number of works, the most substantial being Fort Fisher guarding the New Inlet, and all in all, it was both a desirable prize and a formidable target. Behind its defenses, the town had enjoyed a wartime boom and suffered the attendant difficulties of inflation, increased crime, and general upheaval. Benjamin Butler would hardly be the worst of its visitors.

The expedition turned into the usual military farrago when Butler was involved. With two infantry divisions and a couple of attached artillery batteries, 6,500 strong, the troops went aboard ships on the James, moved down to Fortress Monroe, and from there left for Wilmington, where they were joined by Admiral Porter with an enlarged naval squadron. Lee, on hearing of the departure from Hampton Roads, detached troops from the Army of Northern Virginia and sent them south. He guessed correctly that Wilmington must be the target, and he needed the supplies that came in there. So off went a badly needed division to bolster the city's defenses.

Both sides were slow; the Union forces were delayed by bad weather at sea, and the Confederates by the near breakdown of their rail communications, which necessarily ran inland because the Federals held most of the Carolina low country around the sounds. Nonetheless, Butler got some of his people ashore, took a couple of isolated batteries, and was bombarding Fort Fisher, preliminary to assaulting it, when he received news of the approach of the Confederate reinforcements. At that, he hastily re-embarked his troops, over Porter's remonstrations, and sailed away to Hampton Roads, having captured about 300 prisoners for a loss of 15 wounded and 1 unfortunate drowned.

That finally finished the military career of Spoons Butler. General Grant reported to the president "a gross and culpable failure," and added ominously, "Who is to blame will, I hope, be known." Not only was it known, but the election results were now safely in, and Lincoln no longer needed so much the support of the men who backed Butler. Grant, furious at Butler's casual disregard of his mission and his specific orders, relieved him of command and sent him home to Massachusetts, where he spent the remainder of the war "awaiting orders."

Grant then assigned the same troops and the same mission to Alfred H. Terry, one of the junior commanders in the earlier expedition. A brilliant volunteer soldier, Terry was just too young for enduring Civil War fame, and is better known in connection with the Indian wars of the seventies. He now joined with Porter, and the two got along famously; Porter could be a difficult colleague, but after Butler he was able to cooperate with anyone at all, and the joint commanders worked out an effective plan for the bombardment and storming of Fort Fisher.

The army quickly got four full divisions of troops ashore, three of them white and one black, another straw in the wind indicating the changing nature of the war, the army, and the country. Porter's ships launched an intense bombardment, while the black soldiers sealed off the area from outside rescue. On the afternoon of the 14th of January, the Federals made their assault. Two thousand sailors and marines from the fleet tried to carry the sea face of the fort, and were beaten down with heavy casualties. This turned out to be no more than a diversion, though, as an hour later, Terry launched three full brigades of infantry at the landward side. Advancing through heavy fire—all three brigadiers were badly wounded—the troops carried the parapet and stormed into the fort. The inner works consisted of a series of trenches and traverses, each of which had to be taken in succession, and the fighting went on until well after dark, when Terry committed reserves who finally overran the last defenders. All in all, it was one of the most desperate fights of the whole war, Federal forces sustaining more than 1,000 casualties of the 8,000 involved in the assault, and the entire Confederate garrison being killed, wounded, or taken prisoner.

But it meant the end of Wilmington, the South's last real port. Over the next few days the other works around the city were abandoned, taken, or destroyed. There was much recrimination among Confederate commanders, as to who had failed to support whom, but none of that did any good. It was all too late now.

———

March 25, 1865, turned out to be a day to remember; on that date, though no one could possibly realize it at the time, the Army of Northern Virginia undertook the last offensive operation of its glorious career. This was the opening of Lee's plan to disengage around Petersburg and get his army back into open country. Its immediate target was a large Union work known as Fort Stedman.

The position was a mere 150 yards from the Confederate works, and located at the northern end of Grant's Petersburg lines, fairly close to both the city itself and the Appomattox River, which ran through it on its way to the James. Lee gave the task to John B. Gordon, one of the toughest fighters in an army renowned for such men, now in command of II Corps. Gordon's men were to take the fort in a rush, fan out to carry three smaller works behind it, and open a gate through which 1,000 Confederate cavalry could ride. Their destination was City Point, and the idea was that they could break into the Federal rear areas, tear up communications and burn supplies, and generally create havoc. This was not expected to accomplish anything permanent; it was all just to get Grant to pull back the western end of his line and consolidate a bit, thus allowing Lee to make his major move, his break to the south and west.

In the dark of the early morning, the Confederates crept out and captured the Union picket line, by the simple expedient of pretending to be deserters. This gave them a considerable advantage, and at four o'clock, the main assault swept forward and carried the Union line with a rush. They hit it between Fort Stedman and Battery No. 10, then moved left and right and quickly overran those two works and the men in them, most of whom were captured even before they could tumble out and form up. The Confederates then sent special columns forward to take the secondary works, but got confused in the jumble of tracks and general mix-up behind the front line. In this way they lost their momentum, and the now aroused Federals responded quickly. Both Grant and Meade were away at the moment, but John Parke, the able commander of IX Corps, rallied his units and moved to seal off the breach. A heavy infantry counterattack drove the Confederates back into the fort and Battery No. 10, and by breakfast time they were trapped there, with Union infantry and guns to their front, and other batteries laying down a heavy crossfire on the open space back to their own lines.

By eight o'clock General Lee realized the operation was not going to do any more good, and he sent over orders to retreat. Now, however, it was as dangerous to go back as it was to go forward, and though many of the soldiers took their chances and ran the gauntlet back to their own lines, many more simply surrendered. By mid-morning the Confederates had lost about 3,500 men, almost 2,000 of them prisoners. A remnant still held Fort Stedman, but when Meade got back later in the day, he ordered that cleared out too, and a heavy Federal attack, suffering 1,000 casualties, retook the fort and raised Confederate losses close to the 5,000 mark. As a diversion, the whole thing had not done much good, at a cost Lee's army could ill afford.

Two days later, Philip Sheridan rejoined the Army of the Potomac, his job in the Shenandoah Valley completed; Grant was already putting his army in motion. The Army of Northern Virginia, and the Confederacy, had a mere fortnight left to live.

During these months of waiting and wasting in Virginia, William T. Sherman was steadfastly pursuing his work of destruction. After taking Savannah, and allowing Hardee's garrison to escape north to Charleston, Sherman had refitted his army, which was in remarkably good shape anyway, and turned his attention north to the Carolinas. This was all part of his and Grant's overall plan, and indeed, the operations along the North Carolina coast were conceived with an eye to it. Wilmington fell soon after the taking of Fort Fisher, and the Federal troops there were organized to provide a field force capable of moving inland and supporting Sherman. There were further operations up around New Bern, in Federal hands ever since 1862, with the intent of using that area as a supply base and line once Sherman got that far north. Grant even directed Thomas in Nashville, and General Canby in Alabama, to initiate field operations to keep enemy troops in those areas busy, though in fact little was done there.

Sherman had intended to move into South Carolina as soon as he could organize the Savannah base, but it took him a while to do that, and January proved a very bad month for weather, so it was the 1st of February before he was able to move. By then his army was in fine fettle and the troops were eager to be on the march again. South Carolina held no terrors for them. Quite the contrary: they looked forward to an opportunity to ravage what they considered the heart and soul of the rebellion. If Sherman had made "Georgia howl," his soldiers were determined to make South Carolina scream.

He did have one other problem, as he made ready to march north, and it was indicative of things to come. Sherman, though he marched through the South as a liberator, was, to put it in the best possible light, almost completely uninterested in the fate of the slaves he freed on the way by. His troops largely ignored the blacks, and he himself, though the primary agent of a social revolution of immense consequences, cared little for them. He saw them, if at all, more as a military problem than a social or political one, and in that light he regarded them largely as a nuisance.

A telling and tragic illustration of this occurred on the march to the sea, when one of his units, followed by a large crowd of blacks and pursued by Confederate cavalry, escaped by crossing a river on a pontoon bridge. The soldiers then tore up the treads, leaving the blacks stranded on the far side and at the mercy of the horsemen. Terrified, many of them leaped into the river, several drowned, and the whole scene was one of panic and dismay. Sherman casually dismissed it all as an accident of war, and determinedly supported his field commander in his decision.

But such behavior did not go well with the Radical Republicans in Washington, who suspected Sherman of covert Southern sympathies and of being overtly anti-black. Thus ironically, the man who did much to end the war, and more to engender the subsequent postwar bitterness about how it had been waged, also fell into official disfavor with his own political superiors over his actions. To Southerners he was the vicious and vindictive man who waged war upon women and children; to certain Northern politicians, he was the secret sympathizer who wished to preserve the old social order of the South, and thus subvert the aims for which they—if not everyone—had fought the war. Both Salmon P. Chase and, more importantly, Edwin M. Stanton looked into his conduct, and Stanton made a trip to Savannah to investigate Sherman's attitude toward and treatment of blacks. The antagonism between the two lasted the rest of their lives. Before the war ended, men were fighting over what it meant.

This was the kind of distraction no field commander needed, and the always mercurial Sherman was furious at imputations that he was less than loyal, or that his politics were somehow suspect. He had a war to finish, and he was in fact not interested in much beyond that. When he at last set out on his invasion of South Carolina, both he and his army had blood in the eye.

By now, the first part of February, the Federal forces were so superior numerically, and indeed in every other way, that there was little to impede their progress. Sherman marched more or less due north from Savannah with the same 60,000 men who had accompanied him from Atlanta. When the forces operating out of Wilmington, and those from New Bern, joined in with him, his field forces rose to 80,000, to which might be added several thousands more left in garrisons along the coast and on the successive lines of communication. The Confederates had very little to place in their way. Hardee had about 8,000 men that he had gotten out of Savannah, there were some Georgia militia inland, some South Carolina militia and state troops over the state line, and there were a couple of divisions of regular Confederate cavalry scattered about. General Beauregard was sent down to take command of the whole, but the whole amounted to about 22,000 troops. The South still had good officers, Hardee, G. W. Smith, and Daniel Hill, with Joe Wheeler and Wade Hampton for the cavalry, but it just did not have the bodies anymore, and those it did have were not concentrated.

Just as in Georgia, part of Sherman's plan was to keep the enemy scattered by confusing them as to his intentions. When he came north from Savannah, he did so on the usual broad front, so that it was impossible to tell where he was headed, for Augusta in Georgia, for Charleston on the seacoast, or for Columbia in South Carolina between the other two. The answer was Columbia, and the Federal troops reached it on February 16, after an incredible march through water-logged country. One reason the Confederates failed to concentrate against them, aside from not knowing where they were going, was their confidence that no army could move through the flooded southern part of the state at that time of the year. But Sherman's people just kept on going, building rafts, corduroying roads, producing literally miles of trestle roads as they went. At that stage of the campaign, the axe was far more important than the rifle, and there were a great many men in that army who knew all about axes.

Wade Hampton's cavalry put up a halfhearted resistance in front of Columbia, the capital of South Carolina, but got out of the way as Sherman's right wing came up. The city itself was surrendered by its mayor, and was a terrible mess. Confederate stragglers had looted some homes, cotton bales lay torn open everywhere, blacks wandered around wide-eyed, rejoicing while wondering what on earth had happened to them, and some nervous white citizens set out buckets of corn mash liquor to placate the invaders. Sherman put Oliver Howard in command of the city, and he managed to keep enough soldiers sober to put out some fires in the town's center.

During the night, however, the wind picked up, and casual fires became a major blaze. Through the middle hours of the night the fires grew, mocking all efforts by the soldiers and everyone else to put them out, and by dawn the center of the city, about a third of the whole, was a blackened scar. Many Southerners believed ever after that this was a deliberate atrocity set in train by the arch villian of the Union, a charge made after the war by Wade Hampton to the Senate in Washington.

From Columbia the army marched northeast toward Cheraw, fanning out over the countryside, sweeping all before them and terrorizing the inhabitants. The weather was bad, with unremitting heavy rain, and it was March 3 before Sherman reached his next objective. Hardee, with a few thousand men, was at Cheraw, but he wisely decided he was too weak to fight, and fell back across the state line to Fayetteville in North Carolina.

Sherman's army, which had given pretty free rein to its views on punishing South Carolina, changed its habits when it crossed into North Carolina. The Old North State, a reluctant adherent of the Confederacy at first, had been ultimately one of the most vigorous members of the rebellion, but the soldiers, with their own rough but infallible notions of justice, regarded North Carolinians in a far different light from South Carolinians. March discipline firmed up, the bummers toned down, and North Carolina was treated, at least by the standards of this army, with something approaching military correctness.

Robert E. Lee now sent Joseph Johnston, for several months languishing in enforced idleness, down to supersede Beauregard, though what Johnston was supposed to do, other than what he had always done—retreat—was uncertain. True to form, Johnston decided that (*a*) Sherman was probably heading for Raleigh, and (*b*) there was not much he could do about it. Lee suggested he attack one of Sherman's columns, if he could find an isolated one. Johnston tried to do it, and at Bentonville on March 19 he hit Slocum's wing of the Federal advance.

Bentonville saw the heaviest fighting of the whole Carolinas campaign. Slocum came up against Hampton's cavalry and pushed through it, before being hit by Johnston's infantry, which slammed his men back into a defensive line. Then for the whole afternoon the Confederates launched charge after charge against the Union position, without breaking it. Johnston then drew off and took up a defensive position of his own, while Sherman sent his other troops marching to Slocum's support. The next day both sides held their ground and did some desultory patrolling, but the numerical odds against the Rebels grew longer and longer. On the 21st Sherman sent in a pinning attack while he maneuvered to get around Johnston's flank. Seeing this, the wily Confederate drew off and threw his forces into retreat. He had actually fought a pretty good battle, but like Napoleon in 1814, his army was just too small to accomplish much, and he paid 2,600 casualties for the 1,600 he inflicted.

On the 22nd Sherman took up his march again, and got as far as Goldsboro, where Terry joined him with the troops from Wilmington, raising his numbers to 80,000. Johnston had moved north to Smith-field to cover the approach to Raleigh. While he reorganized his army, and added a few troops from other commands, he waited for the next Federal move.

Instead of marching immediately, however, Sherman went off to Grant's headquarters in Virginia, taking a train down the newly repaired line to New Bern and going by steamer up to City Point in Virginia. There he had a warm reunion with Grant, and the two, along with Admiral Porter, conferred with President Lincoln, who was also visiting the army headquarters. It was a cordial, confident visit, as the two soldiers plotted what looked to be the last campaign of the war; Grant would maneuver Lee out of his lines and chase him southwest; Sherman would destroy Johnston—a matter now of little consequence, he assured his listeners—and move north, and Lee would be pinned between them. Lincoln's contribution was largely to hope there could be as little more bloodshed as possible; he repeated that any terms would be acceptable, if only the Rebels could be got to agree to them and the killing ended. Sherman then returned to his army, and Grant went off to begin the campaign leading toward Appomattox.

In Richmond the Confederate Congress was debating the issue of arming the slaves to fight in defense of their own continued slavery.

Chapter 21

The Collapse of
the Confederacy

WHEN ULYSSES S. GRANT issued marching orders to
the Army of the Potomac for March 29, 1865, and the
armies lurched into motion, every man involved realized
that this campaign would end the war. For the Federal army, it was a
classic maneuver, carried out with a good degree of precision, and
indeed, the events that led to Appomattox constitute one of the great
examples of maneuver and pursuit. Fortunately for the Federals, and
sadly for their foes, it was a maneuver carried out against second- or
even third-class opposition, for the army commanded by Robert E. Lee
was a pale, hollow ghost of what it had been in its glory days. But
that, after all, was the nature of war; it was not a sporting contest, both
sides equally matched and playing a good game to a satisfactory conclusion; it was a grim, deadly contest in which hundreds of thousands
had already suffered, and no man who had watched his friends die in
the Wilderness could now lament the sad state of the Confederacy. The
sooner it was over, the better, for winner and loser alike.

Such was certainly Grant's belief on the matter, and he was determined to press every advantage. In Philip Sheridan, just returned from
the Shenandoah, he possessed a like-minded subordinate, and as Grant
moved, he gave the little fighter command of what was basically his
maneuver arm. As the campaign developed, this shunted George Meade
off to the sidelines, and there was a degree of dissatisfaction among the
commanders and their staffs over this. Meade, however, remained both
a gentleman and a loyal subordinate, and what might have made for
real difficulties in the chain of command was glossed over by the pace
of events, the general good sense of the participants, and above all the

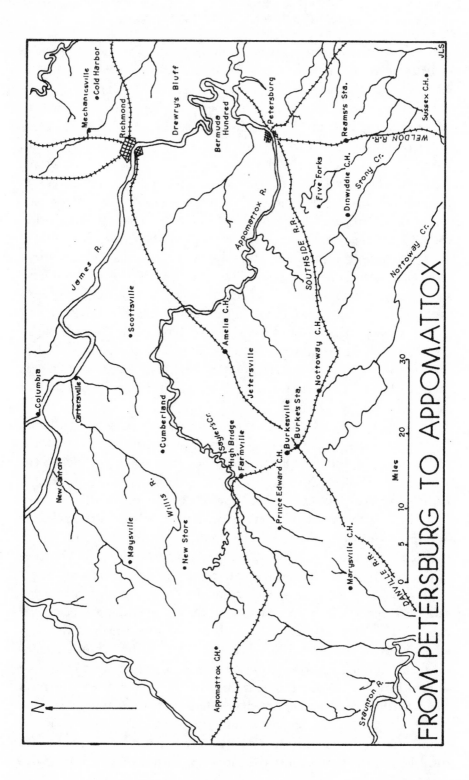

FROM PETERSBURG TO APPOMATTOX

N

Miles
5 10 20 30

knowledge that at last they were winning. There was one unfortunate casualty of this arrangement, but the important thing was getting the war over and done with.

Grant now outnumbered his opponent by about two and a half to one, about 125,000 to 57,000. His command organization was complicated and his troops spread in a long arc from north of the James River all the way around to the southwest of Petersburg. Three corps, XXV under Weitzel, IX under Parke, and VI under Wright, were on the northern and eastern end of this line; then came the Army of the James, now commanded by Edward O. C. Ord, successor to Ben Butler, basically another corps-sized formation, and then extending southwestward were II Corps under Humphreys and V Corps under Warren. Officially, Sheridan commanded only the Cavalry Corps, but Grant soon enlarged his responsibility. As the Federal army moved out into the open, Sheridan took tactical control of the infantry moving along with his troopers. He would have preferred Wright to Warren as an associated infantry commander—both Grant and Sheridan seemed to find Warren a bit too punctilious for their taste—but Warren was there, and it did not seem worthwhile trying to shuffle the corps about for a personality preference.

So, on the 27th and 28th of March Ord put his Army of the James into the line west of the Weldon Railroad, and that freed Humphreys and Warren for a strike. On the 29th the two corps moved out to the south and west, feeling their way along, Humphreys's men making a little loop across Hatcher's Run, Warren's people doing a larger leap-frog out past the Boydton Plank Road toward a little dirt track, the White Oak Road. While the foot soldiers marched carefully along through the wet and rainy weather, the cavalry swung wider yet, covering their flank to the south, where there was no anticipated danger anyway, and heading out even farther. For two days they all moved cautiously, and little happened. On the afternoon of the 31st, a couple of A. P. Hill's brigades put in a small counterattack against Warren's advance, but both sides stopped for the night without much accomplished. Sheridan's troopers, meanwhile, had swung up and moved toward Five Forks, where they bumped into Confederate infantry of Pickett's division. The horsemen were armed with Spencer repeating carbines, which could outfire an infantry rifle by about three or four rounds to one, but even so, infantry were generally much harder to displace than cavalry—hence the contempt with which the former had treated the latter for most of the war—and Sheridan's men made little progress. They bivouacked that night four miles south of Warren's lead troops, around Dinwiddie Court House. The next morning they saddled up and started northwest again, toward Five Forks. Sheridan ordered Warren to come to his support; Warren, already in contact with the enemy, a fact of which Sheridan was ignorant, began to disengage and obey his orders, though it did not seem to him the right thing to do.

On the other side, Lee was trying to organize his army to get it away from Petersburg and Richmond. After the failure of his attempt on Fort Stedman, he knew there was little chance of, and indeed little good to be gained by, retaining his position. His only hope now was to get out, take his army south into North Carolina, and link up with Joe Johnston; this would mean giving up the Confederate capital, but there was no help for it; indeed, he would have to be both skillful and lucky to manage as much as he now intended.

The crucial line for him was the Southside Railroad; it ran more or less west to Lynchburg, and about halfway there it crossed the Danville Railroad, at Burke's Station, running southwest from Richmond to Danville. Lee needed these, especially the Southside, to get the government, his trains, and ultimately his army out of the trap that was now developing. And to keep these lines open, he had to hold Grant at arm's length off the rail line. So by April 1, the vital question was, Could he do it?

That was in the minds of all the commanders as Sheridan's troopers moved once again toward Five Forks. The blue horsemen had three full cavalry divisions, plus a couple of independent brigades that joined in, 13,000 troopers in all, and Warren got his three infantry divisions into contact with them by dint of hard marching, stumbling about on the unfamiliar roads, and a great deal of cursing by noncoms and company officers. George Pickett, with two infantry divisions and the small cavalry corps of Fitzhugh Lee, all told about 19,000 men, wisely fell back on Five Forks and began taking up a defensive position, an L-shaped line in front of the junction with its left flank bent back. Pickett went off to get something to eat, and he and Fitzhugh Lee found a fellow general enjoying some baked shad. They settled down in anticipation of a good meal, the first in some time.

As Sheridan developed the position, he came up with a simple plan: his cavalry would keep the Rebels pinned to their front, while Warren's infantry massed on their left flank and rolled them up. It almost worked, except that the Confederates were not just where the Federals thought they were, and the bad terrain made it very difficult for the infantry to get in position. When Warren's people did advance, they hit open country beyond Pickett's left. Of Warren's three divisions, only that on his left flank came into immediate contact, and while he was on his own right flank getting his men realigned, Sheridan galloped up, took over the left-flank division, and successfully drove the Confederates. Pickett, who had given up his meal and run a gauntlet of fire to get back to his troops, tried to shift units from one end of his line to the other, but the Federal pressure was too strong front, flank, and now rear, and the line finally caved in and collapsed. Those who could drew off, but the Confederates lost more than 5,000 men, a number of guns and standards, and, of course, their hold on the Southside Railroad. The whole was thus a major blow to Lee's slim remaining hopes. Sheridan celebrated his victory by unceremoniously, ungraciously, and quite unjustly relieving Warren of his command.

As soon as the news of this success reached Grant, he realized the time was ripe for bigger things, and ordered a general assault on the Petersburg lines for the next day. As Grant was issuing his orders, Lee was pulling troops out of the works to send off to help Pickett rebuild. He also sent a message to Richmond, to inform President Davis that he could no longer hold his position, and that both Petersburg and the capital would have to be abandoned.

It was April 2, Sunday morning, when this message reached the president. By that time, there was little of official Richmond left anyway; most of the government had left earlier, and Davis had sent his family off three days ago, giving his wife a small pistol and instructing her how to use it. He, and his cabinet, and his aides, were about all that was left. Davis was in St. Paul's Church when the sexton came down the aisle and gave him a message, just received from Lee. He read it impassively, then stood and quietly left the church. For the remainder of the service, cabinet members were summoned and left one by one, the saddest and undoubtedly the most dramatic service ever held in Richmond. Soon the churches were empty all over town, as men and women wandered anxiously and aimlessly back and forth, asking each other for news. Clerks in the War Department were burning papers, and the smell of disaster was in the air.

At first light on that day the Federal troops, 60,000 strong, came surging up out of their trenches and began a general assault on the Petersburg lines. There were less than 20,000 Confederates left to try to stop them, and though the defenses were still formidable, the men left to man them were just too few to hold. Right in front of the city, Parke's IX Corps troops were stopped for a while, but to their west, Wright's people broke the long trench line, turned left, and began rolling the Confederates up. Then Ord's and Humphreys's troops took it up, and with the western end of the line thoroughly smashed, the Union troops about-faced and began moving back toward the city. By mid-afternoon the Confederates were completely done; by then so were the Union men, exhausted from hours of marching, fighting, and storming. The time it took to carry two last bravely defended forts brought the day to an end, and the battle burned down. The Federals had lost nearly 4,000 men, and no one bothered to count the number of Confederates killed, wounded, or, in greater numbers, taken prisoner. Sadly, the dead included A. P. Hill, come back sick for his last fight, and shot through the heart. Lee wept when the news was brought to him. In the darkness, the wounded Confederate army took up its march to the westward.

With Petersburg virtually in his grasp, Grant ordered a further attack upon it, and on Richmond as well, for the next morning. These proved unnecessary. Davis and the last of his government left the capital on the afternoon of the 2nd. That night in Richmond was one of horror, as the city mobs broke into warehouses, arsenals, and liquor stores, got drunk, set fires, and looted what little was left to steal. By the next morning, the good citizens were eagerly awaiting the arrival of their captors, almost their rescuers now, and Federal troops, including some proud black regiments, marched into the city, raised the flag of the United States, and began patrolling the streets to restore order.

All this was now virtually a sideshow, unimportant except that this was the Confederate capital, for Grant was after the real prize now, Robert E. Lee's army, and with it Confederate ability to continue the war. Five Forks had drastically lengthened the odds against Lee getting away, for the Federal victory there levered him off the Southside Railroad as a line of retreat. He must now take his troops due west to Amelia Court House, Farmville, and ultimately Lynchburg. By the fifth, he had most of his army at Amelia Court House, thirty miles west of Petersburg. Davis and his government-in-flight had managed to reach Danville, to the south, but the line was cut behind them, when Union troops reached Burke's Station at the same time that Lee got to Amelia Court House.

The hunt was up now. On the morning of the 6th, Lee's weary men shouldered their rifles and headed west, the long tired columns strung across the rolling hills, men hungry, animals breaking down, wagons gradually being abandoned, a tatterdemalion wreck of a great army. To the south and around the rear hung Union cavalry, snapping at their heels, picking up stragglers. And behind them came the Federal infantry, those long-suffering faithful regiments of the old Army of the Potomac, lengthening their stride now, hastily grabbing rations in the morning, a quick cup of coffee and a couple of biscuits, and On to the day! Gonna catch Bobby Lee at last!

What Grant and Sheridan and Meade and all wanted was to get across the Confederate line of retreat, and to cut them off from the south and west. By mid-day of the 6th, the Confederates were strung out around Sayler's Creek, just east of Farmville, their long wagon train holding up the rear guard of Anderson's III Corps and Dick Ewell's grab bag of about 3,000 troops from the Richmond garrison. The two Confederate commanders halted their men and took up a position, giving the trains time to close up to the advance. But then they got cut off, Federal cavalry hitting their southern flank and infantry closing up from the east on their position. Nothing daunted, the Confederates launched counterattacks—first by garrison troops, later by the last men of the Confederate naval battalion—that temporarily halted the blue-coats. But the pressure kept on mounting, with George Custer's cavalry and their repeating carbines banging away and heavy infantry massing against them, and finally the Confederates broke. Surrounded and harassed from all sides, Ewell ended up surrendering nearly a third of Lee's army.

They were getting close to the end now. An exultant Sheridan wired, "If the thing is pressed I think Lee will surrender," and Lincoln himself wired back, "Let the *thing* be pressed!" On the other side, one of Lee's aides asked where they should stop for the night, and Lee ruefully remarked, Somewhere over the North Carolina line.

They reached Farmville on the 7th, and actually got some rations. Lee then crossed to the north side of the Appomattox River, burning most of the bridges behind him. Humphreys's troops got across at High Bridge, however, and he and Wright kept up the pressure, forcing Lee to deploy to hold them off. Meanwhile, Sheridan, with Ord and Griffin,

Warren's successor, in tow, marched more directly west and got across the Confederate line of retreat near Appomattox Station, where they captured some trains. Lee came up against this on the late afternoon of the 8th, and ordered Gordon's division of infantry and Fitzhugh Lee's cavalry to clear a way through the next morning, the 9th.

Grant had already written to Lee, and over the last two days they had had a carefully courteous exchange of notes. On the 7th Grant had asked Lee to surrender, and Lee had written back asking what terms might be offered. The next day Grant had replied that his only condition would be that officers and men upon surrendering should agree not to fight again until properly exchanged, which both knew was a euphemism for "never." To this Lee had replied that he did not believe his situation as difficult as Grant seemed to think it was, and was therefore not yet prepared to give up. By then it was the morning of the 9th, and Gordon's troops were marching toward Appomattox Station.

It was only when they took up the march that they found there were Federal troops in front of them, but there was no help for it; they had to have supplies. So one last time the shrunken regiments deployed, most of them so small now a whole regiment barely made a company front, and on they came with the morning sun catching the glorious old battle flags. They hit Sheridan's cavalry, and the carbines and rifles broke into a rattle. But then the cavalry gave way, wheeling right and left, and there ahead of them were masses of blue infantry, and there was only one meaning to that: it was all but over now.

With Sheridan, and infantry, in front, and Meade pressing from behind, the Army of Northern Virginia was finished; it could either surrender or be killed where it stood. After some hesitation and discussion among the commanders, they raised a white flag—actually a towel—and reopened communications. It took a while to find Grant, who was in the process of moving forward to join Sheridan, but eventually notes were exchanged, and Grant went to meet Lee at the house of Wilbur McLean, the man who had moved from Bull Run, at Appomattox Court House.

Lee, as always, was impeccably dressed, suffering terribly but armored in the self-possession that never deserted him. Grant, travelworn and just getting over a headache, was almost theatrically shabby. The two men shook hands and began reminiscing about their service in the Mexican War, in the old army. Finally, after a good deal of diffidence on both sides, they got down to business, and Grant wrote out his terms, a simple surrender and officers allowed to retain side arms, men to keep horses and baggage, and that was it. Lee thought the offer generous, and said so, and wrote out an acceptance, and then, with some embarrassment, asked for rations for his men. After some hesitant small talk, Lee left and Grant telegraphed the great news to Washington.

The actual surrender of most of the troops did not come until the 12th, when Joshua Chamberlain, the hero of Little Round Top, was detailed to receive the arms and colors of the various units of the Army of Northern Virginia. One by one the shrunken formations marched past the solid ranks of Federal infantry to lay down their arms. Chamberlain had already decided on his own how to handle this, and as each unit came in, he ordered the Carry Arms, the marching salute. The downhearted Southerners, most with tears in their eyes, responded gratefully to a gesture of honor from men who had endured and suffered as much as they had themselves. Many a regimental color was surrendered as merely a bare pole, as the men had cut the flags up into little pieces to be taken home and cherished for years, until they had rotted away and, like the army that carried them, become but a memory. All day the surrender went on, regiments, divisions, men who had fought through Gettysburg, and Fredericksburg, and Antietam, men who had stood together in the hour of danger and would now stand no more. When it was all over, the blue soldiers and the gray sat down and shared rations while the bands played "Auld Lang Syne."

———

Appomattox Court House and the surrender of Robert E. Lee's army was the most dramatic of the several surrenders at the close of the war, but it was not the last; in fact, it was the first. There were still operations in progress all across the South, and these gradually came to an end, either as they reached a logical military conclusion, or as the news of the Confederacy's collapse reached the respective commanders. Unfortunately, some of these surrenders were more confused, and more colored by the evolving political scene, than Lee's surrender.

While Grant had been so successfully pursuing his Petersburg operations, Sherman had returned to his own army in the Carolinas. Arriving, he divided it into essentially three armies, and made ready to resume his march northward; he had agreed with Grant that he would begin his advance on April 10. His enemy, Joe Johnston, was to the northwest, near Raleigh, his entire army less than the 26,000 or 28,000 in any one of Sherman's three. Before the march began, news came in of the fall of Richmond, and then, soon after the troops moved out, of Davis's flight and Lee's surrender. Davis, from Danville, had issued a proclamation calling upon the Confederacy to open a new phase of the war, essentially guerrilla warfare, but there was little taste for that among the men who had already fought so long and so well, and Lee's surrender put any thought of it out of most minds.

On the 13th, as Federal troops entered Raleigh, Johnston wrote to Sherman asking for terms, and after the usual exchange, they agreed to meet between Raleigh and Durham's Station on the morning of the 17th. Sherman arrived late; as he was about to board the railroad train for the meeting, a coded message came in over the telegraph. He waited for it to be deciphered, and found that President Lincoln had been assassinated on the 14th, and an attempt had been made on Secretary of State Seward, and on other members of the government as well.

This had happened on the night of the 14th–15th; the president, who had returned from a triumphal visit to Richmond, and who was contemplating the happy and successful conclusion of the war, was shot in Ford's Theater by John Wilkes Booth, an actor and ardent Confederate sympathizer. Thinking he was performing an act of patriotic vengeance, Booth probably did the Confederacy the worst service he could conceivably have done; his act threw the government of the United States into the hands of a weak president and a vindictive, Radical Republican Congress.

The repercussions on Sherman were immediate, as an example of what would soon happen. He and Johnston met and soon agreed on wide-ranging terms, some of which transcended the immediate military situation; Sherman, having recently talked with President Lincoln and General Grant, believed he knew what was wanted, and the kind of terms, in a general sense, he thought himself authorized to offer. His position, after all, was substantially different from that of Grant; he was virtually in the middle of the Confederacy, and if he did not make some provision for the continuation of civil authority, the entire area around him might dissolve into some sort of anarchy. However, when he sent his dispatch north to Washington, his agreement was quickly denounced, and Secretary Stanton, riding high in the confused post-assassination capital, publicly chastised Sherman for exceeding his authority. The rebuke was open and stinging, and Sherman never forgave it. Eventually he and Johnston reached an amicable settlement, on April 26, but here was evidence that the Federal victors might well have more difficulty with their political masters than their former enemies.

Other surrenders were slow, depending upon the communications of the country. Substantial cavalry operations were being conducted in Alabama, and it was the first week of May before a surrender was arranged there. On the 10th, President Davis and his few immediate supporters were captured at Irwinville, Georgia. Their makeshift camp was surprised by Federal cavalry, and there was a good deal of confusion; Davis sought to escape in the rush, and unfortunately, as he fled toward the swamp, grabbed the first piece of warm clothing to hand, which turned out to be a woman's shawl. This subsequently gave rise to the canard that he had been captured disguised as a woman. He would spend the next several months in close and unhealthy confinement while the government tried to decide what to do with him.

It was all falling apart now. The worst of the Confederate irregulars, William C. Quantrill, was shot in Kentucky on the same day Davis was captured, the top and bottom of the rebellion going down simultaneously. Across the Mississippi, there was some talk of keeping on with the fight; these people were, after all, Texans and the men who still remembered Bleeding Kansas. It was late June before the last surrender west of the great river occurred. Some Confederates, unrepentant, crossed over into Mexico and vowed to continue the fight. Finally, it was in August that the Confederate cruiser *Shenandoah,* after destroying the American whaling fleet in the Bering Sea, heard of the end of the war.

Thus it was done at last. The Union armies held their great review, marching through Washington, boots and brass polished, bayonets twinkling in the sun, bands playing and colors flying, the thin ranks of the old regiments bringing tears amid the cheers of the viewers. Then they held their last musters, ate ceremonial dinners, exchanged gifts and addresses, and struck their tents, heading for home and dear faces grown unfamiliar through terrible years of war. The Confederates straggled back by twos and threes, no parades and reviews for them, to try to find hungry wives and children, and to rebuild shattered lives. The dream, the nightmare, was over.

Chapter 22

Defeat and Victory

THE GENERATION that fought the Civil War spent the rest of its life trying to absorb the event, and to make sense of what it had done. It was the focal point of men's and women's lives, and as such it deserved, and received, a great deal of reflection. For those who had not participated directly, by virtue of age, condition, or gender, it was, obviously, something they had missed; for those who had taken part in it, and lived through it, it was the occasion of reminiscences and veterans' organizations. For the people of the war generation, and for the millions who came after them, it became a matter of commemoration. Gradually it assumed a centrality in the life of the nation, in the process of defining what the nation was and meant, a centrality that to a large extent it still holds. In almost any town in the eastern United States, the Civil War memorial takes pride of place, even over World War II and even allowing for changing tastes in memorials. The American Revolution, like the eighteenth century generally, seems too distant for any sense of immediate empathy, but the Civil War, with its totality of commitment, with its railroads and its masses of men and matériel, with both its ideology and its romanticism on the one hand, and its practical common sense on the other—Jeb Stuart the last cavalier, and Sam Grant in his baggy trousers and private's blouse—seems something assimilable, something that is still part of Americans even though it happened more than a century ago. There are reasons for this.

Perhaps first among them, it was all America's war; it was fought right in the front yard, and all the casualties, on either side, were American. The costs of winning and losing both had to be debited to

323

the same people. And those costs were tremendous. At the top of the list were the 620,000 men who died, in proportion approximately three Union soldiers for every two Confederates, 360,000 Union soldiers and about 260,000 Confederates. The latter number was about 5 percent of the white population of the Confederacy, and 25 percent of the white males of military age. The Federal deaths represent a smaller proportion of the larger Union resources. Other casualties, wounded, prisoners, and missing, are at the usual ratio of about three to one, so that means another million to a million and a half scarred by the war. Those, of course, are military figures, and leave out of consideration the hundreds of thousands of widows and orphans, and the numerous civilian deaths, almost all of the latter in the South, directly or indirectly attributable to the passage of armies and the devastation of war. Until well after the turn of the century, every town in eastern America had its war widows and its veterans who were missing an arm or a leg. Celebrating heroism, people often forget the hidden ongoing price of pain that ceases only with the death of the last maimed veteran or his widow.

Such costs immediately provoke the question, Was it worth it? What result did the nation gain that compensated for the suffering of the war? The first response that comes to mind is that the question is simply impertinent, if answered only by those—scholars, Civil War buffs, visitors to historic parks—who did not have to pay such costs. Such people are in the position of Civil War re-enactors, who dress up in period costume and shoot each other with blank cartridges, then get together for a barbecue, sham actors in sham warfare. It is easy enough for the writer, sound in body and presumably in mind, to answer that, yes, the war was worth the suffering. Most people can endure other people's suffering with a good deal of equanimity. So the question should be, Did the people who fought, suffered, and lived through the war think it was worth it, and what did they think it meant?

Judging by the memoirs they left behind, the answer is that they did think it was worth the effort and the cost, both on the national and the individual level. President Lincoln believed, as he repeatedly said, that the nation was undergoing "a new birth of freedom," that the United States was a noble experiment, and that men were fighting and dying so that "government of the people, by the people, for the people shall not perish from the earth." Those were noble and lofty aims, and in a nation still dominated by small communities and government of town meetings, they were less imprecise than perhaps they seem today. They were clear enough, anyway, to the Northern men who volunteered by their thousands to fight, and perhaps to die, for them, and to the families who supported and sustained them while they did it. To these men, the Federal Union, the life of the nation as a whole, was worth fighting to preserve. And they gradually came to understand, as indeed did the president himself, that that life, and that vision of what the United States was and meant, could not be sustained in a country in which some men were free and some were slave. If all men were not free, to achieve the natural limits of whatever talents nature or God had given them, then none were truly free. These were of course philosophical or theoretical constructs, and the constraints of daily living, of making a living, meant that such abstractions were seldom achieved in real life. Nonetheless, they were there as the underpinning of what life, individual and national, was all about. We tend, indeed, to think that the average man seldom even thinks in such abstract terms—but it was the average man who volunteered for the war, and fought it, and re-elected Abraham Lincoln to keep on fighting it.

Government of, by, and for the people—old veterans insisted that when President Lincoln spoke that phrase he put the emphasis on "people"—also helps explain the importance of the war in American history, for it was an open-ended aim, not just of the war, but of the nation. One of the reasons the war occurred when it did was because Americans were involved in the process of redefining what "government" and what "people" meant, and one reason for continued discussion of the war, aside from its intrinsic interest, is that they are still doing so. No society is ever static, but few have spent as much time and effort in constant refinement of what society is at any given moment as have Americans. The role of government has constantly changed, and so has the vision of what constitutes the "people." In 1800 "people" meant adult white males possessing certain property qualifications; in 1860 it meant adult white males; after the Civil War it was supposed to mean adult males, and eventually it meant adults; at the end of the twentieth century Americans are busily redefining who is an adult, and working on the concept of family and the protection of those who are not adults. Thus questions addressed in the war are questions still of vital interest to society, questions to which answers are still being sought, in the streets, in the classrooms, and in the courtrooms of America.

Northerners, or more fairly Union men, as there were many in the South who sympathized with and fought for the North, were fighting for the preservation of the Union and, as a necessary entailment, the demise of slavery. And by extension, they were fighting for this open-ended definition of what the United States was all about. What Confederates were fighting for was a different vision, and after the war was over, Southerners and Southern apologists spent a great deal of time and effort justifying what they had done and why they had done it.

The most successful, and the most influential, of these apologia for the South was that produced by the Richmond journalist Edward A. Pollard. During the war he had been vociferously anti-Davis, and he had also written a four-volume history of the war as it was being fought. In 1866 he condensed this into a single volume, which he entitled *The Lost Cause*. The phrase "the Lost Cause" thus passed into Southern mythology, and for at least half a century provided the rationale for what Southerners had done. They had not broken up the Union to protect slavery, but to free themselves from an association they had willingly joined, and had in 1860–61 chosen to leave. In Pollard's view, and that of his Southern readers, the antebellum South represented all or at least the greater part of what was good, cultured, civilized, in America, a rural land of happy yeoman farms as envisaged by Thomas Jefferson. To avoid contamination by, and submergence in, the grasping, avaricious, money-driven world of the Yankee, Southerners had simply opted to leave, as was their right. They had then been prevented from doing so by the overwhelming might of the North, with its capitalists and its mercenaries, and thus Southern cavaliers, fighting gallantly to the end, had ultimately gone down before the crushing masses of lesser men mobilized by a heartless industrial machine society.

This was of course an immensely one-sided view, but like all such, it had just enough verisimilitude in it that it could be accepted, especially by a people who felt themselves abused and mistreated by the oppressive Reconstruction policies imposed on the South in the decade after the war. The Lost Cause, that of honorable men and beautiful women and magnolia blossoms, with contented darkies humming the background music offstage, was the perfect Romantic picture of what the South had been, and what the war had been fought to preserve. Pollard's vision, and the emendations to it by a thousand preachers, editors, and novelists, achieved for the South after the war what Harriet

Beecher Stowe and *Uncle Tom's Cabin* had done for the country before the war: both provided a false image, but an image men and women could embrace, act upon, live with.

In this way, both sides could believe they had contended nobly for a worthy cause; they could all be Americans again. Those who supported the Union could believe that they had been right all along, and that they had vindicated themselves on the battlefield; in the trial by combat, God had indeed upheld the right. But former Confederates could believe that they too had been right, that their vision of America was a valid one, at least for its time, that it was worth testing in war, and they could even entertain the quite contradictory notions that they had both been right to fight, and that it was probably a good thing that they had lost. That required considerable mental or emotional agility, but human beings, as we all know now, are perfectly capable of believing mutually exclusive propositions.

None of this adjustment happened in a vacuum, of course. Life went on, through the years of Reconstruction and on into the Gilded Age, as the country grew ever stronger, larger, richer, more powerful, an exuberant, ebullient America striding confidently toward the new century and the world stage. Under that progress, both Unionist and Confederate could convince themselves that they were, after all, winners in the great struggle of life.

But there were losers. The proud and hopeful assertion that once the black man had a rifle on his shoulder and the letters "U.S." on his belt buckle, he would be a free man and considered the equal of white men proved a sham. Throughout the South, blacks were denied by clever manipulation of the political and legal system the rights they had been officially accorded by the victory of the Union and the laws of the federal government. Freed from legal slavery, they were kept in an economic and political peonage. White southerners actively promoted this, nonsoutherners at the very least passively agreed with it, and blacks themselves lacked the means, through education, economic circumstance, or social or political organization, to do anything about it. Slavery gave way to segregation, and for a century that was about as far as change went. It was not until after the Second World War that real change began.

The passage of time eventually makes all men and women, black and white and everything else, equal, as Carl Sandburg said in *Grass*, and Walt Whitman, the great poet of the Civil War era, said in everything. So the young boys of the war went home to become middle-aged, then old, men; the generals and colonels sat down to write their memoirs, and to prove that everyone had committed errors but they. Few were as honest as old Dick Ewell: "It took a great many mistakes to lose Gettysburg. I made most of them." Most were at pains to prove that someone else, or at least someone else's general, did this or that wrong.

Jefferson Davis, eventually released from prison, settled in Mississippi, looking out over the Gulf Coast, and wrote his memoirs; here at last was the perfect venue, where he could argue with cool logic that he had never been wrong, that the Confederacy had never been wrong. So it went; Confederates discovered a devil, poor old General Longstreet, whom they accused of losing Gettysburg and the war, and a whole host of saints, Lee and Jackson at the head of the list. Union men did even better; they not only wrote memoirs, five of them went on to become presidents of the United States. The last of them was William McKinley, who during the war rose from private to major, was elected president in 1897, and died, ironically, from an assassin's bullet. Joshua Chamberlain, of Little Round Top, became governor of Maine. Oliver Wendell Holmes became a Justice of the Supreme Court, and lived until 1935, but the war remained the defining event of his life. Nathan Bedford Forrest, that incomparable cavalry leader, helped organize the Ku Klux Klan, and Oliver Howard, the unlucky one-armed general, became director of the Freedman's Bureau and had the country's first university for blacks named after him. Gouverneur Warren spent the rest of his life seeking exoneration for his relief from command, and got it just before he died in 1882. Ambrose Burnside died a senator; George Armstrong Custer, the boy general, died at the Little Bighorn. Joe Johnston was a pallbearer at William Tecumseh Sherman's funeral; he stood bareheaded in the rain, and died five weeks later from the chill he caught. The last of the chief Confederate generals, Longstreet, died in 1904; his young widow outlived him by fifty-eight years, and worked building bombers during the Second World War.

So they passed from the scene, first the generals, then the older officers, and finally the young privates and drummer boys and buglers, no longer young at all, but old, old men in faded uniforms of the Grand Army of the Republic or the United Confederate Veterans, riding stiff and straight in automobiles in the parades in Bridgeport or Wilmington, while other young men marched off to other wars. The Grand

Army of the Republic held its last meeting in 1949; sixteen men were still alive of all those thousands who had once worn blue fatigue jackets, and six attended the meeting. The United Confederate Veterans outlasted them; its last reunion, of three men, was held in 1951. Then they were gone, all Americans, all equal, all free at last.

Suggestions for Further Reading

The literature on the Civil War is enormous, and more material is coming out all the time. Not only is there an apparently endless flow of scholarly studies, of this battle, that general, or some particular aspect of the era, but there are even original documentary sources still appearing, as collections of letters and diaries reach public notice. It would be almost a full-time task to stay abreast of new works, let alone catch up on the previous century's production.

In a way this is all illusory, for many earlier works need not be read, having been updated by more thorough modern research and scholarship. For every early work that has stood the test of time, and become a classic either for its writing or for its historical interest, dozens of others have been dated and discarded; for example, Richard A. Sauers in *The Gettysburg Campaign, June 3–August 1, 1863: A Comprehensive, Selectively Annotated Bibliography* (Westport, Conn.: Greenwood, 1982) lists some twenty-eight hundred titles that deal with that one battle alone, and there have been dozens more in the years since his work appeared. These range from full-scale studies to commemorative addresses, and it would be a truly masochistic reader who might try to read them all. None of this is meant to excuse the following list, but is simply offered to explain why the list is as it is. I have been reading Civil War history avidly but unsystematically for nearly fifty years, and more systematically but no less avidly for the last five, since I began working up this book. At the end of it I am still more conscious of all the good books I have not read than of those I have. The Civil War scholar or buff looking at this list will undoubtedly feel the same way, but the list is intended less for those who are already familiar with the literature than for those who may, through youth or leisure time at last, be entering the fascinating world of Civil War study and argument.

First of all, there is available a number of technical or factual compendiums that, while they may not make very good reading, are great browsing material, and are very useful for checking names and dates. As the great American historian Fletcher Pratt once remarked, it seems as if every other Confederate general was named either Lee or Stuart, but at least the Stuarts had the grace to spell their names differently. Among the most useful I have found is Mark M. Boatner III, *The Civil War Dictionary* (New York: David MacKay, 1959), and Patricia L. Faust (ed.), *Historical Times Encyclopedia of the Civil War* (New York: Harper and Row, 1986), while John S. Bowman (ed.), *The Civil War Day by Day* (Greenwich, Conn.: Dorset, 1989), is a helpful almanac. Fascinating capsule biographies of all the generals are in Ezra J. Warner, *Generals in Gray: Lives of the Confederate Commanders*, and *Generals in Blue: Lives of the Union Commanders* (both Baton Rouge: Louisiana State University Press, 1959 and 1964). Also useful is David C. Roller and Robert W. Twyman (eds.), *The Encyclopedia of Southern History* (Baton Rouge: Louisiana State University Press, 1979). A good atlas in indispensable, and as always I have found V. J. Esposito (ed.), *The West Point Atlas of American Wars*, vol. I, 1689–1900 (New York: Praeger, 1959) to be very helpful.

There are several more or less contemporary multivolume histories of the Civil War and the era; pride of place and scholarship must go to Alan Nevins, *The Ordeal of the Union*, 8 vols. (New York: Scribner's, 1947–1971). Bruce Catton, the great historian of the last generation, virtually created a Civil War renaissance in narrative history all by himself; *The Centennial History of the Civil War*, 3 vols. (Garden City, N.Y.: Doubleday, 1961–1965) is but one of his many works, and others are cited below. Where Catton took a generally Northern point of view, Shelby Foote in *The Civil War: A Narrative*, 3 vols (New York: Random House, 1958–1974) takes a generally Southern point of view. The latest of these collections is William C. Davis, *The Imperilled Union 1861–1865*, 3 vols. (Garden City, N.Y.: Doubleday, 1982–). Three- and even eight-volume histories are as nothing, of course, to the original government treatments, and those who are truly caught up in the Civil War will want to refer to what are always known as the "Official Records"; these were collected and published at the turn of the century as U.S. Army, *The War of the Rebellion: Official Records of the Union and Confederate Armies*, 130 vols. (Washington D.C.: U.S. Government Printing Office, 1882–1900), and U.S. Navy, *The War of the Rebellion: Official Records of the Union and Confederate Navies*, 30 vols. (Washington, D.C.: USGPO, 1894–1922). These vast works contained official reports, correspondence, and commentaries, and provided fuel for veterans to argue with each other for years.

Of the many single-volume histories, the one to start and end with is James M. McPherson, *Battle Cry of Freedom: The Civil War Era*, vol. 6 of the *Oxford History of the United States* (New York: Oxford University Press, 1988); this is in some respects a reworking of his earlier *Ordeal by Fire: The Civil War and Reconstruction* (New York: Knopf, 1982), but each has enough material to repay separate reading. There are many studies on the political course of the war, and especially on the crucial years that led to it. An older one now is Avery Craven, *The Coming of the Civil War* (Chicago: University of Chicago Press, 1957); one of the most thorough and readable is David M. Potter, *The Impending Crisis, 1848–1861* (New York: Harper and Row, 1976); two books that define a lifetime's scholarship are Kenneth M. Stampp, *And the War Came: The North and the Secession Crisis, 1860–1861* (Baton Rouge: Louisiana State University Press, 1950), and his *America in 1857: A Nation on the Brink* (New York: Oxford University Press, 1990). A brilliant treatment of the progressive dissolution of the American federation is William H. Freehling, *The Road to Disunion*, vol. 1, *Secessionists at Bay, 1776–1856* (New York: Oxford University Press, 1990). Several other studies that deal with the ever more pressing issues of slavery and potential secession are Elbert B. Smith, *The Death of Slavery: The United States, 1837–1865* (Chicago: University of Chicago Press, 1967); William J. Cooper, Jr., *The South and the Politics of Slavery, 1828–1856* (Baton Rouge: Louisiana State University Press, 1978); Michael F. Holt, *Political Parties and American Political Development: From the Age of Jackson to the Age of Lincoln* (Baton Rouge: LSUP, 1992); and John McCardell, *The Idea of a Southern Nation, 1830–1860* (New York: Norton, 1979). For a history of the whole Confederacy, there are Emory M. Thomas, *The Confederate Nation* (New York: Harper and Row, 1979), and E. Merton Coulter, *The Confederate States of America, 1861–1865* (Baton Rouge: LSUP, 1950).

The issue of slavery has received increasing attention in the last generation. All of the following, of many that might be mentioned, can be read with profit: Hugh G. J. Aitken (ed.), *Did Slavery Pay?* (Boston: Houghton Mifflin, 1971); Robert W. Fogel, *Without Consent or Contract: The Rise and Fall of American Slavery* (New York: Norton, 1989); Roger L. Ransom, *Conflict and Compromise: The Political Economy of Slavery, Emancipation, and the American Civil War* (Cambridge: Cambridge University Press, 1989); Eugene D. Genovese, *The Political Economy of Slavery* (New York: Pantheon, 1965); and Kenneth M. Stampp, *The Peculiar Institution: Slavery in the Ante-Bellum South* (New York: Vintage, 1956). As even these few titles suggest, increasing attention has not meant much agreement on the issue of slavery, and there is still argument over such fundamental points as whether or not slavery was profitable, or how it compared with the free labor of the North. A couple of more specific approaches are Herbert Aptheker, *Abolitionism: A Revolutionary Movement* (Boston: Twayne, 1989), and James M. McPherson, *The Negro's Civil War* (New York: Ballantine, 1965).

———

Turning now to more directly military aspects of the war, there is a large number of studies that attempt to explain why the war took the course that it did; some of these are fairly commonsensical, and some are pretty far-fetched; some are very readable, some less so, but to a military buff, all are interesting. Two very large studies are Herman Hattaway and Archer Jones, *How the North Won: A Military History of the Civil War* (Urbana, Ill.: University of Illinois Press, 1983), and Richard E. Beringer, Herman Hattaway, Archer Jones, and William N. Still, Jr., *Why the South Lost the Civil War* (Athens, Ga.: University of Georgia Press, 1986). Archer Jones has also written *Civil War Command and Strategy: The Process of Victory and Defeat* (New York: Free Press, 1992). Frank E. Vandiver, *Rebel Brass* (Baton Rouge: Louisiana State University Press, 1956), explores the shortcomings of the Confederate command system, while T. Harry Williams, *Lincoln and His Generals* (New York: Knopf, 1952), examines the relationship between the president and his military people. A more current treatment is Joseph T. Glatthaar, *Partners in Command: The Relationship Between Leaders in the Civil War* (New York: Free Press, 1994). While those books deal with men on the same side, the peculiar symbiosis between leaders of the opposite side is examined in Charles Royster, *The Destructive War: William Tecumseh Sherman, Stonewall Jackson, and the Americans* (New York: Knopf, 1991). One of the most remarkable theses on why the war went as it did, and one that has been considered a little too imaginative by most authorities, is Grady McWhiney and Perry D. Jamieson, *Attack and Die: Civil War Military Tactics and the Southern Heritage* (University, Ala.: University of Alabama Press, 1982). Though this might seem an odd place to list the following work, a different perception of Southern defeat is offered in Catherine Clinton and Nina Silber (eds.), *Divided Houses: Gender and the Civil War* (New York: Oxford University Press, 1992). Two interesting collections of the war's issues are Gabor S. Boritt (ed.), *Lincoln the War President,* and *Why the Confederacy Lost* (both New York: Oxford University Press, 1992).

A large number of books deals with the matter of soldiers, their lives and experiences in the war. The starting point for this aspect of the struggle is the two seminal books by Bell I. Wiley, *The Life of Johnny Reb: The Common Soldiers of the Confederacy* (Indianapolis: Bobbs Merrill, 1943), and *The Life of Billy Yank: The Common Soldiers of the Union* (Indianapolis: Bobbs Merrill, 1952). Two more current, highly illustrated treatments along the same line are William C. Davis, *The Fighting Men of the Civil War,* and *The Commanders of the Civil War* (New York: Salamander, 1989 and 1990). Reid Mitchell has written a useful study in *Civil War Soldiers: Their Expectations and their Experiences* (New York: Viking, 1988), paralleled by Gerald F. Linderman, *Embattled Courage: The Experience of Combat in the American Civil War* (New York: Free Press, 1987); for black soldiers, Joseph T. Glatthaar has written *Forged in Battle: The Civil War Alliance of Black Soldiers and White Officers* (New York: Free Press, 1990). That experiences and expectations were startlingly different is illustrated in one of the indispensable books of the war, originally appearing at the turn of the century, Thomas L. Livermore, *Numbers and Losses in the Civil War* (Bloomington, Ind.: Indiana University Press, 1957).

It is in campaign and battle history that the true military buff can wallow to his or her heart's content, for this area of Civil War studies is an ever-swelling stream, of which only a hint can be given here. The stream started early, and one can still read Robert U. Johnson and Clarence C. Buel, *Battles and Leaders of the Civil War,* 8 vols. (New York: Century, 1884–1887) with enjoyment; this collection of battle experiences and memoirs and controversies was one of the great successes of the publishing world, with generals pushing and shoving to get in on it and present their view of what happened to the public. The classic study of the Army of Northern Virginia was Douglas Southall Freeman's *Lee's Lieutenants*, 3 vols. (New York: Scribner's, 1942–1944); this was in essence a companion study to Freeman's *Robert E. Lee*, 4 vols. (New York: Scribner's, 1935–1942), and it seems almost sacrilegious to suggest that these volumes are a bit dated to the modern reader. Then on the other side of the field there is Bruce Catton's *Army of the Potomac Trilogy* (New York: Doubleday, 1951–1953). Several studies take the eastern battles and campaigns in sequence, starting with Stephen W. Sears, *To the Gates of Richmond: The Peninsula Campaign* (New York: Ticknor and Fields, 1992); then John J. Hennessy, *Return to Bull Run: The Campaign and Battle of Second Manassas* (New York: Simon and Schuster, 1993). Antietam has received a great deal of attention, and two good studies are James W. Murfin, *The Gleam of Bayonets: The Battle of Antietam and the Maryland Campaign of 1862* (New York: Thomas Yoseleff, 1965), and Stephen W. Sears, *Landscape Turned Red: The Battle of Antietam* (New York: Ticknor and Fields, 1983). A recent study is Ernest B. Furgurson, *Chancellorsville, 1863: The Souls of the Brave* (New York: Knopf, 1992), and of the many books on Gettysburg, a comprehensive one is Edward B. Coddington, *The Gettysburg Campaign: A Study in Command* (New York: Charles Scribner's Sons, 1979). Noah Andre Trudeau wrote *Bloody Roads South: The Wilderness to Cold Harbor, May–June, 1864* (Boston: Little, Brown, 1989), and Burke Davis covered the closing campaign of the war in *To Appomattox: Nine April Days, 1865* (New York: Rinehart, 1959); an older study of that campaign has recently been reissued in paperback, Joshua L. Chamberlain, *The Passing of the Armies* (New York: Bantam, 1993); by modern standards, Chamberlain's writing style is a bit high-flown, but it is still fabulous reading once one captures the rhythm.

It was once thought that the western campaigns were the poor relation of Civil War studies, but that is certainly no longer the case. A mere sampling will offer the following titles: Benjamin Franklin Cooling, *Forts Henry and Donelson: The Key to the Confederate Heartland* (Knoxville, Tenn.: University of Tennessee Press, 1987), and Peter Cozzens, *No Better Place to Die: The Battle of Stones River* (Urbana, Ill.: University of Illinois Press, 1991). Of many books on Vicksburg, Earl Schenck Miers, *The Web of Victory: Grant at Vicksburg* (New York: Knopf, 1955), is a useful coverage. Glenn Tucker wrote *Chickamauga: Bloody Battle in the West* (Dayton, Ohio: Morningside House, 1984), but this has probably been superseded by Peter Cozzens, *This Terrible Sound: The Battle of Chickamauga* (Urbana, Ill.: University of Illinois Press, 1992). Next comes James Lee McDonough, *Chattanooga—A Death Grip on the Confederacy* (Knoxville, Tenn.: University of Tennessee Press, 1984), and then Albert Castel, *Decision in the West: The Atlanta Campaign of 1864* (Lawrence, Kan.: University Press of Kansas, 1992). James Lee McDonough and Thomas L. Connelly wrote *Five Tragic Hours: The Battle of Franklin* (Knoxville, Tenn.: University of Tennessee Press, 1983), and Connelly also did an outstanding two volumes, *Army of the Heartland: The Army of Tennessee, 1861–1862*, and *Autumn of Glory: The Army of Tennessee, 1862–1865* (both Baton Rouge: Louisiana State University Press, 1967 and 1971). An excellent work on what actually is a new area of study is Alvin M. Josephy, Jr., *The Civil War in the American West* (New York: Knopf, 1992).

––––––

The Civil War era is a gold mine for those who prefer their history in the form of biography or autobiography; though it is indeed a little artificial to separate this list into campaign studies and biographies, when so many books could be included in both sections. Taking the Union first, probably the best one-volume life of Lincoln is Stephen B. Oates, *With Malice Toward None* (New York: Harper and Row, 1977). Recently the Library of America series issued *Abraham Lincoln: Speeches and Writings*, 2 vols. (New York: 1989); no reader can avoid being impressed by Lincoln's clarity of thought and common sense, which shine through his work, and this is the best way to get through the evolution of his ideas and convictions. A fascinating examination of the effects of this evolution is in Mark E. Neely, Jr., *The Fate of Liberty: Abraham Lincoln and Civil Liberties* (New York: Oxford University Press, 1991). The career of his early great rival is covered in Robert W. Johannsen, *Stephen A. Douglas* (New York: Oxford University Press, 1973). Offering further, contemporary, insight, the *Diary of Gideon Welles*, 3 vols. (Boston: Houghton Mifflin) was published in 1903. Fletcher Pratt wrote *Stanton: Lincoln's Secretary of War* (Westport, Conn.: Greenwood, 1970), and Ralph Korngold wrote *Thaddeus Stevens* (New York: Harcourt Brace, 1955). A crucial diplomatic figure is covered in Martin Duberman, *Charles Francis Adams* (Stanford, Cal.: Stanford University Press, 1976); along that line mention might be made here of a new work by Howard Jones, *Union in Peril: The Crisis over British In-*

tervention in the Civil War (Chapel Hill, N.C.: University of North Carolina Press, 1992).

For more specifically military biographies, the place to start on the Union side is undoubtedly with Grant himself. Originally written as he was dying of cancer, *Personal Memoirs of U. S. Grant* (New York: Library of America, 1990) is one of the monuments of American history and literature. It can be nicely supplemented by Horace Porter's personal memoir, *Campaigning with Grant* (New York: Bantam, 1991). The best general biography is William S. McFeely, *Grant: A Biography* (New York: Norton, 1981), and there is any number of other studies; one of the most famous is by the British theorist J. F. C. Fuller, *Grant and Lee: A Study in Personality and Generalship* (Bloomington, Ind.: Indiana University Press, 1957). Bruce Catton's *U. S. Grant and the American Military Tradition* (Boston: Little, Brown, 1954) is still readable.

Sherman's memoirs are very nearly in the same category as Grant's, and were recently reissued as *Memoirs of General W. T. Sherman* (New York: Library of America, 1990); Sherman has had a lot of recent attention, and in addition to Royster's book mentioned above there is John F. Marszalek, *Sherman: A Soldier's Passion for Order* (New York: Free Press, 1993). The other member of the winning trilogy wrote General Philip Sheridan, *Civil War Memoirs* (New York: Bantam, 1991); a recent biography is Roy Morris, Jr., *Sheridan: The Life and Wars of General Phil Sheridan* (New York: Crown, 1992). The reissuing of all these memoirs, most of them a hundred years old now, testifies to the continuing interest in the period.

For the lesser commanders we have Stephen W. Sears, *George B. McClellan: The Young Napoleon* (New York: Ticknor and Fields, 1988), an exquisite dissection for those of us who do not like McClellan. For some of the better commanders, there are Freeman Cleaves, *Rock of Chickamauga: The Life of General George H. Thomas* (Norman, Okla.: University of Oklahoma Press, 1948); Richard E. Winslow III, *General John Sedgwick: The Story of a Union Corps Commander* (Novato, Cal.: Presidio, 1982); and David M. Jordan, *Winfield Scott Hancock: A Soldier's Life* (Bloomington, Ind.: Indiana University Press, 1988). For some of the poorer, there are W. A. Swanberg, *Sickles the Incredible* (New York: Charles Scribner's Sons, 1956); Robert S. Holzman, *Stormy Ben Butler* (New York: Macmillan, 1954); and William Marvel, *Burnside* (Chapel Hill, N.C.: University of North Carolina Press, 1991).

Some slightly lesser known figures are covered in Alice Rains Trulock, *In the Hands of Providence: Joshua L. Chamberlain and the American Civil War* (Chapel Hill, N.C.: University of North Carolina Press, 1992); Liva Baker, *The Justice from Beacon Hill: The Life and Times of Oliver Wendell Holmes* (New York: HarperCollins, 1991); and a new biography by Stephen B. Oates, *A Woman of Valor: Clara Barton and the Civil War* (New York: Free Press, 1994).

Finally in this section, a few selections of the many collections of memoirs and letters: Just released is James M. Greiner, Janet L. Coryell, and James R. Smither, *A Surgeon's Civil War: The Letters and Diaries of Daniel M. Holt, M.D.* (Kent, Ohio: Kent State University Press, 1994). Dale E. Floyd edited *"Dear Friends at Home . . ." The Letters and Diary of Thomas James Owen, Fiftieth New York Volunteer Engineer Regiment, During the Civil War* (Washington, D.C.: Office of the Chief of Engineers, 1985). Stephen W. Sears edited *For Country, Cause, and Leader: The Civil War Journal of Charles B. Haydon* (New York: Ticknor and Fields, 1993), and Robert Hunt Rhodes edited *All for the Union: The Civil War Diary and Letters of Elisha Hunt Rhodes* (New York: Orion, 1985). J. H. Kidd wrote his memoirs in 1901 as *A Cavalryman with Custer* (New York: Bantam, 1991). These few will serve as an introduction to the many.

For the Confederate side, Jefferson Davis himself wrote *The Rise and Fall of the Confederate Government*, 2 vols. (New York: Appleton, 1881); a major biography is Hudson Strode, *Jefferson Davis*, 3 vols. (New York: Harcourt, 1955–1964), and an excellent new one is William C. Davis, *Jefferson Davis: The Man and His Hour* (New York: HarperCollins, 1991). The peculiar relation between the Confederate president and his military men is examined in Stephen E. Woodworth, *Jefferson Davis and His Generals: The Failure of Confederate Command in the West* (Lawrence, Kan.: University Press of Kansas, 1990). In the biography sweepstakes, Southern political leaders have been largely overshadowed by military ones. Lee of course stands at the top of the list, but Freeman's monumental work, cited earlier, should be supplemented by more modern assessments, such as Thomas L. Connelly, *The Marble Man: Robert E. Lee and His Image in American Society* (New York: Knopf, 1977), and Alan T. Nolan, *Lee Considered: General Robert E. Lee and Civil War History* (Chapel Hill, N.C.: University of North Carolina Press, 1991).

For other commanders, there is a wealth of material. Craig L. Symonds has written *Joseph E. Johnston: A Civil War Biography* (New York:

Norton, 1992); Longstreet has received sympathetic treatment in William G. Piston, *Lee's Tarnished Lieutenant: James Longstreet and His Place in Southern History* (Athens, Ga.: University of Georgia Press, 1987), and in Jeffrey D. Wert, *General James Longstreet: The Confederacy's Most Controversial Soldier—A Biography* (New York: Simon and Schuster, 1993). There are dozens of books about Jackson, including the older Burke Davis, *They Called Him Stonewall: A Life of Lt. Gen. T. J. Jackson, C.S.A.* (New York: Fairfax, 1988), and a newer John Bowers, *Stonewall Jackson: Portrait of a Soldier* (New York: Morrow, 1989). James I. Robertson, Jr., wrote *General A. P. Hill: The Story of a Confederate Warrior* (New York: Random House, 1987), and Gary W. Gallagher did *Stephen Dodd Ramseur: Lee's Gallant General* (Chapel Hill, N.C.: University of North Carolina Press, 1985). General insight on Lee and his command relations is in G. Moxley Sorrel, *Recollections of a Confederate Staff Officer* (New York: Bantam, 1992).

For the generals west of the mountains, there is Grady McWhiney, *Braxton Bragg and Confederate Defeat*, 2 vols. (New York: Columbia University Press, 1965); T. Harry Williams did *P. T. Beauregard: Napoleon in Gray* (Baton Rouge: Louisiana State University Press, 1954), and John P. Dyer did *The Gallant Hood* (Indianapolis: Bobbs Merrill, 1950). Michael B. Ballard has written on *Pemberton: A Biography* (Jackson, Miss.: University Press of Mississippi, 1991), and T. Michael Parrish has done *Richard Taylor: Soldier Prince of Dixie* (Chapel Hill, N.C.: University of North Carolina Press, 1992), and on Hardee there is Nathaniel C. Hughes, Jr., *General William J. Hardee: Old Reliable* (Baton Rouge: Louisiana State University Press, 1965). The other end of the scale is recounted in O. S. Barton, *Three Years with Quantrill: A True Story Told by His Scout John McCorkle* (Norman, Okla.: University of Oklahoma Press, 1992). A general picture of Confederate life and arms is in Walter Lord (ed.), *The Freemantle Diary* (Boston: Little, Brown, 1954), and a fuller one of life behind the war is in Mary Boykin Chesnut, *A Diary from Dixie* (Cambridge, Mass.: Harvard University Press, 1980), while some aspects of life on the Union home front are illustrated in Alan Nevins and M. H. Thomas (eds.), *The Diary of George Templeton Strong*, vol. III of *The Civil War, 1860–1865* (New York: Macmillan, 1952).

Finally, for a few titles on the naval side of the war, there is Virgil C. Jones, *The Civil War at Sea*, 3 vols. (New York: Holt, Rinehart, Winston, 1960–1962), James M. Merrill, *The Rebel Shore* (Boston: Little, Brown, 1957), and Thomas P. Nash, Jr., *A Naval History of the Civil War* (New York: A. S. Barnes, 1972). Somewhat more specialized are Richard S. West, Jr., *Mr. Lincoln's Navy* (New York: Longman's Green, 1957), Allen H. Gosnell, *Guns on the Western Waters: The Story of the River Gunboats in the Civil War* (Baton Rouge: Louisiana State University Press, 1949), and Rowena Reed, *Combined Operations in the Civil War* (Annapolis, Md.: U.S. Naval Institute Press, 1978).

———

This list of some hundred-odd titles does no more than scratch the surface; choosing this many from a list that now numbers well over fifty thousand is really a lottery, and in citing these works I am conscious of several hundred more that I have read, enjoyed, and agreed or argued with over the years, and even more conscious of all those worthy books that I have *not* read. Here I can only hope that readers may be inspired to delve ever deeper into this fascinating era. If they are, this effort will have been worthwhile.

Index